DAY HIKING
Olymp
Peninsula

Previous page: Hiker ascending Mount Ellinor-
Lake Cushman in background

Next page: Sprawling alpine meadows above
Appleton Pass

Penstemon growing on Mount Rose's summit
ledges

Meadows above Tubal Cain Mine—Buckhorn Mountain in background

Bailey Range and Hoh River from Bogachiel Peak

Hiker approaching the summit of Colonel Bob Peak on the Petes Creek Trail

Previous page: Clouds burn off above Royal Basin.

Next page: Cinquefoil adds beauty to Baldy-Gray Wolf Peak in background.

DAY HIKING
Olympic Peninsula

national park/coastal beaches/southwest washington

Craig Romano

THE MOUNTAINEERS BOOKS

THE MOUNTAINEERS BOOKS
*is the nonprofit publishing arm of The Mountaineers Club, an
organization founded in 1906 and dedicated to the exploration,
preservation, and enjoyment of outdoor and wilderness areas.*

1001 SW Klickitat Way, Suite 201, Seattle, WA 98134

© 2007 by Craig Romano

First edition, 2007

Manufactured in the United States of America

Copy Editor: Julie Van Pelt
Cover and Book Design: The Mountaineers Books
Layout: Mayumi Thompson
Cartographer: Moore Creative Design
All photographs by the author unless otherwise credited.

Cover photograph: *Mossy trees by Skokomish River*
Frontispiece: *Tarn above Sunnybrook Meadows*

Maps shown in this book were produced using National Geographic's *TOPO!*
software. For more information, go to *www.nationalgeographic.com/topo*.

Library of Congress Cataloging-in-Publication Data
Romano, Craig.
  Day hiking. Olympic Peninsula / by Craig Romano. — 1st ed.
    p. cm.
  Includes bibliographical references.
  ISBN-13: 978-1-59485-047-9
  ISBN-10: 1-59485-047-X
1. Hiking—Washington (State)—Olympic Peninsula—Guidebooks. 2. Olympic Peninsula
(Wash.)—Guidebooks. I. Title. II. Title: Olympic Peninsula.
GV199.42.W2R65 2007
796.5109797'94—dc22
                              2006039135

Table of Contents

SOUTHWESTERN WASHINGTON
Columbia River   42

Long Beach Peninsula   47

Willapa Bay   54

Chehalis River Valley   61

Grays Harbor   68

Black Hills: Capitol State Forest   75

KITSAP PENINSULA
Kitsap Peninsula   88

OLYMPIC PENINSULA: SOUTH
Wynoochee River Valley   108

South Fork Skokomish River Valley   114

OLYMPIC PENINSULA: EAST
North Fork Skokomish River Valley   126

Hamma Hamma River Valley   144

Duckabush River Valley   154

Dosewallips River Valley   163

OLYMPIC PENINSULA: WEST
The Rain Forests   294

OLYMPIC PENINSULA: COAST
Olympic Coast 326

LEGEND

🛣 101	U.S. Highway	▲	Summit
SR 42	State Highway	░	Sand/Mud
▬▬▬	Secondary Road	🌱	Marsh
=======	Unpaved Road	～	River/Stream
== 24 ==	Forest Road	///	Falls
··········	Hiking Route	⛴	Boat Launch
- - - - - - ·	Other Trail	▮	Ranger Station
▬ ·· ▬	State Boundary	▲	Campground
▬ · ▬ ·	Park Boundary	🚏	Picnic Area
①	Hike Number	🕯	Lighthouse
Ⓣ	Trailhead	⚒	Mine

Hikes at a Glance Chart

HIKE	DISTANCE (ROUND TRIP)	DIFFICULTY	HIKEABLE ALL YEAR	KID-FRIENDLY
SOUTHWEST WASHINGTON				
1. Julia Butler Hansen National Wildlife Refuge	5.6 miles	1		x
2. Scarborough Hill	2.8 miles	2	x	x
3. Cape Disappointment	4.2 miles	2	x	x
4. Leadbetter Point State Park: Dune Forest Loop	2.9 miles	1	x	x
5. Leadbetter Point State Park: Leadbetter Point	10.6 miles	3		x
6. Willapa National Wildlife Refuge: Bear River	3.5 miles	1	x	x
7. Willapa National Wildlife Refuge: Long Island	5.75 miles	2	x	
8. Butte Creek Sitka Spruce Grove	1.5 miles	1	x	x
9. Rainbow Falls State Park	up to 3 miles	1	x	x
10. Lake Sylvia State Park	2 miles	1	x	x
11. Chehalis River Sloughs	7miles	1	x	x
12. Johns River State Wildlife Area	2.5 miles	1	x	x
13. Damon Point State Park	4 miles	1	x	x
14. Copalis River Spit	4 miles	1	x	x
15. McLane Creek	1.5 miles	1	x	x
16. Capitol Peak	9 miles	2	x	
17. Mima Mounds	2.75 miles	1	x	x
18. Sherman Creek	9 miles	3	x	
KITSAP PENINSULA				
19. Harstine Island State Park	1.5 miles	1	x	x
20. Twanoh State Park	2.3 miles	1	x	x
21. Mary E. Theler Wetlands Nature Preserve	3.5 miles	1	x	x
22. Penrose Point State Park	2 miles	1	x	x
23. Guillemot Cove	2.5 miles	1	x	x
24. Green Mountain	5 miles	3	x	
25. Gazzam Lake and Close Beach	3.4 miles	2	x	x
26. Hansville Greenway	3.5 miles	1	x	x
OLYMPIC PENINSULA SOUTH				
27. Wynoochee Lake	12 miles	3		
28. Spoon Creek Falls	0.8 mile	2		

Difficulty: 1 = easy, 5 = strenuous

DOG-FRIENDLY	HISTORIC	BEACH HIKING	OLD-GROWTH	SOLITUDE	WILDFLOWERS	CAR CAMPING NEARBY	ALPINE VIEWS
	X			X	X		
	X		X	X			
	X		X			X	
X		X					
		X		X			
				X			
			X	X			
	X		X	X			
	X		X			X	
	X					X	
	X			X			
	X	X					
		X		X			
							X
					X		
X	X						
		X		X		X	
X		X				X	
		X				X	
		X					
					X		X
X							
X							
X			X	X		X	
X				X		X	

HIKE	DISTANCE (ROUND TRIP)	DIFFICULTY	HIKEABLE ALL YEAR	KID-FRIENDLY
29. Spider Lake	2 miles	1	x	x
30. Lower South Fork Skokomish River	10 miles	3	x	
31. Upper South Fork Skokomish River	8 miles	3		
32. Church Creek—Satsop Lakes	6.4 miles	3		
OLYMPIC PENINSULA EAST				
33. Big Creek	4.5 miles	2	x	x
34. Mount Rose	6.4 miles	5		
35. Mount Ellinor	6.2 miles	4		
36. Dry Creek	6 miles	2	x	
37. Copper Creek	5 miles	4		
38. Wagonwheel Lake	5.8 miles	5		
39. Staircase Rapids	4 miles	1	x	x
40. North Fork Skokomish River	11 miles	2		x
40. Flapjack Lakes	15 miles	4		x
41. Elk Lakes	4 miles	1	x	x
42. Lena Lake	6 miles	2		x
43. Lake of the Angels	8 miles	5		
44. Mildred Lakes	9 miles	5		
45. Mount Jupiter	14.4 miles	5		
46. Ranger Hole	2.1 miles	1	x	x
47. Murhut Falls	1.6 miles	1	x	x
48. Duckabush River	10.6 miles	3	x	
49. Dosewallips State Park	3.5 miles	1	x	x
50. Lake Constance	4 miles	6		
51. West Fork Dosewallips River	8.4 miles	2		x
52. Sunnybrook Meadows	12 miles	5		
53. Mount Walker	5 miles	3	x	
54. Fallsview Canyon	1.5 miles	1	x	x
55. Tunnel Creek	8.5 miles	3		
56. Notch Pass and Quilcene Ridge	8.6 miles	4		
57. Lower Big Quilcene River	10 miles	2		x
58. Marmot Pass	10.6 miles	4		
OLYMPIC PENINSULA NORTHEAST				
59. Mount Townsend	8.2 miles	4		
60. Silver Lakes	11 miles	4		
61. Mount Zion	4.6 miles	3		
62. Dirty Face Ridge	7.5 miles	4		
63. Tubal Cane Mine and Buckhorn Lake	12 miles	3		
64. Upper Dungeness River	6.8 miles	2		x

DOG-FRIENDLY	HISTORIC	BEACH HIKING	OLD-GROWTH	SOLITUDE	WILDFLOWERS	CAR CAMPING NEARBY	ALPINE VIEWS
X			X	X			
X			X			X	
X			X	X			
X			X	X			
X						X	
			X	X			X
					X		X
X				X	X	X	
	X		X	X		X	
			X			X	
	X		X			X	
	X		X			X	
X			X	X	X		
X			X				
				X	X		X
			X	X			
				X	X		X
	X					X	
X			X			X	
X	X					X	
			X			X	X
			X		X	X	
			X	X	X	X	X
X					X	X	
X					X	X	
X			X	X			
X	X			X			
X			X				
X			X		X		X
X			X		X		X
X			X		X		X
X					X		X
X				X	X		X
X	X				X		X
X			X				

HIKE	DISTANCE (ROUND TRIP)	DIFFICULTY	HIKEABLE ALL YEAR	KID-FRIENDLY
65. Royal Basin	14 miles	4		
66. Baldy	9 miles	5		
67. Gray Wolf River	8.4 miles	2	x	x
68. Ned Hill	2.2 miles	3		
69. Slab Camp Creek and Upper Gray Wolf River	5.6 miles	3		x
70. Deer Ridge	10.4 miles	4		
71. Gibbs Lake	2.5 miles	1	x	x
72. Anderson Lake	2.2 miles	1	x	x
73. Fort Flagler	5 miles	2	x	x
74. South Indian Island	4 miles	1	x	x
OLYMPIC PENINSULA NORTH				
75. Miller Peninsula and Thompson Spit	5 miles	2	x	
76. Dungeness Spit	11 miles	3	x	x
77. Striped Peak	5 miles	3	x	x
78. Clallam Bay Spit	2.5 miles	1	x	x
79. Lake Angeles	7.4 miles	3		x
80. Heather Park	10 miles	4		
81. Klahhane Ridge	5 miles	4		
82. Sunrise Ridge	5.2 miles	2		x
83. Hurricane Hill (Summer)	3 miles	2		x
83. Hurricane Hill (Winter)	6 miles	4		
84. PJ Lake	1.8 miles	4		
85. Grand Ridge	5 miles	3		
86. Grand Valley	9.8 miles	4		
87. Griff Creek	3.6 miles	4	x	
88. Geyser Valley	7.8 miles	2	x	x
89. Elwha Valley and Lillian River	9.6 miles	3	x	
90. Lake Mills	4 miles	2	x	x
91. Happy Lake	10 miles	4		
92. Boulder Lake	12 miles	4		
93. Appleton Pass	15 miles	5		
94. Spruce Railroad Trail	8 miles	2	x	x
95. Mount Storm King	3.8 miles	4		
96. Marymere Falls / Barnes Creek	2/6 miles	1/3	x	x
97. Pyramid Mountain	7 miles	3		
98. Mount Muller	13 miles	4		
99. Kloshe Nanitch	6.4 miles	4		
100. North Fork Sol Duc River	12.4 miles	3		x

DOG-FRIENDLY	HISTORIC	BEACH HIKING	OLD-GROWTH	SOLITUDE	WILDFLOWERS	CAR CAMPING NEARBY	ALPINE VIEWS
			X		X		X
			X	X	X		X
X			X				
X	X			X	X		
X			X	X	X		
			X	X	X		X
X							
X					X		
	X	X				X	
		X					
X		X		X			
		X				X	
X		X	X	X		X	
X		X		X			
					X	X	
				X	X	X	X
					X		X
					X		X
					X		X
							X
				X	X		X
					X		X
			X		X		X
			X	X	X	X	
	X		X			X	
	X		X			X	
	X		X	X		X	
			X	X	X		X
			X		X		
			X		X		X
	X						
			X				
			X				X
	X		X			X	X
					X		X
X	X			X	X	X	X
			X	X			

HIKE	DISTANCE (ROUND TRIP)	DIFFICULTY	HIKEABLE ALL YEAR	KID-FRIENDLY
101. Sol Duc Falls	5.3 miles	1		X
102. Mink Lake	5 miles	2		X
102. Little Divide	8.6 miles	4		X
103. Deer Lake	7.5 mles	3		
103. Bogachiel Peak	16 miles	5		
OLYMPIC PENINSULA WEST				
104. Bogachiel River	12 miles	3	X	
105. Hoh River—Five Mile Island	10.6 miles	2	X	X
106. South Fork Hoh River—Big Flat	6 miles	1	X	X
107. Queets River	10 miles	4		
108. Sams River	3 miles	1	X	X
109. Quinault National Recreation Trails	3.9 miles	2	X	X
110. Fletcher Canyon	4 miles	3	X	
111. Graves Creek	7 miles	3		
112. Quinault River—Pony Bridge	5 miles	2	X	X
113. North Fork Quinault River— Halfway House	10.2 miles	3	X	
114. Irely Lake	2.2 miles	1	X	X
114. Big Creek	8 miles	3		X
115. Pete's Creek— Colonel Bob Peak	8.2 miles	5		
116. West Fork Humptulips River	10 miles	2		
OLYMPIC PENINSULA COAST				
117. Kalaloch Beach–Browns Point	4 miles	1	X	X
118. Ruby Beach	6 miles	2	X	X
119. Second Beach	4 miles	2	X	X
120. Third Beach	3.6 miles	2	X	X
121. Hole-in-the-Wall	4 miles	1	X	X
122. Quillayute River Slough	1.8 miles	1	X	X
123. Ozette Triangle	9.4 miles	3	X	
124. Shi Shi Beach and Point of the Arches	8 miles	3	X	
125. Cape Flattery	1.5 miles	2	X	X

DOG-FRIENDLY	HISTORIC	BEACH HIKING	OLD-GROWTH	SOLITUDE	WILDFLOWERS	CAR CAMPING NEARBY	ALPINE VIEWS
			X			X	
			X	X		X	
			X	X		X	
			X		X	X	X
			X		X	X	X
			X	X		X	
			X			X	
			X	X		X	
	X		X	X		X	
	X		X	X		X	
			X			X	
X			X	X			
			X	X		X	
			X			X	
	X		X			X	
			X	X		X	
			X	X		X	
			X	X	X	X	X
X			X	X		X	
X		X				X	
X		X					
		X					
		X					
		X				X	
		X	X			X	
		X				X	
		X					

Acknowledgments

In addition to my trusty pick-up and several (now well-worn) pairs of hiking shoes, writing this book would not have been possible without the help and support of the following people.

First, a big thank-you to all of the folks at The Mountaineers Books, especially publisher Helen Cherullo and Hally Swift for giving me the opportunity to be a part of this exciting new series. Thanks, too, to Cassandra Conyers for being so supportive and encouraging in the planning stages of this book. To my series partners, Alan Bauer and Dan Nelson, it is an honor to be working with you. Thanks for your help, and to Alan: thanks for listening to me when I was stressed out! I want to especially thank my editor, Julie Van Pelt, whose professionalism and attention to detail have greatly contributed to making this book a finer volume. I know editors don't usually hear writers say this, but it truly has been a pleasure working with you.

I also want to acknowledge guidebook pioneers Robert L. Wood, Ira Spring, and Harvey Manning for their inspiration and invaluable knowledge. I am honored to be walking in their bootprints.

Thanks to the following land managers who offered their time and insight: Jon Preston of Olympic National Park, Molly Erickson of Olympic National Forest, Susan Graham of Olympic National Forest, Christine Redmond of the Washington State Department of Natural Resources, and Terri L. Butler of the Willapa National Wildlife Refuge. And a special thanks to Jim French of the Olympia Mountaineers for getting me to go to church—Church Creek that is.

Thanks, too, to Lori Lynn Gray and Kristi Agren for their help in finding great places for me to stay in Clallam County. The Washington State Ferry system should be thanking me for helping them make their budget!

Lastly, but most importantly, I want to thank my wife Heather for believing in me and supporting me while I worked hard on this manuscript. Thanks for hiking with me, too, to so many of the special places in this book. And *mille grazie* for the back massages after all my long nights in front of the keyboard.

Preface

I first stepped foot (actually wheel) in Washington State in April 1980. I had bicycled across the country from my home state, New Hampshire, entering the Evergreen State in Pacific County. I immediately fell in love with the raw beauty and expansive wild tidal flats of Willapa Bay. The Washington that I first experienced was the Washington I had always imagined—a land of big timber, big rivers, and a big coastline.

In July 1985 I returned to hike the Cascades. My very first hike, up Cutthroat Pass, yielded stunning alpine views and an up close and personal encounter with four mountain goats.

But it wasn't until September 1989, three months after moving to the Northwest, that I fell for the Olympics—and fell hard. It was on a solo backpacking trip to the High Divide where I experienced a catharsis. Never before had I felt so alive, so full of purpose, and so at ease with myself and the world than in that special corner of the Olympic wilderness. I watched bears splash in a tarn, elk forage in a high basin, a curious coyote sniff out my campsite, and I sat under a blood-red evening sky by an alpine lake listening to a marmot pierce the stillness with his high-pitched whistles. The memory is etched in my mind like it happened yesterday.

Fortunately for me I can return to the High Divide, Willapa Bay, and Cutthroat Pass and enjoy these special places time and again. They've changed little as I've gotten older, their redeeming qualities still present.

Unfortunately for most of my fellow humans, they may never experience these and other beautiful natural places in our special corner of the world. These people have chosen a different path, leading them far from the redeeming qualities of nature. As the world continues to urbanize and as our society grows more sedentary, materialistic, and disconnected from the natural world, life has become less meaningful. Nature may need us to protect it, but we need nature to protect us from an encroaching world of meaningless consumption and pursuits.

Fellow native New Englander Henry David Thoreau proclaimed, "In wildness is the preservation of the world." And I would like to add, "In wildness is the salvation of our souls, the meaning of life, and the preservation of our humanness." So, shun the mall, turn off the TV, skip the casino, and hit the trail. I've lined up 125 magnificent hikes for you to celebrate nature, life, the incredible landscapes of the Olympic Peninsula, and you. Yes, you—go take a hike, celebrate life, and come back a better and more content person.

And if I'm preaching to the choir, help me then to introduce new disciples to the sacred world of nature. For while we sometimes relish our solitude on the trail, we need more like-minded souls to help us keep what little wildlands remain. Help nature by introducing family members, coworkers, your neighbors, children, and politicians to our wonderful trails. I'm convinced that a society that hikes is not only good for our wild and natural places (people will be willing to protect them), but is also good for us (as we live in a healthy and connected way).

Enjoy this book. I've enjoyed writing it. I believe that we can change our world for the better, one hike at a time.

Introduction

Modern life is full of irony. Technology was supposed to set us free, but instead of doing more of our work for us, it has only enabled us to do more work. Remember when we used to talk about the thirty-hour work week? Uh, sounds like science fiction. Americans are working now more than ever, with less vacation time taken and more hours worked than at any time since World War II. Granted, for many this is by choice, as they quest after a big house (or two), a big vehicle (or two), and all the latest gizmos, contraptions, and clutter that they don't have time for anyway. But for many others, working long and hard is a necessity. Health care, energy, education, housing, and food costs aren't getting any cheaper.

This of course helps explain why more and more hikers these days are foregoing multiday backpacking trips in favor of daylong outings. But even if you're not pressed for time, perhaps you prefer day hikes to backpacking for other practical reasons. You can travel lighter, travel farther, and travel with more comfort than if you were schlepping a fifty-pound pack. Day hikes also generally require less planning and fewer hassles when it comes to all of the permits (if any) that might be required these days to recreate on our public lands.

So to help all you hurried and busy and travel-light hikers get your wilderness fixes, turn to this new Day Hiking series. The series sets out to find the best routes in each region that can be enjoyed as day trips. Of course depending on where you live, some destinations may be too far for you to travel to, hike, and travel back from in a day. In that case, look at these trips as daily excursions you can make from that weeklong rental at the coast or from a three-day weekend at a car campground. Again, no backpacking is necessary.

The book you are now holding focuses on hiking routes found throughout the Olympic Peninsula, the Kitsap Peninsula, Grays Harbor County, and the Long Beach Peninsula—basically, all the good day hikes west of I-5 and the Puget Trough and north of the Columbia River. You'll find short walks close to population centers and all-day treks deep into wilderness areas. Beaches, islands, riversides, lakefronts, old-growth forests, alpine meadows, and mountain tops. Hikes perfect for kids, friendly to dogs, popular and remote. New trails, historic trails, and revitalized trails. Where to find wildlife, where to escape crowds, and where to get the best bang for your boot. It's all included in this packed-with-adventure volume.

The Olympic region is home to incredible biological diversity. With a rugged, undeveloped coastline (the largest wilderness coast in the continental United States), the largest tracts of unbroken old-growth forest in the Northwest, the largest undeveloped estuary on the Pacific Coast, and some of the last free-flowing rivers in Washington, it's an area of superlatives in grandeur and ecological importance. Temperate rain forest, glacier-covered mountains, sprawling alpine meadows, and crystal clear lakes can all be found here. Nearly a million acres of this special landscape have been protected as a national park and recognized as a United Nations Biosphere Reserve. While eastern parks like the Great Smoky Mountains and the Everglades lay claim to the most biodiversity, no park comes close to the Olympics when it comes

Opposite: Napping in the backcountry—Satsop Lakes

to biomass. You've never seen so much living matter until you've taken a stroll up an Olympic rainforest valley.

This book will introduce you to trails where you may be able to spot elk, bear, cougar, marmots, coyotes, and otter—both sea and river—as well as whales and seals. Birdlife, too, is abundant and varied. There are eagles, herons, guillemots, dippers, and oystercatchers, as well as marbled murrelets, snowy plovers, pipits, and harlequin ducks.

Hike trails rich in human history as well—along hunting and trade routes favored by First Peoples and on routes used by European explorers, merchants, and pioneers and homesteaders from the east. Retrace famous expeditions and hike to old town sites, fire towers, mines, and Native villages. And like the terrain, the trails that traverse it are just as varied. This book aims to help you find your own discoveries in the incredibly beautiful and diverse landscapes of the Olympic Peninsula region.

USING THIS BOOK

These Day Hiking guidebooks strike a fine balance. They were developed to be as easy to use as possible while still providing enough detail to help you explore a region. As a result, *Day Hiking Olympic Peninsula* includes all the information you need to find and enjoy the hikes, but leaves enough room for you to make your own discoveries as you venture into areas new to you.

Hike Descriptions. Icons at the top of each hike description let you know if this hike is kid-friendly. These hikes are generally easier, pose few if any obstacles, and often consist of natural features that should intrigue and engage youngsters. A dog-friendly icon means dogs are not only allowed, though leashes may be required (dogs must be on a leash in all state parks), but also that the hikes are friendly on your pooch's paws, contain adequate shade and water sources, and in many cases are on

trails that are lightly traveled. The beachcombing icon indicates that the hike is either on a beach or to a beach. Note however that it is unlawful to remove living organisms from several of our beaches. Leave them in place for the health of our coastal ecosystems and for others to enjoy. The historical icon indicates that the hike is of significant human interest in addition to its natural highlights. The Endangered Trail icon spotlights trails that are threatened due to lack of maintenance, motorized encroachment, abandonment, or other actions detrimental to their continuance. A Saved Trail icon denotes where a formerly threatened or abandoned trail has been revived and restored.

 Kid-friendly

 Dog-friendly

 Beachcombing

 Historical

 Endangered trail

 Saved trail

What the Ratings Mean

Every trail described in this book features a detailed "trails facts" section. Not all of the details here are facts, however.

Each hike starts with two subjective ratings: each has a **rating** of 1 to 5 stars for its overall appeal, and each route's **difficulty** is rated on a scale of 1 to 5. This is subjective, based on the author's impressions of each route, but the ratings do follow a formula of sorts. The overall rating is based on scenic beauty, natural wonder, and other unique qualities, such as solitude potential and wildlife-viewing opportunities.

The difficulty rating is based on trail length, the steepness of the trail, and how difficult it is to hike. Generally, trails that are rated more difficult (4 or 5) are longer and steeper then average. But it's not a simple equation. A short, steep trail over talus slopes may be rated 5, while a long, smooth trail with little elevation gain may be rated a 2.

To help explain those difficulty ratings, you'll also find the **round-trip mileage**, total **elevation gain**, and **high point** for each hike. These distances are not always exact mileages—trails weren't measured with calibrated instruments—but the mileages are those used by cartographers and land managers (who have measured many of the trails). The elevation gains report the cumulative difference between the high and low points on the route round-trip. It's worth noting that not all high points are at the end of the trail—a route may run over a high ridge before dropping to a lake basin, for instance.

The recommended **season** is another subjective tool meant to be a guide and not an absolute. Some years, a heavy winter snowpack may not melt in the high country until early September. In other years, the highest trails may be snow-free in June. Many of the hikes in this book can be done year-round, but keep in mind that weather in the winter may not be the best. Again, use the suggested season as a tool to help you plan your trips. But because no guidebook can provide all the details of a trail, nor stay current with constantly changing conditions of trails, stream crossings, and access roads, make sure to call the land manager to get the latest information on conditions before you head out.

To help with trip planning, each hike lists which **maps** you'll want to have on your hike, as well as who to **contact** to get current trail conditions. Hikes in this guidebook primarily use Green Trails and Custom Correct maps, listing USGS maps for areas not covered by these other maps. Green Trails maps use the standard 7.5-minute USGS topographical

maps as their starting point. But where USGS maps may not have been updated since sometimes the 1950s, the Green Trails cartographers have researchers in the field every year, checking trail conditions and changes. Many hikers still use USGS maps, which remain useful for looking at mountains, lakes, contours and the like because natural features don't change rapidly. But man-made features do change, and Green Trails and Custom Correct both do a good job in staying abreast of those changes. These maps are available at most outdoor

Dwight and Lester get ready for a hike.

retailers in the state, as well as at many U.S. Forest Service and national park visitors centers.

Finally, given that we now live in a digital world, **GPS coordinates** for each trailhead are provided—use this both to get to the trail and to help you get back to your car if you get caught out in a storm or wander off-trail.

The route descriptions themselves provide a basic overview of what you might find on your hike, directions to get you to the trail-

WHOSE LAND IS THIS?

Almost all of the hikes in this book are on public land. That is, they belong to you and me and the rest of the citizenry. What's confusing is just who exactly is in charge of this public trust. Over ten different governing agencies manage lands described in this guide.

The largest of the agencies, and those managing most of the hikes in this book, are the National Park Service and U.S. Forest Service. There is an Olympic National Park and an Olympic National Forest. Don't confuse them; they are two different entities with two different objectives.

The Park Service, a division of the Department of the Interior, manages over 900,000 acres as the Olympic National Park. Primary objective: "to conserve the scenery and natural and historic objects and the wildlife therein and to provide for the enjoyment of the same in such a manner and by such means as will leave them unimpaired for the enjoyment of future generations." In other words, the primary focus of the Park Service is preservation.

Contrast that with the Forest Service, a division of the Department of Agriculture, which strives to "sustain the health, diversity, and productivity of the Nation's forests and grasslands to meet the needs of present and future generations." The agency purports to do this under the doctrine of "multiple-use"—the greatest good for the greatest number, frequently resulting in conflict. However, supplying timber products, managing wildlife habitat, and developing motorized and nonmotorized recreation options have a tendency to conflict with each other. Some of these uses may not exactly sustain the health of the forest either.

Olympic National Forest manages over 600,000 acres of land on the national park's periphery. Much has been heavily logged. Five areas within the forest, however, have been afforded stringent protections as federal wilderness areas (see "Untrammeled Olympics" in the Olympic Peninsula: East section).

Other public lands you'll encounter in this book are Washington State Parks, managed primarily for recreation and preservation; Washington State Department of Natural Resources lands, managed primarily for timber harvesting, with pockets of natural area preserves; national wildlife refuges, established to protect wildlife and their habitat; county parks, which are often like state parks but on a regional level; and Washington Department of Wildlife lands, established for wildlife habitat and set aside for hunting and fishing.

It's important that you know who manages the land you'll be hiking on, for each agency has their own fees and their own rules (like for dogs: no in a national park, yes in a national forest, yes but on-leash in state parks). Confusing? Yes, but it's our land and we should understand how it's managed for us. And remember that we have a say in how our lands are managed and can let the agencies know whether we like what they're doing or not.

head, and in most cases additional highlights beyond the actual trails you'll be exploring.

Of course, you'll need some information long before you ever leave home. As you plan your trips, the following several issues need to be considered.

PERMITS AND REGULATIONS

It's important that you know, understand, and abide by them. As our public lands have become increasingly popular, and as both federal and state funding has declined, regulations and permits have become necessary components in managing our natural heritage. To help keep our wilderness areas wild and our trails safe and well-maintained, land managers—especially the National Park Service and U.S. Forest Service—have implemented a sometimes complex set of rules and regulations governing the use of these lands.

Generally, any developed trailhead in Washington's national forests (Oregon too) fall under the Region 6 forest pass program. Simply stated, in order to park legally at these designated national forest trailheads, you must display a Northwest Forest Pass decal in your windshield. These sell for $5 per day or $30 for an annual pass good throughout Washington and Oregon (which constitute Region 6). The Northwest Forest Pass is also required at most trailheads within the North Cascades National Park Complex.

In the Olympic National Park several access areas (Hurricane Ridge, Staircase, Elwha Valley, Lake Ozette, and Hoh rain forest) require a national park entrance fee: currently $15 for a one-week pass, or $30 for an annual pass. Your best bet if you hike a lot in both the national parks and forests is to buy an America the Beautiful–National Parks and Federal Recreational Lands Pass for $80. This pass grants you and three other adults (children under 16 are admitted free) in your vehicle access to all federal recreation sites that charge a

fee. These include: national parks, national forests, national wildlife refuges, and Bureau of Land Management areas, not only here in Washington but throughout the country. I know that who charges what can get confusing, which is why the America the Beautiful Pass makes sense (See Whose Land is this?). Even if you don't hike much, all park and forest pass monies go directly to the agencies managing our lands. It is money well spent. You can purchase passes at national park and forest visitors' centers as well as many area outdoor retailers. They are good for one year from day of purchase.

WEATHER

Mountain weather in general is famously unpredictable, but in the Olympic range—with its multitude of microclimates—you'll be completely baffled (or intrigued). For the most part, the Olympic Peninsula enjoys a moderate maritime climate, influenced by the ocean. Temperature variation fluctuates little between the seasons, thanks in part to the Pacific jet stream. Still, it's not uncommon to have below-freezing temperatures in the winter and periods of hot weather in the summer months. Alpine areas, of course, are subject to more severe conditions, including long periods of below-freezing temperatures accompanied by heavy snowfall.

The entire region is prone to heavy amounts of precipitation, predominantly as rainfall. Rarely does it snow below 2000 feet. When it does, accumulations are usually gone within days. Winter sees the heaviest amount of rainfall, particularly in the western valleys of the Olympic Mountains: the rain forests. Along the coast, low clouds can roll right over, making for drier conditions than just 20 miles inland where the hills begin trapping and wringing out moisture from the clouds.

The eastern slopes of the Olympics, particularly the northeastern corner of the peninsula, enjoy a rainshadow effect. High mountains to the west trap clouds moving eastward, forcing them to release much of their precipitation. These clouds then build up again, collecting moisture farther east to be trapped once more along the western slopes of the Cascades. Locales such as Sequim see as little as 17 inches of rain annually, while the Quinault Valley in the west "enjoys" over 140 inches of annual precipitation.

Bottom line: always prepare for rain and wet conditions while hiking in the Olympics. Being caught in a sudden storm without adequate clothing can lead to hypothermia (loss of body temperature), which is deadly if not immediately treated. Most hikers who have died of exposure (hypothermia) did so not in winter, but during the milder months when a sudden change of temperature accompanied by winds and rain sneaked up on them. Always carry extra clothing layers, including rain and wind protection.

While snow blankets the high country primarily from October to May, it can occur anytime of year. Be prepared. Lightning is rare in the Olympics, but it does occasionally happen. I was once trapped on Mount Ellinor in an electrical episode that reminded me of my days growing up in New Hampshire. If you hear thunder, waste no time getting off of summits and away from water. Take shelter, but not under big trees or rock ledges. If caught in an electrical storm, crouch down—making minimal contact with the ground—and wait for the boomer to pass.

Other weather-induced hazards include the results of past episodes of rain and snow. River and creek crossings can be extremely dangerous after periods of heavy rain or snowmelt. Always use caution and sound judgment when fording.

Be aware of snowfields left over from the previous winter's snow pack. Depending on the severity of the past winter, and the weather conditions of the spring and early summer, some trails may not melt out until well into summer, if at all. The winter of 1999 left most of the Olympic high country blanketed all season. Obstruction Point Road never opened beyond the Waterhole that year. In addition to treacherous footing and difficulties in routefinding, lingering snowfields can be prone to avalanches or slides. Use caution crossing them.

But despite all this talk about rain and snow, the Olympic region enjoys plenty of sunshine too. Midsummer to early autumn is often graced with prolonged dry periods, and it's not unusual to a have a dry week or two in the winter as well.

ROAD AND TRAIL CONDITIONS
In general, trails change little year to year. But change can and does occur, and sometimes very quickly. A heavy storm can cause a river to jump its channel, washing out sections of trail (or access road) in moments. The record rainfall in November 2006 caused flooding, inflicting widespread damage to both trails and access roads. Windstorms can blow down trees by the hundreds, making trails unhikeable. And snow can bury trails well into the summer. Avalanches, landslides, and forest fires can also bring serious damage and obliteration to our trails.

Access roads face similar threats. With this in mind, each hike in this book lists the land manager's contact information so you can phone them prior to your trip and ensure that your chosen road and trail are open and safe to travel.

On the topic of trail conditions, it is vital that we thank the countless volunteers who donate tens of thousands of hours to trail maintenance each year. The Washington Trails Association (WTA) alone coordinates upward of sixty thousand hours of volunteer trail maintenance each year.

As enormous as the volunteer efforts have

become, there is always a need for more. Our wilderness trail system faces increasing threats, including (but by no means limited to) ever-shrinking trail funding, inappropriate trail uses, and conflicting land-management policies and practices.

With this in mind, this guide includes trails that are threatened and in danger of becoming unhikeable. These Endangered Trails are marked with a special icon in this book. On the other side of the coin, we've also been blessed with some great trail successes in recent years, thanks in large part to that massive volunteer movement spearheaded by WTA. These Saved Trails are marked, too, to help show you that individual efforts do make a difference. As you enjoy these Saved Trails, stop to consider the contributions made by your fellow hikers that helped protect our trail resources.

WILDERNESS ETHICS

As wonderful as volunteer trail maintenance programs are, they aren't the only way to help save our trails. Indeed, these on-the-ground efforts provide quality trails today, but to ensure the long-term survival of our trails—and the wildlands they cross—we all must embrace and practice sound wilderness ethics.

Strong, positive wilderness ethics include making sure you leave the wilderness as pure or purer than it was when you found it. As the adage says, "take only pictures, leave only footprints." But sound wilderness ethics go deeper than that, beyond simply picking up after ourselves when we go for a hike. Wilderness ethics must carry over into our daily lives. We need to ensure that our elected officials and public land managers recognize and respond to our wilderness needs and desires. We must make sure that the next generation of Americans has a deep appreciation and respect for the natural world, not an easy task in our urban and materialistic society. If we hike the trails on the weekend, but let the wilderness go neglected—or worse, allow it to be abused—on the weekdays, we'll soon find our weekend haunts diminished or destroyed. Protecting trails and wild areas is a full-time job—and one with many rewards, as any hiker can tell you.

TRAIL GIANTS AND GIVING TREES

I grew up in rural New Hampshire and was introduced to hiking and respect for our wildlands at a young age. I grew to admire the men and women responsible for saving and protecting many of our trails and wilderness areas as I became more aware of the often tumultuous history behind the preservation efforts.

When I moved to Washington in 1989 I immediately gained a respect for Ira Spring and Harvey Manning. Through their pioneering *100 Hikes* guidebooks, I was introduced to and fell in love with the Washington backcountry. I bought the whole series and voraciously devoured them on the trail and on the sofa. I joined the Mountaineers Club, the WTA, and other local trail and conservation organizations so that I could help a little to protect these places and carry on this legacy for future generations.

While I never met Ira Spring, I was honored to work on his last book after he passed away (*Best Wildflower Hikes in Washington*). I believe 100 percent in what he termed "green bonding." We must, in Ira's words, "get people onto trails. They need to bond with the wilderness." This is essential in building public support for trails and trail funding. When hikers get complacent, trails suffer.

And while I often chuckled at Harvey Manning's tirades and diatribes as he lambasted public officials' short-sighted and misguided land practices, I almost always tacitly agreed with him. Sometimes I thought Harvey was a bit combative, a tad too polarizing, and perhaps even risked turning off potential allies. On the other hand, sometimes you have to raise a little hell to get results.

As you get out and hike the trails you find

described here, consider that many of these trails would have long ago ceased to exist without the phenomenal efforts of people like Ira Spring, Harvey Manning, Louise Marshall, Robert Wood, and Greg Ball, not to mention the scores of unnamed hikers who joined them in their push for wildland protection, trail funding, and strong environmental stewardship programs.

When you get home, take a page from their playbook and write a letter to your congressperson or state representative, asking for better trail funding. Call your local Forest Service office to say that you've enjoyed the trails in their jurisdiction and that you want these

Use a privy when available.

routes to remain wild and accessible for use by you and your children.

If you're not already a member, consider joining an organization devoted to wilderness, backcountry trails, or other wild country issues. Organizations like the Mountaineers Club, Washington Trails Association, Volunteers for Outdoor Washington, the Great Peninsula Conservancy, Washington's National Park Fund, Conservation Northwest, and countless others leverage individual contributions and efforts to help ensure the future of our trails and the wonderful wilderness legacy we've inherited. Buy a specialty license plate for Washington's national parks or state parks and let everybody on the way to the trailhead see what you value and are willing to work for.

TRAIL ETIQUETTE

We need to not only be sensitive to the environment surrounding our trails, but to other trail users as well. Many of the trails in this book are open to an array of uses. Some are hiker-only, but others allow equestrians and mountain bikers too (only a couple hikes in this book are open to motorbikes).

When you encounter other trail users—whether they are hikers, climbers, runners, bicyclists, or horse riders—the only hard-and-fast rule is to follow common sense and exercise simple courtesy. It's hard to overstate just how vital these two things—common sense and courtesy—are to maintaining an enjoyable, safe, and friendly situation when different types of trail users meet.

With this Golden Rule of Trail Etiquette firmly in mind, here are other things you can do during trail encounters to make everyone's trip more enjoyable:

- **Right-of-way**. When meeting other hikers, the party going uphill has the right-of-way. There are two general reasons for this. First, on steep ascents hikers may be watching the trail and not notice the approach of descending hikers until they are face-to-face. More importantly, it is easier for descending hikers to break their stride and step off the trail than it is for those who have gotten into a good, climbing rhythm. But by all means if you are the uphill trekker and you wish to grant passage to oncoming hikers, go right ahead with this act of trail kindness.

- **Moving off-trail**. When meeting other user groups (like bicyclists or horseback riders), the hiker should move off the trail. This is because hikers are more mobile and flexible than other users, making it easier for them to step off the trail.
- **Encountering horses**. When meeting horseback riders, the hiker should step off the downhill side of the trail unless the terrain makes this difficult or dangerous. In that case, move to the uphill side of the trail, but crouch down a bit so you don't tower over the horses' heads. Also, make yourself visible so as not to spook the big beastie, and talk in a normal voice to the riders. This calms the horses. If hiking with a dog, keep your buddy under control.
- **Stay on trails**, and practice minimum impact. Don't cut switchbacks, take shortcuts, or make new trails. If your destination is off-trail, stick to snow and rock when possible so as not to damage fragile alpine meadows. Spread out when traveling off-trail; don't hike in line if in a group, as this greatly increases the chance of compacting thin soils and crushing delicate plant environments.
- **Obey the rules** specific to the trail you are visiting. Many trails are closed to certain types of use, including hiking with dogs (in Olympic National Park) or riding horses.
- **Hiking with dogs**. Hikers who take dogs on the trails should have their dog on a leash or under very strict voice command at all times. And if leashes are required (such as in all state parks), then this *does* apply to you. Too

Hardy hikers Steve and Molly on their way to the Mildred Lakes

many dog owners flagrantly disregard this regulation, setting themselves up for tickets, hostile words from fellow hikers, and the possibility of losing the right to bring Fido out on that trail in the future. Remember that many hikers are not fond of dogs on the trail. Respect their right not to be approached by your loveable lab. A well-behaved leashed dog, however, can certainly help warm up these hikers to your buddy.

- **Avoid disturbing wildlife**, especially in winter and in calving areas. Observe from a distance, resisting the urge to move closer to wildlife (use your telephoto lens). This not only keeps you safer, but it prevents the animal from having to exert itself unnecessarily to flee from you.

- **Take only photographs**. Leave all natural things, features, and historic artifacts as you found them for others to enjoy.
- **Never roll rocks off trails or cliffs**. You risk endangering lives below you.

These are just a few of the things you can do to maintain a safe and harmonious trail environment. And while not every situation is addressed by these rules, you can avoid problems by always remembering that *common sense and courtesy are in order.*

Remember, too, that anything you pack in must be packed out, even biodegradable items like apple cores and pistachio shells. "Leave only footprints, take only pictures," is a worthy slogan to live by when visiting the wilderness.

Another important Leave No Trace principle focuses on the business of taking care of business. The first rule of backcountry bathroom etiquette says that if an outhouse exists, use it. While you may be tempted not to (they really aren't that bad—we're not talking city public restrooms here), remember they help keep backcountry water supplies free from contamination and the surrounding countryside from turning into a minefield of human waste decorated with toilet-paper flowers. Composting privies can actually improve the environment. I once spent a summer as a backcountry ranger in which one of my duties was composting the duty. Once the "stew" was sterile, we spread it on damaged alpine meadows helping to restore the turf.

When privies aren't provided, however, the key factor to consider is location. Choose a site at least 200 feet from water, campsites, and the trail. Dig a cat hole. Once you're done, bury your waste with organic duff, sticks, rocks, and a Do Not Enter sign (just kidding about the last one).

WATER
As a general rule you should treat all backcountry water sources. There is quite a bit of debate on how widespread nasties like *Giar-*

dia (a waterborne parasite) are in our water sources. New evidence suggests that the threat is greatly overblown. However, it's still better to assume that all water is contaminated. You don't want to risk it. I have contracted giardiasis on several occasions (in places as diverse as Paraguay and Vermont) and it's no treat—especially for the people around you.

Treating water can be as simple as boiling it, chemically purifying it (adding tiny iodine tablets), or pumping it through one of the new-generation water filters and purifiers. (Note: Pump units labeled as filters generally remove everything but viruses, which are too small to be filtered out. Pumps labeled as purifiers use a chemical element, usually iodine, to render viruses inactive after filtering all the other bugs out.)

CLEANUP
When washing your hands, rinse off as much as you can in plain water first. If you still feel the need for a soapy wash, collect a pot of water from the lake or stream and move at least 100 feet away. Apply a small amount of biodegradable soap to your hands and lather up. Use a bandanna or towel to wipe away most of the soap; then rinse with the water in the pot.

WILDLIFE
Bears
There are an estimated thirty thousand to thirty-five thousand black bears in Washington, and the big bruins can be found in every corner of the state. The Olympics, especially Olympic National Park, is thick with them. Watching bears grazing on huckleberries or splashing in a tarn can be an exciting and rewarding experience—provided, of course, you aren't in the same berry patch or tarn.

Bears tend to prefer solitude to human company, generally fleeing long before you have a chance to get too close. There are times, however, when a bear doesn't hear (or smell) your approach, or when it is more interested in defending its food source or its young than in avoiding a confrontation. These instances are rare, and you can minimize the odds of an encounter with an aggressive bear by heeding the following:

- **Hike in a group** and hike only during daylight hours.
- **Talk or sing as you hike** (Frank Sinatra or Johnny Cash tunes work well). If a bear hears you coming, it will usually avoid you. When surprised, however, a bear may feel threatened. So make noises that will identify you as a human—talk, sing, rattle pebbles in a tin can—especially when hiking near a river or stream (which can mask more subtle sounds that might normally alert a bear to your presence).
- **Be aware** of the environment around you, and know how to identify bear sign. Overturned rocks and torn-up deadwood logs often are the result of a bear searching for grubs. Berry bushes stripped of berries—with leaves, branches, and berries littering the ground under the bushes—show where a bear has fed. Bears will often leave claw marks on trees and, since they use trees as scratching posts, fur in the rough bark of a tree is a sign that says "a bear was here!" Tracks and scat are the most common signs of bear's recent presence.
- **Stay away from abundant food sources and dead animals**. Black bears are opportunistic and will scavenge food. A bear that finds a dead deer will hang around until the meat is gone, and it will defend that food against any perceived threat.
- **Keep dogs leashed and under control**. Many bear encounters have resulted from unleashed dogs chasing a bear: The bear gets angry and turns on the dog. The dog gets scared and runs for help (back to its owner). And the bear follows right back into the dog owner's lap.

Bear Warning

- **Leave scented items at home**—the perfume, hair spray, cologne and scented soaps. Using scented sprays and body lotions makes you smell like a big, tasty treat.
- **Fish cleaning**. Never clean fish within 100 feet of camp.

Cougars

Very few hikers ever see cougars in the wild. I've been tracked by them, but have yet to see one of these elusive kitties. Shy and solitary, there are about 2500 to 3000 of them roaming the entire state of Washington. The Olympics, however, contain one of the highest concentrations in the Northwest.

Cougars and hikers do sometimes encounter each other. To make sure the encounter is a positive one (at least for you), you need to understand these wildcats. Cougars are curious (after all, they're cats). They will follow hikers simply to see what kind of beasts we are, but they rarely (almost never) attack adult humans. If you do encounter a cougar, remember that cougars rely on prey that can't, or won't, fight back. So as soon as you see a cat, heed the following:

- **Do not run!** Running may trigger a cougar's attack instinct.
- **Stand up and face it**. Virtually every recorded cougar attack of humans has been a predator-prey attack. If you appear as another aggressive predator rather than as prey, the cougar will back down.
- **Try to appear large**. Wave your arms or a jacket over your head.
- **Pick up children and small dogs**.
- **Maintain eye contact** with the animal. The cougar will interpret this as a show of dominance on your part.
- **Back away slowly** if you can safely do so.

GEAR

No hiker should venture far up a trail without being properly equipped. Starting with the feet, a good pair of boots can make all the difference between a wonderful hike and a blistering affair. Keep your feet happy and you'll be happy.

But you can't talk boots without talking socks. Only one rule here: wear whatever is most comfortable, unless it's cotton. I prefer a synthetic liner under a wool sock. Cotton is a wonderful fabric, but not the best to hike in. When it gets wet, it stays wet and lacks any insulation value. In fact, wet cotton sucks away body heat, leaving you susceptible to hypothermia. Still, I encounter hundreds of hikers who prefer jeans and cotton T-shirts. I wear synthetics, except for my cap.

While the list of what you pack will vary from what another hiker on the same trail is carrying, there are a few items everyone should have in their packs. Every hiker who ventures into the woods should be prepared to spend the night out with emergency food and shelter. Mountain storms can whip up in a hurry, catching fair-weather hikers by surprise. What was an easy-to-follow trail during a calm, clear day can disappear into a confusing world of fog and rain—or snow. Therefore, every member of the party should pack the Ten Essentials as well as a few other items that aren't necessarily essential, but would be good to have on hand in an emergency.

The Ten Essentials

1. **Navigation (map and compass):** Especially important if you plan on doing any exploring off-trail. But more than just merely having a map and compass, be sure you know how to use them.
2. **Sun protection (sunglasses and sunscreen):** Even in the wet Olympics I always carry sunscreen and sunglasses. At higher elevations your exposure to UV rays is much more intense than at sea level. You can easily burn on snow and near water. Protect yourself.
3. **Insulation (extra clothing):** It may be 70 degrees Fahrenheit at the trailhead, but at the summit it's 45 and windy. Also, storms can and do blow in rapidly. In the high country it can snow anytime of the year. Be sure to carry raingear, wind gear, and extra layers.
4. **Illumination (flashlight/headlamp):** An injury may force you to spend the night—or perhaps you just didn't give yourself enough time to hike out. A good headlamp or flashlight is essential
5. **First-aid supplies:** At the very least your kit should include bandages, gauze, scissors, tape, tweezers, pain relievers, antiseptics, and perhaps a small manual. It is also recommended that you receive first-aid training through a program such as MOFA (Mountaineering Oriented First Aid).
6. **Fire (firestarter and matches/lighter):** And be sure you keep your matches dry. I use sealable plastic bags. A candle can come in handy too.
7. **Repair kit and tools (including a**

knife): The ubiquitous Swiss Army knife is a must. Multitools also work well, but they tend to be a bit heavier. A basic repair kit includes such things as a 20-foot length of nylon cord, a small roll of duct tape, some 1-inch webbing and extra webbing buckles (to fix broken pack straps), and a small tube of superglue. Duct tape is actually my eleventh essential: this stuff can perform miracles, from mending wounds and equipment to creating utensils, hats, you name it! It might not protect me from a nuclear blast, but it'll come in handy for just about any other situation.

8. **Nutrition (extra food):** Always pack in more food than what you need for your hike. If you are forced to spend the night, you'll be prepared. I also always pack a couple of energy bars for emergency pick-me-ups.

9. **Hydration (extra water):** I carry two full, 32-ounce water bottles all the time, unless I'm hiking entirely along a water source. You'll need to carry iodine tablets or a filter, too, so as not to catch any waterborne nasties like *Giardia*.

10. **Emergency shelter:** A space blanket or poncho can easily be transformed into an emergency tent. Consider packing some rope too.

TRAILHEAD CONCERNS

Sadly, the topic of trailhead and trail crime must be addressed. As urban areas continuously encroach upon our green spaces, societal ills follow along. As I write this (July 2006) the hiking community in Washington is in mourning and shock over the tragedy of two women hikers murdered on a trail in the Cascades. While this type of violent behavior is extremely rare (practically absent on most of our public lands, thankfully), it is a grim reminder that we are never truly free from the worst elements of society.

But by and large our hiking trails are safe places—far safer than most city streets. Common sense and vigilance, however, are still in order. This is true for all hikers, but particularly so for solo hikers. (Solo hiking sparks much debate over whether it is prudent or not. I hike solo 90 percent of the time, reaping rewards of deep reflection, self-determination, and a complete wilderness experience. You must decide for yourself.) Be aware of your surroundings at all times. Leave your itinerary with someone back home. If something doesn't feel right, it probably isn't. Take action by leaving the place or situation immediately. But remember, most hikers are friendly, decent people. Some may be a little introverted, but that's no cause for worry.

By far your biggest concern should be with trailhead theft. Car break-ins, sadly, are a far too common occurrence at some of our trailheads. Do not—absolutely under no circumstances— leave anything of value in your vehicle while out hiking. Take your wallet, cell phone, and listening devices with you, or better yet, don't bring them along in the first place. Don't leave anything in your car that may appear valuable. A duffle bag on the back seat may contain dirty T-shirts, but a thief may think there's a laptop in it. Save yourself the hassle of returning to a

Trailhead Crime

busted window by not giving criminals a reason to clout your car.

If you arrive at a trailhead and someone looks suspicious, don't discount your intuition. Take notes on the person and his or her vehicle. Record the license plate and report the behavior to the authorities. Do not confront the person. Leave and go to another trail.

While most car break-ins are crimes of opportunity by drug addicts looking for loot to support their fix, organized bands intent on stealing IDs have also been known to target parked cars at trailheads. While some trailheads are regularly targeted (such as coastal trails on the Olympic Peninsula), and others rarely if at all, there's no sure way of preventing this from happening to you other than being dropped off at the trailhead or taking the bus (rarely an option, either way). But you can make your car less of a target by not leaving anything of value in it.

ENJOY THE TRAILS

Most importantly, though, be safe and enjoy the trails in this book. They exist for our enjoyment and for the enjoyment of future generations of hikers. We can use them and protect them at the same time if we are careful with our actions, as well as forthright with our demands on Congress and state legislators to continue and further the protection of our state's wildlands.

Throughout the twentieth century, wilderness lovers helped secure protection for many of the lands we enjoy today. As we enter the twenty-first century, we must see to it that those protections continue and that the last bits of wildlands are also preserved for the enjoyment of future generations.

If you enjoy these trails, get involved! Trails may wind through trees, but they don't grow on them. Your involvement can be as simple as picking up trash, educating fellow citizens, or writing Congress or your state representative a letter. All of these seemingly small acts can make a big difference. Introduce children to our trails. We need to continue a legacy of good trail stewards. At the end of this book you'll find a list of organizations working on behalf of our trails and wildlands in Washington. Consider getting involved with a few of them.

Happy hiking!

A NOTE ABOUT SAFETY

Safety is an important concern in all outdoor activities. No guidebook can alert you to every hazard or anticipate the limitations of every reader. Therefore, the descriptions of roads, trails, routes, and natural features in this book are not representations that a particular place or excursion will be safe for your party. When you follow any of the routes described in this book, you assume responsibility for your own safety. Under normal conditions, such excursions require the usual attention to traffic, road and trail conditions, weather, terrain, the capabilities of your party, and other factors. Because many of the lands in this book are subject to development and/or change of ownership, conditions may have changed since this book was written that make your use of some of these routes unwise. Always check for current conditions, obey posted private property signs, and avoid confrontations with property owners or managers. Keeping informed on current conditions and exercising common sense are the keys to a safe, enjoyable outing.

—The Mountaineers Books

Opposite: North Head Lighthouse at Cape Disappointment State Park

Columbia River

Entering Washington's northeast corner and exiting through its southwest corner, the mighty Columbia River snakes across the Evergreen State and threads two-thirds of its land mass into one massive watershed. A sustaining life force to the region's First Peoples, the Columbia also allowed explorers and exploiters, settlers, and sailors access to the Pacific Northwest.

A transportation corridor, provider of power, and irrigation source for thousands of acres, the Columbia has changed much since its most famous visitors, Lewis and Clark and their Corps of Discovery, plied it two hundred years ago. And while much of the countryside that clings to the river's shorelines has been radically altered since Boston merchant Robert Gray named the river after his vessel in 1792, wild stretches do still exist.

No dams or large settlements mar the waterway near the Columbia's mouth on the Pacific. And while the legendary salmon runs have sadly yielded to "progress," another kind of progress is being made in restoring some of the area's rich estuaries and bottomland forests. Much of the hilly riverbanks are owned by private timber firms, but a few public and protected parcels grace the Lower Columbia.

On your hikes to these places, prepare to be projected back into the past. Native peoples, explorers, and hardscrabble farmers and fishermen have all left their signatures on this land. An abundant array of wildlife continues to tell the story of this fascinating corner of Washington State.

1 Julia Butler Hansen National Wildlife Refuge

RATING/ DIFFICULTY	ROUND-TRIP	ELEV GAIN/ HIGH POINT	SEASON
★★/1	5.6 miles	None/ 20 feet	June–Sept

50' One-way

0.5 1 1.5 2 2.5 2.8

Maps: USGS Skamokawa, refuge brochure and map available at refuge headquarters; **Contact:** Julia Butler Hansen National Wildlife Refuge, (360) 795-3915, *www.fws.gov /willapa/JuliaButlerHansen*; **Notes:** Dogs prohibited. Wildlife closure Oct 1–May 31; **GPS:** N 46 15.392, W 123 26.181

A flat and easy hike through a rich Columbia River bottomland: explore snaking sloughs and observe a slew of bird and wildlife, including the federally endangered Columbian white-tailed deer.

A Hiker on the "Center Road" in the Julia Butler Hansen National Wildlife Refuge

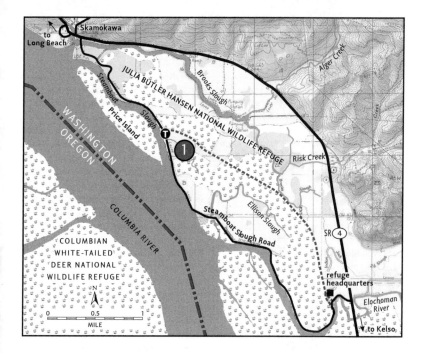

GETTING THERE

From Kelso travel west on State Route 4 for 26 miles to Cathlamet. Proceed for 2 more miles, crossing the Elochoman River and then turning left onto Steamboat Slough Road (signed for the national wildlife refuge). The refuge headquarters is in 0.25 mile—stop and get a map. Continue on Steamboat Slough Road for 3.3 miles. The trailhead for Center Road is on the right, marked by a gate and hiker sign.

ON THE TRAIL

The Julia Butler Hansen Refuge for the Columbian White-Tailed Deer may be a tongue-twister of a name, but at least no ankles will be twisted on this gentle hike. Established in 1972 to protect habitat for the endangered Columbian white-tailed deer, the refuge includes bottomland forests, open pastures, river islands, and lazy sloughs that evoke the American South rather than the Pacific Northwest.

In 1988 the refuge's name was changed to honor Julia Butler Hansen from nearby Cathlamet. Ms. Hansen served twenty-two years in the state legislature and fourteen years in Congress. She was instrumental in establishing the 5600-acre refuge.

Center Road is a gated and grassy "service road." It marches right through the middle of the refuge, offering plenty of opportunities for spotting a few of the three hundred shy deer residing here. Elk, coyotes, otters, herons, eagles, kingfishers, and osprey are all frequently sighted if you come up short in the deer department.

The trail is only open in the summer months, and your best bet for seeing deer is early in the morning or late in the day. Center Road traverses the refuge through mostly open pasture surrounded by wetlands. Take your time to identify birds and scope out camouflaged critters in the grasses.

Center Road ends in 2.8 miles at Steamboat Slough Road near the refuge headquarters. Either retrace your steps or return via the very lightly traveled Steamboat Slough Road for a loop, adding 0.5 mile. Views along the way include wide sweeping Columbia River vistas that enticed Captain William Clark (of Lewis and Clark fame) to exclaim, "Ocian in view!" He was a little premature, but not that far off.

EXTENDING YOUR TRIP

The nearby Skamokawa Vista Park (a county park) makes for an excellent car-camping base, with access to a sandy river beach.

2 Scarborough Hill

RATING/ DIFFICULTY	LOOP	ELEV GAIN/ HIGH POINT	SEASON
★★/2	2.8 miles	650 feet/ 767 feet	Year-round

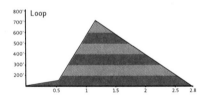

Map: USGS Chinook; **Contact:** Fort Columbia State Park, (360) 642-3078, infocent@parks.wa.gov, www.parks.wa.gov; **Notes:** Dogs must be leashed; **GPS:** N 46 15.251, W 123 55.261

Hike through a rare coastal old-growth Sitka spruce forest. Enjoy sweeping views of the mouth of the Columbia River. After your grunt up Scarborough Hill, *snoop around the meticulously preserved early twentieth-century historic structures of this former military reservation.*

GETTING THERE

From Kelso follow State Route 4 west for 56 miles to Naselle. Turn left (south) onto SR 401, proceeding 12 miles to US 101 at the Astoria-Megler Bridge. Follow US 101 for 3 miles. After emerging from a small tunnel, turn left into Fort Columbia State Park and continue 0.25 mile to the large parking area west of the interpretive center. (From Ilwaco follow US 101 south for 8 miles to the Fort Columbia turnoff.) The Scarborough Trail begins at the far west end of the parking area.

ON THE TRAIL

Fort Columbia State Park sits on a scenic bluff at the mouth of the Columbia River. Established in 1899, the fort was one of several defense installations designed to protect the Columbia from enemy attack.

Never fired upon, Fort Columbia preserves a piece of our history and a good chunk of old-growth forest. While the area never came under enemy attack, the surrounding forests were heavily slain. But within this park's six hundred acres, stately giant Sitka spruce trees still stand—trees that were old when Lewis and Clark paddled by two hundred years ago.

Three hiking trails lead through these centuries-old sentinels. They wind their way up and above the tidy historic military base to 767-foot Scarborough Hill. And while the arboreal giants are the main attraction, occasional gaps in the forest canopy provide satisfying views of the massive mouth of the Columbia—its horizon-spanning jetties, lost-in-time Astoria, Oregon, and lumpy Saddle and Neahkahnie Mountains rising behind it.

Opposite: Giant Sitka spruce along the Scarborough Hill Trail

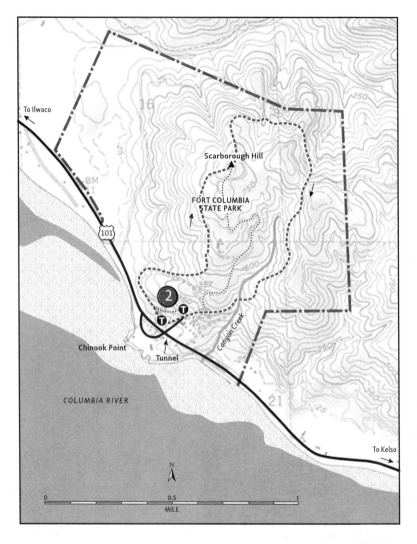

All three trails climb steeply, helping to slow you down in this timeless forest. Start your hike on the Scarborough Trail, winding around some batteries overlooking the Columbia. Then begin climbing. Pass a couple of side trails that veer to the right—they offer short-cut loop options if you're inclined to skip the summit.

Continue through rows of spruce and alder. Admire the glaucous sheen of the alders' smooth trunks contrasted against the spruces' scaly purple bark. After 1.2 miles of twisting and turning through these trees, reach Scarborough Hill's forested summit. For the longer loop back down, take a left, following the Canyon Creek Trail for 1.6 miles back to the base. Expect a good river view among yet more impressive trees. The Military Road Trail departs right, is 0.6 mile shorter, and is much easier on the knees.

EXTENDING YOUR TRIP

Whichever way you decide to return, save some time to explore the historic grounds of the fort before heading home.

Long Beach Peninsula

Extending over 20 miles from the mouth of the Columbia River to the mouth of Willapa Bay is the Long Beach Peninsula, a jutting finger along the Pacific, lined with fine sandy beaches against a backdrop of silver dunes. Ever since Captain William Clark wandered these beaches in November 1805, tourists have been flocking here. In the late nineteenth century, well-heeled Portlanders boarded paddle ships destined downriver to this peninsula. Tidy cottages sprung up in new beach towns: Seaview, Long Beach, and Ocean Park. Oystermen settled the peninsula's northern reaches in Nahcotta and Oysterville, once one of the richest communities in Washington.

"OCEAN IN VIEW!"

Any hiker taking to the trails and beaches of southwestern Washington will be bombarded not only with beautiful scenery, but also with history. In essence, the state's "modern" history began here. In the late 1700s, Vancouver, Meares, Gray, Cook, and others sailed up and down the coastline, mapping, exploring, and trading with Native peoples.

It was Captain John Meares, a British sea merchant, who in 1788 named Cape Disappointment. He was disappointed at not finding the "River of the West." He thought that the mouth of the Columbia was merely a bay. Today, hikers who take to the rugged headlands of Cape Disappointment certainly won't be.

Lewis and Clark spent several wet November days in the region in 1805. Captain William Clark thought he sighted the Pacific near present-day Skamokawa, exclaiming "Ocian in view!" The river mouth that Meares mistook for a bay, Clark mistook for the ocean. Clark was one of the area's first recorded hikers, climbing over North Head at Cape Disappointment and on to Long Beach. Today you can trace his journey on the paved and gravel Discovery Trail that leads from Ilwaco to Long Beach.

Willapa Bay, once known as Shoalwater Bay, helped feed the forty-niners of San Francisco (the gold rushers, not the football players) with succulent oysters. But while Europeans and Americans of European and Asian descent were settling and shaping what would become Pacific, Wahkiakum and Grays Harbor Counties, Native peoples had little to say about this change. On July 1, 1855, at the mouth of the Chehalis River near Grays Harbor, Washington's first territorial governor, Isaac Stevens, brought together coastal tribes to sign a treaty stipulating that they relinquish their land. The tribes didn't capitulate—it wouldn't, however, be Stevens's last attempt.

You can reflect on our state's fascinating and sobering human history while hiking the beaches and trails of southwestern Washington.

Today, beachcombers still enjoy the Long Beach Peninsula, and oyster harvesting is still a viable part of the local economy. For day hikers, the peninsula offers two prime destinations, one on each end of the elongated land form. Cape Disappointment to the south, with its rugged headlands and old-growth forests, is one of Washington's most popular state parks. Leadbetter Point, on the north end, consists of the state's wildest coastline south of Olympic National Park and is a bird watcher's version of heaven.

And while the state still allows vehicles to maraud the peninsula's beautiful beaches (note to legislators: the beaches are no longer needed for mail and goods delivery, State Route 103 does just fine), at Leadbetter Point and Cape Disappointment you and the resident wildlife are free to wander free from exhaust.

3 Cape Disappointment State Park

RATING/ DIFFICULTY	ROUND-TRIP	ELEV GAIN/ HIGH POINT	SEASON
★★★/2	4.2 miles	300 feet/ 250 feet	Year-round

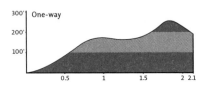

Map: USGS Cape Disappointment; **Contact:** Cape Disappointment State Park, (360) 642-3078, *infocent@parks.wa.gov*, *www.parks.wa.gov*; **Notes:** Dogs must be leashed; **GPS:** N 46 17.136, W 124 03.796

Take the long and scenic way to Cape Disappointment's North Head Lighthouse. Through a salt-sprayed maritime forest, trace part of Captain Clark's hike on the Long Beach Peninsula. From the high headland that houses the 1898 lighthouse, take in breathtaking views that include thundering waves, windswept dunes, and scores of shorebirds skimming the crashing surf.

GETTING THERE

From Kelso follow State Route 4 west for 56 miles to Naselle. Turn left (south) on SR 401, proceeding 12 miles to US 101 at the Astoria-Megler Bridge. Continue on US 101 for 11 miles to Ilwaco and the junction of SR 100. Follow SR 100 (it's a loop, bear left) to Cape Disappointment State Park, and in 2 miles turn left into the park. Drive 0.5 mile to a four-way stop and turn right. Pass the entrance station, and in 0.25 mile turn right again. In 0.4 mile come to the McKenzie Head trailhead and park here.

ON THE TRAIL

There are over 6.5 miles of hiking trails in 1884-acre Cape Disappointment State Park. Once home to Fort Canby, a military reservation established in 1852 (before Washington statehood), the state park was created in the 1950s. Most of its trails are short. All are scenic. The 1.8-mile North Head Trail is the longest, traversing a moisture-dripping old-growth Sitka spruce forest and offering spectacular ocean views along the way. It ties into several other trails, allowing for extended explorations.

The trail to North Head starts through a flat marshy area before heading up onto a small rugged ridge. When Lewis and Clark visited this area, the ridge was a headland protruding into the Pacific. After the North Jetty was built in 1917, this marshy forested area formed through accretion (trapped sand and silt accumulation). The land mass and beaches of Cape Disappointment are growing (and they say land doesn't grow!).

On what can be a muddy trail, climb above the old coastline on this former headland. Giant

Sitka spruces keep you well-shaded, while gaps in the forest canopy offer splendid views down to the "new" beach. In 1.8 miles from the trailhead, come to a parking lot. (Yes, you could have driven to this point—but why? Exercise and nature are good for your body and soul!)

Now hike the 0.3-mile trail down to the North Head Lighthouse for one of the finest maritime settings in all of Washington. Return the way you came.

EXTENDING YOUR TRIP

Continue from the upper parking lot on the Westwind Trail for a 1-mile journey down to Beards Hollow on the beach. After you've returned to your car (or before you head out), consider making the quick 1-mile round trip up McKenzie Head. From this old World War II battery, admire the mouth of the Columbia River and the Cape Disappointment Lighthouse—completed in 1856, it's the state's

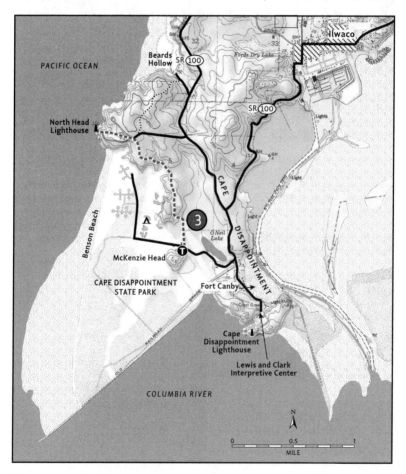

Rugged headlands are one of the highlights in Cape Disappointment State Park.

oldest. The park also offers great car camping, including yurts, if you feel like sticking around to sample a few more of its wonderful trails.

4 Leadbetter Point State Park: Dune Forest Loop

RATING/ DIFFICULTY	LOOP	ELEV GAIN/ HIGH POINT	SEASON
★★/1	2.9 miles	60 feet/ 35 feet	Year-round

Map: USGS Oysterville; **Contact:** Leadbetter Point State Park, (360) 642-3078, *infocent@ parks.wa.gov, www.parks.wa.gov*; **Notes:** Dogs must be leashed; **GPS:** N 46 36.421, W 124 02.629

A great loop any time of year: explore quiet maritime forest and the bird-saturated Willapa Bay shoreline on the wild northern tip of the Long Beach Peninsula. Chances are good that you'll sight bear, deer, or otter along the way.

GETTING THERE
From Kelso follow State Route 4 west for 60 miles to US 101. Head south on US 101 for 15 miles, and just before entering Long Beach turn right (north) onto Sandridge Road (signed "Leadbetter Point 20 miles"). In 11.5 miles come to a junction with SR 103. Continue north on SR 103. In 7.3 miles enter Leadbetter Point State Park. Continue another 1.5 miles to the road end and trailhead. Privy available.

ON THE TRAIL
Leadbetter Point consists of Washington's wildest coastal lands outside of Olympic National

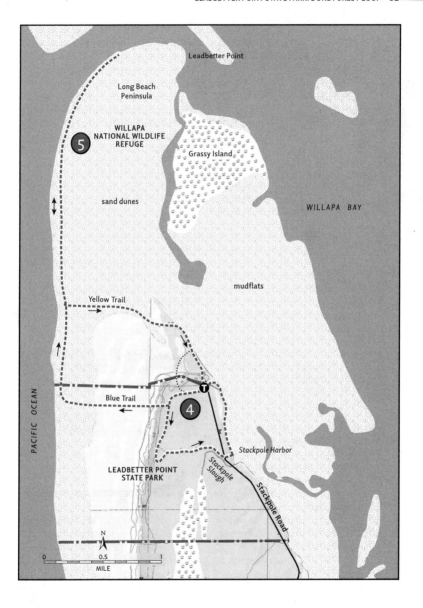

Leadbetter Point

Long Beach
Peninsula

WILLAPA
NATIONAL WILDLIFE
REFUGE

Grassy Island

sand dunes

WILLAPA BAY

mudflats

Yellow Trail

Blue Trail

PACIFIC OCEAN

Stackpole Harbor

LEADBETTER POINT
STATE PARK

Stackpole
Slough

Stackpole Road

N

0   0.5   1
MILE

Pacific Tree Frog—a common resident around Willapa Bay

Park. Undeveloped and untrammeled, over 3000 acres of dunes, salt marshes, and maritime forest and more than 8 miles of vehicle-free ocean and bay beaches are protected within a state park and a national wildlife refuge.

Over 6 miles of trail traverse 1200-acre Leadbetter Point State Park and offer access to both the Pacific and the adjacent Willapa National Wildlife Refuge. While most hikers may be enticed to head directly to Leadbetter Point's wide, sandy ocean beach, the area's real charms lie within its diverse bay and forest ecosystems. The Dune Forest Loop is a great introduction to these wildlife-rich habitats. And if you're looking for a good winter hike in the region, this loop isn't subject to the flooding that keeps the coastal trails under water for half the year.

Start your loop by heading left (west) on the Red Trail, also known as the Dune Forest Loop. Solid tread soon yields to loose sand, slowing your momentum. In 0.5 mile come to a junction with the Blue Trail, which leads 0.8 mile to the Pacific. Continue left, hiking along a sand ridge—an old dune that has since been colonized by shore pine, wax myrtle, salal, and bearberry (kinnikinnick). After another 0.5 mile the trail turns inland (east). As the sound of the surf fades into the distance, Sitka spruce begins to dominate the forest.

In 2.1 miles from the trailhead come to the park access road (and an alternate trailhead). Cross the road, making your way to Willapa Bay. The trail now turns north for 0.8 mile, hugging the shoreline of the bay. Enjoy views of the expansive bay set against a backdrop of rolling, cloud-hugging hills. Birdlife is profuse. Pelicans, marbled godwits, loons, grebes, mergansers—over a hundred species in all ply these waters and saltflats. Eagles can often be spotted on overhanging snags. Mammals are abundant too. If hiking during low tide, scan the mudflats for raccoon, bear, and elk tracks. In 2.9 miles close the loop.

EXTENDING YOUR TRIP

A 1.1-mile interpretive loop, the Bay Trail makes for a nice mileage boost.

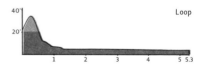

5 Leadbetter Point State Park: Leadbetter Point

RATING/ DIFFICULTY	LOOP	ELEV GAIN/ HIGH POINT	SEASON
★★★/3	10.6 miles	50 feet/ 35 feet	May–Oct

Maps: USGS Oysterville, USGS North Cove, refuge map available at headquarters on US 101 near milepost 24; **Contact:** Willapa National Wildlife Refuge, (360) 484-3482, *www.fws.gov /willapa/WillapaNWR*; **Notes:** Dogs prohibited. Removal of plants or animals from refuge is prohibited. **GPS:** N 46 36.421, W 124 02.629

Hike to the loneliest stretch of beach south of the Olympic Peninsula. Traverse thick maritime forest cloaked in bearberry and salal before emerging on a windswept beach guarded by phalanxes of high dunes. Feeling energetic? Hike all the way to the wild tip of Leadbetter Point for an all-day 10.6-mile journey.

GETTING THERE

From Kelso follow State Route 4 west for 60 miles to US 101. Head south on US 101 for 15 miles, and just before entering Long Beach turn right (north) onto Sandridge Road (signed "Leadbetter Point 20 miles"). In 11.5 miles come to a junction with SR 103. Continue north on SR 103. In 7.3 miles enter Leadbetter

A hiker takes a break from a winter hike at Leadbetter Point

State Park. Continue another 1.5 miles to the road end and trailhead. Privy available.

ON THE TRAIL

Leadbetter Point's forests, salt marshes, its Willapa Bay shoreline, and its mudflats are prime scoping grounds for bird-watchers. This wild northern tip of the Long Beach Peninsula contains some of the best breeding and staging grounds on the entire West Coast for a myriad of species, from snowy owls to snowy plovers. Hikers intent on adding to their bird life lists should take to the area's trails. But if you're intent on stretching your legs, set your sights on Leadbetter's beaches, among the finest in the Pacific Northwest.

Before beginning, take note. Both the ocean and bay beach trails are subject to flooding from November through April. We're talking knee- to thigh-deep of cold tannic water inundating a half-plus mile of each trail. Now, on several occasions, I've donned sport sandals and plodded through the limb-numbing waters. It's sort of fun—like exploring a southern swamp but without the snapping turtles, leeches, and alligators. But unless you have a high tolerance for cold water, wait until the trail dries out sometime in late spring.

From the trailhead head west on the Red Trail (a.k.a. Dune Forest Loop) for 0.5 mile to a junction and take the Blue Trail right. Follow this good path for 0.8 mile through low-lying shrubs and thick maritime forest before breaking out into high dunes adorned with swaying sedges. Reach the beach and behold a wide sandy strand void of people. Head north for 0.5 mile, entering the Willapa National Wildlife Refuge (dogs prohibited beyond this point). Locate the trail sign for the "Yellow Trail (a.k.a. Bear Berry Trail). This is your return route to the trailhead.

You can return from this point for a 3.6-mile loop, or continue trekking on the beach all the way to Leadbetter Point. It's a 3.5-mile journey to the constantly shifting northern terminus of the peninsula. Along the way admire one of the largest undisturbed dune complexes in the state (stay out of them though: endangered snowy plovers nest here). Reach the tip of the peninsula and admire the wild and treacherous mouth of Willapa Bay. After snooping around or taking a quiet beachside nap, retrace your steps back to the Yellow Trail.

This good trail makes a 1.8-mile return via fine stands of shore pine crowded in thickets of bearberry. A short stint along a sandy Willapa Bay beach caps off the hike before delivering you to your point of origin.

EXTENDING YOUR TRIP

During low tide you can continue beyond Leadbetter Point for 1.5 miles on good sandy bayside beach. But don't think about returning to the trailhead via the bay side. Salt marshes, mudflats, and snaking sloughs make travel extremely difficult.

Willapa Bay

Willapa Bay is the second-largest estuary on the Pacific Coast—only San Francisco Bay is larger. But unlike that California estuary, which is home to over seven million people, Willapa Bay is practically deserted. Pacific County, which contains Willapa Bay, has a population of just over twenty thousand. And though settlements along Willapa's shores are among the oldest in the state (Oysterville was founded in 1854), much of the 260-square-mile estuary looks as it did when British captain John Meares first sighted and named it Shoalwater Bay in 1788.

Early settlers were attracted to the region's abundant oyster beds and adjacent timbered hills. They diked the salt marshes for dairy farming. But despite all of this bounty and activity, no big population centers developed and no jetties were ever constructed at Willapa's mouth—dunes and sand bars continue to shift as nature intended.

In 1937 President Franklin D. Roosevelt established the Willapa National Wildlife Refuge, ensuring that a large portion of this prime and productive estuary would remain a healthy ecosystem. The refuge consists of three main parcels (management units), and each one is unique. Leadbetter Point (Hikes 4 and 5) has wild beaches and high dunes. The Lewis and Riekkola Units (Hike 6) consist of reclaimed farmland, extensive mudflats, and the mouth of the Bear River. The Long Island Unit (Hike 7) protects the largest estuarine island on the West Coast and a cedar grove nearly one thousand years old.

Willapa Bay can be hiked all year, but take note: the refuge is managed for hunting and is popular with elk and bird hunters. Plan your hikes accordingly and respect these users—they help fund public-land acquisition and most of them have high conservation ethics. Visit the refuge headquarters along US 101 near milepost 24 for a map and information on the area's wildlife.

Follow the lazy and snaking Bear River to the sprawling mud and salt flats of Willapa Bay. During low tide look out over a landscape that glistens. Listen to it belch and gurgle. Watch herons spear fry, osprey drop from the sky, and otters playfully slide. Observe critters large and small, from grazing elk on the forest edge to singing frogs in trailside pools. On an old dike elevated just a few feet above the flats, dry feet are guaranteed as you hike through this saturated landscape.

6 Willapa National Wildlife Refuge: Bear River

RATING/ DIFFICULTY	ROUND-TRIP	ELEV GAIN/ HIGH POINT	SEASON
★★/1	3.5 miles	None/ 10 feet	Year-round

Round trip

10'

1.75   3.5

Maps: USGS Chinook, refuge map available at headquarters on US 101 near milepost 24; **Contact:** Willapa National Wildlife Refuge, (360) 484-3482, *www.fws.gov/willapa/WillapaNWR*; **Notes:** Dogs prohibited; **GPS:** N 46 21.551, W 123 57.691

Evening clouds reflecting on Bear River

GETTING THERE

From Kelso follow State Route 4 west for 60 miles to US 101. Head 10 miles south on US 101. Immediately after crossing the bridge over the Bear River, turn right (north) onto Jeldness Road (signed "Willapa NWR Lewis Unit"). Proceed 1 mile to the road end and trailhead.

ON THE TRAIL

Start your hike on the dike/trail by passing through a gate and immediately entering a world surrounded by water. With the Bear River on your right and freshwater lagoons on your left, abundant and varied birdlife constantly vie for your attention. But the views are good too. The Bear River Range rises over the eastern flats. To the north, the golden bluffs of Long Island's High Point adds relief to the bay's seemingly featureless horizon.

But as you hike farther along the dike, patterns emerge in the immediate landscape. The river channels into slithering sloughs that

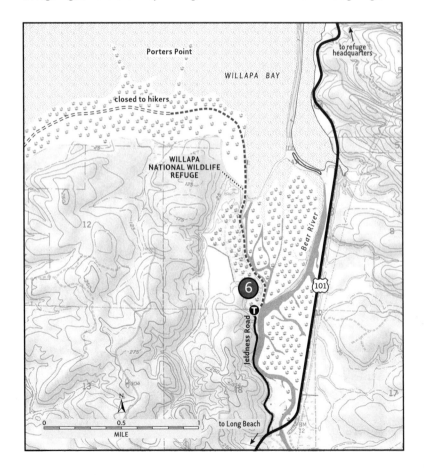

slice through swales of swaying grasses and across mounds of mud. Geese, cormorants, blackbirds, ducks, kingfishers, sparrows—the flats and sloughs are alive with avian activity.

In 0.75 mile a spur trail branches between lagoons, heading for higher ground. In another 0.25 mile a bridge spans a channel, allowing access to the mudflats. Come to yet another bridge in another 0.5 mile. Explore the mud and salt flats—but be sure you're wearing good waterproof boots. The dike/trail continues for another mile, but is open to hikers for only another 0.25 mile. Enjoy good bayside views of the Long Beach Peninsula from the turnaround point.

⑦ Willapa National Wildlife Refuge: Long Island

RATING/ DIFFICULTY	ROUND-TRIP	ELEV GAIN/ HIGH POINT	SEASON
★★/2	5.75 miles	425 feet/ 225 feet	Year-round

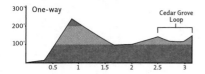

Giant ancient cedar on Long Island

Maps: USGS Long Island, refuge map available at headquarters on US 101 near milepost 24; **Contact:** Willapa National Wildlife Refuge, (360) 484-3482, *www.fws.gov/willapa/WillapaNWR*; **Notes:** Dogs prohibited. Boat needed to access trailhead; heavy hunting activity Sept–Nov. **GPS:** N 46 24.739, W 123 56.385

The largest estuarine island on the entire Pacific Coast, Willapa Bay's Long Island is indeed a special place to hike. Miles of trails and old woods roads traverse this 5460-acre land mass, allowing access to quiet tidal flats, scenic bluffs, hidden sloughs, and old townsites. But the biggest attraction on Long Island is its biggest attraction—a grove of giant cedars almost one thousand years old!

GETTING THERE
From Kelso follow State Route 4 west for 60 miles to US 101. Head south on US 101 for 4.75 miles to Willapa National Wildlife Refuge headquarters. (From Ilwaco follow US 101 north for 13 miles.) Park at the headquarters and launch your watercraft to reach the trailhead on Long Island.

ON THE TRAIL
The hike to Long Island's ancient cedars isn't overly difficult—it's getting to the trail that

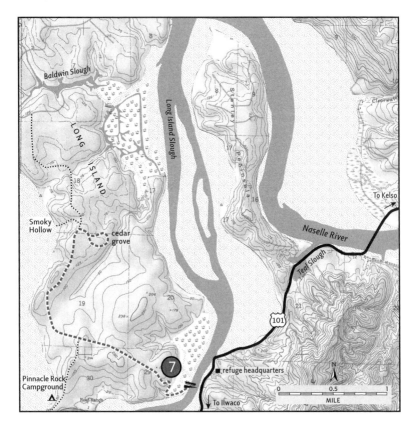

may cause some problems. There's no bridge to the island. You'll need your own canoe, kayak, or other kind of boat to make the short channel crossing to the trailhead. Be sure to check in at refuge headquarters (located across from the boat launch) for bay conditions. Mudflats and weather can make the crossing tricky at times.

Once on the island, secure your watercraft and get hiking! Home to settlements and sawmills during the past century, most of Long Island has been logged. Amazingly, however, a 274-acre tract of old-growth western red cedar was spared from the chainsaw. In 1986

this primeval patch—the last large coastal old-growth forest grove left in Washington—was protected and added to the wildlife refuge. In 2005 the grove was named in honor of Don Bonker, a former congressman from Vancouver who played a major role in preserving these majestic trees.

The road/trail starts off on a beautiful point with nice views south of Willapa Bay's extensive mudflats. Through second- and third-growth forest the trail winds its way inland, climbing a couple of hundred feet in the process. Woodland birds—kinglets, juncos, flycatchers, and chickadees—flit in the regenerating forest.

Long Island is full of life. Bear, elk, deer, and cougar all take residence here.

In 1 mile come to a junction. The trail left leads approximately 0.5 mile to Pinnacle Point, a good place for observing elk. Continue on the main trail, and at 2.5 miles come to another junction. Take the trail right—a cedar sign indicates this way to the Don Bonker Ancient Grove. A few big stumps greet you first—then bang! Complete trees! Giant trees! Ancient trees! An old-growth cathedral of trees and you're the sole parishioner. The trail makes a 0.75-mile loop, touching just the periphery of this special grove so as not to disturb this endangered ecosystem. Walk quietly, walk slowly—enjoy and embrace this forest that has defied the centuries. When you're ready to be projected back into the present, retrace your steps.

EXTENDING YOUR TRIP

Inquire at the refuge headquarters about how to get to nearby Teal Slough. There you'll find another ancient cedar grove. It's smaller, but the trees are grander—some of the largest specimens I have seen in the coastal Northwest. Hike the Salmon Art Trail while at the headquarters. Created by art students from the University of Washington, this unique 0.75-mile interpretive trail is lined with sculptures and images reflecting the area's wildlife.

Old-growth Sitka spruce are the star attraction at Butte Creek

Map: USGS Raymond; **Contact:** Department of Natural Resources, Pacific Cascade Region, (360) 577-2025, *pacific-cascade-region@wadnr.gov, www.dnr.wa.gov*; **Notes:** Dogs must be leashed. Picnic area open Apr 1–Oct 31. Park at gate when picnic area closed; **GPS:** N 46 42.965, W 123 44.557

8 Butte Creek Sitka Spruce Grove

RATING/ DIFFICULTY	LOOP	ELEV GAIN/ HIGH POINT	SEASON
★/1	1.5 miles	200 feet/ 425 feet	Year-round

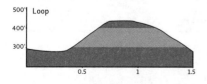

Hike through an old-growth Sitka spruce forest just minutes from the mill town of Raymond. Butte Creek's magnificent ancient grove of trees is a small remnant of the grand forests that once covered the surrounding Willapa Hills.

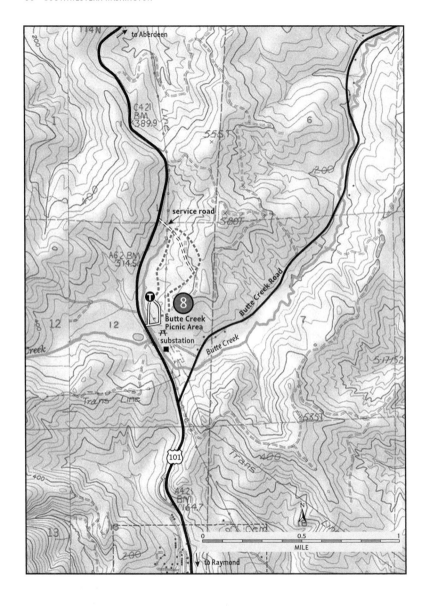

GETTING THERE

From Raymond travel north 2.5 miles on US 101. (From Aberdeen follow US 101 south for 23 miles.) Butte Creek Picnic Area is on the right (east) just beyond milepost 61.

ON THE TRAIL

All along US 101 as it winds around Willapa Bay, timber-company signs announce when the surrounding forest was cut, replanted, and when it will be cut again. Almost the entire Willapa watershed has been logged over at least twice. Green gold, these trees fueled local economies and helped build this nation. But sadly, very little remains of the original forest that once lined the salty marshes and covered the scrappy hills surrounding Willapa Bay.

At Butte Creek, a small but beautiful grove of old-growth Sitka spruce still stands. Here you can hike among stately trees and revel in their majesty. Be thankful that this grove exists, but also lament that we didn't set aside a few others in the area as well.

Start your hike by a sign that says "Unimproved Trail." Don't let that fool you—the trail is very improved, built well and well-cared for but "unimproved" because it can't accommodate wheel chairs. The Butte Creek Trail makes a loop about 1.5 miles long, returning back to the picnic area just to the south of where you began. Various side trails lead off the main path, allowing for shorter loops and variations. The main trail winds its way through a dark forest dominated by spruce with a sprinkling of Douglas-fir and hemlock. Moss carpets everything within this lush environment.

A small stream runs through the parcel, and the main trail crosses it several times on good bridges. The trail runs along Butte Creek for a short distance before crossing a service road, climbing a little, and then looping through a younger forest. The trail then recrosses the service road to remerge in the ancient grove. Cross a creek, come to

an "overlook," and then close the loop on an "improved" trail.

This area was once part of an old homestead. Now, with the cooperation of the Washington State Department of Natural Resources, students from nearby Raymond High School have staked a claim here. They help maintain the trails and facilities of Butte Creek—and hopefully, like you upon hiking this area, they have gained a better understanding and appreciation for our dwindling old-growth forests.

Chehalis River Valley

The Chehalis River forms a big horseshoe in southwestern Washington. Oxbowing and flowing gently through a wide and low valley, it's a lazy river for much of its 100-plus-mile course. From its beginning in the cloud-cloaked Willapa Hills, the Chehalis flows northeast through rural countryside to the small cities of Centralia and Chehalis. Here, surrounded by lush pastures, the river bends westward, cutting a low divide between the Willapa and Black Hills. As the Chehalis gets closer to its outlet, Grays Harbor, it takes on the characteristics of a southern lowcountry river; a waterway lined with moss-draped trees fanning out into a labyrinth of sloughs.

Very little wild country remains along the Chehalis. Logging, farming, and creeping urbanization have taken a toll on the natural communities of this large watershed. Old growth remains only in a few small pockets. Very little remains, too, of the biologically diverse prairies and oak savannas that once graced this river's lower reaches.

Most of the Chehalis River valley remains in private ownership. It's a good river to paddle but a difficult one to discover on foot. Fortunately, there are a few natural gems along this waterway in public ownership. They help preserve some of the rich natural history of this region as well as introduce hikers to this oft-overlooked part of the state.

And while the Chehalis Valley lacks pristine natural areas, it's rich in history. Hopefully someday the area's history will include a chapter on how its forests, prairies, and hills were restored to healthy and vibrant ecosystems.

9 Rainbow Falls State Park

RATING/ DIFFICULTY	ROUND-TRIP	ELEV GAIN/ HIGH POINT	SEASON
★/1	Up to 3 miles	200 feet/ 450 feet	Year-round

Map: USGS Rainbow Falls; **Contact:** Rainbow Falls State Park, (360) 291-3767, *infocent@ parks.wa.gov, www.parks.wa.gov*; **Notes:** Dogs must be leashed; **GPS:** N 46 37.812, W 123 13.911

Hike through some of the last standing old-growth trees in the Chehalis Valley. Admire trails, bridges, and structures built by the Depression-era Civil-ian Conservation Corps (CCC). Once finished hiking, sit by a small cascade and let it lull you to rest.

GETTING THERE

From Chehalis (exit 77 on I-5) follow State Route 6 west for 16 miles to Rainbow Falls State Park. Park on south side of the highway or in the day-use area 0.3 mile from the park entrance.

ON THE TRAIL

This little state park on the upper reaches of the Chehalis River has been attracting visitors since the early twentieth century when it was a community park. Once surrounded by thousands of acres of old-growth forest, the only ancient trees left standing in this region are within the 139 acres of the park. While it's the small cascade, Rainbow Falls, that lures people here, it's the remnant old growth that's the real big attraction.

About 3 miles of interconnecting trail wind through the lush tract of big cedars, hemlock, Douglas-fir, and the occasional Sitka spruce. Beneath the lofty canopy, alders are draped in

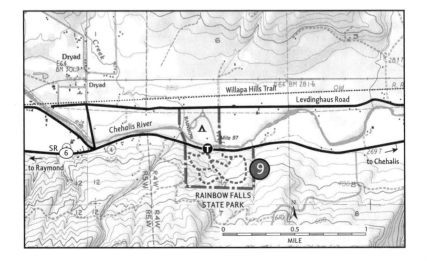

moss and the forest floor is carpeted in oxalis. It's a fairy-tale forest where chickarees and chickadees frolic and flit like gregarious elves in a magical kingdom.

From the trailhead you can set out in several directions and blaze your own course. Trails are signed and you really can't get lost; all trails loop back to the trailhead. The Oxalis

Old-growth cedar at Rainbow Falls State Park

Loop passes by some of the larger trees in the park, while the Woodpecker Trail descends into a small lush ravine complete with a bubbling brook. Hike these trails as a journey—not toward a destination—and enjoy this special tract of remnant wild country.

EXTENDING YOUR TRIP

After your hike, take time to see the rest of the park, including the CCC-built structures and Rainbow Falls, a small cascade tumbling over basalt ledges. If you'd like more hiking, head to the Willapa Hills trailhead located near the campground. This former railroad right-of-way is now a multiuse trail administered by Washington State Parks. Much of the 56-mile trail is still pretty rough, but the 7-mile section from the park to the old Pe Ell Depot is graded with crushed gravel. It makes for a good hike with lots of Chehalis River and Willapa Hills views.

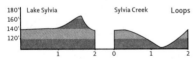

10 Lake Sylvia State Park

RATING/ DIFFICULTY	ROUND-TRIP	ELEV GAIN/ HIGH POINT	SEASON
★★/1	Two 2-mile loops	lake loop 30 feet/ 170 feet creek loop 60 feet/ 140 feet	Year-round

180' Lake Sylvia   Sylvia Creek   Loops
160'
140'
120'
    1   2   0   1   2

Map: USGS Montesano; **Contact:** Lake Sylvia State Park, (360) 249-3621, infocent@parks.wa.gov, www.parks.wa.gov; **Notes:** Dogs must be leashed; **GPS:** N 46 59.841, W 123 35.643

Two 2-mile loops in a 237-acre state park not too far from downtown Montesano. Enjoy an easy hike through mature forest along a sliver of a lake teeming with fish and birdlife. Then amble alongside a babbling creek to appreciate engineers past (those who conducted trains) and engineers present (furry ones who build dams).

GETTING THERE

Exit US 12 in Montesano and head north on Main Street past a traffic light and the scenic county courthouse. Turn left on Spruce Avenue, proceeding three blocks. Turn right on 3rd Street, which eventually becomes Sylvia Lake Road, and drive 1.2 miles to Lake Sylvia State Park. At the park entrance booth turn left, then cross the bridge and park at the day-use area near the ranger residence.

ON THE TRAIL

Lake Sylvia State Park packs a lot of history, natural beauty, and recreation within its tight borders. Once an old logging camp, the area was converted into a park in 1936. The narrow lake was created by damming Sylvia Creek, first for rounding logs and then for providing Montesano's electricity. Plenty of artifacts and evidence remain in the park from its early days. But hikers will be pleasantly surprised to see how well the area's forests have recovered. Mature trees hover above the lake and creek, providing not only a pretty backdrop, but also some great wildlife habitat.

This hike consists of two loops originating from the same origin. Start out near the boat launch, hiking north along Lake Sylvia's west shore on a perfectly level path that once housed tracks for a logging railroad. No gasoline motors are allowed on the lake, providing paddlers and hikers a peaceful environment. Mature evergreens shade the trail while large alders drape over the tranquil waters. The northern end of the lake is marshy, providing good cover for ducks, geese, and herons.

In 1 mile you'll hit an old logging road. Turn

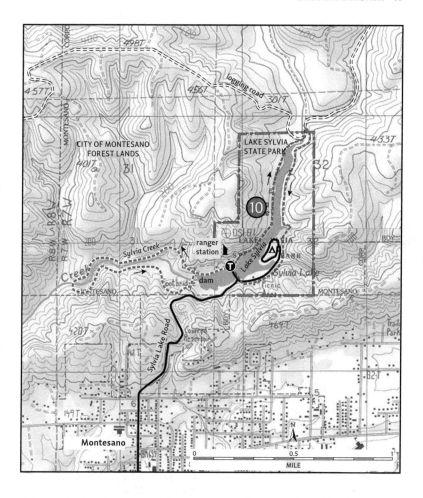

right, cross Sylvia's inlet stream, and then turn right again to hike back along the lake's eastern shore. The return trail is wilder, climbing over bluffs and darting in and out of cool side ravines. You'll emerge in the park's attractive campground (a great weekend base). Walk the campground access road a short distance back to the entrance booth, cross the bridge, and return to your start.

Refill water bottles and head south along the lake for the second loop. Cross a cove on an old railroad bridge (now a beloved fishing spot) and head to the start of the Sylvia Creek Forestry Trail. Follow this 2-mile loop through adjacent City of Montesano City Forest. Along the creek and through cool forests of maple and cedar, keep an eye out for more evidence of past human activity (such as old

An old rail bridge across Lake Sylvia is now a hiker's favorite spot.

springboard cuts and railroad trestles). Look, too, for signs of animal activity. Beaver are active along this stretch of the creek. Close the loop by crossing the old human-built dam that created Lake Sylvia. Enjoy the view before returning to your vehicle.

EXTENDING YOUR TRIP

Nearby Vance Creek County Park in Elma (east along US 12) contains a lovely 0.75-mile paved path around a small pond.

11 Chehalis River Sloughs

RATING/ DIFFICULTY	ROUND-TRIP	ELEV GAIN/ HIGH POINT	SEASON
★★/1	7 miles	None/ 20 feet	Year-round

Map: USGS Central Park; **Contact:** Department of Natural Resources, Pacific Cascade Region, (360) 577-2025, *pacific-cascade-region@wadnr .gov, www.dnr.wa.gov*; **Notes:** Dogs prohibited; **GPS:** N 46 56.692, W 123 39.028

A "slough" of surprises awaits you on this wonderful interpretive trail developed by the Washington State Department of Natural Resources. Journey through the wildlife- and history-rich Chehalis River Surge Plain Natural Area Preserve via an old logging rail bed. Along snaking sloughs and through a tunnel of greenery, you may think you're hiking in Louisiana instead of Washington.

GETTING THERE

From Montesano follow State Route 107 west for 4 miles. Turn right on Preachers Slough Road (signed for hiking) and proceed 0.1 mile to the eastern trailhead. (From Aberdeen travel south on US 101 for 3 miles to Cosmopolis. Just beyond the Weyerhaeuser mill, turn left onto the Blue Slough Road and drive 5 miles to SR 107, passing the western trailhead. Turn left and continue for 1.2 miles to the Preachers Slough Road turnoff.) Privy available.

ON THE TRAIL

From 1910 until 1985, trains rumbled through this saturated bottomland of scaly-barked spruce and speckled-bark alder. A few years back, trail crews from the Cedar Creek Correctional Camp helped transform the abandoned line into a great little trail. Hikers can now get onboard for a trip back in time and into the deep recesses of this productive ecosystem. While chugging along, plan for plenty of stops at the numerous viewing platforms and interpretive plaques along the way.

From the eastern trailhead, start by crossing a swampy pool on a firm bridge and then, with all due respect to the late great Johnny Cash, walk the line. Through a lush understory of vegetation the trail brushes up against Preachers Slough. Winter's lack of greenery allows for better viewing and the guarantee of a mosquito-free journey. In 0.5 mile reach a viewing platform that juts out over the lazy waterway. Just a few miles from the Chehalis River's outlet in Grays Harbor, this area is influenced by tidewaters. As the tide comes in, the heavy saltwater sinks, lifting freshwater to the top and forcing it to flood the surrounding bottomlands—hence the name "surge plain."

Continuing, you'll soon pass a plant restoration area. Lined with a hedgerow of willows and alders, the trail skirts an active farm. At 1.75 miles you'll arrive at a bench and slough overlook. Beyond this point the trail gets less use and may be a bit grassy. Carry on, traversing a marshy area, where copious birds—flycatchers, wrens, and warblers—will serenade you. At 3.5 miles you'll come to the trail's western end at a small parking area and a great overlook

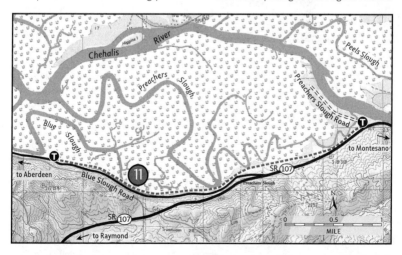

Old pilings in Blue Slough at the end of the Chehalis Surge Plain Trail

of the larger Blue Slough. Entertain thoughts about kayaking this inviting waterway before returning to your car.

EXTENDING YOUR TRIP

On the north bank of the Chehalis River, not far from where you've hiked, is Friends Landing. This Trout Unlimited property includes a 1-mile wheelchair-accessible trail along the river, leading to a pond and through old growth.

Grays Harbor

Grays Harbor is Washington's other great coastal estuary. With a surface area of 60,000 acres it rivals Willapa Bay in both size and ecological importance. But unlike its counterpart to the south, Grays Harbor has been heavily developed. While Willapa Bay sports very little human intrusion, no jetties, and contains thousands of acres of protected shoreline and tideflats, Grays Harbor is a study in contrast.

The eastern reaches of this estuary are highly industrialized. Three cities, Aberdeen, Hoquiam and Cosmopolis, sprawl where the Chehalis River drains into the estuary. These mill cities were once among the largest providers of forest products in the country. Past, sometimes unsustainable logging practices, coupled with rising globalization that favors cheaper imports, left these once-proud cities economically depressed. A century-plus of intense industrialization has also left Grays Harbor's natural communities in a diminished state.

On the estuary's western end, where it meets the Pacific Ocean, resort development has also compromised this great ecosystem. Fortunately, however, for hikers and nature lovers all is not lost. In recent years conservationists have been giving this great waterway some much-needed attention. The Grays Harbor Audubon Society has been protecting shoreline along North Bay near the mouth of the Humptulips River, and the U.S. Fish and Wildlife Service established a 1500-acre national wildlife refuge at Bowerman Basin in 1990.

Grays Harbor is one of the most important staging areas on the entire Pacific Coast for shorebirds. One of the largest concentrations of western sandpipers, dunlins, and dowitchers south of Alaska can be observed here. Grays Harbor offers hikers a handful of other great wildlife-observing locales as well.

Hopefully this region will someday sport

more protected areas, providing this important estuary with not only ecological recovery but perhaps economic recovery in the form of sustainable ecotourism.

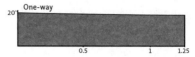

One-way

12 Johns River State Wildlife Area

RATING/ DIFFICULTY	ROUND-TRIP	ELEV GAIN/ HIGH POINT	SEASON
★/1	2.5 miles	None/ 20 feet	Year-round

Map: USGS Hoquiam; **Contact:** Washington Department of Fish and Wildlife, Region 6 Office, Montesano, (360) 249-4628, *http://wdfw .wa.gov/reg/region6.htm*; **Notes:** Dogs must be leashed. Vehicle-use permit required, available from places that sell hunting and fishing licenses. Popular elk and bird hunting area; **GPS:** N 46 53.986, W 123 59.731

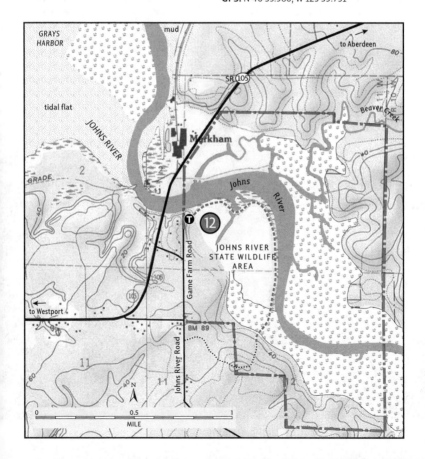

Hike on an old dike along the Johns River into an estuary teeming with birds and elk. The first half of the trail is wheelchair-accessible, offering an easy hike for all.

GETTING THERE

From Aberdeen head west on State Route 105 for 12 miles. Pass the Markham Ocean Spray Plant. Immediately after crossing the Johns River Bridge, turn left onto Johns River Road. In 0.1 mile turn left onto Game Farm Road (signed "Public Fishing"), and in another 0.1 mile turn right into the trailhead parking area. Privy available.

ON THE TRAIL

Developed by the Washington Department of Fish and Wildlife, this popular trail grants hikers and bird-watchers easy access to the 1500-acre Johns River State Wildlife Area. The first 0.6 mile is paved, providing wheelchair-bound hikers the opportunity to enjoy this wildlife-rich area. The pavement also guarantees that the trail won't be muddy during the rainy season, which in Grays Harbor can sometimes be all year.

Hugging this main river of the Grays Harbor basin, the trail traverses an area nearly void of trees. A few lone Sitka spruce and hawthorns punctuate the grasses and reeds of the surrounding estuary. At pavement's end is a blind, but quiet hikers shouldn't need it to observe resident birds. Herons, grebes, terns, geese, and sandpipers are usually easily spotted along the way.

Continue on the now-grassy trail to reach

Tide is in on the Johns River—Johns River Wildlife Refuge

the forest's edge at 1 mile. Scan the reclaimed marshland on your right (west) for members of the resident elk herd. If the big beasties themselves aren't present, plenty of evidence of their passing most certainly will be. Continue another 0.25 mile into the forest to where the trail begins to climb from the floodplain. You can go farther another 0.25 mile to the trail's end on Johns River Road, but in scrappy forest it's hardly worth it. Instead, retrace your steps and explore the diked pasture near the bird blind.

EXTENDING YOUR TRIP
About 2 miles of wooded roads within the wildlife area can be walked on the opposite side of the river. Nearby Westport Lighthouse State Park contains a 1.3-mile paved trail along the Pacific.

13 Damon Point State Park

RATING/ DIFFICULTY	LOOP	ELEV GAIN/ HIGH POINT	SEASON
★★/1	4 miles	None/ 10 feet	Year-round

Loop

Maps: USGS Point Brown, USGS Westport; **Contact:** Ocean City State Park, (360) 289-3553, *infocent@parks.wa.gov, www.parks.wa.gov;* **Notes:** Dogs must be leashed. Snowy plover closure of Damon Point interior Mar 15–Aug 31; **GPS:** N 46 56.774, W 124 07.895

Once an island, now a spit, Damon Point keeps growing thanks to sand accretion (the opposite of erosion). Hike around this protruding land mass for sweeping views that include Mount Rainier and the snowy Olympic Mountains. Observe scores of shorebirds

A hiker reads about the endangered snowy plover before setting out for a hike on Damon Point.

(including endangered snowy plovers), harbor seals, and the remains of a notorious ocean liner. Best of all, enjoy 4 miles of vehicle-free beaches.

GETTING THERE
From Hoquiam head west for 16 miles on State Route 109 to its junction with SR 115. Continue south 2.5 miles on SR 115 to the resort town of Ocean Shores. Proceed south on Point Brown Avenue. In 0.75 mile come to

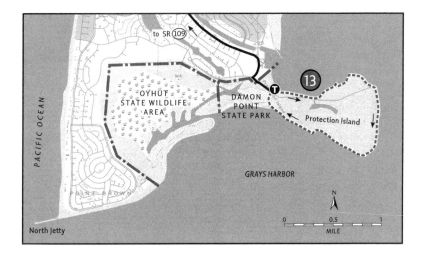

North Jetty

a four-way junction, and continue straight. In 4.5 miles the road bends right, becoming Discovery Avenue. In another 0.25 mile it becomes Marine View Drive. Locate a sign for Damon Point State Park, directing you to turn left onto Protection Island Road. Drive 0.1 mile to the park entrance and trailhead. Privy available.

ON THE TRAIL

Some parks are designed by humans, but nature seems to have had a hand in Damon Point's fate. Named for A. O. Damon, who settled here in 1861, the point has grown to connect with Protection Island, creating a spit 1 mile long and 0.5 mile wide. Washington State Parks then built a road up the middle of the spit. Then nature stepped in, sending a storm to sever the road, providing an outlet for a newly formed pond. Will an island reemerge? Maybe. In the meantime you better get hiking, or you might need a kayak for future visits.

Best hiked at low tide, the trail starts by heading to the bayside beach (to left of closed peninsula road). Turn east for your 4-mile journey around the 61-acre spit. In 0.5 mile you'll come to a creek. In winter, plan on getting your feet wet crossing it. But first, look over to the creek-cut dunes on your right. Wow! There's a half-buried ship hull there. It's the SS *Catala*, shipwrecked in 1965 and just recently visible thanks once again to Mother Nature. The *Catala* has a colorful history, from transporting loggers and miners, to housing world's fair visitors, to onboard offerings of entertaining vices.

Round the first point and come to a nice beach area. On your right is the former picnic area being reclaimed by vegetation, both endemic and invasive. At 2.5 miles you'll round the second point, where you'll be greeted by the fury of coastal winds. Enjoy good views of Westport across the way. Make your way back to the trailhead along a wide beach framed with high rolling dunes. Bald eagles frequently perch on big beached logs lining this stretch of beach. At 4 miles a small trail cuts back to the parking lot.

 Copalis River Spit

RATING/ DIFFICULTY	ROUND-TRIP	ELEV GAIN/ HIGH POINT	SEASON
★★/1	4 miles	30 feet/ 20 feet	Year-round

Maps: USGS Copalis Beach, USGS Moclips; **Contact:** Griffiths-Priday State Park, (360) 289-3553, *infocent@parks.wa.gov, www.parks .wa.gov;* **Notes:** Dogs must be leashed; **GPS:** N 47 06.882, W 124 10.670

Enjoy vehicle-free beach hiking on a quiet spit teeming with birdlife. Located just a few miles from bustling Ocean Shores, the beaches of Griffiths-Priday State Park are often deserted.

GETTING THERE
From Hoquiam head west on State Route 109 for 21 miles to the community of Copalis Beach. At the Green Lantern Tavern turn left onto Benner Road, proceeding 0.2 mile to the park entrance and trailhead. Water and restrooms available.

ON THE TRAIL
One of the quietest stretches of beach south of the Quinault Indian Reservation, the Copalis River Spit makes for a good hike any time of year. Within this 365-acre state park, roads, condos, and other human intrusions are absent.

It used to be a 0.25-mile hike to the beach, but in the late 1990s Conner Creek changed course, extending its route to the sea by nearly 0.5 mile. Now a 0.75-mile hike is required to get to the surf. But what a three quarters of a mile it is! The trail goes through one of the largest dune complexes in the state. Admire the dunes from the trail, though, so as not to disturb the myriad of birds that nest here. Perhaps some day snowy plovers will return.

Follow the wide path through the dunes, eventually coming to a point above Conner

A pair of hikers fight the wind in hiking across dunes on their way to Copalis Spit.

Creek. Continue northward to where the creek turns to empty into the Pacific, and you too are free to reach the sea. On a wide, hard-packed sandy beach, hike 1.25 miles north to the tip of the spit. Copalis Rock, a large sea stack and part of the Copalis National Wildlife Refuge, is visible in the distance.

The spit is often littered with sand dollars, half sand dollars, and quarter sand dollars when the tide is out. Scan overhanging trees along the north bank for eagles and osprey. At low tide it's possible to hike along the ocean side of the river for a short ways. Deep mud will let you know when it's time to turn around.

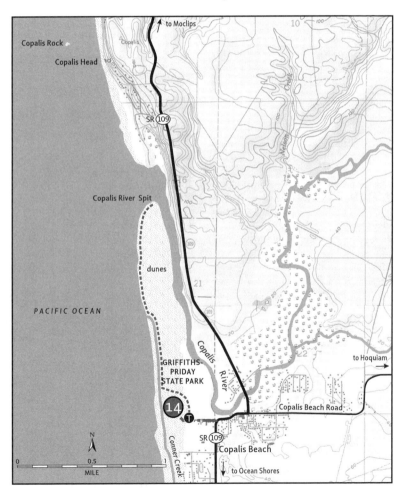

Black Hills: Capitol State Forest

Rising to the southwest of Olympia are the heavily forested Black Hills. Like the Willapa Hills in the state's southwestern corner, the Black Hills are composed of rolling and gentle peaks. The highest summits are just over 2600 feet. But the relief is prominent due to close proximity to the Puget Sound Basin and the Chehalis River valley. Shrouded in green and stroked with smooth contours, these hills look like they belong in Virginia or Pennsylvania.

But they're a unique part of the Washington landscape. Consisting of underlying basalt, the Black Hills actually take their name from a Native American term, *klahle*, describing the dark shadows cast by the ever-changing cloud patterns blown in from the coast. Fires and widespread logging swept through the area in the early part of the twentieth century. During the Great Depression, the state authorized repurchase of the cutover lands.

Today, the Washington State Department of Natural Resources manages over 90,000 acres of the Black Hills as the Capitol State Forest. Primarily a working forest providing a steady stream of timber (converted to income for the state's schools), since 1955 the forest has also been managed for recreation. Over 100 miles of trails traverse the Capitol State Forest. And while many of these are multiuse, the forest provides plenty of motor-free miles for hiking. Actually, all trails are motor-free (and horse-free) from November 1 to March 31.

As the Olympia–South Sound area continues to grow, the Capitol Forest's importance as a backyard wilderness providing clean water, wildlife habitat, and easily accessible recreation also grows. While this forest may lack the ruggedness of other areas in this book, it offers plenty of surprises—from sweeping views to quiet valleys, plenty of history, and a very well-maintained and cared-for trail system.

15 McLane Creek

RATING/ DIFFICULTY	LOOP	ELEV GAIN/ HIGH POINT	SEASON
★★/1	1.5 miles	50 feet/ 60 feet	Year-round

Maps: USGS Little Rock, Capitol State Forest DNR map; **Contact:** Department of Natural Resources, Pacific Cascade Region, (360) 577-2025, *pacific-cascade-region@wadnr.gov*, *www .dnr.wa.gov*; **Notes:** Dogs must be leashed. Trail closed at dusk; **GPS:** N 47 00.046, W 123 00.252

Hikers of all ages, especially children, will love this easy loop, one of the finest nature trails in Western Washington. On good tread and boardwalk this trail takes you on an up-front and personal journey along McLane Creek and an adjacent beaver pond. Plenty of birds and critters will captivate you along the way.

GETTING THERE

From Olympia head west on US 101 for 2 miles, taking the Black Lake Boulevard exit. Proceed left (south) on Black Lake Boulevard. In 3.5 miles the road turns right (west), becoming 62nd Avenue. Continue another 0.7 mile to a stop sign. Turn right on Delphi Road. In 0.5 mile turn left into the McLane Creek Demonstration Forest. Reach the trailhead in 0.4 mile. Privy available.

ON THE TRAIL

The Washington State Department of Natural Resources (DNR) should be commended on this trail. It was clearly developed with environmental sensitivities and with the intent

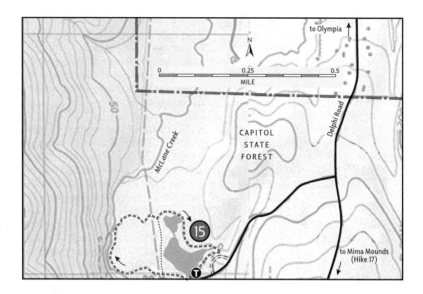

of making it easy for people to connect with nature. If the DNR can only bring some of this same care to other parts of the Capitol State Forest, the possibilities are great.

The McLane Creek Nature Trail consists of a 1.1-mile outer loop and a 0.3-mile connector trail. My recommendation: do a figure-eight and take your sweet time. With interpretive plaques and observation decks along the way, McLane Creek is meant to be savored. Time of day and season will dictate which critters you might observe. Keep your senses keen and you should see plenty anytime you visit.

The trail starts off by skirting a large beaver pond. In springtime the wetland is transformed into a musical marsh thanks to a chorus of blackbirds and an ensemble of tree frogs performing regularly. Cattails and pond lilies punctuate the nutrient-rich wetland. Soon you'll encounter the shortcut trail. Once

part of the Mud Bay Logging Company's rail line, this trail offers more good views of the beaver pond and perhaps a peek of the beavers themselves.

The main trail darts into a dark and gloomy forest of cedar, hemlock, giant maples and over-your-head devil's club. Heading along McLane Creek and twice over it, look for spawning salmon come fall. The trail passes through a hemlock tunnel that children will want to pass through again and again. Next, traverse a skunk cabbage patch before returning to the beaver pond. Take the shortcut trail right or head left to loop around the willow-, alder-, and cascara-lined wetland, returning to the trailhead.

EXTENDING YOUR TRIP

An upper parking lot 0.25 mile from the trailhead provides access to a short loop trail in the Centennial Demonstration Forest.

Opposite: McClane Creek's Beaver Pond is a good place for observing birds.

16 Capitol Peak

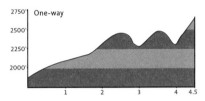

RATING/ DIFFICULTY	ROUND-TRIP	ELEV GAIN/ HIGH POINT	SEASON
★/2	9 miles	1300 feet/ 2659 feet	Year-round

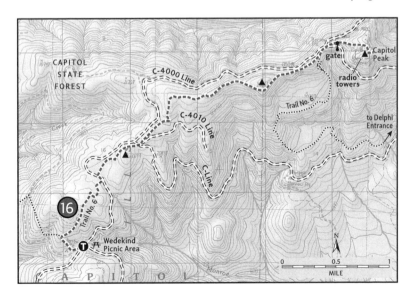

Maps: USGS Capitol Peak, Capitol State Forest DNR map; **Contact:** Department of Natural Resources, Pacific Cascade Region, (360) 577-2025, *pacific-cascade-region@wadnr.gov, www.dnr.wa.gov;* **Notes:** Roads are poorly marked, forest map essential; **GPS:** N 46. 56.909, W 123 11.641

Come for the views: they're quite extensive, from Rainier to the Pacific. Come for the trail: it's well built, not heavily used, and it runs a high ridge for miles. Clad in communication towers, however, the peak may be the highest point on this hike, but it's certainly not the highlight.

GETTING THERE

From Olympia head west on US 101 for 2 miles, taking the Black Lake Boulevard exit. Proceed south on Black Lake Boulevard. In 3.5 miles the road turns west, becoming 62nd Avenue. Continue another 0.7 mile to a stop sign. Turn left on Delphi Road, continuing for 2.2 miles. Turn right on Waddell Creek Road and in 2.7 miles enter the Capitol State Forest. Bear right onto Sherman Valley Road, and in 1.5 miles turn left onto the C Line. Follow this mostly gravel, sometimes paved road for 7 miles to a major junction (just beyond a quarry). Turn left, continuing on the C Line for 1.5 miles to the seriously neglected

Wedekind Picnic Area. Park here. The trail starts on the west side of the C Line.

ON THE TRAIL

Hike this trail and dream of the possibilities for the Capitol State Forest. There's no reason that this 90,000-acre piece of the public domain can't be Olympia's Tiger Mountain. But the area has been long plagued by illegal dumping, shooting, and other problems, causing hikers to shy away. Motorized groups have adopted trails on their half of the forest, and equestrian groups work on nonmotorized trails, but where are the hiking groups? If hikers begin taking more of a vested interest in this forest—volunteering on trail crews, cleanups, and watches—the problems will dissipate. Capitol Forest is getting better, but it's going to take a lot of work from dedicated citizens and some better funding and management from the state to transform this parcel into what it should be—a prime hiking destination.

Contemplate this vision as you hike along the Capitol Crest, the rooftop of the Black Hills. From your high start (1880 feet) hike Trail No. 30 for about 0.3 mile to a junction. Turn right onto Trail No. 6, the Green Line. On very good tread begin a rolling ridgetop romp to Capitol Peak. After about 1.3 miles, cross the C Line that you drove in on. Alternating between fir forests lined with oxalis (pretty white blooms in late spring) and raspberry-cloaked "balds" reminiscent of the southern Appalachians, the trail is a pure delight to travel. Teaser views of the Cascades, Olympics, and Willapa Hills are had along the way.

At 2 miles you'll cross the C Line again, this time at its junction with the C-4000 Line on the left and the C-4010 Line on the right. The trail resumes a few hundred feet up the C-4010. Continue through more fir forests and shrubby openings. After 3 miles pass an old hitching point and then climb a little and drop a little through open forest with more peek-

Nice signing along the trail heading to Capitol Peak

a-boo views. At 3.5 miles, cross another road. The trail, now paralleling two roads, climbs a small knoll above them only to descend where they meet up. Here, at 4 miles from your start, Trail No. 6 heads east, rapidly descending off the ridge.

This is the end of your trail hike. To access Capitol Peak, walk the road north a few hundred feet to a three-way junction. Take the gated middle road and climb steeply to the 2659-foot peak, second-highest summit in the Black Hills.

Under a skyline of communication towers, reach out to sweeping views. To the east are the Cascades, from Mounts Baker to Adams. Rainier is directly in front of you, rising above the Bald Hills. Extending to the north are the finger peninsulas and inlets of the South Sound. To the west, the Satsop Towers rise above the Chehalis Valley, while the Olympics and Pacific Ocean can be seen in the distance. Soak it all in and retrace your steps.

Maps: USGS Little Rock, Capitol State Forest DNR map; **Contact:** Department of Natural Resources, Pacific Cascade Region, (360) 577-2025, *pacific-cascade-region@wadnr.gov*, *www.dnr.wa.gov*; **Notes:** Dogs prohibited. Trail closed at dusk; **GPS:** N 46 54.307, W 123 02.879

17 Mima Mounds

RATING/ DIFFICULTY	ROUND-TRIP	ELEV GAIN/ HIGH POINT	SEASON
★/1	2.75 miles	10 feet/ 225 feet	Year-round

Hike through a landscape that almost appears lunar (except for the vegetation of course). Weave in and out and even over a few of the hundreds of 4- to 6-foot mounds scattered across this Thurston County prairie. How did they get here? Who or what made

Wide open spaces in the prairie that houses the Mima Mounds

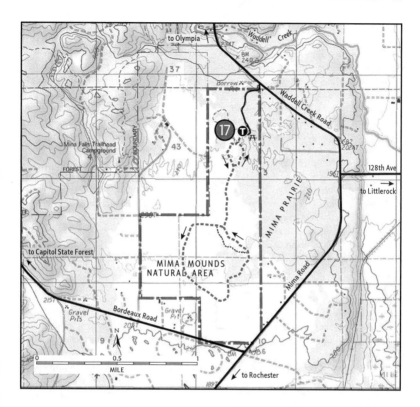

them? You'll most certainly be pondering these thoughts while hiking through this geologically intriguing landscape.

GETTING THERE

From Olympia take I-5 south to exit 95. Follow Maytown Road west for 3 miles to Littlerock. At a stop sign proceed forward (west) on Littlerock Road, which soon turns left (south). Bear right here onto 128th Avenue (signed for the Capitol State Forest). In 0.7 mile come to a T intersection. Turn right onto Waddell Creek Road and drive 0.8 mile. At a sign announcing "Mima Mounds Natural Area," turn left and reach the trailhead in 0.4 mile. Privy available.

ON THE TRAIL

Most visitors to this National Natural Landmark just visit the observation deck and maybe walk the 0.5-mile paved nature loop. But to really appreciate the mysterious nature of the Mima Mounds, take to the trail that loops around this 445-acre preserve. By all means head for the observation deck first to get a look at this bizarre arrangement of "earthen hay bales." Scientists continue to debate the mounds' origins. Was it the thawing and freezing during the last ice age that caused the land to buckle? Or perhaps pocket gophers were at work, having since moved on to haunt golf courses?

Walk the paved path for 0.3 mile to find the trailhead for the prairie loop trail. Once on a soft-surface path, head into the heart of the mounds. The surrounding forest has encroached on the prairie—invasive plants too, like the dreaded Scotch broom. The Washington State Department of Natural Resources and volunteers are trying to restore the prairie to the way it appeared when Native peoples periodically set fires to them, keeping the vegetation in check.

At 0.65 mile pass an old fence line, a remnant of early farming on the mounds. At 0.75 mile come to a junction, and turn right for the loop. Soon pass another junction, a shorter loop option. Continue right, hiking the periphery of the preserve. Enjoy views of Mounts Rainier and St. Helens towering in the distance. At 2.1 miles close the loop and retrace your steps back to the trailhead. The Mima Mounds are exceptionally beautiful in April and May, when prairie flowers such as blue violet, buttercup, and camas paint them in dazzling colors.

18 Sherman Creek

RATING/ DIFFICULTY	LOOP	ELEV GAIN/ HIGH POINT	SEASON
★★/3	9 miles	800 feet/ 1150 feet	Year-round

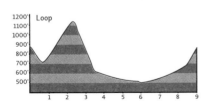

Maps: USGS Little Rock, Capitol State Forest DNR map; **Contact:** Department of Natural Resources, Pacific Cascade Region, (360) 577-2025, *pacific-cascade-region@wadnr.gov, www.dnr.wa.gov*; **GPS:** N 46 55.550, W 123 06.752

One of the best hiking options in the 90,000-acre Capitol State Forest, the Sherman Creek Loop travels up and down two visually appealing valleys. No grand views or grand forest here—just miles of tranquil woods and creekside walking and some historic relics from the golden age of logging. Equestrians and mountain bikers share these trails, but crowding isn't an issue. Come during the week and have this place to yourself.

GETTING THERE
From Olympia take I-5 south to exit 95. Follow Maytown Road west for 3 miles to the community of Littlerock. At a stop sign proceed forward (west) on Littlerock Road, which soon turns left (south). Bear right here onto 128th Avenue (signed for the Capitol State Forest). In 0.7 mile come to a T intersection. Turn left on Mima Road and after 1.5 miles turn right (west) onto Bordeaux Road. Follow this good paved road for 3.5 miles to a Y intersection. Bear right, following the D Line for 0.6 mile to a four-way intersection on a hill crest. Turn right onto the D-4000 Line and follow this good gravel road for 2 miles to its junction with the D-5000 Line, where you'll find the trailhead. Park on the wide shoulder near the junction.

ON THE TRAIL
This loop begins by following the Mima Porter Trail (Trail No. 8) for 0.4 mile down to a junction in the Lost Valley Creek. The trail on your left is your return route. These trails are in excellent shape thanks to the volunteer work of

Opposite: Lush fern growth along tranquil Sherman Creek

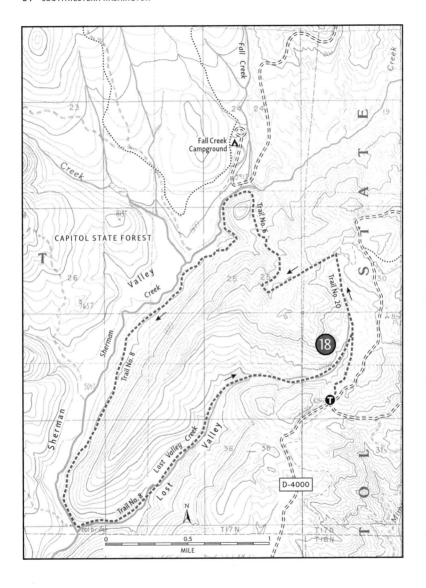

the Backcountry Horsemen (and women) of Washington.

Head right on Trail No. 20. Climbing gradually, pass a few big firs, a lot of skunk cabbage, and an active beaver pond. In 1.4 miles come to a junction with Trail No. 6, the Green Line. Turn left and follow this good trail. Climb a bit more, and after crossing a logging road enter a mature second-growth forest. Begin a long descent into the Sherman Creek valley. At 2.6 miles emerge from the forest to cross a recent cut. Notice the temperature change. Notice Capitol Peak and Larch Mountain in front of you. Notice, too, that there are no larches on Larch Mountain. Hmm.

At 3.25 miles reach the lovely Sherman Creek valley, where you'll come to another trail junction. The trail right crosses the creek (bridge out as of summer 2006) and heads to the Fall Creek trailhead and onward to the Capitol Crest. You'll want to continue left on Trail No. 8 for an enjoyable journey down the valley. Plenty of lunch spots along the way will entice you to take a break.

After about 3 miles of hiking along the creek you'll come to an old trail junction. There used to be a trailhead on the other side of the creek, but it and the road no longer exist. This decommissioning has helped return a little solitude to this region. The trail now leaves Sherman Creek to follow Lost Valley Creek upstream. This is the best part of the loop. Under a canopy of moss-draped alders and big cedars, the trail uses an old logging railroad bed. After 1 mile of heading up Lost Valley Creek, look for trestle remnants. Look, too, along the creek for relics from the old logging days. Broken bricks and porcelain plates litter the area. Be sure to leave these artifacts for others to enjoy.

Hike about 1.5 more miles upstream back to the junction with Trail No. 20. Turn right and follow Trail No. 8 for 0.4 mile back to your vehicle.

BUILDING A DIFFERENT CAPITOL IN OLYMPIA

The Capitol State Forest has long been a place where Olympia hikers come to hike. But soon they'll be able to hike to the Capitol State Forest. A so-called Capitol-to-Capitol trail is being developed to link the city with the forest. Starting at the state capitol campus, the new trail will thread together local schools, including the Evergreen State College, and city parks to reach the sprawling state forest.

Overseen by the Washington State Department of Transportation, the trail has long been advocated by various community groups. School groups, local volunteers, and inmates from the Cedar Creek Corrections Center (located within the state forest) have already developed sections of the trail. And while it will be years before this project is complete, it is a major step in the right direction—providing greenbelts in the Olympia region.

As suburbia continues to sprawl across the countryside and the average American's waistline continues to sprawl as well, greenbelt trails like the Capitol-to-Capitol are all the more important for the health of our communities and their residents. These trails connect parks and preserves and provide people places to exercise close to where they live. As fuel prices continue to soar and open space continues to dwindle, places like the Capitol State Forest will only grow in importance. Making them more accessible should be a priority for both government and community leaders.

Opposite: Scads of oyster shells litter the beach at Guillemot Cove.

Kitsap Peninsula

Jutting into Puget Sound like a big arrowhead, the Kitsap Peninsula is Washington's second great peninsula. With over 240 miles of coastline, and attached to the mainland by an isthmus less than 2 miles wide, Kitsap can feel like an island. But despite its geographical isolation, its proximity to Seattle and Tacoma via ferries and bridge has led to its development. Out of the state's thirty-nine counties, Kitsap ranks thirty-sixth in size but is the second most densely populated, with nearly 600 people per square mile (only King County is more densely populated).

While development continues to transform much of the peninsula's rural charm into suburbia, all is not lost. Large expanses remain fairly wild. Along Hood Canal on the peninsula's western shoreline, large tracts of beach and quiet coves remain unmolested by development. But it won't stay this way without citizen involvement calling for conservation measures. The Great Peninsula Conservancy, a land trust in the county, has been instrumental in protecting thousands of acres of key shoreline, forest, and lakefront. The Kitsap County Parks Department has also accelerated its land acquisitions.

Surrounded by water and within the shadows of the Olympic Mountains, the Kitsap Peninsula truly is a beautiful place. Hikers will be pleasantly surprised to find that just beyond the suburban sprawl radiating from Bremerton, some fine hiking destinations await.

19 Harstine Island State Park

RATING/ DIFFICULTY	LOOP	ELEV GAIN/ HIGH POINT	SEASON
★★/1	1.5 miles	200 feet/ 175 feet	Year-round

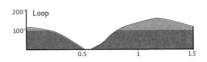

Map: USGS Longbranch; **Contact:** Jarrell Cove State Park, (360) 426-9226, *infocent@ parks.wa.gov, www.parks.wa.gov*; **Notes:** Dogs must be leashed; **GPS:** N 47 15.741, W 122 52.227

Hike down into a lush ravine to a deserted beach on an island that has resisted time. Quiet Harstine Island State Park may very well be the best-kept secret in Puget Sound. After combing the tranquil beach, take to the park's even quieter woodland trails.

GETTING THERE

From Shelton, drive State Route 3 east for 11 miles. Turn right on Pickering Road (signed "Harstine Island and Jarrell Cove SP") and follow it for 3.3 miles. Bear left, cross Harstine Island Bridge, and come to a T junction. Go left on North Harstine Island Drive and in 3 miles come to a four-way junction. Turn right onto East Harstine Island Road North and in 1 mile turn left on Yates Road. Follow this dirt road for 1 mile to the park entrance on the right. The trailhead is 0.25 mile farther. Privy and picnic tables available.

ON THE TRAIL

Short and oh so very sweet, this hike will bring you back to a time when most of Puget Sound's shoreline wasn't wall-to-wall homes. One of the largest islands in the South Sound, Harstine has resisted much change. Still rural. Still quiet. Still special. Harstine Island State Park assures that 300 acres of this prime place will remain protected from development.

There are two ways to get to the beach. Both are fairly short, but there's no hurry: take the trail on the east end of the parking lot to get a little preview before dropping to the shoreline, peeking through gaps in the thick forest to see what lies ahead. In 0.25 mile be-gin your descent into a cool and dark ravine graced with big cedars and firs. Come to a junction: left to the beach, right to more trails. Head to the beach first. Drop deeper into the ravine, cross a pretty little creek, and in 0.1 mile emerge on a crowd-free beach. Lounge,

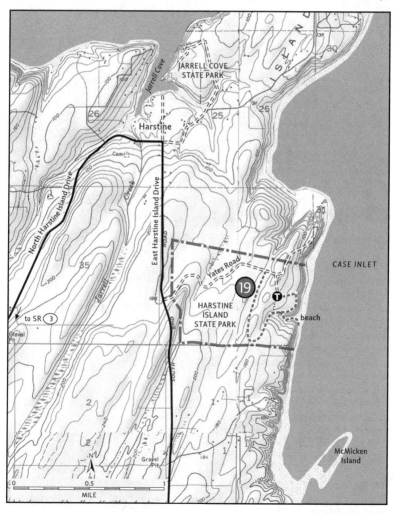

McMicken Island in the background from Harstine Island State Park's inviting beach

beachcomb, or if the tide is low hike south below the forested bluffs.

When you're beached out, return to the junction to explore the park's uplands. Climb out of the ravine and pass a few ancient cedars spared the ax. In 0.25 mile from the junction reach another junction. The trail right heads back to the parking lot in 0.25 mile. Go left on a good trail lined with bearberry and salal under a canopy of mature second growth. In 0.1 mile the main trail bears right; continue on it. Enjoy a peaceful woods hike, emerging on Yates Road in 0.5 mile. Turn right and return to your vehicle by walking this road for a little less than 0.4 mile.

EXTENDING YOUR TRIP
At low tide it's possible to walk the beach all the way to McMicken Island State Park (about a mile away). But note that the shore is private property; don't get stuck by an incoming tide. Nearby Jarrell Cove State Park has a nice campground and a 1-mile nature trail.

20 Twanoh State Park

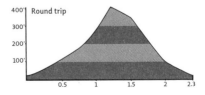

RATING/DIFFICULTY	ROUND-TRIP	ELEV GAIN/HIGH POINT	SEASON
★/1	2.3 miles	375 feet/400 feet	Year-round

Round trip

Map: USGS Mason Lake; **Contact:** Twanoh State Park, (360) 275-2222, *infocent@parks.wa.gov, www.parks.wa.gov*; **Notes:** Dogs must be leashed; **GPS:** N 47 22.644, W 122 58.431

Enjoy an easy hike along a salmon-spawning stream in a lush emerald ravine. Twanoh is derived from the Skokomish people, meaning "gathering place." Twanoh State Park protects 182 acres of prime Hood Canal real estate—a perfect place for hikers and wildlife to gather.

GETTING THERE
From Bremerton head west on State Route 3 to Belfair. Continue west on SR 106 for 7.75 miles to Twanoh State Park. Turn left into the campground entrance; day-use parking is before the camping information station. The (signed) trailhead is on the south side of the entrance, at Twanoh Creek Bridge.

ON THE TRAIL
This hike begins with Twanoh Creek immediately at your side. Through a verdant tunnel of rhododendron and cedar, begin working your way up the small ravine that houses this bubbling waterway. The surrounding forest was logged over a century ago. Clumps of ferns engulf springboard-notched cedar stumps smothered in moss. In 0.3 mile come to a junction. Continue forward; you'll be returning on the trail on your right.

At 0.75 mile the trail begins to climb out of the ravine. Notice the vegetation change on the forest floor to salal and kinnikinnick, an indication that less moisture is being trapped here than near the creek. After two switchbacks, crest the top of the ravine. Now away from the raucous creek, begin a slow descent in quiet forest. At 1.25 mile the trail yields to an old woods road. At 1.5 miles you'll come to the state park group camp.

Turn right and pick up the trail again. Beneath a few big old Douglas-firs and clusters of leathery-leaved rhododendrons, begin dropping back into the damp ravine. At 2 miles reach the creek and the first trail junction. Turn left and return 0.3 mile to your vehicle.

EXTENDING YOUR TRIP
After your hike follow Twanoh Creek to its small delta on Hood Canal. Comb the beach or go for a swim in some of the warmest saltwater in the state. Check out the Civilian Conservation Corps buildings in the park. Twanoh's shaded creekside campground makes a perfect weekend retreat.

Little Twanoh Creek flowing after a winter storm

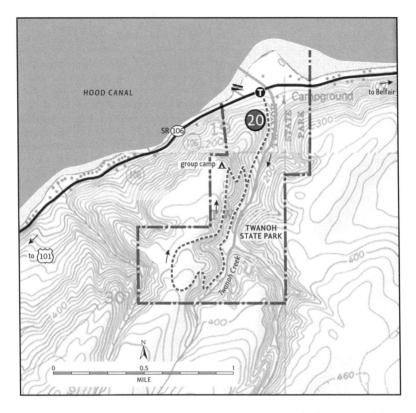

HOOD CANAL

SR 106

group camp

to 101

TWANOH STATE PARK

Twanoh Creek

Campground

to Belfair

STATE PARK

N

0   0.5   1
MILE

Mary E. Theler Wetlands Nature Preserve

RATING/ DIFFICULTY	ROUND-TRIP	ELEV GAIN/ HIGH POINT	SEASON
★★/1	3.5 miles	40 feet/ 50 feet	Year-round

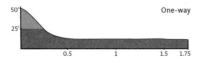

One-way

Maps: USGS Belfair, wetlands map available online; **Contact:** Mary E. Theler Wetlands and Community Center, (360) 275-4898, theler@ hctc.com, www.thelercenter.org/wetlands; **Notes:** Dogs prohibited. Trail open dawn to dusk; **GPS:** N 47 26.286, W 122 50.194

Spend a couple of hours or all day exploring a wildlife-rich estuary at the farthest reaches of fjordlike Hood Canal. Let eagles, osprey, herons, otters, and deer captivate you on this hike through grassy wetlands and along the Union River.

GETTING THERE

From Bremerton head west on State Route 3 to Belfair. Proceed 1 mile beyond the junction with SR 300 to the Mary E. Theler Community Center (and sign for the nature trail), located on your right. Park at community center. The trailhead is located in the northwest corner of the parking lot. Privy available.

ON THE TRAIL

Among the many legacies that Sam and Mary Theler left the town of Belfair was land for a Masonic Lodge, church, and school. Out of the 70 acres deeded to the North Mason School District arose the Mary E. Theler Wetlands Nature Preserve. Serving an educational role for area school children, the wetlands have also become the area's prime hiking destination.

Start your visit by passing under the wel-come arch and proceeding 0.25 mile to the Wetlands Project Center. If it's open, take time to visit to gain a better appreciation and understanding of the complex ecosystem you are about to explore. Children—heck, adults too—will appreciate the hands-on exhibits.

Several trails radiate from the Wetlands Project Center. All are pleasurable to walk and are wheelchair-accessible. The Sweetwater Creek and Alder Creek Trails make 0.25-mile loops. The South Tidal Marsh Trail extends 0.25 mile onto a boardwalk into Hood Canal. It's ideally positioned for spotting birds among the grasses and reeds and for viewing the Olympic Mountains in the background.

The Union River Estuary Trail offers the

A hiker stopping to observe birdlife at the Theler Wetlands

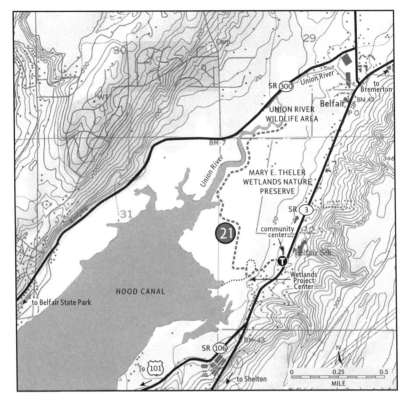

longest and best hike in the preserve. Along an old dike the trail elbows across open wetlands—tidal marsh on the left, freshwater marsh on the right. Through a tunnel of shrubs and along active farmland, the trail makes a beeline for the mouth of the Union River. In 0.5 mile you'll reach the river.

The trail then turns right (northeast) to hug this nutrient-rich waterway for one more mile. Just beyond the 1-mile mark is a small picnic area and restroom. At the trail's terminus are two short spurs—the one left leads to the river's edge for prime waterfowl and salmon-spawning viewing. Return to the Theler Wetlands at different times of the year to

fully appreciate the life cycles at work in this ecologically important preserve.

22 Penrose Point State Park

RATING/ DIFFICULTY	LOOP	ELEV GAIN/ HIGH POINT	SEASON
**/1	2 miles	140 feet/ 140 feet	Year-round

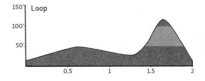

Map: USGS Fox Island; **Contact:** Penrose Point State Park, (253) 884-2514, *infocent@ parks.wa.gov, www.parks.wa.gov*; **Notes:** Dogs must be leashed; **GPS:** N 47 15.500, W 122 44.736

Saunter out on this small peninsula for stunning views of Mount Rainier rising over Puget Sound. Let eagles and kingfishers announce your passing. Admire contorted bluffs, big Doug-firs, and a procession of passing watercraft.

GETTING THERE

From Gig Harbor head north on State Route 16. Exit in Purdy, following SR 302 west for 5.3 miles. At a traffic light bear left onto Key Peninsula Highway and proceed for 9 miles. Turn left (east) onto Cornwall Road (approximately 1.5 miles south of the village of Home). In 0.5

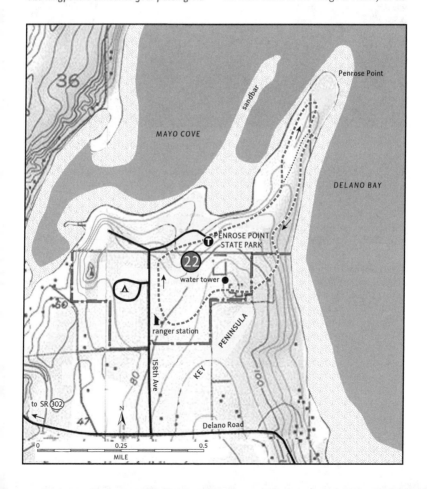

On clear days Mount Rainier can be seen rising above Delano Bay from Penrose Point.

mile turn right (south) onto Delano Road and continue 0.8 mile to a four-way intersection. Turn left (north) on 158th Avenue and in 0.3 mile enter Penrose Point State Park. Proceed 0.4 mile to the day-use parking area and trailhead. Water and restrooms available.

ON THE TRAIL

One of the prettiest state parks on Puget Sound, this old estate-turned-park draws visitors mostly for its lovely beaches, campsites, and grassy shore-abutting picnic grounds. But there are a couple of miles of nice hiking trails here too. They wind through mature woodlands, along a mountain-reflecting coastline and over a quiet hillside.

Located on the Key Peninsula, a subpeninsula of the Kitsap Peninsula, Penrose Point is a little off the beaten path. And the paths through the park aren't well beaten either, but they're well defined and well maintained. Start your hike at the main trailhead signed as

Junction A. You'll be returning here via a circuitous route.

Through a forest of maples and alders the trail climbs slightly on a bluff above Mayo Cove. Go left at Junction B and in 0.25 mile arrive at Junction C. Turn left here for a trip around Penrose Point. Amble under a canopy of massive Doug-firs and flaky rusted-bark madronas. Views are limited, but in 0.75 mile you'll come to another junction—you guessed it, D. Take the short spur that heads south to a beach. Wham! There's Mount Rainier staring right at you from across Delano Bay. Framing the bay is Fox Island to the southeast and Anderson Island to the southwest.

Retrace back to Junction D and then head west along a nice shoreline trail. After about a third of a mile you'll arrive at Junction E. Turn left for a little climb over a quiet wooded knoll, pass a water tower, and then start to descend. At Junction F turn right and proceed under big maples to Junction H (what happened to

G?). Turn right and after about 0.25 mile you'll reach Junction A to close the loop. You've now lettered in hiking!

EXTENDING YOUR TRIP

You can easily spend all day at Penrose Point. Heck, all night too—the park's campground is quite inviting. More hiking can be done on a series of nature trails along Mayo Cove. At low tide look for Native American petroglyphs on an exposed spit in the inner cove. You can also hike around Penrose Point on the beach during low tide—it's slow going, but worth the opportunity to see contorted bluffs shaped by tides and winter storms.

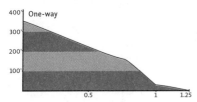

23 Guillemot Cove

RATING/ DIFFICULTY	ROUND-TRIP	ELEV GAIN/ HIGH POINT	SEASON
★★★/1	2.5 miles	350 feet/ 350 feet	Year-round

```
400'  One-way
300'
200'
100'
              0.5            1    1.25
```

Maps: USGS Holly, nature preserve map available at trailhead; **Contact:** Kitsap County Parks, (360) 337-5350, *www.kitsapgov.com /parks/regionalparks/guillemot_cove_county _park.htm*; **Notes:** Dogs prohibited; **GPS:** N 47 36.942, W 122 54.456

One of the best-kept secrets on the Kitsap Peninsula, this county nature preserve protects almost 200 acres of stunning beach and stately forest on Hood Canal. Hike to a secluded cove teeming with seabirds. With The Brothers looming high above and directly across the *canal, you may have to reel your jaw back in before heading home.*

GETTING THERE

From Bremerton follow Kitsap Way (State Route 310) for 3 miles to Kitsap Lake. Turn left on Northlake Way and proceed for 1 mile. Turn left onto the Seabeck Highway, following it for 3 miles. Then turn left on Holly Road, continuing for 5 miles to a junction. Turn right (north) on Seabeck-Holly Road, and after 3 miles turn left onto Miami Beach Road (no kidding). In 1

Boyce Creek cuts across mudflats as it flows into Hood Canal at Guillemot Cove.

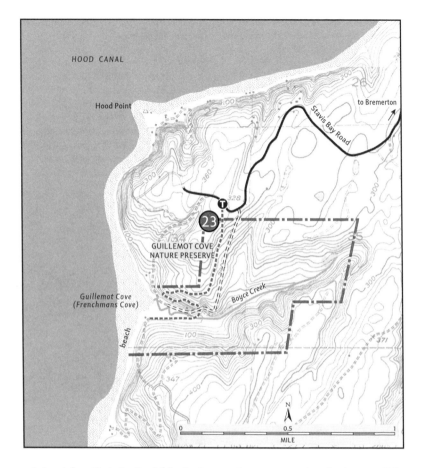

HOOD CANAL

Hood Point

to Bremerton

Stavis Bay Road

23

GUILLEMOT COVE
NATURE PRESERVE

Guillemot Cove
(Frenchmans Cove)

Boyce Creek

beach

N

0   0.5   1
MILE

mile bear left on Stavis Bay Road, following it for 4.5 miles to the Guillemot Cove Nature Preserve. Park on the right; the trail begins across the road.

ON THE TRAIL

A former private estate in a quiet corner of Hood Canal, Guillemot Cove is now one of the crown jewels of Kitsap County Parks. Managed as a nature preserve, it's open to passive recreation. As surrounding shoreline

continues to succumb to development, Guillemot Cove's value as a refuge for wild critters and people seeking wildlands immensely appreciates.

Before setting out, grab a map at the trailhead kiosk. On good tread and through mature forest the trail drops about 350 feet on its way to the quiet cove. Ignore side trails that veer left (they head to the access road), continuing on the signed Sawmill Trail. After passing through a beautiful flat of alders garnished with bouquets of ferns, the trail turns east. Now named the Margaret Trail, it drops sharply into a cool ravine shaded by cedar, hemlock, and the occasional yew.

After rounding a switchback, emerge in the heart of the old estate, 1 mile from the start. A decaying residence and barn grace the surrounding pasture. An information kiosk presents your hiking options. Best choice? Cross the Boyce Creek Bridge on the Beach House Trail. In 0.25 mile the old beach house appears and—no surprise here—so does the beach. And what a beach! The Brothers, perhaps the most identifiable of all Olympic peaks, tower directly above Hood Canal. Five hundred feet deep and a mile across, Hood Canal is Washington's grand fjord.

At low tide Boyce Creek slithers across a muddy oyster bar. Scores of shorebirds scamper for succulent oyster shooters. Bald eagles sit watch on tall firs on the water's edge. Explore the rocky and mucky beach, but be mindful of delicate critters exposed to your crushing feet at low tide. And while you're enjoying this special place you may be thinking, "What's a guillemot?" It's a penguinlike seabird—and yes, they're here.

EXTENDING YOUR TRIP

There are several more miles of hiking trails in the preserve. Try the 0.5-mile Ridge Trail or the 1-mile Maple Tree Trail for solitude. Children will enjoy the 0.25-mile trail to the cedar stump house, domicile to a desperado during the Depression.

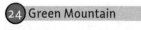

24 Green Mountain

RATING/ DIFFICULTY	ROUND-TRIP	ELEV GAIN/ HIGH POINT	SEASON
*/3	5 miles	1000 feet/ 1639 feet	Year-round

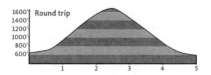

Maps: USGS Holly, USGS Wildcat Lake, state forest trail map available at trailhead; **Contact:** Department of Natural Resources, South Puget Sound Region, (360) 825-1631, *southpuget .region@wadnr.gov*, *www.dnr.wa.gov*; **Notes:** Trails are multiuse and open to motorized recreation; **GPS:** N 47 33.104, W 122 49.598

Climb the second-highest peak on the Kitsap Peninsula for good views of Puget Sound, the Seattle skyline, and Mount Rainier. Of course there are views of the Olympics too, and on the way down you'll get a pretty darn good look at them. This is a working forest, but most of the way is shaded by a cool canopy of evergreens.

GETTING THERE

From Bremerton follow Kitsap Way (State Route 310) for 3 miles to Kitsap Lake. Turn left on Northlake Way, proceeding for 1 mile. Turn left onto the Seabeck Highway and follow it for 3 miles. Then turn left on Holly Road, proceeding for 3 miles. Turn left (south) onto Tahuya Lake Road and in 1.25 miles bear left onto Gold Creek Road. The trailhead is in 2 miles on your left. Privy available.

ON THE TRAIL

Along with neighboring Gold Mountain, Green Mountain makes up the rooftop of the Kitsap Peninsula. Granted, at a grand ol' elevation of 1639 feet it isn't exactly nosebleed-inducing. But Green offers enough relief above the surrounding low country—and sits right in the middle of the peninsula—to offer an eagle's-eye view of a lot of saltwater and snowcapped mountains.

The good news is that Green Mountain is accessed by several well-maintained trails and is surrounded by over 6000 acres of state forest. The bad news is that the trails are open to motorcycles and ATVs. Now, I don't want to deny these users their rights to this piece of the public domain. I just would like to see a hiker's-only route here among the miles of motorized trails. Being in Bremerton's backyard and as one of the largest tracts of undeveloped land on the Kitsap Peninsula, Green Mountain is far more valuable than as a simple speedway for the throttle-inclined. Meanwhile, come here on a weekday for exhaust-free wandering. Let your mind wander too. Could Green someday become Bremerton's Tiger Mountain?

On the Gold Creek Trail, begin your hike in a recently cut area. Forested Green Mountain looms in front of you. In 0.4 mile enter cool forest along chattering Gold Creek. A few minutes later, cross the creek on a good bridge, then turn left at a junction. Shortly after, encounter another junction—on the left is the Plummer Trail, your return route. Hang a right, staying on the Gold Creek Trail.

Through a leathery dark-green understory of salal, bearberry, madrona, and rhododendron (visit in mid-May for the floral show), begin climbing. At 1 mile the trail splits (not shown on map). Either way works—they meet again soon enough. Limited views of the Olympics tease through the trees. At 1.5 miles reach a junction. The left (signed for Green Mountain Camp) is your return route. Continue right and in 0.25 mile come to

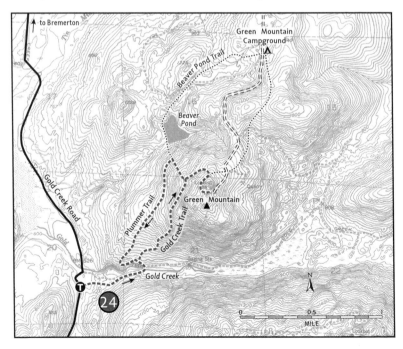

Excellent views of the Olympics can be had from the Plummer Trail.

another junction. Take the trail right, signed "Vista." Follow it past the summit parking lot (only open weekends in the summer), and in 0.4 mile reach the summit.

Find a few picnic tables and a rocky overlook. The once-sweeping vista of the Olympics is being crowded out by new growth. (Call in the loggers! It *is* a working forest.) Views eastward over Bremerton, Puget Sound, and out to the Cascades remain decent though. The real treat, however, is on the return.

Retrace your steps 0.65 mile to the junction signed for Green Mountain Camp. This is the Beaver Pond Trail. Follow it for about 0.5 mile, dropping a few hundred feet to the junction with the Plummer Trail. The Beaver Pond (more a grassland than wetland) is to the right, about 0.25 mile farther. Take the Plummer Trail left to return. Built by the Backcountry Horsemen, it's the best hiking trail on Green Mountain.

After 0.5 mile you'll skirt a recent clear-cut. The view here of Lake Tahuya and the eastern Olympic front is absolutely awesome. Savor it—then continue another 0.5 mile back to the Gold Creek Trail. From this familiar junction it's 0.5 mile back to your vehicle.

EXTENDING YOUR TRIP

Green Mountain can be hiked using the 4-mile Wildcat Trail, but it's rocky and receives heavy ATV use. The Beaver Pond Trail extends for 3 miles and is a fairly quiet option for making a longer loop when combined with the Gold Creek Trail and 2 miles of the Wildcat Trail.

25 Gazzam Lake and Close Beach

RATING/ DIFFICULTY	ROUND-TRIP	ELEV GAIN/ HIGH POINT	SEASON
★★/2	3.4 miles	500 feet/ 380 feet	Year-round

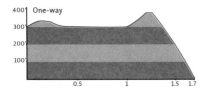

Map: USGS Bremerton East; **Contact:** Bainbridge Island Parks, (206) 842-2306, *www.biparks.org/parks/gazzamlake.html*; **Notes:** Dogs must be leashed; **GPS:** N 47 36.583, W 122 33.836

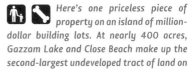

Here's one priceless piece of property on an island of million-dollar building lots. At nearly 400 acres, Gazzam Lake and Close Beach make up the second-largest undeveloped tract of land on Kitsap County's Bainbridge Island. Managed as a natural preserve by the Bainbridge Island Parks Department, it's a prime hiking spot in heavily populated Puget Sound.

GETTING THERE

From the Bainbridge ferry terminal proceed north on State Route 305 for 0.25 mile, turning left (west) at the first traffic light onto Winslow Way. Continue for 0.5 mile through a business district. Turn right (north) onto Grow Avenue, and in 0.3 mile at a four-way stop turn left (west) onto Wyatt Way. In 0.6 mile Wyatt Way turns left and becomes Eagle Harbor Drive. In 0.3 mile bear right onto Bucklin Hill Road. In another 0.3 mile bear right, and in 0.2 mile bear left onto Lynwood Center Road. Continue for 1 mile and turn right (west) onto Baker Hill Road. In 0.8 mile turn right (north) onto gravel Deerpath Lane (signed "Gazzam Lake"). Proceed for 0.2 mile to the southernmost trailhead. (A northern trailhead is closer to the lake and beach; continue on Bucklin Hill Road, Vincent Road, and then Marshall Road to reach it.)

ON THE TRAIL

This is not the shortest way to Gazzam Lake. It can easily be reached by a 0.25 mile hike from the northern Marshall Road trailhead. But hey, we're here to hike! Start by heading down the gated dirt road to two rather unattractive water towers and then through a scrappy patch of invasive species. Just wait—in 0.25 mile it gets better when you enter healthy forest. Now on good trail, encounter a junction. Take the right path for a slightly longer hike, or veer left to get right to the point. At 0.6 mile (0.8 if you went right) the trails meet back up.

Quiet and remote Close Beach in Gazzam Lake Park

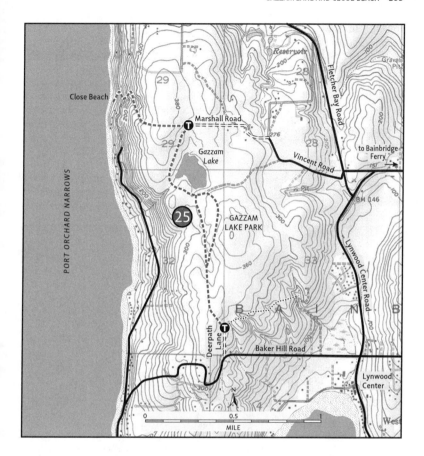

Through a nice forest of cedar and maple, approach Gazzam Lake. Spur paths lead down to the wooded shore. At 1 mile the best of them leads to a small open area complete with a bench. Watch for buffleheads, cormorants, and eagles among the avian residents of this 14-acre lake.

Leave the lake and head north for about 0.1 mile, coming to a junction. The trail right leads to the Marshall Road trailhead. Head left for the best part of this hike. Crest a small hill and begin a steep descent. After 0.6 mile ar-

rive beneath a canopy of big firs to a secluded little beach on Port Orchard Narrows. Pull out your lunch, plop down on a log, and enjoy the sweet smell of salt air along with views of the Kitsap Peninsula and the Olympic Mountains rising behind.

Thanks to the Bainbridge Island Land Trust, $2.5 million was raised to purchase this 550 feet of shoreline and 64 acres of upland, adding it to Gazzam Lake Park. Hikers are sure to get many returns on this wise investment!

EXTENDING YOUR TRIP

From the southern trailhead you can follow Peters Trail northeast for 0.5 mile through a greenbelt of cedars and firs. The Grand Forest, a Bainbridge Island park located a few miles to the north, has several miles of good trails traversing its 240 acres.

Maps: USGS Hansville, trail map available at meadow kiosk; **Contact:** Kitsap County Parks, (360) 337-5350, *www.kitsapgov.com /parks/regionalparks/hansville_greenways _county_park.htm*; **Notes:** Dogs must be leashed; **GPS:** N 47 54.529, W 122 33.381

26 Hansville Greenway

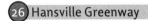

RATING/ DIFFICULTY	ROUND-TRIP	ELEV GAIN/ HIGH POINT	SEASON
★/1	3.5 miles	100 feet/ 180 feet	Year-round

Hike on an old logging railbed through an emerging greenbelt on the northern tip of the Kitsap Peninsula.

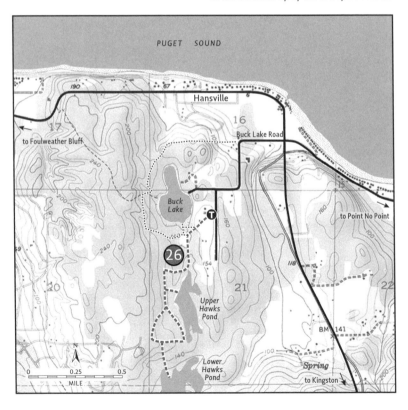

Wildlife observation deck on the Hansville Greenway

Lakes, bogs, and wildlife observation platforms await you. A good network of trails allows for plenty of options in this quiet park.

GETTING THERE

From Poulsbo take State Route 307 northeast to SR 104. Continue east on SR 104 for 1.5 miles to a four-way intersection and traffic light. (From Kingston follow SR 104 west for 2.5 miles.) Turn left (north) on Hansville Road, driving 7.5 miles. Turn left (west) on Buck Lake Road (signed for Buck Lake County Park and Hansville Community Center). Proceed for 0.8 mile, passing boat launch access in Buck Lake County Park. The trailhead is located in the southwest corner of a ball field. Water and restrooms available, except in winter.

ON THE TRAIL

Here's what can happen when concerned local citizens come together to work with a governing agency toward a common conservation goal: the Hansville Greenway. Back in the 1990s the Hansville Greenway Association along with Kitsap County Parks began acquiring land for a nature preserve in the relatively undeveloped northern reaches of the peninsula. By 2005 they had preserved 200 acres and built 3 miles of trail. Having recently secured grant monies, these managing bodies are working on doubling the size of the preserve and trail system.

Meanwhile, there's plenty of ground to explore. Start by heading through the Welcome Wood to the meadow kiosk (at 0.3 mile). Head south through Otter Meadow and continue under stately firs, passing the Muskrat Swamp. Come to a trail junction at Alder Hollow (at 0.6 mile). Turn left (south) on a wide trail on what was once part of a narrow-gauge logging railway built in the 1920s.

Come to a junction (at 0.7 mile). The trail left leads for 0.3 mile to a planked resting area overlooking Upper Hawks Pond (actually more of a swamp), affectionately called Quiet Place. Continue south on the railroad trail to another junction (at 0.8 mile). Head left, skirting wetlands and traversing pleasant woods to arrive at yet another trail junction (at 1.3 miles). Turn left and head 0.25 mile to Lower Hawk's Pond, where you'll find a beautiful elevated wooden observation platform perfect for scoping this eutrophic waterway. In addition to the myriad of birds that live in and along this nutrient-rich body of water, look for bear, coyotes, and deer.

Return to the main trail and take a left. Shortly after, come to a junction. The trail left leaves the preserve; bear right instead and within 0.25 mile come to the railroad trail again. Turn left and retrace your steps back to the trailhead.

EXTENDING YOUR TRIP

From the meadow kiosk to Bear Meadow Vista on Buck Lake is 1 mile. You can continue from the meadow another 0.7 mile to the community of Hansville. Nearby Point No Point County Park and Foulweather Bluff Nature Conservancy Preserve have nice, albeit short, hiking trails through gorgeous coastal settings.

Opposite: Mossy milepost on Lower South Fork of the Skokomish Trail

Wynoochee River Valley

One of the largest watersheds (218 square miles) on the southern flank of the Olympic Peninsula, the Wynoochee has been intensively logged since the 1940s. Its steep slopes are marred by roads, massive cuts, and landslides, revealing some of the worst examples of industrial forestry practices in the state.

Before World War II the Wynoochee was mainly a wilderness of unbroken old-growth forests. Miles of trails led through some of its lonely valleys and to a few of its scenic peaks. But as the big trees succumbed to chain saws, most of the trail system was uprooted as well, leaving hikers little reason to visit this once-great valley.

Still, while most of the old trails were destroyed, an excellent new one was built when the river was dammed for flood control. And now that logging in the Olympic National Forest has been greatly reduced, in part because globalization favors cheaper foreign imports, the Wynoochee is slowly healing. Fragments of some of the great trails can still be followed. Perhaps part of the recovery of this vast area will include reopening former trails to reintroduce hikers to the region, thereby instilling a new sense of stewardship for this long-abused and neglected part of our natural heritage.

27 Wynoochee Lake

RATING/ DIFFICULTY	LOOP	ELEV GAIN/ HIGH POINT	SEASON
★★/3	12 miles	1150 feet/ 950 feet	Late July–Oct

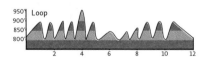

Map: Green Trails Grisdale No. 198; **Contact:** Olympic National Forest, Hood Canal Ranger District, Quilcene, (360) 765-2200, www

.fs.fed.us/r6/olympic; **Notes:** Fording of the Wynoochee River is safe only during low flow in late summer. Alternative trail with bridge adds 4 miles to loop; **GPS:** N 47 23.414, W 123 36.146

Enjoy an up-and-down route around the forested shores of man-made Wynoochee Lake. From quiet coves, look out across clear waters to craggy peaks and scrappy hills. Traverse numerous groves of old-growth forest harboring some of the largest Douglas-firs left in the Olympic National Forest. Encounter plentiful signs of deer, bear, and elk, attesting to their abundance. Along the eastern shore, the trail can be accessed at several points from Forest Road 2270 for shorter kid-friendly and winter hiking options.

GETTING THERE

From Montesano travel north on Wynoochee Valley Road for 17 miles. The pavement ends and the road becomes Forest Road 22. Continue north for 17 more miles to a major intersection. Turn left (still on FR 22) and after 0.5 mile turn right onto FR 2294, driving 1.2 miles to Coho Campground. Park in the day-use area. The trail begins near the boat launch.

ON THE TRAIL

Before starting, catch a glimpse of the lake from the boat launch. Dammed by the Army Corps of Engineers in 1972 for flood control and now managed by Tacoma Power, the lake almost appears natural, lined with tall timber and surrounded by rugged hills. The Forest Service developed the loop trail shortly after the lake's creation and the Tacoma Urban League has done a good job maintaining it.

The trail skirts the campground to join the Working Forest Nature Trail. This 0.5-mile path soon veers to the left, while the lakeshore trail travels through thick timber on a

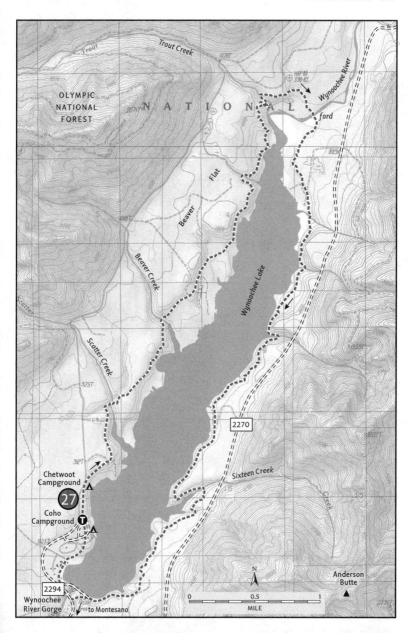

level terrace. A side path heads right to the Chetwoot Campground, accessible only by foot and watercraft.

After a mile the trail drops into the first of many ravines to cross a creek, and then it climbs back out. Get used to this pattern—it'll repeat itself a dozen times, contributing to a cumulative elevation gain well over 1000 feet. Undulate between thick second growth and mature groves of towering hemlocks and firs. Oxalis carpets the forest floor.

At 2 miles the trail traverses alder-lined Beaver Flat, a marshy and gravelly bottom-land. At 4 miles the trail cruises by some big cedars and then begins a steep climb on a high slide-prone bank above the lake. There are good views here of the lake below and of the upper Wynoochee River valley to the north. Mount Church and Capitol Peak stand out in the east.

Drop rapidly to Trout Creek and find a series of rocks to hop across. Climb another steep bank and then descend into a lush forested grove housing some monster firs. Over 140 inches of rain fall upon the Wynoochee annually, making it no small wonder why so many giants grace this valley.

At 5.5 miles reach a junction. Head right across a wide gravel bar to ford the river. Look for a shallow spot to make the crossing. If it can't be done safely, either head back or take the alternative bridged trail (to the left at the junction), adding 4 miles to your already long hike.

Once across, head south along the generally more attractive eastern shore through large pockets of old growth, across steep ravines of crashing creeks, and by good lake-viewing gaps in the forest. At 9 miles come to a spur road leading to the shore. Turn left to pick up the trail again. Sixteen Creek at 10 miles marks your last ravine drop. Two miles

beyond, the trail reaches the dam. Cross the Wynoochee River gorge on the road bridge and complete the loop by passing through the day-use area. A quick dip may be in order before returning home.

28 Spoon Creek Falls

RATING/ DIFFICULTY	ROUND-TRIP	ELEV GAIN/ HIGH POINT	SEASON
★★/2	0.8 mile	200 feet/ 1000 feet	July–Oct

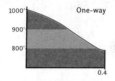

Map: Green Trails Grisdale No. 198; **Contact:** Olympic National Forest, Hood Canal Ranger District, Quilcene, (360) 765-2200, *www .fs.fed.us/r6/olympic*; **GPS:** N 47 21.227, W 123 33.912

❌ 🥾 *Here's a trail to literally get your feet wet hiking. Drop into a cool box canyon—one of many on the south flank of the Olympics—then splash your way to the bottom of a spectacular waterfall. Lots of fun on a hot day in late summer when the creek flow is low and passage is safe, this should never be attempted during periods of heavy rain. During times when the creek is roaring, the falls can safely be seen from a viewing area above.*

GETTING THERE

From Montesano travel north on Wynoochee Valley Road for 17 miles. The pavement ends and the road becomes Forest Road 22. Continue north for 17 more miles to a major intersection. Proceed north for 0.1 mile, turning right

Opposite: The Wynoochee River flowing into Wynoochee Lake, as seen from a high shoreline bluff

onto FR 23 and driving 2.5 miles. The trailhead is on the right, 0.1 mile beyond the bridge over the West Fork Satsop River. Park on the shoulder. The trail is unmarked and begins behind a large post.

ON THE TRAIL

While this hike is short and may not warrant a trip in itself because of its long access, it makes for a nice add-on while visiting nearby Wynoochee Lake. Many of the creeks and rivers in the southern Olympics traverse deep forbidding box canyons. Glimpses of some, like the West Fork Dosewallips and Wynoochee River gorges, can be had from bridges high above. Here's an opportunity to experience one of these magnificent gorges from down below.

Wear nonslip rubber boots or an old pair of hiking shoes you don't mind getting wet—and take along trekking poles for balance for this short and fun jaunt. The trail dives into a cool grove of old-growth cedar and hemlock adorned with a thick understory of

Opposite: Spoon Creek Falls as seen from the canyon floor

salal. Cascading Spoon Creek interrupts the tranquility of the surrounding forest. In 500 feet a short path leads left to a viewpoint of the falls dropping into the gorge below. The vista is growing over and does little justice to the beautiful falls—only from below can you truly revel in its beauty.

Continue down the trail, coming to another limited-view viewpoint. This one is of the impressive West Fork Satsop River gorge. Now on a wedge of high ground between the two hidden waterways, drop rapidly, coming to a point on Spoon Creek just above its confluence with the West Fork Satsop. Begin working your way up the cool chasm on gravel bars, through ripples, and around pools to the base of Spoon Creek Falls. Find a dry rock to sit on and ponder the falls' glory or refresh yourself in a pool at its base.

EXTENDING YOUR TRIP

If confident in creek-bed hoofing, head down Spoon Creek a short ways to the West Fork Satsop River. Snoop around a little in the remote canyon. Looking for dry land travel? The western terminus of the Church Creek Trail leading to the Satsop Lakes (Hike 32) can be reached by following nearby Forest Road 2372 for 5 miles.

LOGGING THE ANNALS OF HISTORY

About 1 mile south of Lake Wynoochee a large sign on the side of Forest Road 22 marks where Camp Grisdale once stood. Developed in 1946 by the Simpson Timber Company, Grisdale was unlike other logging camps—it was designed to stay in one place. Over fifty fully-serviced homes, a school, bowling alley, and baseball field comprised the complex. In 1986, after forty years of operation, Simpson closed Grisdale. It was the last residential logging camp in the continental United States and its closure was the end of an era in Pacific Northwest history.

Nothing remains of Grisdale. Douglas-firs nearly twenty years old occupy the site. You can see a scale replica of the camp on display at the Mason County Historical Museum in Shelton. While it's easy to romanticize this colorful part of Northwest history, the age when timber was king in Washington certainly left its mark on the landscape, and in particular on the southern flank of the Olympics.

These forests need rejuvenation, and so do the economies of the communities that once relied on the timber from these hills. Perhaps it's time to enter a new era, of sustainable timber harvesting based on ecologically sound principles and friendly to recreation. Perhaps, too, new camps can be established in these parts, employing men and women to help rehabilitate the surrounding scarred forests and mountains, and maybe even revive a trail or two.

South Fork Skokomish River Valley

Like the Wynoochee Valley, this southern flank valley has been heavily cut over. In 1946, with little regard to recreation and preservation, the Forest Service signed an exclusive agreement with the Simpson Timber Company, granting them a ninety-nine-year lease to log and manage a huge portion of public land (our land)—in essence turning it into a private tree farm.

It's easy to lament the loss of thousands of acres of primeval forest, and hundreds of miles of trail, but fortunately a few fragments of trail and uncut tracts have survived. With marketplace changes now favoring foreign timber, and new environmental laws favoring protecting roadless areas, there just might be some hope for preserving what little wildlands remains in the South Fork Skokomish River drainage.

Get to know this neglected valley by hiking beside this major Olympic Peninsula river. A good trail severed in two by a logging road offers excellent hiking among old-growth giants along the river. And while forests along the southern section of this trail have been intruded upon, they are recovering. The northern trail traverses some of the finest old-growth forest remaining within the Olympic National Forest. It needs to be protected in an expanded Wonder Mountain Wilderness. Hike it, cherish it, then help do something about protecting this beautiful and important piece of our natural heritage.

29 Spider Lake

RATING/ DIFFICULTY	LOOP	ELEV GAIN/ HIGH POINT	SEASON
★/1	2 miles	250 feet/ 1400 feet	Year-round

Map: Green Trails Mt Tebo No. 199; **Contact:** Olympic National Forest, Hood Canal Ranger District, Quilcene, (360) 765-2200, *www.fs.fed .us/r6/olympic*; **GPS:** N 47 24.407, W 123 26.409

Saunter around a small lake tucked snugly in a narrow valley on the Skokomish–Satsop River divide. And while this placid body of water has appeal in its own right, it's the surrounding forest that is the main attraction. An exceptional grove

Old-growth forest graces Spider Lake, a gem in a sea of clearcut hills.

of ancient giants graces Spider Lake's tranquil shores. Pleasant any time of year, this hike glows pearly white in early summer when dwarf dogwood and queen's cup blossoms blanket the forest floor.

GETTING THERE

From Shelton travel north on US 101 for 7 miles, turning left (west) at milepost 340 onto the Skokomish Valley Road (signed

"Skokomish Recreation Area"). Follow this good paved road for 5.5 miles, bearing right at a V intersection onto Forest Road 23. In 1 mile the pavement ends; in another 1.5 miles it resumes; and in another mile enter Olympic National Forest. Continue for 6 miles on FR 23 to a signed junction. Bear left, continuing on now-unpaved FR 23 for 8 miles. A pullout on the left with a sign high on a large fir reading "Spider Lake" marks the trailhead.

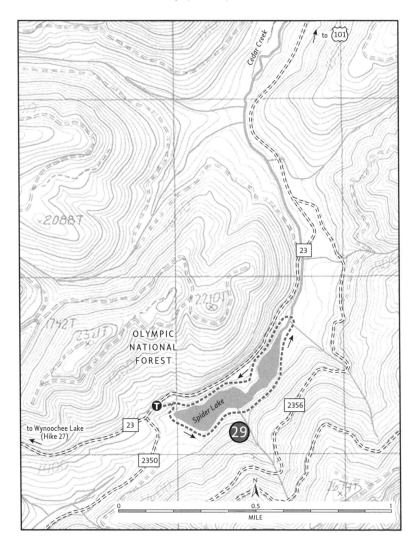

ON THE TRAIL

While the trailhead may lack amenities, the trail is top-notch. In the mid-1990s trail builders resurrected a portion of an old trail (lost to decades of clear-cutting and road building) and constructed brand new tread to form a 2-mile loop around the lake. Trailblazing aficionados may find the loop's three bridges noteworthy for their durability and aesthetics.

The trail starts on a wide track by dropping steeply 100 feet to a point just above the lakeshore. Here the loop begins. Turn right (although either direction will work), ambling above the green waters of the lake and beneath the emerald canopy of ancient behemoths. Fishing spots and viewpoints are encountered along the way. Soon the trail climbs a bit across a steep side slope. Cross a high log bridge, drop back down to lake level, and then pass a big beaver hut. After traversing a marshy area you'll come to an unmarked junction. Take the trail left, crossing the outlet stream (the trail right goes to an alternative trailhead, unmarked and often muddy).

Return along the western shoreline, the trail hugging closer to water level. Gaze up at the surrounding ridges. The intensively logged surroundings offer quite a contrast to the virgin groves you've been hiking through. Fortunately, the web of life has remained strong at little Spider Lake.

The South Fork of the Skokomish flows heavily during winter rains.

30 Lower South Fork Skokomish River

RATING/ DIFFICULTY	ROUND-TRIP	ELEV GAIN/ HIGH POINT	SEASON
★★★/3	10 miles	575 feet/ 850 feet	Year-round

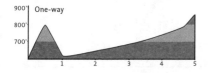

Maps: Green Trails Mt Tebo No. 199, Custom Correct Mount Skokomish–Lake Cushman; **Contact:** Olympic National Forest, Hood Canal Ranger District, Quilcene, (360) 765-2200, *www.fs.fed.us/r6/olympic*; **Notes:** Northwest Forest Pass required; **GPS:** N 47 25.143, W 123 19.780

⊛ ◤ *Big trees, a big river, and a big chance of seeing some big elk if you venture far enough up this well-built and well-maintained trail. You won't be alone on this popular path; mountain bikers*

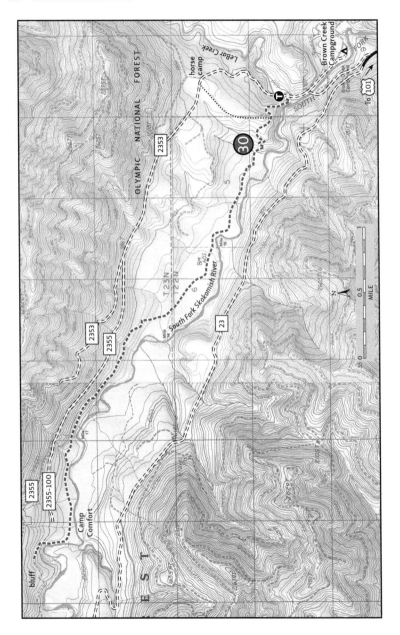

and equestrians like it too. But if you saunter during the week or in the quiet months of the year, only the roar of the river will interrupt the silence.

GETTING THERE

From Shelton travel north on US 101 for 7 miles, turning left (west) at milepost 340 onto Skokomish Valley Road (signed "Skokomish Recreation Area"). Follow this good paved road for 5.5 miles, bearing right at a V intersection onto Forest Road 23. In 1 mile the pavement ends; in another 1.5 miles it resumes; and in another mile enter Olympic National Forest. Continue for 6 miles on FR 23 to a signed junction and turn right onto FR 2353. In 0.5 mile cross the South Fork Skokomish River, coming to a four-way intersection. Turn left, continuing on FR 2353 for 0.3 mile to the trailhead. Privy available.

ON THE TRAIL

The South Fork Skokomish River Trail No. 873 immediately gets down to business, making a steep little climb of about 300 feet. Rounding a high bluff above the roaring river below, the trail enters a magnificent old-growth grove of Doug-firs, some over five hundred years old. In 0.4 mile and nearing the crest of the bluff, a spur trail heads right to the Le Bar Creek Horse Camp. Stay on the path left to a series of short, steep switchbacks, dropping back to the valley floor. After hopping across a side creek (at 1 mile) you'll traverse a beautiful glade of mossy maples and alders.

More old fir giants are soon encountered, as well as a few stumps of cedar giants that were sent to the mills many years ago. At 2 miles pass a campsite, site of an old ranger guardhouse. A half mile farther you may get your feet wet crossing a side creek in a large outwash. The next creek crossing (at 3 mile), however, comes with a nice bridge.

Venturing slightly away from the river you'll pass some old slides and then drop back again

toward the roaring waterway and more old growth. Encounter several more creek crossings, a nice cascade, and then at 4.3 miles come to a junction. The trail right leads to FR 2355-100. The short spur left leads to Camp Comfort, a wonderful place set on a scenic gravelly river bar. It's a good spot for lunch or for whiling away lazy summer days.

If you have any energy left, continue along the trail for another 0.75 mile to an incredible overlook of the river on a bluff high above a big bend.

EXTENDING YOUR TRIP

The South Fork Trail continues for another 5 miles, making longer hikes possible or a 10-mile one-way if you can arrange a pickup at the northern trailhead. Nearby Brown Creek Campground makes for a good base camp for exploring the valley. Kids will enjoy the 0.8-mile nature trail around wildlife-rich Brown Creek Beaver Pond.

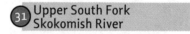

31 Upper South Fork Skokomish River

RATING/ DIFFICULTY	ROUND-TRIP	ELEV GAIN/ HIGH POINT	SEASON
★★★/3	8 miles	1100 feet/ 1800 feet	June–Sept

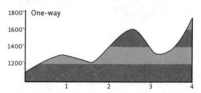

Maps: Green Trails Mt Tebo No. 199, Custom Correct Mount Skokomish–Lake Cushman; **Contact:** Olympic National Forest, Hood Canal Ranger District, Quilcene, (360) 765-2200, *www.fs.fed.us/r6/olympic*; **Notes:** Road closed Oct 1–Apr 30 to protect wildlife; **GPS:** N 47 28.765, W 123 27.125

Venture up a valley as wild as any in the adjacent national park. Marvel at the sheer height, girth, and biomass of some of the biggest trees you'll ever lay eyes on. Watch in awe as the churning, tumbling Upper South Fork Skokomish crashes and squeezes through a narrow box canyon. And while the Upper South Fork lacks federal wilderness protection, this area is nothing but pure Olympic wilderness.

GETTING THERE

From Shelton travel north on US 101 for 7 miles turning left (west) at milepost 340 onto Skokom-

A trusty bridge across the South Fork of the Skokomish River

ish Valley Road (signed "Skokomish Recreation Area"). Follow this good paved road for 5.5 miles, bearing right at a V intersection onto Forest Road 23. In 1 mile the pavement ends; in another 1.5 miles it resumes; and in another mile enter Olympic National Forest. Continue for 6 miles on FR 23 to a signed junction. Bear left on now-unpaved FR 23, proceeding 4.4 miles. Turn right onto FR 2361 and follow it for 5 miles to its end at the trailhead.

ON THE TRAIL

From the large parking area the Upper South Fork Skokomish River Trail heads north and the Lower South Fork Trail takes off south (see Hike 30). Though the lower trail is not a bad option, make sure you're on the Upper South Fork path. Start by hiking 0.5 mile on a grassy old roadbed to a small clearing that once served as the trailhead. Once on bona fide trail enter a world dominated by a turbulent river and towering conifers.

In 0.75 mile you'll emerge on a narrow shelf, river thundering but nowhere in view. Carefully creep to the edge of the trail and peer straight down. Directly below you the South Fork careens through a tight chasm, its booming waters occasionally interrupted by the high-pitched call of a rapids-loving dipper.

At 1.2 miles cross Rule Creek on a big log bridge. Shortly afterward span the South Fork on another big log bridge. Climbing above the tumultuous waterway, weave through a procession of old-growth giants that'll leave your neck sore from constantly cocking it upward. Why this area lacks wilderness protection is, as you can now attest, not for lack of qualifying criteria. During the free-for-all logging frenzy of the 1970s and '80s, Big Timber had their axes trained on these beauties. When you return home, log a request to your senators about giving these arboreal elders some much deserved respect by permanently protecting them.

Cross numerous side streams (plan on wet

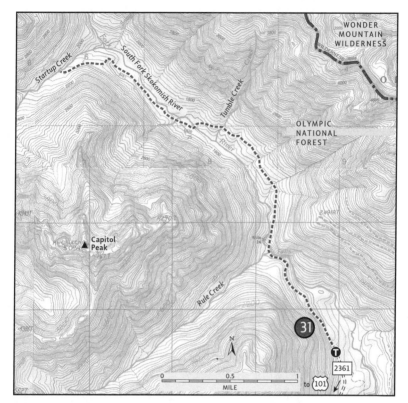

feet in early season) before recrossing the South Fork on another big log bridge at 2.25 miles. The gravel bars here make for a good lounging area. But more wild country calls out to be explored. Continue farther up the valley through mossy glens and tranquil flats, and right alongside the ever-impressive river. At about 3.25 miles the trail pulls away from the river and begins climbing. The tread gets rockier and brushier. At 4 miles you'll come to Startup Creek. This is a good spot to turn around; beyond, the trail deteriorates to not much more than a way path on its rugged journey to Sundown Pass in Olympic National Park. Enjoy lunch by the pretty tumbling waterway before heading back.

EXTENDING YOUR TRIP

While in the neighborhood, head a ways down the Lower South Fork Skokomish Trail. The Church Creek Shelter Trail veers off right, leading to some good camp spots.

32 Church Creek–Satsop Lakes

RATING/ DIFFICULTY	ROUND-TRIP	ELEV GAIN/ HIGH POINT	SEASON
★★/3	6.4 miles	2300 feet/ 3200 feet	June–Sept

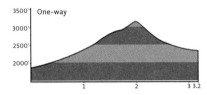

Maps: Green Trails Mt Tebo No. 199 and Grisdale No. 198; **Contact:** Olympic National Forest, Hood Canal Ranger District, Quilcene, (360) 765-2200, *www.fs.fed.us/r6/olympic*; **Notes:** Road closed Oct 1–Apr 30 to protect wildlife; **GPS:** N 47 26.928, W 123 29.437

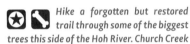 *Hike a forgotten but restored trail through some of the biggest trees this side of the Hoh River. Church Creek* epitomizes why the southern flank was cherished (and nearly completely cutover) by the big timber companies. Towering Douglas-firs reach dizzying heights, and wide-girth cedars and hemlocks hundreds of years old line the trail from end to end. And while the Satsop Lakes make a satisfying destination—peaceful and scenic—it's the forest that's the star of this hike.

GETTING THERE

From Shelton travel north on US 101 for 7 miles, turning left (west) at milepost 340 onto Skokomish Valley Road (signed "Skokomish Recreation Area"). Follow this paved road for 5.5 miles, bearing right onto Forest Road 23. In 1 mile the pavement ends; in another 1.5 miles it resumes;

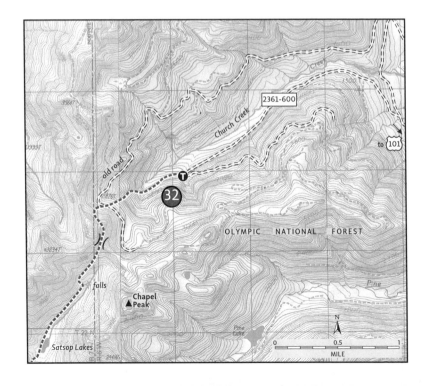

and in another mile enter Olympic National Forest. Continue for 6 miles on FR 23 to a signed junction. Bear left on now-unpaved FR 23, proceeding 4.4 miles. Turn right onto FR 2361 and follow it for 3.4 miles to FR 2361-600 on your left (if you cross Church Creek, you've gone too far). Follow this spur 2.2 miles to a hairpin turn. The trailhead is located on your right.

Zachary inspects Satsop Lake for aquatic activity.

ON THE TRAIL

Once extending from the South Fork Skokomish River all the way to the Wynoochee River, over the years the Church Creek Trail has been whittled to a fraction of its former length. By the late 1990s the Forest Service abandoned it. But Church Creek was resurrected in 2005 thanks to the Olympia Mountaineers. They adopted it, restoring it to a top-notch trail.

From the unimposing trailhead, immediately enter a cathedral forest of buttressed cedars and spires of fir. Cascading Church Creek, audible but not visible, adds a soothing aria to this sanctuary. Named not for a house of worship, but in honor of Frederic Church of the 1890 O'Neil Expedition, the name's alternate meaning is nevertheless apropos, for this truly is a sacred place.

Under a lofty canopy supported by gigantic beams, your attention will be diverted upward for most of this hike. Good thing, too, for these old-growth giants will take your mind off of the stiff climb when a series of switchbacks kicks into gear. The trail comes close to Church Creek on several occasions, but the plummeting waterway remains hidden in a deep ravine.

The forest understory soon unfolds into a boundless huckleberry patch—visit in August to reap the bounty. In early summer, fawn lilies, calypso orchids, and marsh marigolds brighten this emerald world. Hop over a handful of small creeks and after about 1.5 miles reach a decommissioned road (elev. 2800 ft). This entire basin was once slated for the mills. Turn right for 500 feet, once again picking up the trail. Through a more open forest continue climbing, reaching the 3200-foot divide between the South Fork Skokomish and Satsop Rivers after another 0.5 mile. A humongous hemlock with two pistol-butted limbs stands sentry.

Through a forest of silver fir, the trail rapidly descends. Pass a lovely cascade that fans into a steep ravine. Giant cedars and Doug-firs are once again encountered as the trail levels out. At 3.2 miles and after losing 1000 feet of elevation, emerge in a grassy opening that houses the largest of the five Satsop Lakes. A gravel outwash area makes for a good lunch spot. Keep your eyes on the lake for surfacing newts—the lake is home to thousands of them. Roam around the lake and notice no outlet. Water seeps to the Satsop River via a cavernous basalt basin.

EXTENDING YOUR TRIP

Four other lakes are hidden in the surrounding forest if you feel inclined to find them. The trail also continues for 0.3 mile under more giant trees, ending at FR 2372. But save some energy for the climb back.

Opposite: Heather negotiates Whitehorse Creek on her way to Lake of the Angels.

North Fork Skokomish River Valley

Like its southern counterpart, the North Fork Skokomish River has seen its share of human meddling. Intensive logging, a hydro dam, and housing developments mar its lower reaches. But the upper watershed, protected within Olympic National Park, is pure wilderness.

Owing to the presence of Lake Cushman and close proximity to Olympia, Shelton, and Bremerton, this valley sees a fair amount of recreational usage. Trails like those to the Staircase Rapids and Mount Ellinor can get downright busy. But there are plenty of other options for solitude seekers. Big Creek and Copper Creek, two of the Olympic National Forest's newest trails, have yet to be discovered.

The North Fork Skokomish offers a diverse arrangement of hiking options too. Choose from challenging peak-bagging to lazy river jaunts. Head to quiet backcountry lakes or along crashing cascading creeks. Hike trails trodden by prospectors and explorers, elk and cougars. While parts of this valley have succumbed to modern development, most of it remains as wild as it was when Lieutenant Joseph P. O'Neil led one of the first exploratory missions across this region in 1890.

33 Big Creek

RATING/ DIFFICULTY	LOOP	ELEV GAIN/ HIGH POINT	SEASON
★★/2	4.5 miles	900 feet/ 1870 feet	Year-round

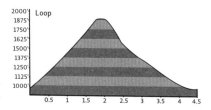

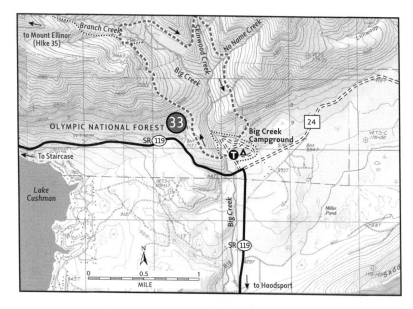

Map: Custom Correct Mount Skokomish–Lake Cushman; **Contact:** Olympic National Forest, Hood Canal Ranger District, Quilcene, (360) 765-2200, *www.fs.fed.us/r6/olympic*; **Notes:** Northwest Forest Pass required; **GPS:** N 47 29.599, W 123 12.661

In the shadows of Mount Ellinor, enjoy this circuitous route around the Big Creek drainage. There are plenty of pretty resting and contemplation spots along the way. Plenty of cascades too, along Big Creek and the smaller creeks feeding into it.

GETTING THERE

From Shelton travel north on US 101 for 15 miles to Hoodsport. Turn left (west) onto State Route 119, proceeding 9.3 miles to a T intersection with Forest Road 24. Make a sharp left and immediately turn right into the Big Creek Campground. The trailhead is located near the picnic shelter.

ON THE TRAIL

Save this hike for a hot summer day when shaded glens offer respite from the midday rays. Forested all the way, and always within earshot of tumbling water, the Big Creek Trail makes a fine rainy-day hike too. Constructed entirely by volunteers, this relatively new addition to the Olympic National Forest trail inventory is sure to gain in popularity.

Utilizing many old roads, the crew put together an interesting loop guaranteed to make you walk away with a better appreciation of the beauty of cascading waters. Start your journey by walking west through the picnic area and to the Big Creek Nature Trail. This trail circles the campground for a 1-mile loop. But you've got bigger plans, so cross Big Creek on a good bridge and come to a junction. Turn left on Trail No. 827.1 and start the big loop.

Clockwise is the preferred direction for an

Cascading Big Creek

easier-on-the-knees descent. On a well-built and well-shaded trail begin ascending above the creek. Mileposts and resting benches grace the way. After 1 mile the grade gets steeper. Mount Washington hovering above can occasionally be seen through gaps in the forest canopy. At 1.7 miles you'll come to a junction. You can continue straight on the loop, or take an interesting side trip dropping to the confluence of Big and Branch Creeks. Here you'll find good lunch rocks among the two tumbling waterways.

Continuing on the main loop, soon come to a junction with the Mount Ellinor Trail. This is the long and challenging way to the popular peak. Next comes a scenic crossing of Branch Creek on a good bridge. A few steps ahead and another good bridge is encountered, this one spanning Big Creek above a gorgeous cascade. The loop now begins descending, skirting some big boulders and granting good views of roaring Big Creek.

At 2 miles another side trail drops to the confluence of Big and Branch Creeks. Following an old road, the main loop works its way 2 miles back to the campground, but not before spanning scenic Skinwood and No Name Creeks, passing the giant firs that loggers forgot, and catching a glimpse of Mount Ellinor rising above the watershed. At 4 miles this lovely loop ends at the Big Creek Nature Trail. Return to the main trailhead by following the nature trail 0.5 mile in either direction.

EXTENDING YOUR TRIP

Stay awhile by spending a peaceful night in the spacious Big Creek Campground. Take an evening hike on the 1-mile Big Creek Nature Trail. Nearby Hoodsport Trail State Park (milepost 3 on SR 119) offers 2 miles of quiet interlocking trail often void of two-legged visitors.

34 Mount Rose

RATING/ DIFFICULTY	ROUND-TRIP	ELEV GAIN/ HIGH POINT	SEASON
★★★/5	6.4 miles	3500 feet/ 4301 feet	June–Oct

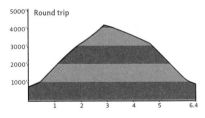

Maps: Green Trails Mt Steel No. 167, Custom Correct Mount Skokomish–Lake Cushman; **Contact:** Olympic National Forest, Hood Canal Ranger District, Quilcene, (360) 765-2200, www.fs.fed.us/r6/olympic; **GPS:** N 47 29.734, W 123 16.055; **Notes:** Trail was closed in 2006 due to the Bear Gulch Fire. Call ahead for status of trail.

With all due respect to the Bard, what's in a mountain? That which we call Mount Rose by any other name would still be as steep. This is a challenging hike—one of the steepest trails in the Olympics. Great for conditioning, Rose offers a few scenic rewards too, from beautiful high-elevation old-growth forests to a knockout view of Lake Cushman from 3500 feet directly above it. Consider Rose an alternative to Mount Ellinor. When half of Olympia is crowding Ellinor's summit like goats at a salt lick, you just might be savoring the sweet offerings of Rose all by yourself.

GETTING THERE

From Shelton travel north on US 101 for 15 miles to Hoodsport. Turn left (west) onto State Route 119, proceeding 9.3 miles to a T intersection with Forest Road 24. Make a sharp left. In 1.7 miles the pavement ends. Continue on FR 24 for 1 more mile to the trailhead, located on your right.

ON THE TRAIL

Start by crossing a cascading creek and heading up an old road. Enjoy it, for it's the only level walking you'll see on this hike. Now begin the grind. On good tread, start switchbacking to the heavens. Yes, the grade is steep, but it used to be worse. Over a decade ago a dedicated volunteer trail crew reconfigured much of the way.

A carpet of salal lines the trail. Uniform second growth with a few remnant giants (survivors of early twentieth-century fires) offer

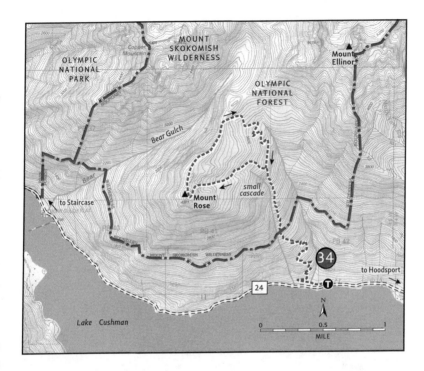

needed shade. At 0.3 mile pass through a pair of towering Doug-firs that act as a gateway. Despite the roar of a distant creek, the slope is dry, as evidenced by the few madronas and manzanita bushes.

At 1 mile and after 1000 feet of climbing, a bench with a view of Lake Cushman invites a break. Catch your breath and continue. After 0.1 mile enter the Mount Skokomish Wilderness. Ironically, the trees are now smaller and less impressive. Perhaps it's due to thinner soils, for the way gets even steeper. At 1.6 miles enter a cool forest of hemlock. A short spur trail leads left to a little cascade, although it may be dry by late summer.

In another 0.25 mile reach the summit loop junction (elev. 3050 ft) along with a small plaque honoring the crew that built this trail.

Take the left trail—it's shorter and steeper, leaving the longer and more gradual option for the descent, relieving your knees.

The summit loop climbs 1300 feet in just over 1 mile, mostly through cool old growth. At 2.9 miles from the trailhead reach the 4301-foot forested summit. Don't despair, a small vertigo-inducing rock outcropping juts out of the forest providing a panoramic payoff. Directly below, waters sparkling, is Lake Cushman. Lightning Peak and Timber Mountain rise majestically behind it. Wonder Mountain and Church Peak are just off to the right. The Skokomish delta, Black and Willapa Hills, and Mount Rainier are all visible from this pulse-raising promontory. Through silver snags and white pines the deep valley of the North Fork Skokomish can also be glimpsed.

Spiraling view of Lake Cushman from Mount Rose's summit

After your rosy outlook continue on the loop. Along a forested ledge, the trail makes a 1.7-mile saner return to the loop junction. Enjoy glimpses of Copper Mountain, but the real point of interest is a colonnade of four silver firs about halfway down the trail. They have grown so close together they appear fused. Now, test your trekking poles before careening down the mountain.

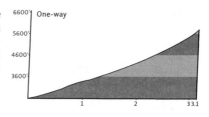

35 Mount Ellinor

RATING/ DIFFICULTY	ROUND-TRIP	ELEV GAIN/ HIGH POINT	SEASON
★★★★★/4	6.2 miles	3200 feet/ 5944 feet	July–Oct

Maps: Green Trails Mt Steel No. 167 and The Brothers No. 168, Custom Correct Mount Skokomish–Lake Cushman; **Contact:** Olympic National Forest, Hood Canal Ranger District, Quilcene, (360) 765-2200, *www.fs.fed .us/r6/olympic*; **Notes:** Northwest Forest Pass required; **GPS:** N 47 30.396, W 123 13.925

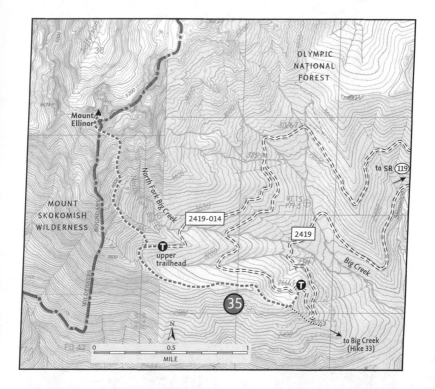

An Olympic classic—bag this peak for one of the most supreme views this side of Hood Canal. From the jagged summit peer deep into the heart of the Olympic wilderness or out across Lake Cushman and Puget Sound to the Cascades spanning the eastern horizon. All of this comes at a price, however—the trail to Ellinor is steep and tough.

GETTING THERE

From Shelton travel north on US 101 for 15 miles to Hoodsport. Turn left (west) onto State Route 119 and proceed 9.3 miles to a T intersection with Forest Road 24. Turn right onto graveled FR 24, proceed 1.6 miles, and turn left onto FR 2419. After 4.8 miles come to the lower trailhead. The upper trailhead can

A hiker descends the steep slopes of Mount Ellinor; Lake Cushman is in the background.

be reached by continuing on FR 2419 for 1.6 miles to a junction. Turn left on FR 2419-014 and follow it 1 mile to the upper trailhead.

ON THE TRAIL

Yes, there is an upper trailhead that shortens this hike by 3 miles and knocks 900 feet of elevation off. But why start there? The whole idea is to go hiking, not get to the mountain the shortest way possible. By beginning on the lower trailhead you get a chance to warm up for a very steep ascent, and you get to enjoy one of the finest old-growth groves this side of Copper Creek. Plus you get 1.5 miles of quiet hiking, avoiding the crowds flocking to the upper trailhead.

Begin by immediately entering a cool forest of old-growth hemlock and Douglas-fir. As the trail skirts the edges of old clear-cuts, teaser views promise what lies ahead. In about 0.5 mile the trail from Big Creek comes in from the left (the long, long way up Ellinor). Ascending steadily, the trail winds 1 mile up a heavily forested ridge to meet the upper trail at 3900 feet. The trail right descends 400 feet to meet the upper trailhead in 0.3 mile.

Now, hopefully warmed up and limber, prepare for some serious work. The incline gets steeper while the terrain gets rougher. At 2.5 miles (4600 feet) trees yield to meadows and views begin. But to quote the late not-so-great 1970s rock band, BTO, "B-b-baby, you ain't seen nothing yet!"

The winter climbing route veers right. Continue left, ascending open meadows and rocky gardens. Years ago, going beyond this point was a tricky scramble. But thanks to the hard work of the Mount Rose Volunteer Trail Crew a trail was carved into the steep mountain face, making the ascent much safer and more manageable.

Continue huffing and puffing, traversing a very steep slope. Now just a short distance from your objective, clamber north up a rocky ridge until finally, at 3.1 miles from and nearly two-thirds of a mile above the lower trailhead, reach Ellinor's magnificent summit. Wipe your brow, gulp some water, and prepare to be wowed. One mile directly below is Lake Cushman, rippling waters shining right back at you. Lots of saltwater twinkles below too, with Puget Sound and Hood Canal clearly visible. The Cascades fill the eastern horizon, with Rainier dominating the show. Percolating St. Helens is visible to the south.

Turn your attention north and westward to a diorama of jagged Olympic peaks. Washington, Pershing, and Stone, like a lineup of generals, flank Ellinor to the north. Lincoln, Cruiser, Gladys, and Copper guard her to the west. Gaze down into the vertigo-inducing Jefferson Creek valley and spot an inviting but isolated pond. You can sit on this summit for hours learning much about western Washington's geography.

EXTENDING YOUR TRIP

If you're a purist or really looking for a challenge, hike to Ellinor starting at the Big Creek Campground (see Hike 33). A new trail replicating part of the old route from Lake Cushman was recently built by a volunteer trail crew. The stats: 12.4 miles round trip and 5000 feet of vertical gain.

36 Dry Creek

RATING/ DIFFICULTY	ROUND-TRIP	ELEV GAIN/ HIGH POINT	SEASON
*/2	6 miles	800 feet/ 1600 feet	Year-round

Maps: Green Trails Mt Tebo No. 199, Custom Correct Mount Skokomish–Lake Cushman; **Contact:** Olympic National Forest, Hood Canal Ranger District, Quilcene, (360) 765-2200, *www.fs.fed.us/r6/olympic*; **Notes:** Trail begins on a private road, respect adjacent private property; **GPS:** N 47 30.088, W 123 19.235

★ 🦴 *Save this trail for a wet fall or spring morning. Quiet woods and a lack of fellow hikers should give you some good wildlife-observation opportunities. During the hot days of summer the Dry Creek Trail may still be enjoyed, but chances are you won't want to venture far from the inviting shores of Lake Cushman.*

GETTING THERE

From Shelton travel north on US 101 for 15 miles to Hoodsport. Turn left (west) onto State Route 119, proceeding 9.3 miles to a T intersection with Forest Road 24. Make a sharp left. In 1.7 miles the pavement ends. Continue on a good gravel road (FR 24) and in 3.7 miles come to a junction. Turn left on FR 2451, crossing a causeway, and in 0.4 mile find the trailhead on your left.

ON THE TRAIL

The Dry Creek Trail was saved from obscurity a few years ago, thanks to the Washington Trails Association. Tenacious volunteers helped reopen this old trail in an area of the

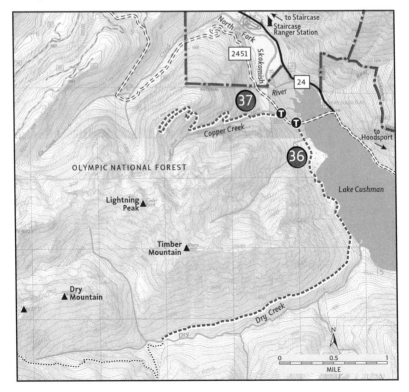

Olympic National Forest, long overlogged and underhiked. The trail traverses a low ridge through mostly second-growth forest. Nothing particularly grand or alluring here, just miles of lightly traveled terrain.

Start by walking 0.3 mile down a private road lined with summer cabins. Once on real trail, begin a 1-mile trot along Lake Cushman. Enlarged in the 1920s when the City of Tacoma built a dam on it for power, hundreds of acres of prime old growth was cut and the area flooded. At 0.8 mile come to a good access point for exploring the stump-laced lakeshore.

At 1 mile a small bluff offers a good vantage for viewing Mount Rose across the lake's reflective waters. Now, pulling away from the lake, start climbing. Soon you'll come to a spur trail heading left. It leads to a campsite on Dry Creek at its outlet into Cushman—a great lunch spot or turnaround point for those intent on enjoying more of the lake than the hike.

The Dry Creek Trail now climbs steadily on an old road, creek in sound but not in sight. After about a mile of uphill grunting, the trail levels out under a canopy of alders. In midspring it's lined with thousands of trilliums, bleeding hearts, and violets. At 3 miles, with the roar of Dry Creek now quite loud, the trail finally comes upon it. The old footlog spanning it was wiped out years ago. Dry Creek, as you can see, is far from dry, and crossing it can be treacherous. Find yourself a good lunch rock and enjoy the torrent before turning around.

EXTENDING YOUR TRIP

If you can safely cross the creek, you can continue hiking farther. The trail enters old-growth forest, climbing 2000 feet to a pass beneath Dry Mountain, where there are limited views. Beyond the pass (2.5 miles from the creek crossing), it's a 1.5-mile drop to the upper trailhead near Le Bar Creek.

Mount Rose rises above Lake Cushman.

37 Copper Creek

RATING/ DIFFICULTY	ROUND-TRIP	ELEV GAIN/ HIGH POINT	SEASON
★★★/4	5 miles	2400 feet/ 3200 feet	May–Oct

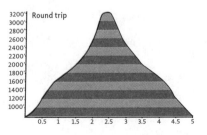

Map: USGS Lightning Peak; **Contact:** Olympic National Forest, Hood Canal Ranger District, Quilcene, (360) 765-2200, *www.fs.fed .us/r6/olympic*; **Notes:** Maps don't show this new trail; **GPS:** N 47 30.325, W 123 19.587

⭐🏠 *Climb alongside crashing Copper Creek through a deep and narrow ravine on a steep trail. Explore an old mine site, and then continue onward through primeval forest to a high and narrow shoulder of Lightning Peak.*

GETTING THERE

From Shelton travel north on US 101 for 15 miles to Hoodsport. Turn left (west) onto State Route 119, proceeding 9.3 miles to a T intersection with Forest Road 24. Make a sharp left. In 1.7 miles the pavement ends. Continue on a good gravel road (FR 24) and in 3.7 miles come to a junction. Turn left on FR 2451, crossing a causeway. In 0.8 mile, just after crossing Copper Creek, find a small parking area on your left. The trail begins on the east side of Copper Creek.

ON THE TRAIL

Built originally in 1915 by prospectors searching for copper and manganese, this long-abandoned trail was recently rebuilt by a group of volunteers. Integrating some of the original tread, this new trail is just as steep and challenging as the original—just as wild and beautiful too. While miners clambered along the vertical slopes encompassing Copper Creek, loggers shunned them. Some of the finest old-growth forest in the Skokomish Valley can be found on this hike.

Make sure your legs are limber, for this trail immediately gets down to business. Start climbing into the narrow and dark ravine cut by Copper Creek. At 0.2 mile you'll cross the thundering waterway on a good bridge. Just below, look over on the west side of the ravine wall to spot a shaft from the Brown Mule Mine. Use caution if you wish to further explore it.

The way gets steeper, forging directly up an outwash. At 0.4 mile stop to take in the breathtaking beauty of a cascading tributary plummeting from high above. Now working your way up an increasingly narrow ravine, you'll be hard-pressed to hear anything above the roaring creek pummeling the earth by your feet. When you think the trail can't get any steeper, it does. Through a series of tight switchbacks, climb above the creek on the western slope of the ravine.

At 1 mile from the trailhead, and in a grand forest of giant cedar and Douglas-fir, the trail eases a bit. At 1.4 miles you'll come to a junction. The trail left leads a short distance back

Giant cedars grow in the steep ravine along Copper Creek.

to Copper Creek and to the site of the old Apex Mine. The trail right climbs another 700 feet in 0.75 mile, coming to another junction. Here the Ridge Loop takes off for a 0.5-mile rough route to a 3200-foot shoulder on Lightning Peak. Views are limited on the forested ridge, but a few dizzying glimpses of Lake Cushman and the Elk Creek basin can be had. Rest up and brace yourself for a knee-burning descent.

38 Wagonwheel Lake

RATING/ DIFFICULTY	ROUND-TRIP	ELEV GAIN/ HIGH POINT	SEASON
**/5	5.8 miles	3200 feet/ 4100 feet	Mid- June–Oct

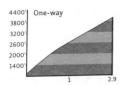

Maps: Green Trails Mt Steel No. 167, Custom Correct Mount Skokomish–Lake Cushman; **Contact:** Olympic National Park, Wilderness Information Center, (360) 565-3100, *www .nps.gov/olym*; **Notes:** Dogs prohibited. National park entry fee; **GPS:** N 47 30.966, W 123 19.655

It's one of the steepest trails in Olympic National Park, a trailhead sign warns (or boasts). Over 3000 vertical feet are gained in less than 3 miles. With tight switchbacks to no switchbacks, the grade is brutal. Then once you stop climbing, you get to traverse a brushy avalanche chute. When you arrive at Wagonwheel Lake, you realize it's no chrome hubcap—just a tiny forest-ringed pond with nary a good place to soak your feet. But if you can muster some energy to climb the open ridge behind it, this hike goes to four stars, and all that sweat and pain will be worth it.

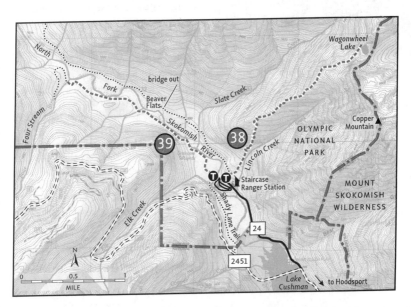

Wagonwheel Lake in early summer

GETTING THERE

From Shelton travel north on US 101 for 15 miles to Hoodsport. Turn left (west) onto State Route 119, proceeding 9.3 miles to a T intersection with Forest Road 24. Make a sharp left. In 1.7 miles the pavement ends. Continue on a good gravel road (FR 24) and in 3.7 miles come to a junction. Turn right and drive 1.2 miles to the Staircase Ranger Station. Trailhead parking is on your right, across from the campground. Water and privies available.

ON THE TRAIL

Despite its grueling statistics, little Wagonwheel Lake gets its fair share of visitors. Rather, its attempted share. Many hikers comprehend 2.9 miles, but not 3200 vertical feet. It's an insane combination, bringing many an unconditioned hiker to his knees and back to the trailhead unfulfilled. If you're ready for the challenge, however, carry on!

Through a lush understory of shoulder-high ferns and salal, ease into the climb. After about 0.25 mile, break out onto a dry ledge and get down to business. Pass an old mining bore on your right (which is more interesting than an old boring miner). Relentlessly, the trail attacks the steep slope in a series of short, tight switchbacks. Through mostly second-growth fir, a few white pines and rhododendrons break the monotony of the forest. The monotony of the climb however, is rarely broken. At about 1.5 miles, nearby a small ledge with a limited view of the valley, enter a cooler forest of hemlock.

The trail now gets even steeper—gone are the switchbacks. Hikers like me who grew up scaling the peaks of the Northeast will feel right at home. We'll also be reminded of how much we don't miss those straight-up-the-mountain trails. After 2 miles and 2 quarts of sweat, the trail miraculously levels out. Now through old-growth fir and hemlock, skirt a steep slope, breaking out onto a brushy avalanche chute. Work your way across slumping tread, enjoying views of Mount Lincoln and the Sawtooth Range.

Reenter cool evergreen forest, cross Wagonwheel's outlet creek, and finally—at 2.9 miles—arrive at the little tarn. A small sunny bench above the lake makes for a good place to collapse. But if you have any oomph left, locate a primitive path taking off from the main trail at the lake. It goes for 0.5 mile straight up the 4700-foot ridge to the north. From its meadows punctuated with silver snags, enjoy a breathtaking panorama that includes the following peaks: Pershing, Washington, Ellinor, Copper, Lincoln, Skokomish, and The

Brothers. Even little Wagonwheel looks great from up here.

39 Staircase Rapids

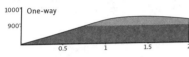

RATING/ DIFFICULTY	ROUND-TRIP	ELEV GAIN/ HIGH POINT	SEASON
★★/1	4 miles	150 feet/ 950 feet	Year-round

Maps: Green Trails Mt Steel No. 167, Custom Correct Mount Skokomish–Lake Cushman; **Contact:** Olympic National Park, Wilderness Information Center, (360) 565-3100, *www.nps .gov/olym*; **Notes:** Dogs prohibited. National park entry fee. Staircase road closed in winter, park at picnic area and hike 1 mile up road or hike 1 mile along Shady Lane Trail from Copper Creek trailhead; **GPS:** N 47 30.946, W 123 19.798

Stand in awe watching the swift-moving waters of the North Fork Skokomish River barrel and thunder over a series of cascades. A great hike anytime of year, Staircase Rapids is especially impressive during the spring runoff. Hikers of all ages will be delighted on this easy and captivating hike.

GETTING THERE
From Shelton travel north on US 101 for 15 miles to Hoodsport. Turn left (west) onto State Route 119, proceeding 9.3 miles to a T intersection with Forest Road 24. Make a sharp left. In 1.7 miles the pavement ends. Continue on a good gravel road (FR 24) and in 3.7 miles come to a junction. Turn right and drive 1.2 miles to the Staircase Ranger Station. Trailhead parking is on your right, across from the campground. Water and privies available.

ON THE TRAIL
The trek to Staircase Rapids is a heck of a lot easier today than it was in 1890 when Lieutenant Joseph O'Neil, accompanied by a group of scientists, led an army expedition here. The O'Neil Party was intent on traversing the Olympic Peninsula. Lacking the wonderful trails that now grace the region, O'Neil and company cut a mule trail up the North Fork Skokomish River to help transport supplies to base camps along the way. Among the many findings that this expedition would report was

The North Fork of the Skokomish River goes through a series of rapids and cascades at Staircase Rapids.

a realization that this wild area deserved to be protected. In his trip report O'Neil wrote that the Olympic interior would serve admirably as a national park. Nice forward thinking, Lieutenant O'Neil—I salute you.

From the main parking area, cross the North Fork Skokomish on a solid bridge to begin this hike, which follows part of the original O'Neil Mule Trail. Immediately pass a side trail that leads left to the small hydro plant that powers the ranger station. About 0.1 mile beyond, pass another side trail. This path leads to what was once an incredibly large cedar. Today it leads to an incredibly large windfall. The old cedar yielded to a winter storm in the late 1990s.

A few more minutes of gentle hiking delivers you to the riverbank. As you begin marching up the valley, a series of roaring rapids and frothing falls awaits you. Follow the thundering river from one mesmerizing spot to another. At 0.8 mile is a junction. The trail right leads to a bridge that has been out since the mid-1990s. If the Park Service ever gets the funding to replace it, the bridge will once again provide a nice loop option. Meanwhile, ask Congress how they find billions of dollars for boondoggles but not a few thousand for trails.

Continue your hike up the river valley on the much quieter and less-used Four Stream Trail. Soon come to Beaver Flats, a nice spot to soak your feet in the refreshing river. Next, pass through a forest of silver and charred snags, thanks to a wildfire created by a careless camper in the late 1980s. New greenery is growing in, so the views of Mount Lincoln rising over the valley won't be around much longer.

Emerging back in mature forest, the trail follows alongside a much calmer river. At 2 miles the trail drops down to Four Stream, which for most of the year is too high, cold, and fast to ford. The trail doesn't go much farther anyway, making this a good spot to turn around.

EXTENDING YOUR TRIP
Back at the ranger station consider hiking the Shady Lane Trail. This 1-mile path heads down the North Fork Skokomish valley to FR 2451 through some of the biggest and oldest trees in the Staircase area. There's an old mine and some good river views along the way as well.

40 North Fork Skokomish River and Flapjack Lakes

Big Log Camp

RATING/DIFFICULTY	ROUND-TRIP	ELEV GAIN/HIGH POINT	SEASON
★★★/2	11 miles	700 feet/1550 feet	Mar–Nov

Flapjack Lakes

RATING/DIFFICULTY	ROUND-TRIP	ELEV GAIN/HIGH POINT	SEASON
★★★/4	15 miles	3200 feet/3900 feet	Mid-June–Oct

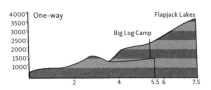

Maps: Green Trails Mt Steel No. 167, Custom Correct Mount Skokomish–Lake Cushman; **Contact:** Olympic National Park, Wilderness Information Center, (360) 565-3100, www.nps.gov/olym; **Notes:** Dogs prohibited. National park entry fee; **GPS:** N 47 30.966, W 123 19.655

Your choice: An easy all-day hike along a roaring wild waterway embraced by coniferous giants, or a very long all-day hike to a pair of subalpine lakes in the shadows of the jagged Sawtooth Range. Neither hike is particularly difficult; they just require endurance and some good aerobic conditioning because of their lengths. No

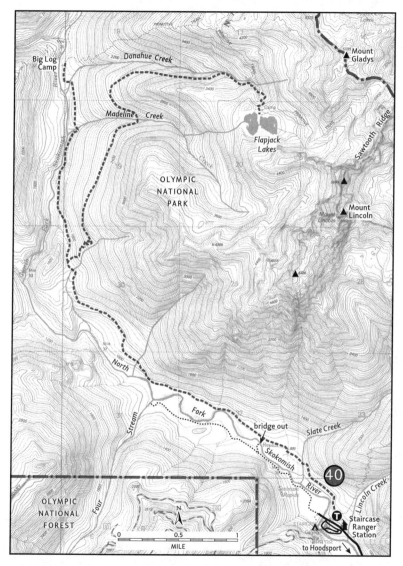

matter your destination, though, you'll have plenty of company. The North Fork Skokomish River valley has been attracting legions of hikers ever since Lieutenant O'Neil and his boys passed this way shortly after Washington became a state.

GETTING THERE

From Shelton travel north on US 101 for 15 miles to Hoodsport. Turn left (west) onto State Route 119, proceeding 9.3 miles to a T intersection with Forest Road 24. Make a sharp left. In 1.7 miles the pavement ends. Continue on a good gravel road (FR 24) and in 3.7 miles come to a junction. Turn right and drive 1.2 miles to the Staircase Ranger Station. Trailhead parking is on your right, across from the campground. Water and privies available.

ON THE TRAIL

The North Fork Skokomish Trail will satisfy your hiking desires whether you amble up it for 1 mile or 10. The first 3.5 miles were once a road. Decommissioned in the early 1970s, it now makes for a wide and well-graded path. The trail follows part of the O'Neil Party's 1890 exploratory route. Several months after the famous Press Expedition, which traversed the Olympic interior from north to south, Lieutenant O'Neil led a group of scientists and soldiers across the Olympics from east to west.

Immediately start with a view up the wild valley. At 0.5 mile cross Slate Creek, fed by a little lake high on Mount Lincoln. Cross a luxuriant bottomland of massive cedars and firs—a few big big-leaf maples too! Cross a small creek and large outwash area, and at 1 mile come to the Staircase Rapids Trail. The bridge has been out for years. If it ever gets replaced, this trail makes a nice loop for children and those short on time.

The main trail continues right, coming within earshot and eyesight of the tumbling North Fork. A few nice riverbank flats can be accessed along the way. At 1.25 miles pass the Slide Camp access, leading to good camp and picnic sites on the river. Proceed past remnants of a 1986 slide and emerge at the edge of a 1985 burn. Thanks to a careless camper,

1400 acres of our old-growth heritage went up in flames. Thankfully, nature forgives, and the area has been nicely recovering.

At 2 miles emerge on a small rise in the burnt-over area, which offers good views of the bowing river. Now climbing gradually, move away from the waterway through a forest of new greenery and resilient giants sporting blackened trunks. At 3.4 miles reach the junction to Flapjack Lakes at Spike Camp (elev. 1450 ft).

Big Log Camp: For Big Log Camp, head straight, soon returning to the riverbank and more impressive old growth. At 5.5 miles arrive at a junction. Big Log Camp is to your left, a great place to while away the afternoon by the river.

Flapjack Lakes: For Flapjack Lakes, head right, climbing out of the valley. After a few switchbacks, the trail turns north, skirting a slope and gradually gaining elevation. At 5.5 miles, cross Madeline Creek. Skirt another hillside and then work your way up the Donahue Creek ravine. The way, now considerably steeper, parallels the cascading creek. At 7 miles the climb eases and you reach a junction with the trail that heads to Black and White Lakes and Smith Lake.

Continue right and after 0.5 mile reach the two Flapjack Lakes (elev. 3900 ft). Ringed by subalpine forest and framed by the rugged spires of the Sawtooth Range, the lakes serve up a hearty helping of views. In this popular place, please help mitigate environmental degradation by practicing Leave No Trace principles.

EXTENDING YOUR TRIP

Why not stay awhile in the North Fork Skokomish Valley? Base-camp right on the river at the national park campground at Staircase. A week's worth of day hikes await you.

Opposite: Plenty of good river resting spots can be found along the North Fork of the Skokomish River.

UNTRAMMELED OLYMPICS

While much of the Olympic National Forest has been heavily roaded and logged, nearly 90,000 acres of the forest's 633,000 acres (15 percent of forest) have been protected as federal wilderness. Bowing to a rising public environmental consciousness, Congress passed the Wilderness Act in 1964, one of the strongest and most important pieces of environmental legislation in our nation's history.

Recognizing that parts of our natural heritage should be altered as little as possible, the Wilderness Act afforded some of our most precious wild landscapes a reprieve from exploitation, development, and harmful activities such as motorized recreation. Even bicycles are banned from federal wilderness areas. Wilderness is "an area where the earth and community of life are untrammeled by man," states the act, "where man himself is a visitor who does not remain."

Only Congress can designate an area as wilderness. While the Olympic National Forest had no shortage of qualifying lands back in 1964, not one single acre was protected. A powerful timber industry with friends in both political parties made sure all of the Olympic National Forest remained on the chopping block.

Finally, in 1984, a sweeping wilderness bill was passed and signed into law, creating five wilderness areas in the Olympic National Forest:

Wonder Mountain, 2349 acres
Colonel Bob, 11,961 acres
Mount Skokomish, 13,105 acres
The Brothers, 16,682 acres
Buckhorn, 44,258 acres

Conservationists argued (rightfully) that these new areas were too small to afford ample protection for imperiled species like the spotted owl. Old-growth logging continued in the Olympics, leaving very little of the national forest left in an untrammeled condition

But now that the Washington timber industry is a fraction of what it once was, it's time to consider adding the last remaining roadless areas of the Olympic National Forest to the wilderness system. Conservationists have identified nearly 70,000 acres suitable for wilderness inclusion. Some tracts, like the South Quinault Ridge and Moonlight Dome, contain some of the finest unprotected stands of old-growth forest left on the Olympic Peninsula. Whether these lands remain untrammeled and wild for future generations is all a matter of public opinion and political will.

Hamma Hamma River Valley

Native Americans named the Hamma Hamma, which means "big stink," in reference to the smell of thousands of rotting carcasses left behind by spawning salmon. And while your carcass may be slightly sweaty upon finishing a hike in this popular Olympic valley, your adventure won't stink at all.

A handful of backcountry lakes, all in pretty settings, are yours to explore in this watershed. Some are easy to reach and attainable by just about anyone who puts on a pair of hiking boots, while others require effort, determination, and a little bit of self-punishment.

Most of this valley succumbed to heavy logging and forest fires over the twentieth century, but the upper reaches are as wild and rugged as any place in the Olympics. Two federal wilderness areas assure that the remote corners of the Hamma Hamma and its tributaries will remain much as they did during the days of the big stinks.

Maps: Green Trails The Brothers No. 168, Custom Correct Mount Skokomish–Lake Cushman; **Contact:** Olympic National Forest, Hood Canal Ranger District, Quilcene, (360) 765-2200, *www.fs.fed.us/r6/olympic*; **Notes:** Northwest Forest Pass required at FR 2401 trailhead; **GPS:** N 47 34.757, W 123 07.239

41 Elk Lakes

RATING/DIFFICULTY	ROUND-TRIP	ELEV GAIN/HIGH POINT	SEASON
**/1	4 miles	500 feet/1300 feet	Year-round

Hike along a sunny canyon and through primordial old growth to two little lakes bursting with ducks and herons. The Elk Lakes are easily accessible off of Jefferson Creek Road (Forest Road 2401), explaining their popularity with weekend anglers. But by taking this "back way" you're guaranteed a quiet journey to the lakes and lots of big cedars and firs to admire along the way. You'll also get to hike on

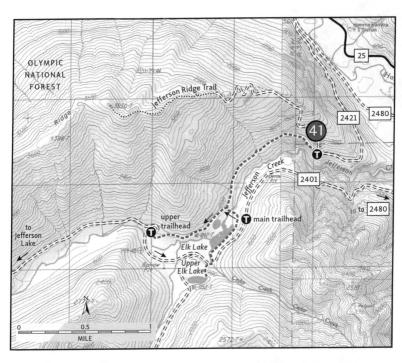

Jefferson Creek at Elk Lake outlet

a remnant of an old trail that once spanned the entire valley.

GETTING THERE

From Hoodsport travel US 101 north for 14 miles. At milepost 318 turn left (west) onto Hamma Hamma River Road (Forest Road 25). Continue for 6.5 miles to a signed junction (passing a Forest Service campground). Turn left onto FR 2480, cross the Hamma Hamma, and in 0.1 mile turn right onto an unsigned road (FR 2421). Follow this primitive but drivable road 1.6 miles to a pullout on your left and park. The trail begins where the road makes a sharp turn right. If FR 2421 is too rough, stay on FR 2480 for 3 more miles, turn right onto FR 2401, and proceed 2.5 miles to the main trailhead.

ON THE TRAIL

Find the unmarked but well-maintained trail that heads west through a tunnel of second-growth greenery. Within minutes you'll emerge on a dry hillside, realizing you are standing some several hundred feet above roaring Jefferson Creek. Born in the snowfields of Mount Ellinor and her rugged neighbors, the creek crashes through a steep and narrow canyon before draining into the Hamma Hamma.

Admire various wildflowers that paint the landscape as you traverse the sun-kissed canyon wall. In early summer, rhododendrons add to the array of colors. A few flaky-barked madronas also vie for attention.

Enter old-growth forest, immediately feeling a temperature contrast. After a series of slight ups and downs you'll arrive at a junction at 1.1 miles. Head right, through a grove of monster cedars, to Elk Lake. Depending on the season the lake may be a wet grassy swale or a pretty reflecting pool. Regardless of water level, plenty of birdlife will be present.

Continue along the shore, stopping occasionally to inventory its residents. Beyond the quiet lake, the mostly level trail follows Jefferson Creek through more impressive old growth. At 1.9 miles from your start, you'll reach the upper trailhead on FR 2401. Retrace your steps or follow the road left for 0.5 mile, picking up the trail again just after crossing Cedar Creek. Upper Elk Lake is reached on a short path that leaves from the road section.

Head left, dropping back down to the main lake. Expect more good shoreline probing and big-tree gazing. In 0.4 mile from the road, reach a junction. The right trail leads 0.1 mile to the main trailhead. Head left, crossing Jefferson Creek on a sturdy log bridge. Just beyond is a familiar junction. Turn right for the 1.1-mile return to your vehicle.

EXTENDING YOUR TRIP

The nearby Jefferson Ridge Trail may be worth a visit if you're up for good views and a challenge. It's a steep slog through a cutover slope. The road leading up to it is steep as well, requiring a high-clearance vehicle. Looking for something easier? Beyond Elk Lake on FR 2401 is little Jefferson Lake, reached by a 0.25-mile path.

42 Lena Lake

RATING/ DIFFICULTY	ROUND-TRIP	ELEV GAIN/ HIGH POINT	SEASON
★★/2	6 miles	1300 feet/ 2000 feet	Apr–Nov

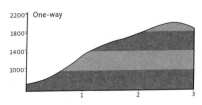

Maps: Green Trails The Brothers No. 168, Custom Correct Mount Skokomish–Lake Cushman; **Contact:** Olympic National Park, Wilderness Information Center, (360) 565-3100, *www.nps .gov/olym*; **Notes:** Northwest Forest Pass required; **GPS:** N 47 35.984, W 123 09.071

An extremely popular backcountry lake surrounded by ancient timber and ringed with designated campsites complete with fire rings—don't expect a wilderness experience on this hike. You'll encounter all walks of life on this wide, well-groomed, and easy-graded trail that delivers the masses to Lena Lake. Those willing to expend a little more energy can push farther into wilder and quieter places. But if you're intent on Lena, expect lots of company unless you visit in the waning days of autumn.

GETTING THERE

From Hoodsport travel US 101 north for 14 miles. At milepost 318 turn left (west) onto Hamma Hamma River Road (Forest Road 25). Continue for 7.5 paved miles to the trailhead. Privy available.

ON THE TRAIL

The day hike to Lena Lake is one of the most popular in the Olympics. As one of the easiest trails to a backcountry lake, and with developed campsites, it attracts throngs of backpackers,

Lena Lake from the big lunch boulder

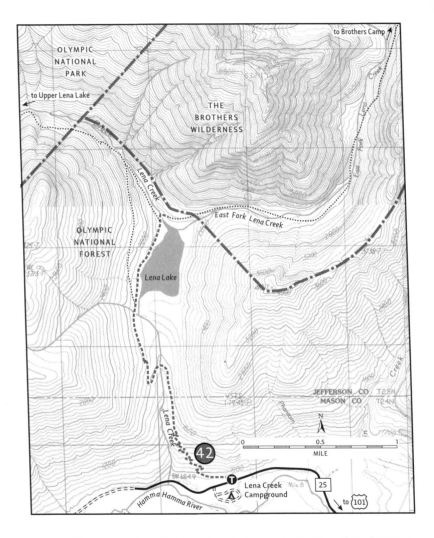

too, especially neophytes. And while this good-sized body of water nestled among old-growth firs and cedars is fairly scenic, there's just too much detracting from it.

The trail is badly scarred by ding-a-lings cutting switchbacks. The Forest Service has had to construct railings along the way to discourage these ne'er-do-wells. And litter? Expect to see beer cans and cigarette butts tossed along the way. Finally, the fire pits are nuisances, encouraging the denuding of shoreline vegetation.

So, is it worth it? Yes, but keep in mind the ambience. Perhaps find some teachable moments along the way to help correct the ways of less-than-enlightened backcountry travelers. Carry a trash bag with you. Gain bigger rewards than the view. Be a shining example to others. With that said, enjoy the hike.

The trail takes off in second-growth timber, climbing gently and carefree. Lena Creek can be heard crashing in the distance. After about a mile, come to impressive old growth. As the trail nears Lena Creek, prepare for a surprise. You soon find yourself standing on a bridge over missing waters. Lena Creek makes a subterranean passage below, leaving you standing high and dry over a mossy, rocky draw.

Now winding around and below a ledge, the trail makes a final push to the lake. At 3 miles a junction is reached. Venture right, and within a few hundred feet encounter an inviting sunny ledge that provides a resting spot and a wonderful view of Lena Lake 100 feet below.

The trail continues, descending to the shoreline and passing one overused campsite after another. A half mile beyond where Lena Creek tumbles into the lake makes for a scenic lunch spot.

EXTENDING YOUR TRIP

Strong hikers have two options beyond Lena Lake. Head 4 miles up the Lena Creek valley to Upper Lena Lake in Olympic National Park (dogs prohibited). Upper Lena, surrounded by alpine meadow and rocky peaks, is quite a contrast from the lower lake. It's a tough hike of nearly 4000 vertical feet from the trailhead.

The second option, and a good choice on a rainy day, is to follow The Brothers Trail along the subterranean East Fork Lena Creek through the Valley of the Silent Men in The Brothers Wilderness. You'll encounter lots of old growth and a few climbers on their way to and from The Brothers, one of the most recognized Olympic peaks from the Seattle

waterfront. It's a 3-mile journey to The Brothers Camp, beyond which only prepared and experienced climbers should venture.

Other kid-friendly hikes in the vicinity include the 1.3-mile Living Legacy Interpretive Trail at the Hamma Hamma Campground and the 0.25-mile Hamma Hamma Beaver Pond Trail located a few miles up FR 25.

43 Lake of the Angels

RATING/ DIFFICULTY	ROUND-TRIP	ELEV GAIN/ HIGH POINT	SEASON
★★★★/5	8 miles	3400 feet/ 4950 feet	Late July– mid-Oct

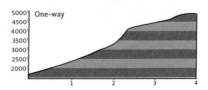

Maps: Green Trails The Brothers No. 168 and Mt Steel No. 167, Custom Correct Mount Skokomish–Lake Cushman; **Contact:** Olympic National Forest, Hood Canal Ranger District, (360) 765-2200, *www.fs.fed.us/r6/olympic*. Olympic National Park, Wilderness Information Center, (360) 565-3100, *www.nps.gov /olym*; **Notes:** Dogs prohibited at national park boundary (at 3.2 miles); **GPS:** N 47 35.016, W 123 14.083

Cupped in a high cirque on snowy, craggy Mount Skokomish, Lake of the Angels in the Valley of Heaven is one of the prettiest alpine lakes in the Olympics. But reaching this divine destination first requires a passage through hell. The trail was laid out by climbers—it's brutally steep and requires use of hands in one short section going over a headwall. It's not dangerous, but hikers skittish on ledges may want to opt for another trail. For those who work hard to get to this celestial setting, expect one of the most dramatic backdrops in the Olympics as your reward.

GETTING THERE

From Hoodsport travel US 101 north for 14 miles. At milepost 318 turn left (west) onto the Hamma Hamma River Road (Forest Road 25). Continue for 12 miles (the first 7.5 miles of which is paved) to the trailhead.

ON THE TRAIL

Named in honor of Carl Putvin, an early pioneer, trapper, and explorer, the Putvin Trail is as rugged and daring as its namesake. The first 1.4 miles, however, is relatively easygoing, traveling along tumbling Boulder Creek and crossing two narrow ravines before emerging on an old roadbed (elev. 2400 ft). From this point on, the trail climbs more than 2000 feet in 1.7 miles.

A quarter-mile beyond the old road, the trail enters the Mount Skokomish Wilderness, wasting no more time in heading to the heavens. With Whitehorse Creek crashing trailside, it's up, up and away. At 3500 feet enjoy a brief respite from climbing by traversing a brushy avalanche chute at the base of a large headwall.

As Whitehorse Creek plummets over the sheer wall in a series of breathtakingly beautiful cascades, the trail looks for a way to get over the wall. Angling to the northeast it ascends a series of ledges, some requiring handholds to thrust you upon the rim of the headwall. You made it! Now enjoy an alpine world flush in wildflower-bursting meadows and frog-fortified tarns high on a bench above the Hamma Hamma Valley. Enjoy views, too, of imposing Mount Pershing across the valley and Hood Canal and the Cascades in the distance.

At 3.2 miles enter Olympic National Park.

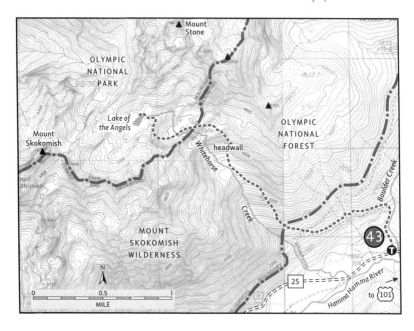

Frozen much of the year, Lake of the Angels is still a heavenly place.

Negotiate a crossing of Whitehorse Creek, and then make one final steep grunt over a snowfield and through thick greenery to the heavenly Lake of the Angels (elev. 4950 ft). Perched in an open basin scoured by ice and snow, the setting is spectacular. Cascading waters fed by perpetual snowfields stream down polished rock faces and over terraced ledges. Resident marmots pierce the mountain air with their warning whistles.

EXTENDING YOUR TRIP

The scene is quite sublime, and it's easy to while away the day in such a stunning setting. But if the hike in didn't beat you up, follow scramble paths higher to slopes on 6434-foot Mount Skokomish and 6612-foot Mount Stone. Remember, though, that while this alpine environment is indeed rugged, it is also fragile. Avoid tramping across the heather meadows.

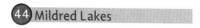

44 Mildred Lakes

RATING/ DIFFICULTY	ROUND-TRIP	ELEV GAIN/ HIGH POINT	SEASON
★★★/5	9 miles	2500 feet/ 4100 feet	July–Oct

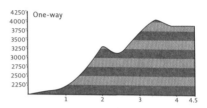

Maps: Green Trails Mt Steel No. 167, Custom Correct Mount Skokomish–Lake Cushman; **Contact:** Olympic National Forest, Hood Canal Ranger District, Quilcene, (360) 765-2200, www.fs.fed.us/r6/olympic; **Notes:** Northwest Forest Pass required; **GPS:** N 47 34.517, W 123 15.672

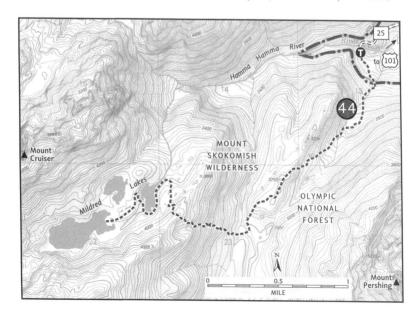

Three beautiful backcountry lakes tucked in a hidden valley surrounded by craggy summits await you at the end of this arduous hike. A boot-beaten path that leaves you beat, the Mildred Lakes Trail was forged by tenacious fishermen and masochistic hikers. An entanglement of roots, slippery rocks, and an up-and-down course that defies logic, this hike is definitely about the destination, not the journey. But boy is the fishing good, and that's what lures most visitors to these aquatic gems.

GETTING THERE

From Hoodsport travel US 101 north for 14 miles. At milepost 318 turn left (west) onto the Hamma Hamma River Road (Forest Road 25). Continue for 12 miles (the first 7.5 miles of which is paved) to the trailhead. Privy available.

ON THE TRAIL

Everything you've heard or read about this hike is true: it's a bear. Never officially constructed, this trail resembles little more than a way path, especially the second half. We're talking no-frills hiking here. Beginning at the end of the Hamma Hamma Road near a dramatic gorge and waterfall (did you peek over the bridge?), Mildred Lakes Trail no. 822 immediately enters the Mount Skokomish Wilderness.

Winding through recovering wilderness (the area was logged decades ago), the first mile or so is easy enough. But once you cross a large avalanche chute, the misery begins. Around fallen logs, over fallen logs, and straight-up rocky and rooty slopes the trail climbs a 3200-foot ridge. Mount Pershing looms in the southeast.

Through hemlock and huckleberry the trail hightails it off the ridge, dropping 250 feet into a cool forested glen graced by a rushing creek. Cross it on a questionable log (or wade), and within two minutes come to another creek crossing, this one much easier. Now the way

A clearing morning at the lower Mildred Lake

gets tricky and even tougher. Ascending a steep ridge, upward mobility is temporarily halted upon coming to a ravine. Using roots as handholds, drop 25 feet into the dank draw before resuming the taxing climb. After clambering over rock, root, and ledge—and gaining 1000 feet in elevation—the insanity ends on a 4100-foot heather-draped ridge crest. Wander along the open ledge, enjoying excellent views of Mount Cruiser and the Sawtooth Range, but no lakes.

Your punishment isn't actually over. Drop 200

feet through marshy mosquito breeding grounds before finally coming to the first lake (elev. 3800 ft). Set in deep old timber with a backdrop of rugged summits, the scene is serene and it's all yours—you deserve it. Scramble over more root and rock to the far side of the lake for good fishing and resting posts. Share the abundant trout with the resident osprey.

If not totally spent, consider checking out the other two lakes. To reach Upper Mildred, one of the largest backcountry lakes in the Olympics, cross Lower Mildred's inlet stream and follow a rough path for 0.3 mile. The third Mildred can be reached by following a rudimentary path north from the upper lake's outlet creek.

REALLY GETTING MY GOAT

Quick! Name a nonnative invasive species in the Olympic Mountains, a species that has altered the natural environment. Humans, obviously. How about Scotch broom, purple loosestrife, Robert's geranium, and mountain goats? Mountains goats? Yes, mountain goats, those furry lovable alpinists and members of the cattle family (Bovidae). They don't belong here.

The mountain goat, indigenous to the Cascades and Rockies, was never native to the Olympic Mountains, isolated as they are by the Puget Trough. In the 1920s, before the establishment of Olympic National Park, a dozen goats from Canada were introduced into the Olympics for hunting purposes. Then in 1938 the national park was established, prohibiting hunting in much of the Olympic range. The goat population exploded, reaching 1500 by the early 1980s.

Foraging on plants endemic to the Olympic Mountains (which had never adapted to munching mountain goats), the furry invasives threatened the fragile alpine ecosystems, and the Park Service called for their removal. Big problem, though: the public loved coming up to Hurricane Ridge to watch the critters (my suggestion: go to a zoo). Park plans for the goats' removal were often controversial and contentious, calling for such measures as allowing a hunt and sterilizing the animals. Ultimately a removal program began in which over four hundred of the goats were tranquilized and helicopter-evacuated.

The program, while successful in its objective (mountain goat removal), fell under budget cuts and some loud (and often misguided) criticism and backlash. Now, let me make this clear. I love mountain goats too, but in their natural environment. I love lions and rhinos as well. But in Africa, not Washington.

Current estimates for invasive goats in the Olympics stand somewhere around three hundred. Meanwhile, the native goat population in Washington's Cascades has plummeted from nine thousand in 1960 to around three thousand today. It seems to me like two problems can be solved pretty easily here. Hey you, Olympic goats! They have a whole wilderness area named after you guys in the South Cascades. How about if we help you move? I hear the views are great and the meadows simply succulent.

Duckabush River Valley

From its origins in the glaciers and tarns near O'Neil Pass deep within Olympic National Park, the Duckabush River cuts one of the great deep valleys of the Olympics' eastern front.

But unlike the Hamma Hamma, Skokomish, and Dosewallips Rivers, which have roads that run along beside them, only 6 miles of the Duckabush Valley is penetrated by road. That leaves over 20 miles of wilderness river valley accessible only to those on foot or horseback.

While deep forays into the Duckabush Valley require backpacking, day hikers can still enjoy this ripe-with-rapids tumbling blue-green river. A couple of great short hikes lead to a spectacular waterfall and a secluded chasm. Or enjoy a wilderness experience by sauntering just a few miles up the 20-mile Duckabush River Trail. And for strong hikers looking for a good challenge, the Mount Jupiter Trail provides an eagle's-eye view of nearly the entire watershed—from its snowy mountainous origin to its terminus in Hood Canal.

Arnica on Mount Jupiter

45 Mount Jupiter

RATING/ DIFFICULTY	ROUND-TRIP	ELEV GAIN/ HIGH POINT	SEASON
★★★★/5	14.4 miles	3600 feet/ 5701 feet	Mid-June– Oct

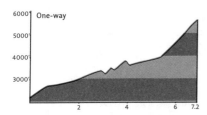

Maps: Green Trails The Brothers No. 168, Custom Correct The Brothers–Mount Anderson; **Contact:** Olympic National Forest, Hood Canal Ranger District, Quilcene, (360) 765-2200, www.fs.fed.us/r6/olympic; **Notes:** Road subject to changes and closures due to logging on adjacent private lands. Road closed for wildlife management Oct 1–May 1; **GPS:** N 47.698, W 122.993

A long, bone-dry, and at times steep trek to a former lookout site atop Mount Jupiter, where you'll be treated to sweeping views of the Olympic eastern front, Puget Sound, Mount Rainier, and other Cascade peaks of prominence. Situated between Mount Constance and The Brothers, Jupiter also gives an eagle's-eye perspective of the Duckabush and Dosewallips Valleys, two of the Olympics' great green portals into its hinterlands. Pack plenty of water, and if the summit seems a bit out of reach, there are plenty of views to be had on bumps and knolls along the way.

GETTING THERE

From Quilcene drive south on US 101 for 13.5 miles to Mount Jupiter Road (Forest Road 2610-010), located on the right exactly 2.5 miles beyond the Dosewallips State Park entrance. (If you're coming from the south, the turnoff is just shy of a mile north of Duckabush Road.) Follow Mount Jupiter Road for 3.5 miles and turn left on FR 2610-011. Continue on this steep and rough road 3 miles to the trailhead.

ON THE TRAIL

Starting in a recently logged over area, Trail No. 809 (scheduled to be rehabilitated by the Washington Trails Association in the near future) winds its way through private

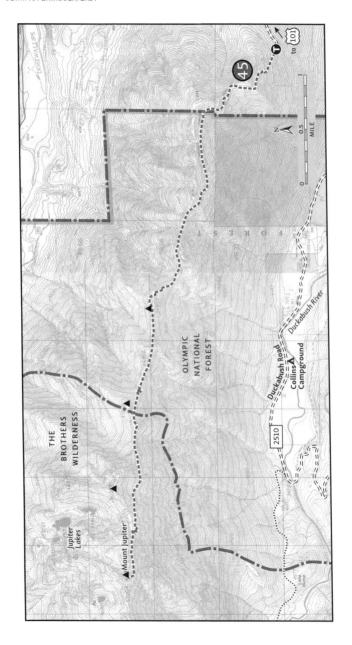

timberlands before entering the Olympic National Forest in just under 1 mile. Through thick forest wrapped in rhodies and salal, peek-a-boo glimpses hint at the visual rewards awaiting persistent hikers.

After a little bit of climbing, the trail rides the ridge crest, undulating between the Dosewallips and Duckabush watersheds (but no water along the trail) and dipping and blipping along the way. At 3.5 miles pass a small promontory providing a view down to the Duckabush Valley. After a few more mild descents and ascents (which will seem major on the return), the trail ratchets up the climbing.

With a thinning forest canopy and more open ledges, bigger and better views assure you it's worth carrying on. Upon entering The Brothers Wilderness at 5.5 miles (elev. approx. 4000 ft), the trail gets down to business, switchbacking relentlessly up a basalt ledge and dry open slopes. At 7.2 long miles, reach the 5701-foot sunny summit.

You worked too hard not to stick around. Kick back—the views are incredible in every direction, from waves of craggy Olympic peaks to the west, to waves of saltwater in the Puget Basin to the east. Seattle's skyline shimmers in the afternoon sunlight. A series of remote tarns, the Jupiter Lakes, sparkle in north-facing cirques directly below. While Mount Jupiter is nowhere near being one of the Olympics' highest summits, its positioning along the eastern front and its isolation from other peaks gives it a bit of distinction. Perhaps the Roman god who lent his name to this summit may actually even prefer the views from here than from remote and chilly Mount Olympus.

46 Ranger Hole

RATING/ DIFFICULTY	ROUND-TRIP	ELEV GAIN/ HIGH POINT	SEASON
★/1	2.1 miles	200 feet/ 320 feet	Year-round

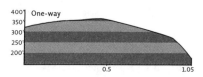

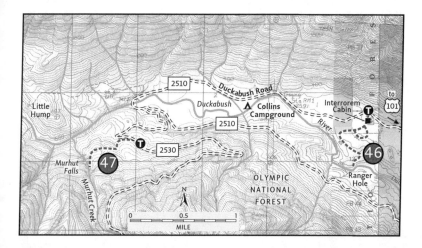

Turbulent waters in the Ranger Hole

Map: Custom Correct The Brothers–Mount Anderson; **Contact:** Olympic National Forest, Hood Canal Ranger District, Quilcene, (360) 765-2200, *www.fs.fed.us/r6/olympic*; **Notes:** Northwest Forest Pass required; **GPS:** N 47 48.897, W 122 59.661

From a historic ranger station, travel back into the early days of the Olympic National Forest. Then amble under moss-draped trees to an isolated gurgling fishing hole on the Duckabush River.

GETTING THERE

From Shelton drive north on US 101 for 37 miles. (From Quilcene drive US 101 south for 15 miles.) At milepost 310 turn left (west) onto Duckabush Road (signed "Duckabush Recreation Area"). Drive 3.6 miles to the Interrorem Cabin, located on your left. Park here for the trailhead. Water and privy available.

ON THE TRAIL

This short trail leads to, not along, the Duckabush—stoking your anticipation as it cuts its way through a dense and dank forest delivering you to a sunny ledge above the tumbling and churning river. But before you make a beeline to the river, a little historical appreciation is in order. Start by admiring the Interrorem Cabin. Built in 1907, this structure is the oldest Forest Service dwelling on the Olympic Peninsula. Interrorem served as a ranger station, a base for Works Progress Administration and Civilian Conservation Corps workers, and a fire guard station. Currently it's rented out by the Forest Service for the public to use overnight. Be sure to respect the privacy of any guests who may be staying in the cabin while you're visiting.

The first overnighter at Interrorem was Ranger Emery Finch. Mr. Finch, an avid fisherman, was responsible for building the

Ranger Hole Trail—a path to his favorite fishing spot, the ranger's fishing hole. The trail leads 0.8 mile to that revered spot. Through mature second growth (cut circa Finch's tenure) the good path climbs a little hump then makes a slow descent toward the river. In April hundreds of trilliums line the way. As the Duckabush's roar becomes more audible, the trail makes a steep drop, emerging at the famed fishing spot.

While the fishing isn't what it used to be, you'll still catch some good views of the river. The Duckabush crashes through a narrow chasm here. Frothy gurgling waters crash up against the narrow cleft. Be sure to keep small children nearby while admiring this landmark. On your return, take the 0.3-mile interpretive loop for more information on the Interrorem Cabin and the Ranger Hole.

EXTENDING YOUR TRIP
Consider spending a night in the historic Interrorem Cabin. The nearby National Forest Collins Campground, located along the Duckabush River, also makes for a nice evening stay.

47 Murhut Falls

RATING/ DIFFICULTY	ROUND-TRIP	ELEV GAIN/ HIGH POINT	SEASON
★★/1	1.6 miles	300 feet/ 1050 feet	Year-round

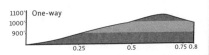

Maps: Green Trails The Brothers No. 168, Custom Correct The Brothers–Mount Anderson; **Contact:** Olympic National Forest, Hood Canal Ranger District, Quilcene, (360) 765-2200, www.fs.fed.us/r6/olympic; **GPS:** N 47 40.616, W 123 02.360

On this newer trail in the Hood Canal Ranger District, you'll marvel not only at the beauty of the 130-foot falls, but also at the trail work done to get you there.

GETTING THERE
From Shelton drive north on US 101 for 37 miles. (From Quilcene drive US 101 south for 15 miles.) At milepost 310 turn left (west) onto Duckabush Road (signed "Duckabush Recreation Area"). Drive 6.3 miles to a junction just beyond the Duckabush River Bridge (the pavement ends at 3.6 miles and you'll pass Collins Campground

Murhut Falls plunges through a narrow chasm.

at 5 miles). Bear right (signed "Murhut Falls"), following a good gravel road for 1.3 miles to the trailhead. Park on the left in a small pullout.

ON THE TRAIL

Most of this 0.8-mile trail uses an old logging road. Nothing unusual about that—just that so many roads-turned-trail are rutted and rocky, lined with scrappy alders and not always that visually appealing. Not this trail! Real care went into building the smooth tread, developing proper water drainage, and making this path aesthetically pleasing.

Of course, the real allure to hiking this trail is Murhut Falls. Surprisingly, these now-accessible falls are relatively unknown and undiscovered. Pitched back in a hidden and narrow ravine, it's understandable that these falls were missed by early traipsers.

Follow the good trail for a short climb of about 250 feet. Before making the short drop into the ravine, catch a glimpse or two through the trees of Mount Jupiter across the Duckabush Valley.

At this point, Murhut's roar is quite loud. Descend 50 or so feet into the damp, dark, cedar-lined ravine—and behold, Murhut Falls crashing before you. The upper falls drops over 100 feet while the lower one crashes about 30. Save this hike for spring when snowmelt adds to the falls' intensity and flowering rhododendrons line the trail.

Maps: Green Trails The Brothers No. 168, Custom Correct The Brothers–Mount Anderson; **Contact:** Olympic National Forest, Hood Canal Ranger District, Quilcene, (360) 765-2200, www .fs.fed.us/r6/olympic; **Notes:** Northwest Forest Pass required; **GPS:** N 47 41.125, W 123 02.403

Explore one of the quieter Olympic Peninsula river valleys. Quiet, that is, if you don't count the Duckabush River's constant belching, crashing, and churning as it tumbles over giant boulders and squeezes through narrow rocky clefts.

GETTING THERE

From Shelton drive north on US 101 for 37 miles. (From Quilcene drive US 101 south for 15 miles.) At milepost 310 turn left (west) onto Duckabush Road (signed "Duckabush Recreation Area"). Drive 6 miles (the pavement ends at 3.6 miles and you'll pass Collins Campground at 5 miles). Pass the horse unloading area and turn right onto Forest Road 2510-060 to reach the trailhead. Privy available.

ON THE TRAIL

Duckabush River Trail No. 803 travels over 20 miles into the heart of the Olympic Peninsula, but a trip of 3, 4, or 5 miles up this good path will certainly deliver plenty of scenery, solitude, and perhaps a chance to spot bear or elk.

The trail begins on an old roadbed through uniform second-growth fir. After 1 mile of gentle climbing, the trail enters The Brothers Wilderness Area. Drop 200 feet, and then follow an old logging railroad grade, cutting through a mossy wonderland on an almost perfectly flat path. A few remnant old firs greet you along the way. Finally, in about 2 miles, the river comes into view. A half mile farther delivers you to an absolutely gorgeous spot where emerald giant cedars and firs hang over rows of chugging white water. This mesmerizing spot is a good place to turn around if you don't feel inclined to

48 Duckabush River

RATING/ DIFFICULTY	ROUND-TRIP	ELEV GAIN/ HIGH POINT	SEASON
★★★/3	10.6 miles	2300 feet/ 1750 feet	Year-round

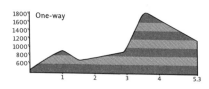

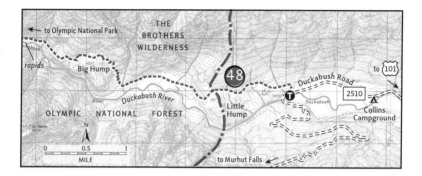

make the 1000-foot climb up the Big Hump.

For hikers hankering to hike the Hump, the trail twists and turns using tight switchbacks to ascend this valley obstacle. Thanks to a southern exposure, madrona and manzanita can be found scattered beneath the fir and hemlock. At about 3.5 miles, emerge onto a ledge with a spectacular view east down the river and out to the Cascades. To the south, impressive St. Peters Dome hovers over the Hump. More spectacular than the view, however, is the spring floral show. Come here in April for batches of fawn lilies lining the ledges. In May, the rhodies flaunt their blossoms.

Feel like continuing? Encounter one more outcropping before cresting the Hump. Then, through impressive old growth, the way descends a much cooler north slope. In about 5.3 miles and after dropping 650 feet, the trail once again reaches the river level. Here, at a well-worn camping area near a series of impressive rapids, is a great spot to call it quits. Enjoy the view. Watch for darting dippers. Be sure to rest up, for you'll need to head over the Hump one more time before going home.

EXTENDING YOUR TRIP

Feeling energetic? You can continue hiking farther into the Duckabush wilderness. After 6 miles, enter Olympic National Park (dogs prohibited). Four miles beyond is Ten Mile Camp.

Winter in the Duckabush Valley

THE BEAR ESSENTIALS

The Olympic Peninsula is one of the best places in Washington for observing bears. Usually your encounter will only involve catching a glimpse of his bear behind. But occasionally the bruin may actually want to get a look at *you*. In very rare cases (and I repeat, rare) a bear may act aggressively. If you did everything right (see "Bears" in the introduction) and Yogi appears to be agitated, heed the following advice, compliments of fellow guidebook writer and man of many bear encounters, Dan Nelson:

- Respect a bear's need for personal space. If you see a bear in the distance, make a wide detour around it, or if that's not possible (i.e., if the trail leads close to the bear) leave the area.
- If you encounter a bear at close range, remain calm. Do not run, as this may trigger a predator/prey reaction from the bear.
- Talk in a low, calm manner to the bear to help identify yourself as a human.
- Hold your arms out from your body, and if wearing a jacket hold open the front so you appear to be as big as possible.
- Don't stare directly at the bear—the bear may interpret this as a direct threat or challenge. Watch the animal without making direct eye-to-eye contact.
- Slowly move upwind of the bear if you can do so without crowding the bear. The bear's strongest sense is its sense of smell, and if it can sniff you and identify you as human, it may retreat.
- Know how to interpret bear actions. A nervous bear will often rumble in its chest, clack its teeth and "pop" its jaw. It may paw the ground and swing its head violently side to side. If the bear does this, watch it closely (without staring directly at it). Continue to speak low and calmly.
- A bear may bluff-charge—run at you but stop well before reaching you—to try to intimidate you. Resist the eager desire to run from this charge, as that would turn the bluff into a real charge and you will *not* be able to outrun the bear (black bears can run at speeds up to 35 miles per hour through log-strewn forests).
- If you surprise a bear and it does charge from close range, lie down and play dead. A surprised bear will leave you once the perceived threat is neutralized. However, if the bear wasn't attacking because it was surprised—if it charges from a long distance, or if it has had a chance to identify you and still attacks—you should fight back. A bear in this situation is behaving in a predatory manner (as opposed to the defensive attack of a surprised bear) and is looking at you as food. Kick, stab, punch at the bear. If it knows you will fight back, it may leave you and search for easier prey.
- Carry a 12-ounce (or larger) can of pepper spray bear deterrent. The spray—a high concentration of oils from hot peppers—should fire out at least 20 or 30 feet in a broad mist. Don't use the spray unless a bear is actually charging and is in range of the spray.

Dosewallips River Valley

Forming one of the great passages into the heart of the Olympic interior, the Dosewallips River cuts a deep and narrow valley through the range's eastern front and is fed by three main forks. The middle one, Silt Creek, originates high on Mount Anderson at the Eel Glacier, the largest glacier in the eastern Olympics.

Flowing within the shadows of some of the loftiest peaks on the peninsula, the Dosewallips is surrounded by supreme alpine beauty. Long a haven for backpackers, this wild valley offers day hikers a few choices. But the river is prone to raging tantrums—its periodic floods often claim tread, bridge, and access road. Since 2002 the valley has been off-limits to all but the strongest day hikers because of a devastating road washout (see "All Washed Up" in this Dosewallips River Valley section). Day hiking around the river's terminus at Hood Canal, however, remains inviting and accessible to all hikers.

49 Dosewallips State Park

RATING/ DIFFICULTY	LOOP	ELEV GAIN/ HIGH POINT	SEASON
★/1	3.5 miles	400 feet/ 420 feet	Year-round

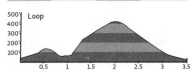

Maps: USGS Brinnon, state park map available at park; **Contact:** Dosewallips State Park, (360) 796-4415, *infocent@parks.wa.gov*, *www .parks.wa.gov*; **Notes:** Dogs must be leashed; **GPS:** N 47 41.277, W 122 54.166

Well-known for family-friendly camping and great shell fishing on Hood Canal, unbeknownst to many visitors the 425-acre Dosewallips State Park offers good hiking too. There are over 5 *miles of trail within the park, and the Steam Donkey Loop is an especially attractive hike. Offering glimpses of the Dosewallips River, passing by tumbling creeks, and traversing quiet stands of tall timber, this loop can be enjoyed by most hikers, young and old. Relics of the area's bygone logging days can be witnessed along the way too, adding a historic perspective to peaceful rambling.*

GETTING THERE

From Quilcene drive US 101 south for 12 miles to the Dosewallips State Park entrance at milepost 307, 1 mile south of Brinnon. (From Shelton drive US 101 north for 40 miles.) Day-use parking is on the east side of the highway. Cross the highway (use caution) and walk 0.2 mile on the campground access road to the trailhead, located on your left.

ON THE TRAIL

Legend has it that Dos-wail-opsh was a Twana Indian who was turned into a mountain, forming the source of the Dosewallips River. From his lofty position in the Olympic Mountain wilderness, this transformed Native American did well by creating one of the peninsula's most wild and scenic rivers. At Dosewallips State Park, you can enjoy with ease a bit of the river's grandeur and bounties.

Start your loop by crossing a little bridge that spans a cedar-studded creek. Traverse a lush bottomland of stately maples and cottonwoods. Speckled-barked alders and slowly decaying stumps of slain giants also line the way. Turn right at a junction following signs for Maple Valley (you'll be returning on the trail to the left). Cross a babbling brook before bolting up a small ridge rife with rhododendrons.

Soon the Dosewallips River comes into audible range. In winter it roars. Drop to a junction and head left (the right fork returns to the campground). Now traverse Maple

Valley, a luxuriant alluvial plain punctuated with majestic big-leaf maples. The trail then leaves the bottomland, making a short and steep climb to drier ground dominated by Doug-fir.

Skirt a clear-cut along the park boundary before making a turn south. Intersect a fire road (which can be used for a shorter loop) and continue along the park's western periphery. Gently climbing through maturing second growth, cross a series of soothing creeks spanned by delightful bridges, one with a colorful name describing an embarrassing incident.

Crest the ridge to begin a long descent on an old woods road through stands of cedar. At 2.75 miles you'll skirt a small dammed pool, whose waters were used to power the steam donkeys this trail was named for. These machines were used by loggers in the early twentieth century to power winches for yarding and loading large logs at a railway landing. The old railroad bed can be reached by continuing your hike, not far after recrossing the fire road. It's hard to imagine all this past activity. The surrounding forest has recovered nicely since the railroad's decommissioning in 1913.

Just beyond the pool lies the first junction you passed. Turn right here to return to your vehicle.

EXTENDING YOUR TRIP

Dosewallips State Park offers great camping, including platform tents, and the park makes a good base for exploring the adjacent Olympic National Park and Forest. The Dosewallips River drains into Hood Canal, creating a productive

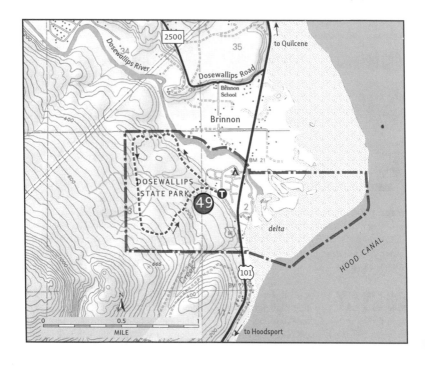

The Steam Donkey Loop includes a few nice vistas of the Dosewallips River.

delta and estuary. The short trail to the delta is rewarding. An observation deck helps you spot seals and the abundant birdlife that call this park home.

50 Lake Constance

RATING/ DIFFICULTY	ROUND-TRIP	ELEV GAIN/ HIGH POINT	SEASON
★★★/6 (beyond strenuous)	4 miles	3300 feet/ 4650 feet	Late June–Oct

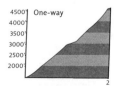

Maps: Green Trails The Brothers No. 168, Custom Correct Buckhorn Wilderness; **Contact:** Olympic National Park, Wilderness Information Center, (360) 565-3100, *www.nps .gov/olym*; **Notes:** Dogs prohibited. Requires scrambling skills; **GPS:** N 47 44.00, W 123 09.14

A secluded tarn tucked in a cleft high on Mount Constance, this little lake's setting is awesome. Gaze into turquoise waters reflecting sheer cliff faces spiraling to the heavens. But to reach this stunning scene, you too must spiral to the heavens. The trail is a climber's path, requiring stamina, sure footing, and the use of hands. The elevation gain is insane: 3300 feet in 2 miles. To those prepared and skilled, this hike can be rewarding; to others it can be dangerous.

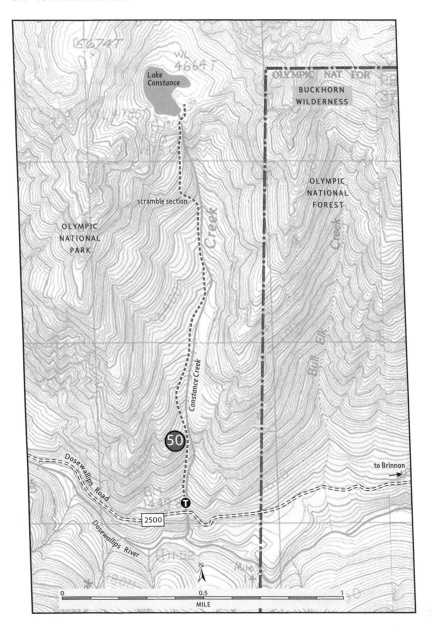

GETTING THERE

From Quilcene follow US 101 south 11 miles to Brinnon, 1 mile north of Dosewallips State Park. (From Shelton drive US 101 north for 41 miles.) Turn right (west) on Dosewallips Road and drive 13.5 miles. The trailhead is located 0.5 mile within the national park, just after crossing Constance Creek, and there is limited parking on the shoulder. **Note:** In the winter of 2002 the Dosewallips Road washed out 9.7 miles from Brinnon. The road may or may not reopen (see "All Washed Up" in this Dosewallips River Valley section). Without this road, an additional 7.6-mile hiking or bicycling round trip is required to access the trailhead.

ON THE TRAIL

When you get right down to it, there are only two bad sections to this route: the first half and the second half. From the get-go the trail wastes no time in testing the laws of gravity. However, despite its arduous approach, Lake Constance is a popular destination for bivouacking alpinists as well as for a substantial number of tenacious hikers.

Head straight up the extremely narrow draw cut by Constance Creek, clambering over root and rock. Big Doug-firs tower above, keeping the hillside anchored and preventing slumping into the Dosewallips. Under a canopy of mature evergreens and along the crashing, bashing creek, the way is cool despite its south-facing aspect. Pass by numerous picturesque cascades—many are fine destinations in themselves if you find yourself questioning continuing.

Giant boulders litter the forest floor, including a couple of mini Rocks of Gibraltar. After gaining 1600 feet in just over 0.75 mile, the trail grants you a reprieve. Enter a tranquil glen, where even Constance Creek takes a break from working hard. The relief is brief though; the trail resumes its mountainside at-

tack with even more fury. As the valley closes in, the trail has no choice but to go right up the creek bed. It's a rocky, brushy affair and, depending on water flow, wet as well.

The worst of this gauntlet is next. The route leaves the creek, ascending straight up the wall of the narrow draw. It's steep but not exposed. Using your hands and "spider strength," scale up the abrupt slope. Occasionally look back at The Brothers hovering in the distance. Finally, at the brink of exhaus-

The hike to Lake Constance is tough, but the scenery is amazing beneath towering Mount Constance.

tion, on what is probably the 2 hardest miles of your hiking career, enter the hidden basin housing Lake Constance. Its beauty should take away what little breath you have left.

Despite such a rugged setting beneath the Olympic Mountains' third-highest summit, the lakeshore is fragile. Please walk lightly and respect areas closed for restoration. Walk 0.3 mile on a trail along the eastern shore to an open area of talus and boulders for a good place to sit in the sun above the lake. Nurse those knees for the descent.

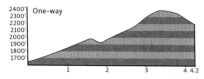

51 West Fork Dosewallips River

RATING/ DIFFICULTY	ROUND-TRIP	ELEV GAIN/ HIGH POINT	SEASON
**/2	8.4 miles	900 feet/ 2400 feet	May–Oct

Maps: Green Trails The Brothers No. 168, Custom Correct The Brothers–Mount Anderson; **Contact:** Olympic National Park, Wilderness Information Center, (360) 565-3100, www

.nps.gov/olym; **Notes:** Dogs prohibited; **GPS:** N 47 44.19, W 123 10.13

Rhododendrons, old growth, and a river that "talks" to you most of the way. The West Fork Dosewallips River spends much of its time on this hike hidden, flowing through a deep narrow canyon. But its constant commotion can continuously be heard through the surrounding primeval forest. At times it bellows, at times it serenades, but it's always a trailside companion. At Big Timber Camp the river swings by, allowing the two of you to become better acquainted.

GETTING THERE

From Quilcene follow US 101 south 11 miles to Brinnon, 1 mile north of Dosewallips State Park. (From Shelton drive US 101 north for 41 miles.) Turn right (west) on Dosewallips Road and drive 15 miles to its end at a campground and ranger station. Privy available. **Note:** In the winter of 2002 the Dosewallips Road washed out 9.7 miles from Brinnon. The road may or may not reopen (see "All Washed Up" in this Dosewallips River Valley section). Without this road, an additional 10.6-mile hiking or bicycling round trip is required to access the trailhead.

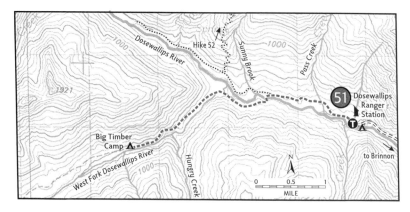

ON THE TRAIL

This is a delightful hike on gentle terrain—perfect for introducing neophytes to the splendors of the Olympic backcountry or as an early season warm-up. Amble this way in June and see Washington's state flower, the showy Pacific rhododendron, at its finest.

Start on the Dosewallips River Trail, a major

The Dosewallips Terrace Trail makes for a nice addition to the West Fork Trail.

portal to Olympic National Park's vast wilderness interior. Immediately cross Station Creek as it rushes down from Mount Constance. Reach a junction with the Dosewallips Terrace Nature Trail, which heads down to the river and loops back to the main trail in 0.75 mile—a nice variation for the return.

Through dry Douglas-fir forest garnished with salal and rhododendrons, the trail winds above the river. Elk trails periodically pierce the route. These well-worn paths attest to the abundant presence of these majestic beasts. At 1.4 miles come to a junction. Bear left (signed "Anderson Pass"), dropping 100 feet to the Dose Forks Campground and a sturdy bridge over the glacier-silt-clouded Dosewallips River.

Briefly climbing, the way contours around a steep slope, offering a view to the confluence of the Dosewallips and its West Fork. At 2.4 miles reach a bridge that spans a deep slot canyon; the West Fork thunders below. Now high above the west bank of the West Fork, the trail ascends slopes of stilted conifers and lush rhodies. After reaching a bench (elev. 2400 ft) several hundred feet above the river, the trail slowly descends to Big Timber Camp, set amid big boulders and, yes, big timber, sort of. But the real treat is that this spot sits along the river.

EXTENDING YOUR TRIP

For real big timber, continue up the trail another 2.4 miles to the pleasing Diamond Meadow Camp (elev. 2700 ft). The route wavers up and down and is primarily away from the river.

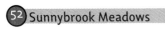

52 Sunnybrook Meadows

RATING/ DIFFICULTY	ROUND-TRIP	ELEV GAIN/ HIGH POINT	SEASON
★★★★/5	12 miles	4000 feet/ 5650 feet	Mid-June –Oct

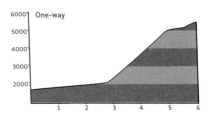

Maps: Green Trails Tyler Peak No. 136, Custom Correct Buckhorn Wilderness; **Contact:** Olympic National Park, Wilderness Information Center, (360) 565-3100, www.nps .gov/olym; **Notes:** Dogs prohibited; **GPS:** N 47 44.19, W 123 10.13

Hike to the lonely high divide between two of the Olympic Mountains' tallest sentinels, Mounts Constance and Mystery. Watch the entire deep emerald Dosewallips Valley unravel before you. And mountains! Towering crags of snow and ice: The Brothers, Anderson, Elk Lick, Diamond, and LaCrosse pack the southern horizon. At your feet, dazzling displays of wildflowers grace sun-kissed slopes. It's a stiff climb to Sunnybrook Meadows, but the expansive views and sprawling meadows are sure to brighten your day.

GETTING THERE

From Quilcene follow US 101 south 11 miles to Brinnon, 1 mile north of Dosewallips State Park. (From Shelton drive US 101 north for 41 miles.) Turn right (west) on Dosewallips Road and drive 15 miles to its end at a campground and ranger station. **Note:** In the winter of 2002 the Dosewallips Road washed out 9.7 miles from Brinnon. The road may or may not reopen (see "All Washed Up" in this Dosewallips River Valley section). Without this road, an additional 10.6-mile hiking or bicycling round trip is required to access the trailhead.

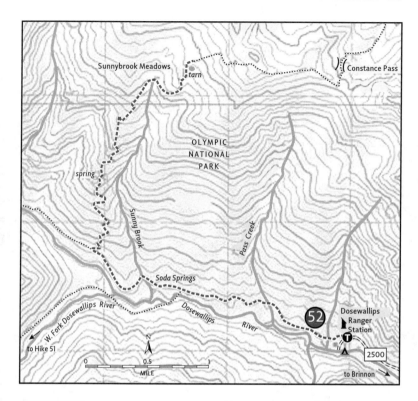

ON THE TRAIL

Consider the first 2.5 miles of this hike a warm-up. Starting on the well-groomed Dosewallips Trail, enjoy easy walking through cool forest. At 1.4 miles bear right at a junction (signed "Hayden Pass"). Pass Soda Springs and, if lucky, observe salt-craving deer relishing the seeps. Soon afterward, Sunny Brook is crossed in a deep dark glen, a far cry from its solar-enriched upper reaches.

At 2.5 miles leave behind this gentle hiking and the Dosewallips River Trail for the Constance Pass Trail (elev. 2200 ft). This lightly used but well-defined trail takes off through salal-choked forest up a steep rib via a series of short switchbacks. The forest is dry,

with many openings in the canopy providing impressive window views stoking you for the grand payoff.

Pass through a rhody jungle where, at about 3600 feet, a reliable spring bubbles from the ground (the only water until the meadows). The climb now stiffens through a hot rocky corridor. But stands of mature mountain hemlock soon bring shaded relief. After 2.5 miles of relentless climbing the trail breaks out into a wet meadow (elev. 4900 ft). In another 0.1 mile a tumbling brook lined with yellow monkey flowers invites sipping and face-splashing.

The trail rounds a high basin cut by a myriad of tributaries that collectively become Sunny Brook. As the trail darts between

subalpine forest and expanding meadows, the views grow. To the south over the verdant Dosewallips Valley, snowfields clinging to The Brothers and Elk Lick Mountain shimmer in the afternoon sun. Keep climbing—it gets better. Through thick greenery splattered

ALL WASHED UP

Most hikers will probably agree that far too many roads mar our national forests. Most hikers probably support decommissioning many of these past relics of the age of unsustainable logging, and converting a handful of them to trails. But what most hikers don't agree on is what to do after a washout or series of washouts renders an access road to a favorite trailhead impassable.

Such is the case with the Dosewallips Road. The winter of 2002 dealt the road some serious damage in the form of a 300-foot washout. Repairing the road would require serious capital (hard to come by in these days of cash-strapped forest and parks budgets) and some realigning. Furthermore, the realignment could mean losing some old-growth trees and possibly increasing sedimentation in the river.

Conservationists and some hikers, seeing a silver lining in the washout, point out that critical salmon habitat, degraded when the road was first designed, could now be properly restored. They also argue that enough old growth has been cut. They see the Dosewallips Road ripe for becoming an all-season low-country hiking trail.

Other hikers disagree. They argue that repairing the road can be done with minimal impact to the environment and that the cost is justified due to the popularity of the valley. Two well-loved car campgrounds and a beloved trailhead providing easy access to a remote corner of Olympic National Park are unnecessarily being held off-limits to thousands of recreationists, they argue. They also point out that most people lack the time and physical energy now required to access these popular park trails.

The Forest Service initially supported rebuilding the road, but has since withdrawn its original plan, calling for an environmental impact statement before proceeding further. Local communities support rebuilding the road, stating that Jefferson County has lost its only east-side access to the national park. Local businesses have been hard hit due to a serious decline in valley visitors. The Washington Trails Association and other trail and conservation organizations, on the other hand, support converting the road to trail. The washout has done more than just sever the road. It has divided the hiking community.

This guidebook author supports reopening the road. There seems to be a bigger threat than losing a few old trees (which is always unfortunate): dwindling access to public lands. If the tax-paying public can't access their lands, will they continue to vote to support them? So much of Olympic National Park is already off-limits to day hikers. Sure, you can hike or mountain bike the road to the Dosewallips trailhead—parts are pretty. But much of it is a slog, and the extra mileage is beyond many day hikers' physical limits.

When the hiking community becomes deeply polarized on issues such as rebuilding the Dosewallips Road, how will it come together to support much larger (and I might add, more important) habitat-protecting initiatives such as new wilderness legislation?

Opposite: The alpine views are amazing on the way to Sunnybrook Meadows.

with a mosaic of colors, work your way up to a tiny little tarn (elev. 5500 ft). Watering hole for resident marmots, breeding ground for resident mosquitoes, and feeding ground for resident frogs, it's a beautiful oasis tucked beneath a barren ridge.

Just to the south find a small rise offering sweeping views to the south. Look straight across to Anderson Pass flanked by glacier-harboring Mounts Anderson and LaCrosse. Look west toward Hayden Pass. Look all around and savor the solitude.

EXTENDING YOUR TRIP

Continue another mile, climbing 1000 more feet to the stark crest of the divide. Some of the finest views in the Olympics can be had from this wind-swept crest, including Mount Constance staring down at you from across the alpine tundra.

Quilcene River Valley

A rugged area of easily accessible trails, the Quilcene Valley offers a wide array of hiking options, from very easy to challenging. Blessed with mild temperatures and moderate amounts of annual precipitation, the valley makes a good choice for year-round adventures.

Much of the surrounding heavily timbered steep ridges have succumbed to the chain saw, but the forests are recovering as the timber industry has gone into a deep decline on the Olympic Peninsula. Mount Walker and Quilcene Ridge, both heavily logged in the past, now offer delightful hiking through unbroken forest.

The upper reaches of both the Big and Little Quilcene Rivers lie within the 44,000-acre Buckhorn Wilderness, the largest protected area within the Olympic National Forest. Both the Tunnel Creek and Marmot Pass Trails take hikers into the Buckhorn, to some of the wildest and prettiest forest and alpine zones in the eastern Olympics.

53 Mount Walker

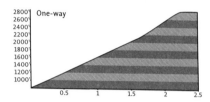

RATING/ DIFFICULTY	ROUND-TRIP	ELEV GAIN/ HIGH POINT	SEASON
★★/3	5 miles	2000 feet/ 2804 feet	Year-round

Map: USGS Mount Walker; **Contact:** Olympic National Forest, Hood Canal Ranger District, Quilcene, (360) 765-2200, *www.fs.fed.us/r6 /olympic*; **Notes:** Road gated in winter. Parking limited; **GPS:** N 47 46.536, W 122 54.824

Hovering over the glacial trough known as Hood Canal, Mount Walker is the easternmost peak in the Olympic Mountains. From its two summits you can gaze out over the Puget lowlands to the Seattle skyline and beyond. Or cast your eyes westward on the jagged Buckhorn Wilderness peaks, including mighty Mount Constance.

GETTING THERE

From Quilcene drive US 101 south for 5 miles. (From Shelton follow US 101 north for 47 miles.) Just north of milepost 300, turn left (east) onto Mount Walker Road (Forest Service 2730) and proceed 0.25 mile to the trailhead. When the road is closed, park at the gate.

ON THE TRAIL

Washington's state flower, the coast rhododendron, grows in profusion along the steep dry slopes of Mount Walker. For much of the year the rhodies merely add a layer of dark green to the forest understory. But come late spring this hardy shrub calls for attention as it begins to blossom, speckling the surrounding firs and hemlocks with rosy-purple bouquets. By June, vibrant violet bell-shaped blossoms ring throughout the emerald forest. Mount Walker is one of the best places in the state to witness this floral show.

But if you can't come for the blossoms, Mount Walker makes for a great winter hike. With the summit road closed, you won't have

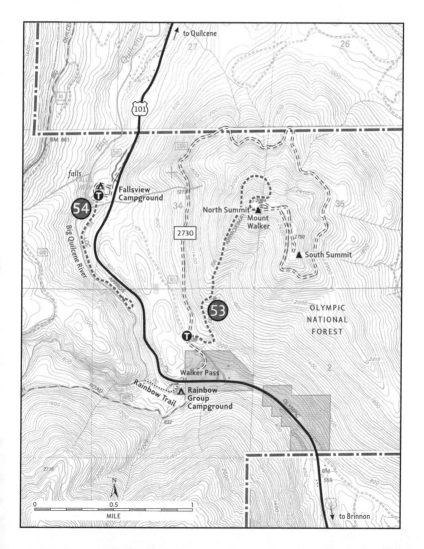

Looking south from Mount Walker out over Hood Canal and the Toanados Peninsula

to worry about sharing those far-fetched Puget Sound views with very many people. The trail is hiker only; it's short but steep, well maintained and well traveled.

Immediately begin climbing through a tunnel of rhodies under a uniform canopy of second-growth cedar and hemlock. Look up occasionally to see if you can locate any of the old wire and insulators that once serviced a fire tower on the summit. After about 1.5 miles small ledges begin to break the monotony of the forest and tease with limited views.

The grade eases slightly, and after 2 miles and 2000 feet of climbing you emerge at the North Summit viewpoint. Views are limited here. They're much better at the South Summit, reached by walking the graveled Summit Road for 0.5 mile and then following a small trail to the breathtaking panorama of Puget Sound. Stare straight down to Dabob Bay and the Toanodos Peninsula. Behind, Green and Gold Mountains rise on the Kitsap Peninsula.

Mount Rainier adds a snowy backdrop. And if you're here in June, the whole scene will be framed with fragrant purple boughs.

For a variation on the return, if the road is closed (winter) consider descending on it. It loops 4 miles around the mountain, offering more sweeping views of the surrounding territory.

54 Fallsview Canyon

RATING/ DIFFICULTY	ROUND-TRIP	ELEV GAIN/ HIGH POINT	SEASON
★/1	1.5 miles	300 feet/ 400 feet	Year-round

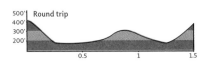

Map: USGS Mount Walker; **Contact:** Olympic National Forest, Hood Canal Ranger District, Quilcene, (360) 765-2200, *www.fs.fed.us/r6*

/olympic; **Notes:** Access is at Fallsview Campground. Northwest Forest Pass required; **GPS:** N 47 47.373, W 122 55.697

From a popular campground off of a busy highway, escape the commotion in a hidden little canyon along the Big Quilcene River, shielded from the outside world as if in deep wilderness. Enjoy the serenading river's rapids and in springtime enjoy a floral show of blossoming lilies, honeysuckle, and rhododendrons. Fallsview Canyon makes a great evening hike if camping nearby, or a nice break from the road if traveling by.

GETTING THERE

From Quilcene drive US 101 south for 4 miles to Fallsview Campground. (From Shelton follow US 101 north for 48 miles.) Enter the campground, turning left to the day-use/picnic area. When the campground is closed, park at the gated entrance.

ON THE TRAIL

Before beginning this little hike, walk the adjacent short Fallsview Loop Trail. Leading to a promontory above the canyon, gaze straight down to the roiling Big Quilcene River. Cast your attention straight across the canyon too, to an unnamed creek cascading 100 feet into it. OK, now that you've gotten the falls view promised by this hike, it's time for the canyon part of the trip.

Plunging quickly, the trail loses 200 feet of elevation in 0.1 mile. Frothing white water comes into view as the trail lands alongside the thundering Big Quilcene River on the lush canyon floor. Here within the chasm the river's roar amplifies, ricocheting off the guarding walls.

Under a canopy of maples veiled with mosses, follow the rushing river upstream. Stop periodically to be mesmerized by the frothing waters—churning, turning, chugging, and frug-

ging ("frugging"? Why not!). In 0.5 mile come to a side trail on your left; it's a loop that you'll be returning on, though the Forest Service's literature about this hike hasn't gotten around yet to showing it. Continue alongside the Big Quilcene enjoying yet more rapids; then loop around and make your return. Don't forget about the small climb awaiting you at the finish.

EXTENDING YOUR TRIP

Would you like to explore the canyon a little more? Across from the Mount Walker Road, a mile south on US 101, is the Rainbow Group Campground (park at the Mount Walker gate across the highway). From this campground you can access the 0.5-mile Rainbow Trail. Follow this quiet path to the Big Quilcene and another unnamed creek cascading into the canyon.

Blooming rhododendron in Fallsview Canyon

55 Tunnel Creek

RATING/ DIFFICULTY	ROUND-TRIP	ELEV GAIN/ HIGH POINT	SEASON
**/3	8.5 miles	2450 feet/ 5050 feet	Late June–Nov

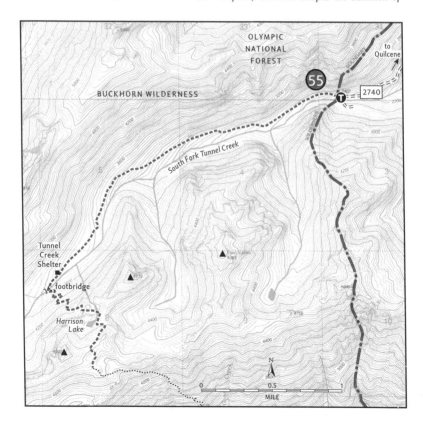

Maps: Green Trails Tyler Peak No. 136, Custom Correct Buckhorn Wilderness; **Contact:** Olympic National Forest, Hood Canal Ranger District, Quilcene, (360) 765-2200, www .fs.fed.us/r6/olympic; **Notes:** Northwest Forest Pass required; Forest Service may decommission 2 miles of access road, creating a longer hike; **GPS:** N 47 46.892, W 123 03.127

Located within the 44,000-acre Buckhorn Wilderness, Tunnel Creek is one of the quietest trails in the Olympic rain shadow. Perhaps because it doesn't lead to a major lake or peak, this trail escapes the attention of

A fallen giant on the Tunnel Creek Trail

many hikers. It didn't escape the attention of the Washington State Department of Transportation, however—they featured the creek on the cover of the 2002–2003 official state highway map.

GETTING THERE

From Quilcene drive US 101 south for 1.5 miles. (From Shelton follow US 101 north for 50.5 miles.) Turn right (west) onto Penny Creek Road. After 1.5 miles bear left onto Big Quilcene River Road (Forest Road 27). Follow it for 3 miles and turn left onto FR 2740, continuing for nearly 7 miles to trailhead.

ON THE TRAIL

For nearly 3 miles this delightful trail follows the South Fork Tunnel Creek through a tunnel of towering old-growth hemlocks and fir. The hike is perfect on a misty morning or a sweltering afternoon, as the ancient trees do a good job of regulating the temperature, keeping you either warm or cool. The old but restored shelter at 2.7 miles makes for a good turnaround point. But if you have extra energy, continue farther up the trail.

At 0.25 mile you'll cross the cascading creek on a sturdy bridge. Stop to admire its tumbling waters. Now shifting gears, the trail begins to steeply climb 1000 feet, reaching daylight at tiny Harrison Lake. Climb just a little bit more to take in an up-close-and-personal view of Mount Constance's impressive vertical east face. In 0.4 mile from the lake the trail reaches a ridge crest, maxing out at 5050 feet. You can scramble along the rocky ridge a little ways to better appreciate Constance's towering presence.

EXTENDING YOUR TRIP

Continue on the trail 3.25 miles to the Dosewallips River for a one-way trip of 7.5 miles. But ask yourself if you cherish your knees. It's a 4500-foot plunge to the valley, an insanely steep descent that only a mountain goat can love.

56 Notch Pass and Quilcene Ridge

RATING/ DIFFICULTY	ROUND-TRIP	ELEV GAIN/ HIGH POINT	SEASON
★★/4	8.6 miles	3000 feet/ 2500 feet	Apr–Nov

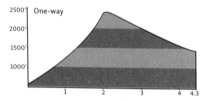

Map: USGS Mount Walker; **Contact:** Olympic National Forest, Hood Canal Ranger District, Quilcene, (360) 765-2200, www.fs.fed.us/r6 /olympic; **GPS:** N 47 49.579, W 122 56.324

Retrace an old Native American route through a tight pass high on Quilcene Ridge. In the 1930s Roosevelt's Tree Army, the Civilian Conservation Corps, constructed a good trail over the centuries-old route. By the 1960s, however, the trail was abandoned. Then in the 1990s a Forest Service wilderness crew, the Quilcene Ranger Corps, and a Washington Trails Association work party restored and reopened it. The way is steep, and there aren't many views, but a hike through Notch Pass is a walk back into time.

GETTING THERE

From Quilcene drive US 101 south for 1.5 miles. (From Shelton follow US 101 north for 50.5 miles.) Turn right (west) onto Penny Creek Road. After 1.5 miles bear left onto Big Quilcene River Road (Forest Road 27). Proceed for 1 mile, taking a right on an unmarked

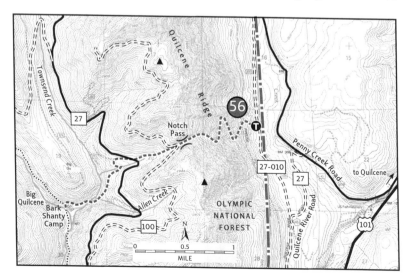

WTA "Memorial Bench"

dirt road (FR 27-010). Continue for 1.4 miles to the trailhead, where there's limited parking on the right shoulder.

ON THE TRAIL

Back in New Hampshire where I first took to the trail, we call mountain passes "notches." So you can imagine the confused faces I get when I continuously reverse a feature of this hike by calling it Pass Notch. But no matter how you arrange it, Notch Pass is a steep little climb. So before you put another notch in your hiking belt, it's going to cost you 2000 vertical feet in just over 2 miles.

The trail immediately starts off steep and there's no reprieve until the pass. Via long switchbacks work your way up a salal- and fir-covered slope. Much of Quilcene Ridge went

up in flames in the 1930s. Fire-scarred cedars and charred stumps and snags attest to the past conflagration. In 0.5 mile come to a Washington Trails Association memorial bench.

Continue climbing through thick forest, occasionally broken with limited views out to Mount Walker. After 1 mile cross a sometimes-flowing creek, the only water source this side of the ridge. After relentlessly gaining elevation, enter the dark notch of a pass at 2.1 miles. Now high on Quilcene Ridge (elev. 2500 ft), pass through a tunnel of tightly packed trees. Emerge in daylight to find yourself on an old logging road. Kind of anticlimactic, huh?

The best is yet to come, provided you don't mind losing 1000 feet of elevation and regaining it all on your return. Cross the road and descend through a scree-covered and ledgy mininotch. At 2.7 miles emerge on FR 27 (elev. 2200 ft). The trail resumes across the road, a few hundred feet to the right. Walk the road a couple of hundred feet more for some good views of Mounts Townsend and Constance.

On the trail, hike through a mixture of new and old growth adorned in rhodies, descending into the Townsend Creek valley. At 3.5 miles marvel at the Mosquito Rock erratic before crossing cascading Allen Creek. About 0.1 mile beyond, in a luxuriant ravine crowded with ancient conifers, reach Townsend Creek. Cross it, continuing on a rough-and-tumble last 0.5 mile to the Lower Big Quilcene Trail just above the Bark Shanty Bridge. Plenty of good lunch spots can be found in the vicinity along the Big Quilcene.

EXTENDING YOUR TRIP

Amble up or down the Lower Big Quilcene Trail if you'd like (Hike 57). Arrange for a one-way hike over Notch Pass and out the Big Quilcene.

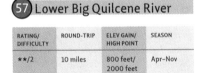

57 Lower Big Quilcene River

RATING/ DIFFICULTY	ROUND-TRIP	ELEV GAIN/ HIGH POINT	SEASON
★★/2	10 miles	800 feet/ 2000 feet	Apr–Nov

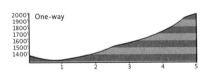

Maps: Green Trails Tyler Peak No. 136, Custom Correct Buckhorn Wilderness; **Contact:** Olympic National Forest, Hood Canal Ranger District, Quilcene, (360) 765-2200, www

.fs.fed.us/r6/olympic; **Notes:** Northwest Forest Pass required; **GPS:** N 47 47.013, W 122 57.895

The Big Quilcene Trail to Marmot Pass (Hike 58) is one of the most popular trails in the Olympic National Forest. What many hikers don't realize is that it was once twice as long. The road delivering them to the trailhead severed it in two. Good news, though, the entire trail still exists, the eastern 6 miles now known as the Lower Big Quilcene Trail. And although not in the Buckhorn Wilderness, it's still quite wild in places. Much of the route runs through a rugged canyon cloaked in primeval forest. And while past logging has eaten away at the periphery, plenty of ancient groves grace the way.

GETTING THERE

From Quilcene drive US 101 south for 1.5 miles. (From Shelton follow US 101 north for 50.5 miles.) Turn right (west) onto Penny Creek Road. After 1.5 miles bear left onto Big Quilcene River Road (Forest Road 27). Drive 3 miles, coming to a junction. Continue right on FR 27 and after 0.4 mile turn left onto FR 27-080. Follow this narrow dirt road 0.5 mile to the trailhead. Privy available.

ON THE TRAIL

Starting at an elevation of 1400 feet, the Lower Big Quilcene River Trail climbs a mere 1200 feet in its entire 6.2-mile journey. Besides making for an easy trek, the low elevation is ideal for an early-season hike. But if you wait until early summer, you'll be rewarded with blooming rhododendrons. The trail passes by old camp and shelter sites, testaments to when there was no shorter option to Marmot Pass.

A good day-hike objective is Camp Jolley, 5 miles out. But hikers not intent on putting in that many miles can cut their hike in half by

Opposite: Bark Shanty Bridge over the Big Quilcene River

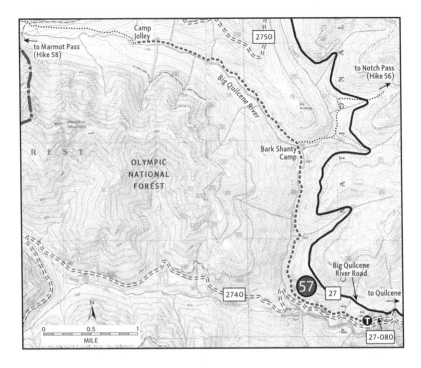

opting for Bark Shanty Camp. No matter how far you venture, the Lower Big Quilcene offers one of the best low-country valley hikes in the eastern Olympics.

The trail starts high above the river on an old roadbed. Walking is fast and easy on this well-groomed and well-graded path. After a slight descent in the first mile the trail enters a steep-walled canyon. After another mile the trail finally meets up with the roaring river, crossing it on a good bridge. Along the rushing waterway and through beautiful groves of towering old growth, reach Bark Shanty Camp at 2.6 miles, a great place to stare at the rapids or cut some z's under an ancient tree.

The trail continues, however, recrossing the river and heading farther up the valley. Just

beyond the old wooden bridge is the western terminus of the Notch Pass Trail (see Hike 56). Continue through a series of old rapidly recovering clear-cuts , and then at 4 miles enter the forest primeval once more. Keep your boots dry crossing a series of side creeks, and at 5 miles arrive at Camp Jolley. Take a break by bubbly Jolley Creek before happily making your way back to the trailhead.

EXTENDING YOUR TRIP

The trail continues for 1.2 miles, terminating on FR 2750. If you can arrange for it, hiking one way is a good option. Another option is to saunter from Bark Shanty up the first 0.5 mile of the Notch Pass Trail to a beautiful lush gorge along Townsend Creek.

58 Marmot Pass

RATING/ DIFFICULTY	ROUND-TRIP	ELEV GAIN/ HIGH POINT	SEASON
★★★★★/4	10.6 miles	3500 feet/ 6000 feet	July–Nov

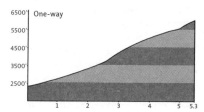

Maps: Green Trails Tyler Peak No. 136, Custom Correct Buckhorn Wilderness; **Contact:** Olympic National Forest, Hood Canal Ranger District, Quilcene, (360) 765-2200, www .fs.fed.us/r6/olympic; **Notes:** Northwest Forest Pass required; **GPS:** N 47 49.669, W 123 02.445

If for some terrible reason you are only allowed one hike in the Olympics in your lifetime, this should be it. The trail to Marmot Pass captures the very essence of what makes the Olympics so special, and so darned pretty. Towering old growth, a tumbling pristine river, resplendent alpine meadows, and horizon-spanning views that include majestic snow-clad craggy spires— they're all part of this amazing hike. And it gets even better—being in the Olympic rain shadow, Marmot Pass is often kissed with sunbeams while nearby ridges swirl with clouds.

GETTING THERE

From Quilcene drive US 101 south for 1.5 miles. (From Shelton follow US 101 north for 50.5 miles.) Turn right (west) onto Penny Creek Road. After 1.5 miles bear left onto Big Quilcene River Road (Forest Road 27). Drive 9.25 miles, turning left on FR 2750. Continue 4.75 miles to the trailhead. Privy available.

ON THE TRAIL

While Upper Big Quilcene River Trail No. 833.1 gains 3500 feet in its 5.3-mile journey to 6000-foot Marmot Pass, the climb is quite agreeable. The grade is mostly moderate, the tread smooth, and the scenery is spectacular throughout the hike, enabling you to easily overlook any discomfort along the way.

Immediately enter the Buckhorn Wilderness and a magnificent stretch of primeval forest. For 2.5 miles the trail winds its way through hulking hemlocks and colossal cedars and firs hundreds of years old, all while the Big Quilcene River keeps you company. Mossy overhanging boulders and numerous gurgling

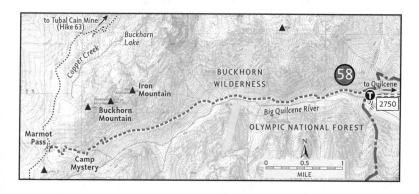

the-sun slopes. Rocky knobs sit on the steep ridge above like gargoyles on a medieval cathedral, while slender stalks of fireweed dance in the gentle breezes whisking down from the pass. At 4.5 miles enter groves of yellow cedar and subalpine fir. Inviting Camp Mystery, with its dual springs, makes a good spot for refueling.

Next break out into a meadowed corridor painted in red, white, and purple flowers and pockmarked with marmot burrows. Skirt beneath a steep rock face, emerging at a small hanging valley just below the open pass. One final push and—voilá!—you're standing on one of the supreme viewing spots in the Olympics. Gaze east to Hood Canal, Puget Sound, and the Cascades. The Dungeness Valley spreads out below to the west, flanked by a wall of some of the highest summits in the Olympics—Mystery, Deception, and the Needles.

The high slopes are dry and open here, quite different from the rest of the Olympics—looking more like the Cascades' eastern slopes. The rainshadow environment allows lodgepole and whitebark pines to grow here. Clark's nutcracker, a jaylike bird, roosts in the subalpine forests, feeding on pine nuts. Listen for their raucous call, a rare sound in the Olympics.

EXTENDING YOUR TRIP

There are many exploring options from this lofty outpost. A rough way path leads 1 mile and climbs 900 feet to the 6998-foot summit of Buckhorn Mountain, from which views are stupendous, including great perspectives of Mount Constance. One-way trips with car shuttles include heading down to Boulder Camp and out the Dungeness Valley (Hike 64) or across the barren alpine tundra of Buckhorn's north ridge and out the Tubal Cain Mine Trail (Hike 63).

Chris and Tikka head down from Marmot Pass.

side creeks greet you along the way.

At Shelter Rock Camp (elev. 3600 ft) the trail parts ways with the Big Quilcene, making a short and steep ascent away from the valley floor. About a mile beyond, the forest yields to open avalanche chutes and scree slopes fanning down from Buckhorn and Iron Mountains. Enjoy breathtaking views of the rugged surroundings from these hot-in-

Opposite: Alpine tundra and flower gardens on Mount Townsend's summit

The Rain Shadow

You'll find not only some of the Olympic Peninsula's best weather in its extreme northeast, but also some of its best hikes. Thanks to rings of mountains to the west trapping clouds and marine air, this region enjoys a rainshadow effect. The Buckhorn Wilderness and adjacent areas of Olympic National Park often see sunny skies while valleys and peaks to the west are soaked in moisture.

But it's not just milder weather that makes this region shine. There's an abundance of good trails leading to ancient forests, alpine lakes, and lofty peaks exploding with meadows and views. And with trailheads generally starting at higher elevations than in other regions of the Olympics, the pain required to get to such spectacular places is eased a little.

You'll also hike through the best countryside in Washington for observing the state flower, the Pacific rhododendron. Flower buffs and other botanically inclined hikers will also appreciate the wide array of wildflowers (including all of the Olympics' endemics) and forests reminiscent of the east slopes of the Cascades.

59 Mount Townsend

RATING/ DIFFICULTY	ROUND-TRIP	ELEV GAIN/ HIGH POINT	SEASON
★★★★★/4	8.2 miles	2900 feet/ 6280 feet	June–Nov

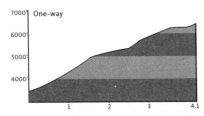

Maps: Green Trails Tyler Peak No. 136, Custom Correct Buckhorn Wilderness; **Contact:** Olympic National Forest, Hood Canal Ranger District, Quilcene, (360) 765-2200, www .fs.fed.us/r6/olympic; **Notes:** Northwest Forest Pass required; **GPS:** N 47 51.385, W 123 02.153

One of the most hiked summits in the Olympics, and it's easy to see why this peak is so popular. Easy access, a long hiking season, and unparalleled views of Puget Sound and the eastern half of the Olympics give Mount Townsend quite an edge. Of the three trails leading to its summit, Trail No. 839 is the route most taken. It's not the shortest way, but it offers incredible biological diversity and one of the best built and maintained trails in the Buckhorn Wilderness.

GETTING THERE

From Quilcene drive US 101 south for 1.5 miles. (From Shelton follow US 101 north for 50.5 miles.) Turn right (west) onto Penny Creek Road. After 1.5 miles bear left onto Big Quilcene River Road (Forest Road 27). Drive 13.5 miles, ignoring the sign at 12.5 miles for the Mount Townsend Trail (that's the lower trail to Sink Lake). Turn left onto FR 27-190 and in 0.75 mile come to the trailhead.

ON THE TRAIL

Most hikers intent on reaching the 6280-foot open summit opt to begin their journey from the upper trailhead. This saves 1.2 miles and 600 feet of elevation gain, but at the expense of missing a beautiful old-growth forest and Sink Lake, a small body of water that causes tumbling Townsend Creek to disappear.

If you opt to skip the glories of the old growth, start from the upper trailhead (elev. 3400 ft). the well-worn path climbs steadily through a stately grove of fir and hemlock adorned with Pacific rhododendrons. In 0.5 mile the trail enters the Buckhorn Wilderness. Soon afterward the terrain opens up and the views begin. Through flower

Stunning alpine gardens and views into the Buckhorn Wilderness are visible from Townsend's open summit ridge.

gardens and by cascading creeks the trail pushes toward the clouds. Over two dozen switchbacks will keep you heading in the right direction: that's up!

At 2.5 miles come to a small pine and fir grove nestled on a knoll, where tiny (and in season, buggy) Windy Lake is hidden just off the trail. Continue onward, passing the Silver Lakes Trail (Hike 60) junction at 3 miles (elev. 5500 ft) and leaving the trees behind. As you ascend higher on Townsend's slopes, alpine tundra rolls out.

After another 0.5 mile of climbing from the Silver Lakes turnoff, reach the expansive and open summit plateau. Ground-hugging juniper and brilliant clumps of cinquefoil and phlox carpet this high country. Amble 0.5 mile farther, yielding to eagles and angels. A short side trail leads right to the mountain's highest point.

Puget Sound with its labyrinth of islands, bays, and channels sprawls below. Watch ferries ply azure waters. Gaze out at the Seattle skyline to glass and metal twinkling in the afternoon sunlight. A fortress of Cascade peaks, punctuated by the snowy volcanoes, occupies the eastern horizon. To the north lie Dungeness Spit, Discovery Bay, the San Juan Islands, and Vancouver Island. To the west, nothing but pure Olympic wilderness—jagged peaks and deep green valleys. It should be apparent why this peak remains so well-loved.

EXTENDING YOUR TRIP

The main trail continues along the broad open mountaintop to Townsend's northern, slightly lower summit. If a car shuttle can be

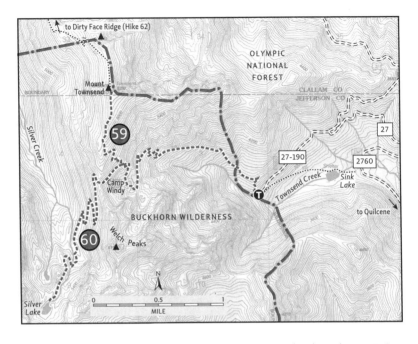

arranged, consider hiking down the Little Quilcene River Trail either via Little River Summit (3.5 miles) or Dirty Face Ridge (3.7 miles; see Hike 62).

60 Silver Lakes

RATING/ DIFFICULTY	ROUND-TRIP	ELEV GAIN/ HIGH POINT	SEASON
★★★★/4	11 miles	3400 feet/ 5700 feet	June–Nov

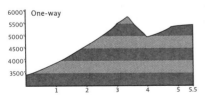

Maps: Green Trails Tyler Peak No. 136, Custom Correct Buckhorn Wilderness; **Contact:** Olympic National Forest, Hood Canal Ranger District, Quilcene, (360) 765-2200, www .fs.fed.us/r6/olympic; **Notes:** Northwest Forest Pass required; **GPS:** N 47 51.385, W 123 02.153

Mount Townsend certainly has its loyal legion of fans. Lofty, prominent, and easily accessible, this northeastern Olympics mountain rarely receives a reprieve from clunking boots and clanking poles. But the scene is quite different at Silver Lakes, nestled in a remote cirque just south of the mountain. These two little alpine lakes receive a fraction of Townsend's traffic. And the scenery? It's as sublime and inspiring as that found at the nearby busy summit.

GETTING THERE

From Quilcene drive US 101 south for 1.5 miles. (From Shelton follow US 101 north for 50.5 miles.) Turn right (west) onto Penny Creek Road. After 1.5 miles bear left onto Big Quilcene River Road (Forest Road 27). Drive 13.5 miles, ignoring the sign at 12.5 miles for the Mount Townsend Trail (that's the lower trail to Sink Lake). Turn left onto FR 27-190 and in 0.75 mile come to the trailhead.

ON THE TRAIL

Getting to these quiet little lakes requires hiking the first 3 miles of the Mount Townsend Trail (Hike 59). With over 2600 feet of elevation to gain, it's a stiff little climb to the Silver Lakes Trail junction. Most hikers who have made it this far, having expended a considerable amount of energy, remain determined to see the top of Mount Townsend. That the lakes lie another 2.5 miles away and 600 feet below helps deter them from changing their plans.

But if solitude beckons, follow the Silver Lakes Trail through open forest, climbing 200 feet to a small notch on Townsend's southern shoulder. Before descending, look back east for a great view of Windy and Sink Lakes directly below. To the west, enjoy a sweeping view of the Silver Creek valley. The lakes, however, are not visible. They're hidden behind a small wooded knob.

Across a steep and barren slope (except in early summer when wallflowers paint it yellow), descend into the valley following a couple of long switchbacks. After 2 miles (5 miles from the trailhead), reach Silver Creek. Its sparkling and cascading waters invite you to follow it to its source. So begin climbing again, and through openings in the forest look back for a few good glimpses of Mount Townsend.

A half mile from the creek crossing, the terrain opens up as you enter the Silver Lakes basin. The upper lake lies right in front of you. Its

Silver Lake on a misty afternoon

waters shimmer in the afternoon sun, rippling from the soft breezes. Scout the shores for a warm rock to rest on. Enjoy the lake's tranquility, broken only by trout jumping in pursuit of a morsel.

EXTENDING YOUR TRIP

It's easy to while away the time at this delightful spot, deep within the Buckhorn Wilderness. But if the 5.5 miles in didn't spend you, plenty of exploring options await. The high ridge to the south can be reached by following a primitive trail. The lower lake is reached by another primitive trail found on the small ridge near the upper lake's outlet.

61 Mount Zion

RATING/ DIFFICULTY	ROUND-TRIP	ELEV GAIN/ HIGH POINT	SEASON
★★★/3	4.6 miles	1300 feet/ 4274 feet	May–Nov

Maps: Green Trails Tyler Peak No. 136, Custom Correct Buckhorn Wilderness; **Contact:** Olympic National Forest, Hood Canal Ranger District, Quilcene, (360) 765-2200, www .fs.fed.us/r6/olympic; **Notes:** Northwest Forest Pass required; **GPS:** N 47 55.368, W 123 01.564

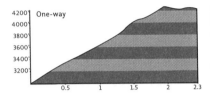

Hike a short and to-the-point trail to an isolated peak on the fringe of the Olympics. Enjoy views out over glistening Puget Sound, with its ferries and Seattle skyline. But there's more. From Zion's summit follow a ridgeline trail to a series of ledges, a promised land of sweeping views of lofty Mount Townsend and the towering and jagged Gray Wolf Ridge. Make a pilgrimage in June and be rewarded with a kingdom of brilliantly blooming rhododendrons.

GETTING THERE

From Quilcene drive US 101 north for 1.5 miles, turning left (west) onto Lords Lake Loop Road. In 3.5 miles turn left at a junction at Lords Lake (a public water supply). Continue for 0.7 mile, entering the Olympic National Forest. Bear right on gravel Forest Road 28 and climb 4.75 miles to an unmarked junction at Bon Jon Pass (pass the junction with FR 27). Bear right on FR 2810 and in 2.3 miles come to the Mount Zion trailhead. Privy available.

ON THE TRAIL

On a well-built and well-maintained trail, begin in a mature forest of fir and hemlock. The way is pretty straightforward. The trail angles up the mountain, steeply at times, but never at an insane angle. The way is dry, lined with salal and under a tunnel of rhododendrons. Mount Zion ranks as one of the supreme rhody hikes in the Olympics.

Big blackened snags stand as reminders to the large-scale fires that swept over this corner of the Olympic National Forest many decades ago. After marching up a ridge, the trail

Craig enjoys the view from Zion's ledges.

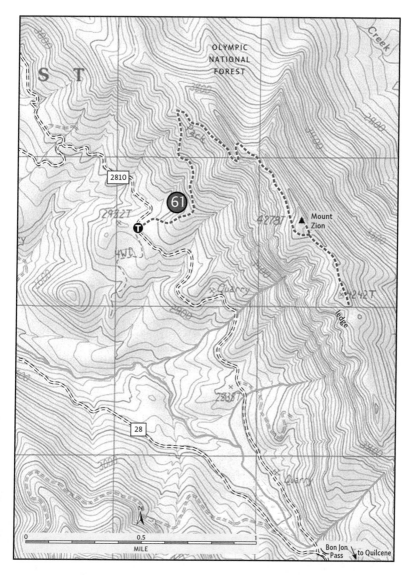

sweeps west and then makes a wide sweep back to the east, steadily gaining elevation. Negotiate a short series of switchbacks be-

fore skirting a series of basalt ledges.

At 1.8 miles, arrive on the rocky summit. A fire tower perched here until 1975. The surrounding forest has slowly been encroaching upon the view, blocking much of what was once a supreme vista. Mount Baker, the San Juan Islands, Puget Sound and the Quimper Peninsula can still be seen over the tops of tenacious conifers. But for the premiere showing—the promised views—carry on a little farther.

Locate a trail heading southeast from the summit and follow it. Pass a spring that once provided water for the fire-lookout personnel. Continue on good tread and after 0.5 mile of fairly level hiking emerge on a huge outcropping, your portal to panoramic pleasures. Using caution, climb a little onto the open ledge, and then enjoy the view. Mount Townsend dominates the southern horizon, while the rocky high wall of the Gray Wolf Ridge commands the western sky. It's a heavenly view, and what you'd expect from a mountain named Zion.

62 Dirty Face Ridge

RATING/ DIFFICULTY	ROUND-TRIP	ELEV GAIN/ HIGH POINT	SEASON
★★★★/4	7.5 miles	3000 feet/ 6280 feet	June–Nov

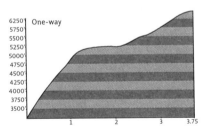

Maps: Green Trails Tyler Peak No. 136, Custom Correct Buckhorn Wilderness; **Contact:** Olympic National Forest, Hood Canal Ranger District, Quilcene, (360) 765-2200, www .fs.fed.us/r6/olympic; **GPS:** N 47 53.139, W 123 05.377

Short and steep but loaded with views long and sweet from one of the Olympics' most popular peaks. You'll have plenty of solitude along Dirty Face Ridge— most hikers shun it for the two other approaches to Mount Townsend. Ledges galore offering views into the heart of the Buckhorn Wilderness may even distract you enough that you leave Townsend's summit to the masses.

GETTING THERE

From the west end of the Hood Canal Bridge, drive State Route 104 to its end and veer north onto US 101. Proceed 16 miles and turn left onto Louella Road (just before reaching the Sequim Bay State Park entrance). In 1 mile turn left on Palo Alto Road, continuing for 6 miles. Bear right at a junction onto Forest Road 2880. The road descends and crosses the Dungeness River, coming to another junction in 1.7 miles, where you turn left on FR 2870. In 2.6 miles bear right at a junction to continue on FR 2870 (formerly called FR 2860). Drive 10 miles to the Tubal Cain Trail parking area. The trail begins 0.15 mile farther along FR 2870, from the left side of the road.

ON THE TRAIL

This trail gives you no time to warm up, climbing steeply from the get-go. Through a tunnel of rhododendrons remarkably reminiscent of the southern Appalachians, you may find yourself humming "Smoky Mountain Sunrise" on the ascent. But after crossing a damp little draw (last water) and angling up to the ridge to the first viewpoint, it's pure Pacific Northwest mountain scenery.

A succession of viewpoints follow as the trail rapidly gains elevation as it heads for the ridge crest. Enjoy precious glimpses below of the Silver and Copper Creek valleys. Buckhorn Mountain with its twin-peaked horns guards the head of the emerald valleys, and the Gray Wolf Ridge with its pack of peaks paces the western horizon.

The grade finally eases. Alternating between lodgepole pine groves and crumbling basalt ledges, the trail heads southeast toward Mount Townsend, lupines lining the way. Look for Piper's bellflower, a rare Olympic endemic clinging to several of the rocky outcrops. Junipers creep along the outcrops too; common on the east slopes of the Cascades, this member of the cypress family thrives in this dry corner of the Olympic Peninsula.

At 2 miles a large ledge (elev. 5200 ft) invites lounging and is a good place to turn around if your intent was a short adventure. Otherwise continue 0.25 mile in cool silver fir forest, coming to a junction. Say goodbye to solitude. Turn right, following fellow hikers on a wide path 1.3 miles to Mount Townsend's windswept and tundra-cloaked summit. Be sure to touch upon the north peak (via a short spur trail). This former fire lookout site provides a stunning view of Puget Sound's plethora of islands, peninsulas, bays, and coves.

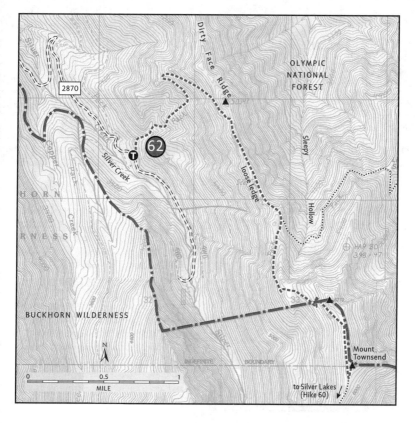

Good views of Buckhorn and Iron Mountains from Dirty Face Ridge

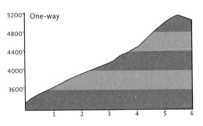

63 Tubal Cain Mine and Buckhorn Lake

RATING/ DIFFICULTY	ROUND-TRIP	ELEV GAIN/ HIGH POINT	SEASON
★★★/3	12 miles	2000 feet/ 5200 feet	June–Oct

Maps: Green Trails Tyler Peak No. 136, Custom Correct Buckhorn Wilderness; **Contact:** Olympic National Forest, Hood Canal Ranger District, Quilcene, (360) 765-2200, *www.fs.fed.us/r6/olympic*; **GPS:** N 47 53.173, W 123 05.497

Retrace a packer's trail to a mine dating from the 1890s. Peer into dark forbidding shafts and saunter past relics left over from boomtown settlements that went bust. But the real find is the miles of wildflower-studded meadows beyond the mine. Rhododendrons too—traverse a jungle of them on the trail's lower reaches.

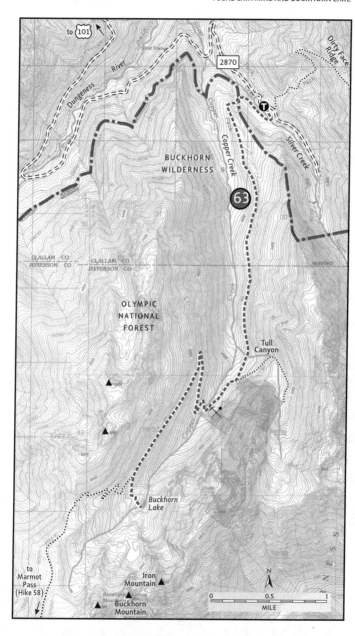

to 101

Dungeness River

2870

Dirty Face Ridge

T

BUCKHORN WILDERNESS

Copper Creek

Silver Creek

63

CLALLAM CO
JEFFERSON CO

CLALLAM CO
JEFFERSON CO

OLYMPIC
NATIONAL
FOREST

Tull Canyon

to Marmot Pass (Hike 58)

Buckhorn Lake

Iron Mountain

Buckhorn Mountain

N

0   0.5   1
MILE

GETTING THERE

From the west end of the Hood Canal Bridge, drive State Route 104 to its end and veer north onto US 101. Proceed 16 miles and turn left onto Louella Road (just before reaching the Sequim Bay State Park entrance). In 1 mile turn left on Palo Alto Road, continuing for 6 miles. Bear right at a junction onto Forest Road 2880. The road descends and crosses the Dungeness River, coming to another junction in 1.7 miles, where you turn left on FR 2870. In 2.6 miles bear right at a junction to continue on FR 2870 (formerly called FR 2860). Continue 10 miles to the trailhead.

ON THE TRAIL

Start on a well-groomed track, passing the Silver Creek Shelter (which once provided refuge to wayfarers before FR 2870 shortened the journey) and crossing Silver Creek on a log bridge shortly afterward. After 0.5 mile enter the Buckhorn Wilderness; then turn southward, entering the Copper Creek valley. Skirting slopes high above the creek, the trail travels through a tunnel of rhododendrons and thick stands of second-growth conifers. Occasional breaks in the forest canopy offer previews of the high country lying ahead.

After 3 miles of easy but monotonous walking (except in early summer when the rhodies' purple reign dazzles and delights), come to a junction. The trail left climbs steeply 0.7 mile into Tull Canyon. Among the surprises that await you if you explore this rugged rift are the ruins of an old mining town and the remains of a crashed World War II–era military plane. Immediately up the trail and visible from the junction is a mine shaft. It's extremely dangerous to enter, so best to just imagine what deep dark secrets it possesses (or once possessed).

A half mile beyond, in dank, scrappy forest, is the site of yet another old mining town, now a popular backcountry camping area. Rusted relics lie scattered about—some have been revived, serving the needs of imaginative campers. The Tubal Cain Mine lies just to the left. It is a private inholding within the wilderness and is still active (somewhat); respect all postings and leave any equipment alone.

Besides, you have little time to snoop around with miles of meadows waiting for your arrival. Leap across Copper Creek and begin climbing the valley's west wall via a series of short (followed by one long) switch-

Great views of Buckhorn Mountain along the Tubal Cain Mine Trail

backs. Now, thanks to a series of past forest fires and avalanches, enjoy 2 miles of hip-hopping through the harebells. Other blossoms too—a full spectrum of colors streaks the hillside.

Twin-peaked Buckhorn Mountain with Iron Mountain by its side hovers over the far end of the valley. At 5.5 miles reach a junction. The trail left drops 150 feet, heading 0.5 mile to little Buckhorn Lake tucked in thick timber. The lake isn't much, but Copper Creek is pretty enough to make the trip worth it.

EXTENDING YOUR TRIP
The Tubal Cain Trail continues beyond Buckhorn Lake for 3.2 miles to Marmot Pass. Traversing more meadows, rock gardens, and alpine tundra, it climbs a high shoulder of Buckhorn Mountain. Views are far-reaching and amazing, especially of the Dungeness Valley.

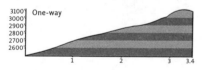

64 Upper Dungeness River

RATING/ DIFFICULTY	ROUND-TRIP	ELEV GAIN/ HIGH POINT	SEASON
★★★/2	6.8 miles	600 feet/ 3100 feet	May–Nov

Maps: Green Trails Tyler Peak No. 136, Custom Correct Buckhorn Wilderness; **Contact:** Olympic National Forest, Hood Canal Ranger District, Quilcene, (360) 765-2200, www.fs.fed.us/r6/olympic; **Notes:** Northwest Forest Pass required; **GPS:** N 47 52.676, W 123 08.217

A delightful hike through ancient timber along the crystal-clear Dungeness River—save this one for a hot or rainy day. Quite possibly the easiest 3.4 miles of wilderness trail in the Olympics, the

Upper Dungeness is ideal for introducing neophytes and youngsters to the backcountry. Handy dandy Camp Handy with its restored shelter provides cover on overcast days, allowing you to enjoy your lunch while droplets run down the cedar shingles.

GETTING THERE
From the west end of the Hood Canal Bridge, drive State Route 104 to its end and veer north onto US 101. Proceed 16 miles and turn left onto Louella Road (just before reaching the Sequim Bay State Park entrance). In 1 mile turn left on Palo Alto Road, continuing for 6 miles. Bear right at a junction onto Forest Road 2880. The road descends and crosses the Dungeness River, coming to another junction in 1.7 miles, where you turn left on FR 2870. In 2.6 miles bear right at a junction to continue on FR 2870 (formerly called FR 2860). Continue 6.5 miles to the large parking area just past the Dungeness River Bridge. Privy available.

ON THE TRAIL
The Upper Dungeness River Trail begins right beside the tumbling and crashing river, never letting it out of eyesight or earshot for the entire journey to Camp Handy. Through a magnificent stand of sentinel Douglas-firs—200 feet tall and several hundred years old—the trail is well sheltered. Embrace its air-conditioning effects on warm sunny days and embrace its protecting qualities on overcast ones.

A couple of times the trail comes close enough to the river to allow mesmerizing glances into its frothy cascading waters. After 1 meditative mile arrive at a junction. The trail right travels 6.5 miles along Royal Creek to Royal Lake (Hike 65). Turn left instead, crossing Royal Creek on a sturdy log bridge, and immediately enter the Buckhorn Wilderness.

Through cool glens of Doug-fir and hemlock, across numerous side creeks, and along seeps spawning salmonberries, the trail parallels the majestic river. Raucous rapids and placid pools entice you to slow down and marvel at the beauty. In 2.6 miles the trail crosses the river. In 2006 the log bridge sustained serious damage from winter runoff. Hopefully the Forest Service has replaced it. If not, cross with caution.

Once across, the trail pulls away from the river, the chattering of resident birds no longer drowned out by the thunderous waterway. At 3.2 miles reach an unmarked junction. Head right to a lovely meadow on the Dungeness, home to Camp Handy. If the weather is agreeable, head to the wide gravel bar for views and

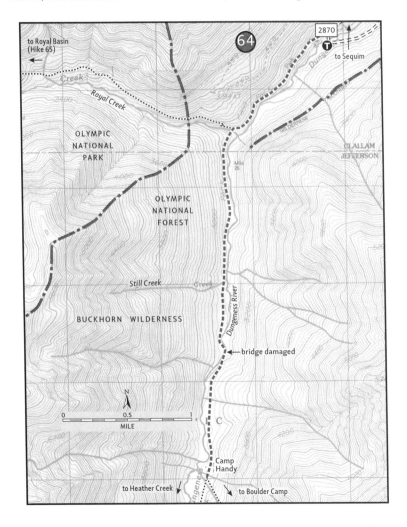

The Camp Handy Shelter is inviting on an overcast day.

feet-soaking. If it's raining, take to the shelter. Be prepared, however, to fend off snack-sneaking chipmunks.

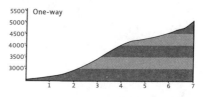

EXTENDING YOUR TRIP

The Upper Dungeness Trail leaves the river valley and continues for over 3 miles, climbing 1800 feet to Boulder Camp in the shadows of Mount Constance. It's an incredibly scenic journey. The Heather Creek Trail begins 0.3 mile from Camp Handy and travels for over 3 miles along a lonely and wild Dungeness and then its tributary, Heather Creek. The trail isn't regularly maintained, and it requires a river crossing 1 mile from the turnoff.

Maps: Green Trails Tyler Peak No. 136, Custom Correct Buckhorn Wilderness; **Contact:** Olympic National Park, Wilderness Information Center, (360) 565-3100, *www.nps.gov/olym*; **Notes:** Northwest Forest Pass required. Dogs prohibited at national park boundary (at 1.3 miles); **GPS:** N 47 52.676, W 123 08.217

65 Royal Basin

RATING/ DIFFICULTY	ROUND-TRIP	ELEV GAIN/ HIGH POINT	SEASON
★★★★★/4	14 miles	2650 feet/ 5100 feet	Late June–mid-Oct

Hike to a beautiful alpine lake flanked by some of the highest, craggiest snow- and ice-covered peaks in the Olympic Mountains. The trip is long, but much of the way is gentle, through primeval forests and along a crashing, milky creek fed by glaciers high above. Though Royal Lake is popular with backpackers, by day hiking you'll leave less of an impact on both the fragile alpine environment and your body (with less pack weight!). If you're not up for the whole trek, any distance along this delightful trail will satisfy your wilderness urges.

GETTING THERE

From the west end of the Hood Canal Bridge, drive State Route 104 to its end and veer north onto US 101. Proceed 16 miles and turn left onto Louella Road (just before reaching the Sequim Bay State Park entrance). In 1 mile turn left on Palo Alto Road, continuing for 6 miles. Bear right at a junction onto Forest Road 2880.

The road descends and crosses the Dungeness River, coming to another junction in 1.7 miles, where you turn left on FR 2870. In 2.6 miles bear right at a junction to continue on FR 2870 (formerly called FR 2860). Continue 6.5 miles to the large parking area just past the Dungeness River Bridge. Privy available.

ON THE TRAIL

From a large trailhead parking area resembling a hiker's Grand Central Station, start on the Dungeness River Trail on a gentle grade through ancient groves of towering fir. In 1 mile (elev. 2700 ft) head right at a junction signed "Royal Basin." (The trail left leads up

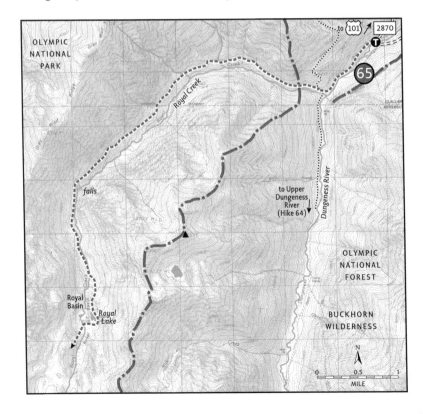

the Dungeness, see Hike 64). In another 0.25 mile pass the trail to Baldy taking off on your right (Hike 66). Shortly afterward enter Olympic National Park.

Through thick forest carpeted in moss and landscaped with rhododendrons, the trail heads gracefully up the Royal Creek valley. Not always within sight, but always close by, the creek crashes and churns through the deep narrow vale. You'll need to hop over several tributaries in the first couple of miles, but none pose any problems.

In about 2.7 miles cross the first of several brushy avalanche chutes. As nettles zap some smarts into you, look up at the fortress of towering peaks flanking the valley. At 5 miles the way steepens. The trail ascends rocky and open slopes, granting impressive views both up and down the U-shaped valley while a royal carpet of wildflowers rolls out beneath you.

Climb above a yellow cedar–graced headwall with Royal Creek furiously cascading over it. Now following along a much gentler creek, the grade eases as the trail enters the hanging valley housing Royal Lake. With 7000-foot giants, Mounts Clark and Walkinshaw, casting their shadows upon you, traverse willow flats and a lovely meadow basin, passing a backcountry camping area (elev. 4700 ft) at 6.3 miles.

Royal Creek is soon crossed on a sturdy log bridge. One short climb is your last hurdle before arriving at regal Royal Lake (elev. 5100 ft) in 7 well-earned miles. Majestic peaks hold court above the quiet body of water. In early summer the shoreline is adorned in purple regalia, thanks to thousands of blossoming shooting stars. A short trail goes around the lake. Wander it, sharing splendid shoreline lunch spots with deer, chipmunks, and marmots.

EXTENDING YOUR TRIP

Strong day hikers can continue another mile, climbing 500 feet higher into the magnificent

Royal Lake reflecting the beauty of the Royal Basin

upper Royal Basin. Explore deep blue tarns reflecting a ring of rugged rocky peaks clad in snow and ice, including Mount Deception (elev. 7788 ft), second-highest mountain in the Olympics.

66 Baldy

RATING/ DIFFICULTY	ROUND-TRIP	ELEV GAIN/ HIGH POINT	SEASON
★★★★★/5	9 miles	3700 feet/ 6550 feet	June–Oct

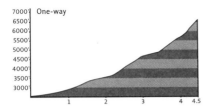

Maps: Green Trails Tyler Peak No. 136, Custom Correct Buckhorn Wilderness; **Contact:** Olympic National Forest, Hood Canal Ranger District, Quilcene, (360) 765-2200, www.fs.fed .us/r6/olympic; **Notes:** Northwest Forest Pass required; **GPS:** Lower Maynard Burn trailhead N 47 52.173, W 123 09.149

What could be more beautiful than hiking into Royal Basin? How about hiking above it and getting an eagle's-eye view into that glacially carved valley flanked by towering spires and icy summits. The hike to Baldy is brutal—it's one of the steepest trails in the Olympics (perhaps only Lake Constance is steeper; see Hike 50). One section gains over 2500 feet of elevation in 2 miles. But for your sweat and toil you are rewarded with one of the supreme views on the peninsula: from Olympus to Constance, countless islands and mountains, and broad emerald valleys. And at your feet, a brilliant alpine tundra flower garden.

GETTING THERE

From the west end of the Hood Canal Bridge, drive State Route 104 to its end and veer north onto US 101. Proceed 16 miles and turn left onto Louella Road (just before reaching the Sequim Bay State Park entrance). In 1 mile turn left on Palo Alto Road, continuing for 6 miles. Bear right at a junction onto Forest Road 2880.

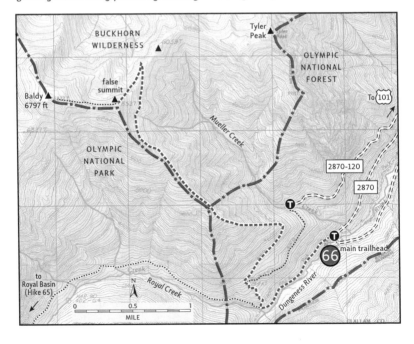

A pair of hikers work their way up Baldy's summit.

The road descends and crosses the Dungeness River, coming to another junction in 1.7 miles, where you turn left on FR 2870. In 2.6 miles bear right at a junction to continue on FR 2870 (formerly called FR 2860). Continue 6.5 miles to the large parking area just past the Dungeness River Bridge. Privy available.

ON THE TRAIL

This hike is physically demanding. It should only be attempted by hikers with sure feet and strong lungs. Start on the gentle Dungeness River Trail through a cool forest of towering fir. In 1 mile turn right and head toward Royal Basin. In another 0.25 mile head right again—a sign points the way to Baldy via the Lower Maynard Burn Trail. Here the fun stops and the work begins.

Snake up salal-choked switchbacks, climbing 300 feet in 0.4 mile to a former road now cloaked in grasses and daisies. It's possible to get to this point by hiking 1 mile up this road from FR 2870-120 (formerly called FR 2860-120; 1.75 miles north of the Dungeness trailhead) and saving 500 feet of elevation gain. But you risk compromising your vehicle's tires and paint job.

Head left up the grassy road-trail, crossing numerous boggy patches sporting showy orchids and monkey flowers. In 0.6 mile, just after passing through a tunnel of encroaching young firs, the trail to Baldy takes off left (elev. 3480 ft). It's easy to miss. Unmarked but well-defined, this is the Maynard Burn Trail, created decades ago by the Forest Service as a bulldozed fire-protection lane. It climbs straight up (and I mean straight up) a dry steep rib , gaining 2600 feet in 2 miles. Make sure your water bottles are full.

Grind your way up the insanely steep grade, gasping for air and thanking the surrounding forest for keeping you shaded and lessening the pain. In 0.75 mile enter the Buckhorn Wilderness. Hike 0.5 mile more of wicked climbing, then savor a reprieve. The trail leaves the Cat track (elev. 5200 ft) for a saner approach, skirting a high slope above the Mueller Creek drainage. Trees thin and views begin. After 0.5 mile of dare I say delightful hiking, emerge in an alpine meadow adorned in wildflowers. Asters, lupine, penstemon, and phlox paint the landscape a purple mountain majesty.

Traverse a high bowl, coming to a clump of lodgepole pines. The tread fades, but it's just a short distance over open meadows to the 6200-foot saddle between Baldy and Tyler Peak. The view, like the hike, will take your breath away. Mount Constance and Warrior Peak dominate the southern horizon over the sweeping emerald Dungeness Valley. Look northeast over hundreds of islands, American and Canadian. North to Sequim, Sequim Bay, Victoria, and Dungeness Spit. To the northwest, Blue Mountain, Elk Mountain, and Mount Angeles fill the viewfinder.

Clamber 0.25 mile and 350 more vertical feet to Baldy's false summit for a jaw-slackening view down into Royal Basin. Mount Olympus, too, can be seen.

EXTENDING YOUR TRIP

Experienced off-trail travelers can continue another 0.6 mile over alpine tundra to 6797-foot Baldy for a 360-degree visual show second to none in these parts of the Olympic high country.

67 Gray Wolf River

RATING/ DIFFICULTY	ROUND-TRIP	ELEV GAIN/ HIGH POINT	SEASON
★★/2	8.4 miles	800 feet/ 1500 feet	Year-round

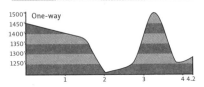

Maps: Green Trails Tyler Peak No. 136, Custom Correct Buckhorn Wilderness; **Contact:** Olympic National Forest, Hood Canal Ranger District, Quilcene, (360) 765-2200, *www.fs.fed .us/r6/olympic*; **GPS:** N 47 58.022, W 123 07.644

Perfect for a winter leg-stretcher or a spring woodland flower hike, this easy trail will appeal to most hikers, young and old. Through groves of old-growth conifers, over cascading creeks, and hugging the lush banks of the Gray Wolf River, the trail marches up a quiet canyon in the Buckhorn Wilderness. Plenty of good

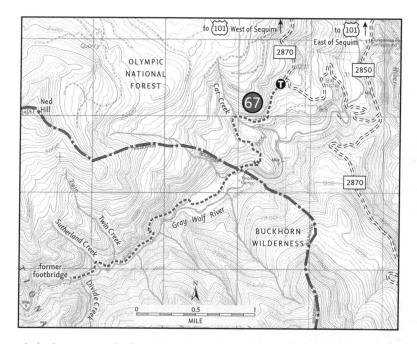

picnic sites, too, can be found along the tumbling, churning river. And there's always an excellent chance of spotting a big critter along the way.

GETTING THERE

From the west end of the Hood Canal Bridge, drive State Route 104 to its end and veer north onto US 101. Proceed 16 miles and turn left onto Louella Road (just before reaching the Sequim Bay State Park entrance). In 1 mile turn left on Palo Alto road continuing for 6 miles to a junction. Bear right at a junction onto Forest Road 2880. The road descends and crosses the Dungeness River, coming to another junction in 1.7 miles. Turn right on FR 2870, cross the Gray Wolf River, and arrive at the trailhead after 1.8 miles. (Alternatively, from US 101 west of Sequim, turn left/south on Taylor Cutoff Road, turn right on Lost Mountain Road, and

then turn left on FR 2870 and drive 5.5 miles to the trailhead.)

ON THE TRAIL

A new beginning and an abrupt ending have changed this trail considerably since the 1990s. From the small parking lot, start downhill on new trail, formerly a logging road. A series of slides forced this reroute. The new trail starts away from the river, but its slope-side route provides some nice views of Maynard Mountain and the portal to the Gray Wolf Canyon.

After 0.5 mile of gentle walking, enter mature forest. The Cat Creek Loop Trail takes off to the left. An alternative route, it drops steeply through an ancient cedar grove, and then follows a portion of the old Gray Wolf Trail to return to the main trail about 0.5 mile farther. It's worth the walk, increasing the sweat factor only slightly.

Gray Wolf River flowing strongly on a spring morning

The main trail leaves the old roadbed, entering a cool old-growth forest of fir and hemlock and accelerating its drop to the river. At 1.5 miles enter the Buckhorn Wilderness, the river growing louder. Finally reach the wild waterway and traverse a sun-kissed bottomland that invites naps and snack breaks.

At 2.5 miles leave the river bottom to climb diagonally up a steep hillside. A few breaks in the trees provide views up to lofty Gray Wolf Ridge and down into the canyon. Dropping back to river level, feel a cool breeze embrace you as the trail heads along the surging waterway. At 3.5 miles, after some of the nicest riverside hiking on this side of the Olympics, the trail once again climbs a steep hillside.

Enjoy good views of the Gray Wolf crashing through a tight canyon gorge. Make your way back to river bottom, and at 4.2 miles call it quits as the trail ends at a narrow gorge that once housed a high bridge. Noted Olympic guidebook writer and legend Robert Wood once observed, "The bridge was built high enough to preclude its destruction from floods." This was probably the only time Mr. Wood wasn't correct—a torrent in the early 1990s washed it away.

Fording the river here is extremely dangerous. If you want to further explore the Gray Wolf Valley, use the Slab Camp Creek Trail (Hike 69). But that's for another time. Right now, sit by the lovely waterway, letting its rapids mesmerize and its resident dippers entertain you.

68 Ned Hill

RATING/ DIFFICULTY	ROUND-TRIP	ELEV GAIN/ HIGH POINT	SEASON
★/3	2.2 miles	850 feet/ 3450 feet	May–Nov

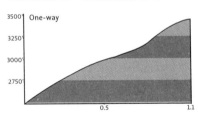

Maps: Green Trails Tyler Peak No. 136, Custom Correct Buckhorn Wilderness; **Contact:** Olympic National Forest, Hood Canal Ranger District, Quilcene, (360) 765-2200, *www.fs.fed .us/r6/olympic*; **GPS:** N 47 58.085, W 123 11.262

 Enjoy a short but steep trip to a historic fire lookout on the edge

of the Buckhorn Wilderness. With limited views awaiting you, you might question, why go? A hike in early summer provides the answer. Through an unbroken tunnel of showy rhododendrons splashing the hillside in shades of purple and pink, Ned Hill will leave a lasting imprint in your mind's eye. And aside from dazzling bouquets dangling along the trail, chances are you'll have this entire wild garden to yourself.

GETTING THERE

From Sequim head west 2.5 miles on US 101. Turn left onto Taylor Cutoff Road (just after

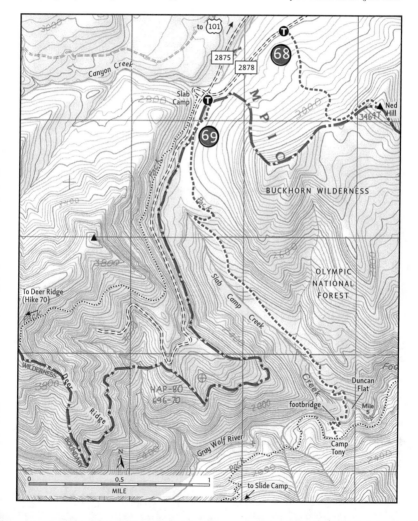

crossing the Dungeness River). In 2.6 miles bear right onto Lost Mountain Road. In another 2.6 miles turn left onto dirt Forest Road 2870. After 1 mile enter the Olympic National Forest, coming to a junction. Bear right on FR 2875 and stay on it for 3.5 miles until an intersection at primitive Slab Camp. Turn left, following FR 2878 for 0.4 mile to the trailhead, located on your right. There is limited parking on the left shoulder just east of the trailhead.

ON THE TRAIL

From its unimposing start, the Ned Hill Trail takes off on a steep climb through a jungle of rhododendrons, salal, and Oregon grape. This

Historic old fire tower and blooming rhododendrons on Ned Hill

trail was built in the 1930s in a no-nonsense fashion to service a makeshift fire lookout after much of the area went up in smoke a few years prior. Eventually the forest recovered, the lookout became obsolete, and the trail was abandoned. In the 1990s, long-time Forest Service employee Jim Halvorsm reopened the trail.

For a trail only slightly longer than a mile, it may knock the wind out of you with its 30 percent grade in places. Those benches along the route may now seem practical. On soft tread often covered in moss, work your way up this little peak, a guardian of the Gray Wolf River valley.

Blackened and silver snags, testaments to the great fire of yesteryear, periodically punctuate the emerald green canopy of the succession forest. After 1.1 long miles, come to Ned Hill's summit and its decaying provisional fire lookout. A gate encloses it. Please stay off of the structure for your safety and the preservation of this historic relic. Besides, the forest has grown up around it, obscuring the wide views it once granted. If you snoop around Ned a bit you may get a few peek-a-boo views of Deer Ridge, Maynard Peak, and Baldy. Of course, all of those rhody blossoms will keep you in awe.

69 Slab Camp Creek and Upper Gray Wolf River

RATING/ DIFFICULTY	ROUND-TRIP	ELEV GAIN/ HIGH POINT	SEASON
★★★/3	5.6 miles	1100 feet/ 2540 feet	May–Nov

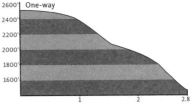

Maps: Green Trails Tyler Peak No. 136, Custom Correct Buckhorn Wilderness; **Contact:** Olympic National Forest, Hood Canal Ranger District, Quilcene, (360) 765-2200, *www.fs.fed .us/r6/olympic*; **GPS:** N 47 57.926, W 123 11.628

An upside-down trail letting you cruise to your destination and then pay for it later. Even though you must climb more than 1000 feet on your return, the grade is fairly gentle and the tread is smooth. With a new bridge in place across the Gray Wolf River, the Slab Camp Creek Trail offers the best and easiest way into the upper reaches of this wilderness valley. The trees are big, the river impressive, and company is scarce.

GETTING THERE

From Sequim head west 2.5 miles on US 101. Turn left onto Taylor Cutoff Road (just after crossing the Dungeness River). In 2.6 miles bear right onto Lost Mountain Road. In another 2.6 miles turn left onto dirt Forest Road 2870. After 1 mile enter the Olympic National Forest, coming to a junction. Bear right on FR 2875 and in 3.5 miles come to an intersection at primitive Slab Camp. Park here. The trail begins on the south side of road.

ON THE TRAIL

From a 2500-foot saddle between Deer Ridge and Ned Hill, the Slab Camp Creek Trail begins its delightful descent into the Gray Wolf River valley. A mosquito-breeding marsh at the trailhead may have you picking up the pace before you're warmed up. Immediately enter the Buckhorn Wilderness, winding your way through a thick forest of second-growth hemlock. Much of this area succumbed to major fires early in the twentieth century.

After about 0.5 mile of level walking, begin descending. Through open forest lined with an understory of leathery-leaved rhododen-

New bridge on the Slab Camp Trail allows access to the upper Gray Wolf River valley.

drons, salal, and Oregon grape, catch some good views of Deer and Gray Wolf Ridges hovering over the valley.

At about 1.5 miles the grade eases. Slab Camp Creek now bubbles alongside the trail. As you descend deeper into the Gray Wolf Valley, bigger and older trees become the norm. Evidently a cooler and moister microclimate helped protect these trees from the ravages of wildfire.

With the Gray Wolf River now audible but not

yet visible, the trail makes a final, somewhat steep drop to the valley floor. Cross cascading Slab Camp Creek on a good bridge on your way down. At 2.8 miles emerge in a rich bottomland known as Duncan Flat, with towering cedars. Here a scattering of campsites along the tumbling and thundering Gray Wolf River make good lunch and nap spots.

A little beyond the flats the trail crosses the Gray Wolf on a sturdy iron-beamed bridge, which was flown in and constructed in 2005. More camp and contemplation sites can be found on the other side of the mighty river. A quarter mile beyond the bridge, the Slab Camp Creek Trail ends at Camp Tony on the Gray Wolf River Trail. With the bridge out downriver on this major trail, don't expect to encounter very many fellow hikers if you continue to further explore this wild valley.

EXTENDING YOUR TRIP

Continue up the Gray Wolf River Trail for lonely wandering. Although much of the trail between Camp Tony and the Olympic National Park boundary is on a slope high above the river, the country is wild and beautiful. Slide Camp, 2.5 miles from the bridge, is a good objective, and the park boundary is 1 mile farther.

Maps: Green Trails Tyler Peak No. 136 and Mount Angeles No. 135, Custom Correct Buckhorn Wilderness; **Contact:** Olympic National Forest, Hood Canal Ranger District, Quilcene, (360) 765-2200, *www.fs.fed.us/r6/olympic.* Olympic National Park, Wilderness Information Center, (360) 565-3100, *www.nps.gov/olym*; **Notes:** Dogs prohibited at national park boundary (at 3.6 miles); **GPS:** N 47 57.926, W 123 11.628

You can easily drive to Deer Park via a snaking gravel road from Port Angeles. So why hike this somewhat steep trail? Here are five good reasons. One: access to Deer Park, since the road is often closed until July. Two: wildflowers that grow along this trail in profusion, both in numbers and varieties. Three: absolute solitude for most of the way. Four: spectacular views of the entire Grey Wolf River valley and its towering peaks. And five: you'll earn it all, something you simply can't do from the seat of your SUV.

GETTING THERE

From Sequim head west 2.5 miles on US 101. Turn left onto Taylor Cutoff Road (just after crossing the Dungeness River). In 2.6 miles bear right onto Lost Mountain Road. In another 2.6 miles turn left onto dirt Forest Road 2870. After 1 mile enter the Olympic National Forest, coming to a junction. Bear right on FR 2875 and in 3.5 miles come to primitive Slab Camp and park here. The trail begins south of the camp on the west side of the road.

ON THE TRAIL

This lightly used but well-defined trail starts out gentle enough through a dry forest of Douglas-fir, layered with rhododendrons and carpeted by salal and kinnikinnick. At 1.5 miles reach an unmarked junction with a "short-cut" trail that leads 0.5 mile back to the road (about 1.6 miles from Slab Camp).

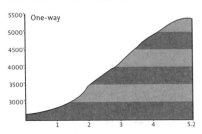

70 Deer Ridge

RATING/ DIFFICULTY	ROUND-TRIP	ELEV GAIN/ HIGH POINT	SEASON
★★★/4	10.4 miles	2800 feet/ 5360 feet	June–Nov

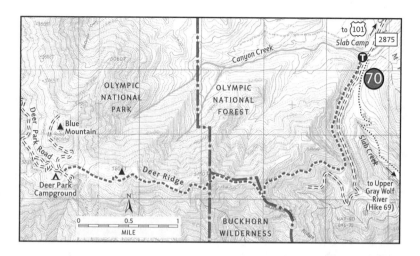

Gray Wolf Ridge from Deer Ridge

The easy strolling ends as the way steepens. Pass a spring and consider topping off your water bottle. This is the only water along the trail after the snows melt. At about 2.75 miles reach an open rib and your first breathtaking views of the Gray Wolf Valley. A bench has been placed here in memory of longtime trail volunteer and Sequim resident Phil Hall. It is

THIS IS COUGAR COUNTRY

While eastern Washington is clearly cougar country (home to Washington State University), this University of Washington alum has had to accept that so is the Olympic Peninsula. But the cougars that roam these hills don't don red and gold—they're wild cats. And they're proliferating. Cougar populations throughout the state have been increasing. No surprise, so have sightings. Cougar encounters, thankfully, are still rare. But it's important to know how to react just in case you do have a run-in with this elusive predator.

Fellow guidebook writer and WSU alum Dan Nelson, a Cougar, who grew up in cougar country, offers the following advice if you should run into one of these cats:

Cougars are curious animals. They may appear threatening when they are only being inquisitive. By making the cougar think you are a bigger, meaner critter than it is, you will be able to avoid an attack (the big cats realize that there is enough easy prey that they don't have to mess with something that will fight back). Keep in mind that fewer than twenty fatal cougar attacks have occurred in the United States in the past since the early twentieth century (on the other hand, more than fifty people are killed, on average, by deer each year—most in auto collisions with the deer).

If the cat you encounter acts aggressively:

* Don't turn your back or take your eyes off the cougar.
* Remain standing.
* Throw things, provided you don't have to bend over to pick them up. If you have a water bottle on your belt, chuck it at the cat. Throw your camera, wave your hiking stick, and if the cat gets close enough, whack it *hard* with your hiking staff (I know of two cases where women delivered good, hard whacks across the nose of aggressive-acting cougars, and the cats immediately turned tail and ran away).
* Shout loudly.
* Fight back aggressively.

You can minimize the already slim chance of having a negative cougar encounter by doing the following:

* Don't hike or run alone (runners look like fleeing prey to a predator).
* Keep children within sight and close at all times.
* Avoid dead animals.
* Keep a clean camp.
* Keep dogs on leash and under control. A cougar may attack a loose, solitary dog, but a leashed dog next to you makes two foes for the cougar to deal with—and cougars are too smart to take on two aggressive animals at once.
* Be alert to the surroundings.
* Use a walking stick.

indeed a great place to be honored.

Now, through open forest and dry rocky slopes, the trail reaches higher. At 3.6 miles enter Olympic National Park. The next 1.6 miles of trail travel through some of the most scenic hiking terrain in this corner of the Olympics. Through parklands, meadows, and basalt outcroppings, the trail weaves its way to Deer Park, delivering breathtaking views at every bend in its course. Gaze out to barren Baldy and Gray Wolf Peak. Admire the jagged summits of Mounts Walkinshaw, Clark, Deception, and Mystery, some of the loftiest summits on the Olympic Peninsula.

Peer down into the emerald valleys of the Gray Wolf River and of Grand and Cameron Creeks to some of the largest concentrations of old-growth forests in western Washington. And at your feet? Flowers! Find arnica, phlox, pearly everlasting, stonecrop, chocolate lily, paintbrush, columbine, yellow violet, wallflower, buttercup, cinquefoil, rockslide larkspur, and many more.

At 5.2 miles you'll come to a junction with the Three Forks Trail at the Deer Park Campground, high on a grassy shoulder of Blue Mountain. If you're there before the road opens it'll just be you and the deer enjoying the scenery.

EXTENDING YOUR TRIP
Walk up the Deer Park road a mile or so to the 0.5-mile Rainshadow Nature Trail on the summit of 6007-foot Blue Mountain. Enjoy incredible views that range from Vancouver Island to the Cascade mountains to Grand Ridge.

Quimper Peninsula
Extending 7 miles north into the Strait of Juan de Fuca and Puget Sound, the Quimper Peninsula is at the marine crossroads of western Washington and makes up the northeasternmost point of the Olympic Peninsula. The weather is mild here because of the Olympic rain shadow, with annual precipitation rarely exceeding 20 inches. This small peninsula is also home to one of the state's oldest and most charming communities, Port Townsend.

Over half of Jefferson County's thirty thousand residents live in communities on the 4-mile-wide by 7-mile-long peninsula. But much of the area is still graced with farms and large green swaths. Several state parks and an active land trust have helped assure that a good portion of the peninsula remains in a natural state.

As a hiker you won't find anything challenging here. But there are plenty of miles of good trail and shoreline to be explored, accessible to anyone with a little motivation. The region is particularly attractive for winter outings when other areas of the Puget Sound Basin are pelted with rain and the high country is buried in snow.

71 Gibbs Lake

RATING/ DIFFICULTY	LOOP	ELEV GAIN/ HIGH POINT	SEASON
★/1	2.5 miles	160 feet/ 480 feet	Year-round

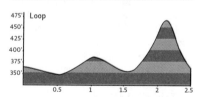

Map: USGS Center; **Contact:** Jefferson County Parks, (360) 385-2221, www.myrecdept.com/wa /porttownsend; **Notes:** Dogs must be leashed; **GPS:** N 47 58.222, W 122 48.646

 Hike around a tranquil little lake nestled in the hills just south of bustling Port Townsend. Amble through peaceful groves of fir and cedar. Savor the sweet smell of blossoming rhododendrons in the spring. Watch nervous ducks swim across

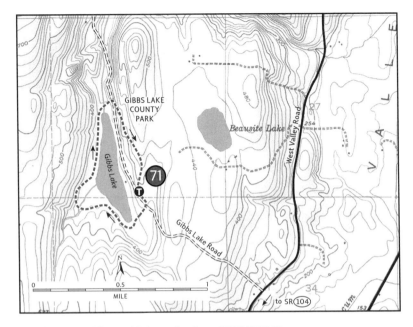

placid waters while songbirds nesting in shoreline reeds hum sweet melodies. Gibbs Lake is a sanctuary for man and beast. But it almost didn't turn out this way. Thanks to negotiations by the Jefferson Land Trust, the Washington State Department of Natural Resources ceased logging here and converted the 669-acre haven into a county park.

GETTING THERE

From the west end of Hood Canal Bridge, drive State Route 104 west for about 9.5 miles and take the Center Road exit (signed "Quilcene, Port Townsend"). Turn right (north), following Center Road for 1.7 miles. Turn left (west) on Eaglemount Road and in 0.25 mile turn right (north) onto West Valley Road. Proceed for 1.6 miles. Turn left (west) onto Gibbs Lake Road (signed "County Park"), following this narrow road for 1 mile to the trailhead, located on the right (signed).

ON THE TRAIL

Over nine trails crisscross the forested hills surrounding Gibbs Lake. Most appeal more to mountain bikers and equestrians than to hikers, but the 1.75-mile Lakeside Trail combined with Jack's Track makes for a delightful hike. The trailhead kiosk marks the point where you'll be returning on this loop. Start your hike on the well-defined trail leaving from the southwest corner of the parking lot.

Cross the access road after 500 feet. Now in damp forest logged during the Depression years, slowly drop to an alder and big fir flat. At 0.5 mile Gibbs Lake can be made out through the trees, but the trail courses away from it, crossing several creeks to ascend drier ground. After 1 mile the lake comes in view once more. Soon afterward, pass two massive Doug-firs, mysteriously granted a stay of execution while their neighbors ended up planked and boarded.

More big trees, including a grove of mature

cedars, are soon encountered. At 1.5 miles work your way through a small wetland. Notice the Sitka spruce, common along the coastal strip but an anomaly in the dry forests of the Olympic rain shadow. At 1.75 miles the Lakeside Trail crosses Gibbs's outlet creek, ending at a dirt road. Pick up Jack's Track across the roadway to the right.

Gibbs Lake on a quiet winter morning

The trail makes a steep little climb onto a bluff above the lake. Stay left at a trail fork. At the next junction keep right. Soon afterward approach a five-way signed trail intersection. Head right on the trail (not on the old woods road), emerging in a parking lot after 0.1 mile. Your vehicle is in the next lot. Pick up the trail again to close the loop after a few more minutes of hiking.

EXTENDING YOUR TRIP

A short trail leading to a grassy picnic spot on the lake takes off from the road a few hundred feet north of the main parking lot. Bring your lunch (and your swimsuit in the summer).

72 Anderson Lake

RATING/ DIFFICULTY	LOOP	ELEV GAIN/ HIGH POINT	SEASON
★★/1	2.2 miles	80 feet/ 320 feet	Year-round

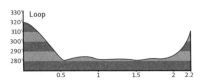

Maps: USGS Port Townsend South, state park map available at trailhead; **Contact:** Fort Flagler State Park, (360) 385-1259, infocent@parks.wa.gov, www.parks.wa.gov; **Notes:** Dogs must be leashed. Open Apr 30–Oct 31, otherwise park on road; **GPS:** N 48 1.095, W 122 48.326

Nestled in a quiet valley just 1 mile east of Discovery Bay is Anderson Lake, a 70-acre quiet body of water teeming with fish and wildlife. Once the centerpiece to farmland owned by William F. Anderson, the lake along with surrounding fields and forest are now part of a 410-acre

Tranquil Anderson Lake

state park. Aside from Anderson's former home and a few outbuildings, the property is in a natural state. Where cattle once grazed, you now have free reign to discover the simple beauty of this tranquil little spot on the Quimper Peninsula.

GETTING THERE

From Port Townsend head west on State Route 20 for 6.5 miles, turning left (east) onto Anderson Lake Road. Proceed 1 mile to the park entrance. (From the west end of Hood Canal Bridge drive SR 104 west for about 5 miles to SR 19. Head north for 9 miles on SR 19 to a four-way stop in Chimacum. Continue 1 mile on SR 19 turning left/west onto Anderson Lake Road. The park entrance is 1.7 miles farther.) Water and restrooms available.

ON THE TRAIL

Over 7 miles of multiuse trail (open to horseback riders, mountain bikers, and hikers) traverse this lovely little park. The 2.2-mile hike around Anderson Lake will appeal to hikers of all walks of life—young and old, fast and slow. From the parking lot and boat launch, walk 0.3 mile down the gravel access road through rolling pasture to a trail crossing. The trail heading right is the Olympic Trail, a rolling woodland romp. You want the trail that takes off left, the Savage Memorial Trail, named in honor of former state and U.S. Representative Charles R. Savage of Shelton.

On well-built trail, travel through mature stands of fir and cedar, making your way to the lake's outlet stream. Cross it on a sturdy bridge and come to a junction. Take the trail bearing left, the Lakeside Trail. Now enjoy a 1.5-mile shoreline-clinging journey that undulates through forest and along grassy banks as it rounds the lake. Look for critters small and large who take up residence in this protected habitat. The lake's placid waters often reflect

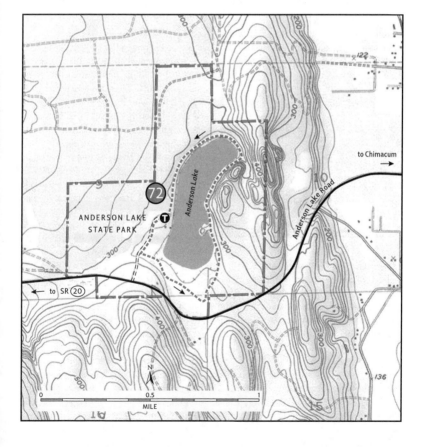

puffy white clouds framed by firs and alders.

When you're not absorbing the subtle beauty of the lake, tune your senses to the forest. In spring, trilliums and wild strawberry blossoms carpet the forest floor. Honeysuckle and thick stands of waxy-leaved rhododendrons crowd the lofty evergreens. By May, the rhodies' showy flowers burst onto the scene. A dazzling arrangement of white, rose, and purple blossoms are sure to mesmerize you. At 2.2 miles you'll arrive at the boat launch, completing your loop.

EXTENDING YOUR TRIP

Consider sampling some of the park's woodland trails. Many loops can be made. The lake is also open to nonmotorized boating, so bring your canoe or kayak along.

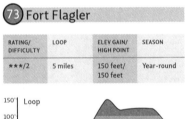

73 Fort Flagler

RATING/ DIFFICULTY	LOOP	ELEV GAIN/ HIGH POINT	SEASON
★★★/2	5 miles	150 feet/ 150 feet	Year-round

Maps: USGS Nordland, state park map available at trailhead; **Contact:** Fort Flagler State Park, (360) 385-1259, *infocent@parks.wa.gov*, *www.parks.wa.gov*; **Notes:** Dogs must be leashed. Beach sections may be impassable during very high tides; **GPS:** N 48 05.724, W 122 43.386

History is full of irony. Five grand military installations originally established to protect Puget Sound from foreign invaders are now peaceful idylls: *witness Forts Ebey, Casey, Worden, Townsend, and Flagler. Fortunately, they never saw combat. Fortunate, too, that with their decommissioning in the 1950s they were converted to state parks that now protect over 2300 acres and 9 miles of prime Puget Sound coastline. At 780 acres, Fort Flagler on the northern tip of Marrowstone Island is the largest, consisting of over 3.5 miles of shoreline. It offers one of the finest beach hikes in the state. And if that isn't enough, there are miles of trails weaving through quiet forest and historic grounds to keep you more than content.*

GETTING THERE

From Port Townsend head west for 5 miles on State Route 20 to SR 19. Continue south (straight) on SR 19, turning left (east) in 3.5 miles onto SR 116. (From the west end of Hood Canal Bridge drive SR 104 for about 5 miles to SR 19. Head north for 9 miles on SR 19 to a four-way stop in Chimacum. Turn right onto Irondale Road, proceeding 1.6 miles to SR 116 in Port Hadlock.) Follow SR 116 east for 10 miles to its end at Fort Flagler State Park (don't miss SR 116's left turn about a mile beyond the Irondale Road–SR 116 intersection). Proceed through the park entrance, turning left at a four-way intersection in 0.5 mile. Continue 1.4 miles to the road's end at a large day-use parking area. Water and restrooms available.

ON THE TRAIL

With over 7 miles of trail and 3.5 miles of coastline, hiking options are many at Fort Flagler. The following loop samples a few of the many facets of this wonderful seaside park. You'll walk on a wide beach with sweeping views out to islands, mountains, bays, and inlets. And you'll walk upon towering bluffs graced with stately trees and harboring relics that tell a century's worth of stories about life at Fort Flagler. Throw in some seabirds, frolicking deer and rabbits, and

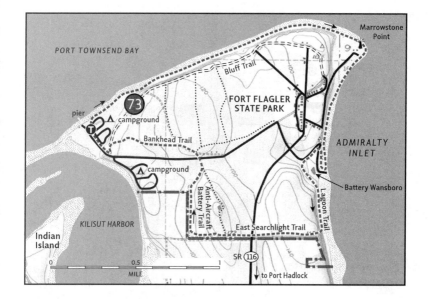

a surprise or two and you've got yourself quite a hiking lineup to look forward to.

Start your adventure on the wide cobblestone-strewn beach. Head east, enjoying a grand view across Port Townsend Bay to the Victorian city of Port Townsend. Admire Whidbey Island's lofty chalky bluffs hovering in the distance. An impressive fortress of bluffs soon begins to tower right above you as well. Gaze up at the tall trees teetering on them—there's a good chance a bald eagle or two will be peering down at you. After 1.5 miles of beach strolling, round Marrowstone Point. Enjoy a knock-out view of Admiralty Inlet with its flotilla of vessels plying choppy waters.

Continue hiking on a wide sandy beach, coming to an old weather-battered pier at 2.25 miles. It's time now to sample Flagler's interior. Find the trail leading from the beach 0.25 mile to the Battery Wansboro, perched high on a bluff. Via a series of short interconnect-ing trails, work your way back to your starting point. Follow the Lagoon Trail for 0.5 mile to the East Searchlight Trail. Turn right, proceeding 0.5 mile to the Anti-Aircraft Battery Trail. Then continue 0.7 mile to the Bankhead Trail, turning left, for an 0.8-mile hike back to your vehicle.

En route you'll pass a handful of historic structures and pass through quiet groves of fir, cedar, maple, and alder. It's quite peaceful. Ironic, considering this land was set aside for war.

EXTENDING YOUR TRIP

The 1.5-mile bluff trail makes a nice alternative if you prefer not to hike the beach (or can't because of a high tide), and plenty of other trails connect to the ones mentioned in this hike. Pick up a park map. Fort Flagler also makes for a nice place to spend the night, offering snuggly campsites, historic-home rentals, and a hostel.

Beach at Fort Flagler State Park

74 South Indian Island

RATING/ DIFFICULTY	ROUND-TRIP	ELEV GAIN/ HIGH POINT	SEASON
★★/1	4 miles	50 feet/ 50 feet	Year-round

One-way

Map: USGS Nordland; **Contact:** Jefferson County Parks, (360) 385-2221, *www.myrecdept .com/wa/porttownsend*; **Notes:** Dogs must be leashed; **GPS:** N 48 01.912, W 122 43.748

Hike through a forest of madronas and Doug-firs to a long sandy beach with impressive views of Mount Rainier towering in the distance. Walk out on a narrow spit. Explore a lagoon flourishing with birds. Watch playful seals ply harbor waters or comb the shoreline of this delightful maritime park. Jefferson County's South Indian Island Park is one of the best-kept secrets on the Olympic Peninsula.

GETTING THERE

From Port Townsend head west for 5 miles on State Route 20 to SR 19. Continue south (straight) on SR 19, turning left (east) in 3.5

miles onto SR 116. (From the west end of Hood Canal Bridge drive SR 104 for about 5 miles to SR 19. Head north for 9 miles on SR 19 to a four-way stop in Chimacum. Turn right onto Irondale Road, proceeding 1.6 miles to SR 116 in Port Hadlock.) Follow SR 116 east for 3 miles (don't miss SR 116's left turn about a mile beyond the Irondale Road–SR 116 intersection). Immediately after crossing the bridge to Indian Island, turn right into a small parking area for South Indian Island County Park. Privy available.

South Indian Island lagoon and beach

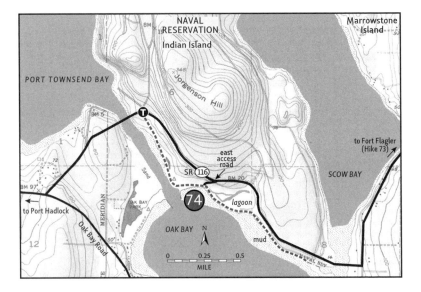

ON THE TRAIL

Once connected to the Quimper Peninsula by a low stretch of land, Indian Island was cut off in 1913 when Port Townsend merchants had a channel dredged. But it was the U.S. Navy that cut most of this landmass off from the public by establishing an ammunition storage depot here. Fortunately, a narrow strip along the south shore of the island has been established as parkland. And what a park!

From the grassy bluff picnic area, find the trailhead at the edge of a thicket. Through a tunnel of vegetation the trail heads south, down along Portage Canal. In late spring enjoy the fragrance and blossoms of primrose and honeysuckle. The trail brushes up against some marshy openings, ideal for seeking out eagles

and herons. It then climbs back up a bluff, ending at the park's east access road after 0.5 mile.

Your hike, however, continues. Turn right, walking the road 0.25 mile and dropping off the bluff to reach an inviting beach. Over 1 mile of shoreline waits for your bootprints. You may have to do a little rock hopping or get your feet wet crossing the small creek draining a lagoon. Once across, continue east on a sandy spit complete with mini dunes and big views. Aside from Rainier grabbing most of your attention, watch for myriad species of birds flitting in the lagoon and bobbing in the bay.

Walk to where a narrow strip of beach connects Indian to Marrowstone Island. Here the public beach ends. Turn around and enjoy your shoreline stroll all over again.

Opposite: Placid Deer Lake above the Sol Duc Valley

olympic peninsula: north

Strait of Juan de Fuca

The portal to Puget Sound, the 100-mile-long Strait of Juan de Fuca acts as a transition zone between the Pacific Ocean and Washington's great inland waterway. And like all transition zones, diversity is legion. From dry Doug-fir forests in the rain shadow to dew-dripping salty spruce groves at its mouth, Juan de Fuca's landscapes change radically and dramatically moving from east to west. And while the mood is always maritime, alpine scenery adorns the backdrop. The snowcapped Cascade peaks or Vancouver Island's rugged ranges are always in view across this long arm of the Pacific.

Though the strait is populated along its more gentle eastern fringes, its western reaches are wild and sparsely settled. But this waterway is a busy place, a super highway for thousands of tankers and vessels plying their way to ports in Victoria, Vancouver, Seattle, Tacoma, and a handful of other destinations.

On the trails and beaches of Juan de Fuca, however, it is possible to seek out quieter waters. The western reaches are lightly visited, while winter casts a quiet shadow upon the entire region. And year-round, the hiking is always rewarding.

75   Miller Peninsula and Thompson Spit

RATING/ DIFFICULTY	ROUND-TRIP	ELEV GAIN/ HIGH POINT	SEASON
**/2	5 miles	360 feet/ 360 feet	Year-round

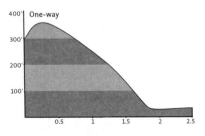

Map: USGS Gardiner; **Contact:** Sequim Bay State Park, (360) 683-4235, *infocent@parks .wa.gov, www.parks.wa.gov*; **Notes:** Restricted parking, don't block Northwest Technical Industries access road. State park development underway, hiking routes may change; **GPS:** N 48 04.659, W 122 56.542

Explore a cool lush ravine that leads to a remote beach on the Strait of Juan de Fuca. Walk along the shore under towering bluffs to a spit littered with drift logs and watched over by a battalion of eagles. Take in clear views of Protection Island, a bird sanctuary at the mouth of Puget Sound, difficult to see from most other shoreline points. Welcome to the Miller Peninsula, destined to become Washington's next grand state park.

GETTING THERE

From the west end of the Hood Canal Bridge, drive State Route 104 to its end and veer north onto US 101. Continue on US 101 for 11 miles to the Clallam–Jefferson County line near milepost 275. (From Sequim head east 10 miles on US 101.) Turn right (north) on Diamond Point Road (signed "Airport"), proceeding 2.2 miles. Where the road makes a sharp left turn, park in a small pullout on the right. The hike begins on a gated road on the opposite side of the road—use caution crossing.

ON THE TRAIL

Once considered for a nuclear power plant, and once almost sold to a Japanese company for development into a golf resort, this former Washington State Department of Natural Resources timberland and magnificent piece of coastal property has not always been revered by state officials. But Washington's citizens have, and the property was transferred to the state parks division. After sitting idle for 15 years the state plans to have the park's

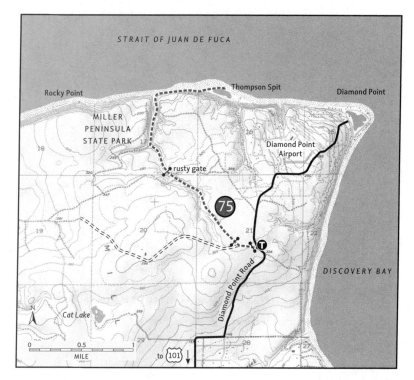

facilities developed in time for the agency's centennial in 2013. Meanwhile, the Washington Trails Association has helped clear a trail through the property so you can start exploring and get a preview of just what this 2800-acre prime piece of public land has to offer.

Start your sneak peek by walking up the Northwest Technical Industries access road for 0.2 mile to an old gated road on your right. Follow this nice woodlands byway through a thick stand of second growth. After 1 mile come to a junction with another old road and head right. Immediately come to another road junction and go left.

Shortly afterward approach an old rusty gate (at 1.3 miles). Pass it, descending into a rhododendron-lined gully. Soon you'll notice a

sign indicating the way to the beach. Head right on a refurbished trail compliments of the WTA.

Wind your way 0.4 mile through a lush narrow ravine graced with remnant old-growth fir and cedar. Rays of light begin penetrating the forest, and the sound of the surf grows louder. At 1.75 miles from the trailhead, reach a long and deserted but wildly beautiful beach. If the tide is high, plop your bum on a driftwood log and let the surf serenade you. If the tide is out, walk the cobbled beach right (east) under a fortress of high bluffs capped in thick forest.

Protection Island's chalky bluffs shine across choppy waters. Mount Baker's snowy cone rises above the San Juan Islands. After 0.75 mile of beach strolling, come to log-littered Thompson Spit and its bird-rich lagoon. Eagles, buffleheads,

A WTA work crew constructs a new trail at Miller Peninsula State Park.

geese, herons, and blackbirds go about their business in the brackish waters, while oyster-catchers and harlequin ducks ply the shoreline. Stay for a while, but give yourself enough time to return before the tide does. Contemplate and rejoice in the new trails and camping facilities this emerging state park will soon provide.

76 Dungeness Spit

RATING/ DIFFICULTY	ROUND-TRIP	ELEV GAIN/ HIGH POINT	SEASON
★★★★/3	11 miles	130 feet/ 130 feet	Year-round

Maps: USGS Dungeness, refuge maps available at trailhead; **Contact:** Dungeness National Wildlife Refuge, (360) 457-8451, *www .fws.gov/pacific/refuges/field/wa_dungeness .htm*; **Notes:** $3 per family entry fee (Golden Eagle Pass accepted). Closed at sunset. Dogs prohibited. Hike may be difficult in highest tides; **GPS:** N 48 08.480, W 123 11.395

No need to head all the way to the Pacific if it's a good beach hike you seek. One of Washington's best saltwater strolls is along its "north coast," the Strait of Juan de Fuca. Actually, this hike heads directly into the strait on the longest coastal spit in the continental United States. A narrow strip of sand, dune, and beached logs, the Dungeness Spit protrudes over 5 miles straight into the strait. Prone to breaching during storms, the spit is also resilient and well-established—and well-hiked and loved by those who explore it.

GETTING THERE

From Sequim head west on US 101 for 5 miles. (From Port Angeles drive east for 12 miles.) Turn right (north) at milepost 260 onto oddly named Kitchen-Dick Road. At 3.3 miles, Kitchen-Dick sharply turns right, becoming Lotzgesell Road. In another 0.25 mile, turn left on Voice of America Road (signed "Dungeness National Wildlife Refuge, Dungeness Recreation Area"). Proceed through the Clallam County park and campground, and in 1 mile come to the trailhead. Water and restrooms available.

ON THE TRAIL

The Dungeness Spit was formed by wind and water currents that forced river silt and glacial till to arch into the Strait of Juan de Fuca. Over the centuries the spit has grown to over 5 miles. You can hike all the way to the tip,

where a lighthouse has been keeping guard since 1857. The extreme tip, however, like the Dungeness Bay side of the spit, is closed to public entry to protect important wildlife habitat. Because the spit is protected and managed as a wildlife refuge, many recreational activities are restricted. Please respect areas closed to public visitation.

Try to do this hike during low tide for easier walking. Lying within the Olympic rain shadow, the spit receives less than 20 inches of rainfall annually, making it a great winter destination when surrounding areas are socked in. Pack your binoculars too, as the bird-watching is supreme. Over 250 species have been recorded on the spit and in Dungeness Bay, including many that are endangered or threatened. Marbled murrelets, harlequin ducks, and snowy plovers frequent the area.

Follow the refuge trail 0.5 mile through cool maritime forest. Before descending to the beach, take in sweeping views of the spit

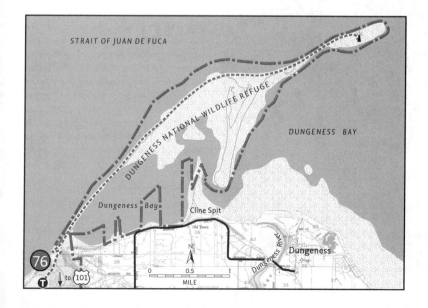

from an overlook. Now drop 100 feet, emerging at the base of tall bluffs and at the start of the spit. It's a straightforward hike to the lighthouse. Pack plenty of water and sunscreen. If the 11-mile round trip seems daunting, any distance hiked along the spit will be rewarding.

If you head south from the trail, you can wander for over a mile on oft-deserted beaches under golden bluffs. Mount Angeles hovering in the distance may very well lure you this way. No matter which way you venture, expect some of the best beach hiking around.

EXTENDING YOUR TRIP
The 630-acre wildlife refuge borders a 216-acre Clallam County park that contains developed campsites with awesome views. A 1-mile trail along a high bluff weaves through the park and makes for a great sunset hike.

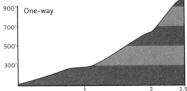

77 Striped Peak

RATING/ DIFFICULTY	ROUND-TRIP	ELEV GAIN/ HIGH POINT	SEASON
★★/3	5 miles	850 feet/ 950 feet	Year-round

One-way

Map: Green Trails Joyce No. 102; **Contact:** Salt Creek County Park, (360) 928-3441, ccpsc@ olypen.com, www.clallam.net/CountyParks/html /parks_saltcreek.htm; **GPS:** N 48 09.731, W 123 41.914

Two adventures in one await you at Striped Peak. First, hike to a 1000-foot peak rising above the Strait of Juan de Fuca. Watch liners and vessels ply this passageway connecting Puget Sound to the Pacific against a backdrop of craggy peaks on Canada's Vancouver Island. Then head directly to the strait to explore a series of tide pools up close. Hike a steep trail down to a remote cliff-enclosed cove, or leisurely wander across a sandy beach on a picturesque bay.

GETTING THERE
From Port Angeles follow US 101 west for 5 miles to State Route 112. Turn right on SR 112, heading west for just over 7 miles. Turn right (north) onto Camp Hayden Road, following it 3.5 miles to Salt Creek County Park. Enter the park, pass the entrance booth, and immediately turn right for trailhead parking.

Approaching Dungeness Spit from bluff above

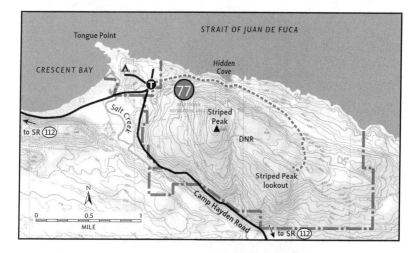

ON THE TRAIL

Port Angeles residents have long known that some of the finest coastal scenery around can be found at nearby Salt Creek County Park. A one-time army post known as Camp Hayden, Clallam County Parks now manages the property complete with campground and trails. A 1500-acre Washington State Department of Natural Resources (DNR) tract encompassing 1166-foot Striped Peak abuts the park to the east. Although heavily logged, the steep northern slopes of the mountain were spared, allowing you to hike amid huge Douglas-firs hundreds of years old.

The well-built but poorly marked trail takes off though a stand of big firs just to the northeast of the parking area. Hugging the hillside and not far from the coastline, wind through forested flats while listening to waves splash up against ledge and bluff. Continue deeper into the forest, climbing a bench high above the crashing surf. Enter a primeval grove of towering hemlocks, firs, and cedars. If access weren't so prohibitively difficult, these ancient giants surely would have been logged.

After twisting beneath one big tree after another, the trail climbs to a small dizzying viewpoint of an isolated cove 200 feet below. Be careful while admiring this vista! If you continue, keep skittish dogs and children nearby as the trail rounds the cove high above, coming to a side trail at 1 mile. The trail left drops rapidly to the remote cove. It's worth the effort, but other beaches in the park can be more easily accessed.

The main trail continues up a damp ravine—a dense fern alley—and uniform second growth replaces the big trees. Cross numerous side creeks that flow down the dark slope. Turning south, the trail climbs steeply, skirting an old cut to emerge on a dirt road at 2.4 miles (elev. 900 ft). Follow the road right a short distance to a viewpoint over a vast expanse of saltwater and Canadian soil. Mount Baker, the San Juans, and Port Angeles can all be seen to the east. Unfortunately, past visitors arriving by motor have not left the summit too appealing, leaving scads of trash behind. (Put the litterers on a chain gang to pick up after themselves!)

It's possible to return to the trailhead via a series of DNR roads, but it's a confusing route

Tongue Point is worth exploring after hiking adjacent Striped Peak.

and often not very scenic, so best to return the way you came.

EXTENDING YOUR TRIP

Back within the park, be sure to sample the short trails leading to the Tongue Point Marine Sanctuary and the flowerpot sea stacks of Crescent Bay. Consider spending the night and letting the surf sing you to sleep.

78 Clallam Bay Spit

RATING/ DIFFICULTY	ROUND-TRIP	ELEV GAIN/ HIGH POINT	SEASON
★★★/1	2.5 miles	None/ 20 feet	Year-round

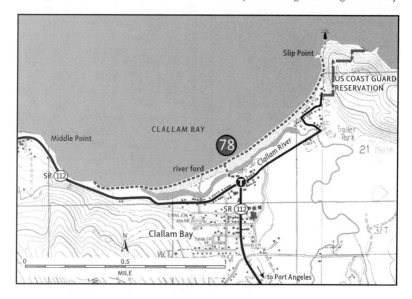

Map: USGS Clallam Bay; **Contact:** Clallam County Parks, (360) 417-2291; **Notes:** Dogs must be leashed; **GPS:** N 48 15.269, W 124 15.635

 A wild and deserted ocean beach on the Strait of Juan de Fuca? With big waves and lots of marine and bird life, Clallam Bay Spit feels like it should be on the Pacific. But when you look across its rough waters and see a sea of mountains on the horizon, your geographic inclinations are set "strait"! Clallam Bay Spit is a breathtakingly beautiful place to catch a sunset or just to wander aimlessly. Best of all, this "north coast" beach is never crowded. Your fellow hikers are too busy heading to nearby Ozette.

GETTING THERE

From Port Angeles follow US 101 west for 5 miles to the junction with State Route 112. Turn right (west) on SR 112, continuing 44 miles to the community of Clallam Bay. (Alternatively, take US 101 to Sappho and drive SR 113 north to SR 112 and then on to Clallam Bay. This way is longer, but not as curvy.) In Clallam Bay look for a sign indicating "Clallam Bay

Beautiful beaches on Clallam Spit—Slip Point in background.

Community Beach." Located on your right, the turnoff is near an auto center and across the street from a closed grocery. The trailhead is located at a large parking area. Water and restrooms available.

ON THE TRAIL

When Washington State Parks acquired this 33-acre property, the state cooperated with Clallam County Parks to make sure that you, the intrepid hiker, would have easy access to this magnificent parcel. They constructed a wonderful little 0.25-mile trail and a picturesque wooden arch bridge over the Clallam River, enabling access to a 1-mile-long sandy spit.

In the winter of 2003, Mother Nature had a few things to say about beach access, throwing a storm that caused the river to shift and breach the spit. The bridge was also rendered useless, as it was now surrounded by water. And just when the parks department was about to construct a new bridge, the river shifted again. So, before you head this way, contact Clallam County Parks about the status of the spit. There are public access points both east and west of the main entrance, so this wonderful beach is not going to keep you away that easily.

Assuming the bridge is back in place, amble down the short trail, span the fickle Clallam River, and behold one of the finest stretches of beach in the Evergreen State. Wander west for 0.5 mile toward rocky Middle Point (you may have to wade the Clallam River en route—easy in summer, dangerous in winter). Turn around and kick sand for a mile all the way to the headland at Slip Point, home of a coast guard station and lighthouse. When the tide is low you can comb the pools left behind.

You can spend hours on Clallam Bay Spit just walking back and forth and staring into the surf. But make sure you stay for a sunset on one of your visits. It's simply radiant.

EXTENDING YOUR TRIP

Over 7 miles of public tidelands can be wandered near the Sekiu River and Shipwreck Point a few miles west of Clallam Bay. Washington State Parks has also acquired property along the Hoko River, about 3 miles west of Sekiu, which has 0.5 mile of nice sandy beach at its mouth.

KLAHOWYA TILLICUM

Many place names on the Olympic Peninsula, like much of the Pacific Northwest, come from the Chinook Jargon. Not an actual language, Chinook is a collection of several hundred words drawn from various Native American tribal languages as well as from English and French. It was used as a trade language among Native peoples, Europeans, and European Americans in the Pacific Northwest throughout the nineteenth century. A unique part of our Northwest cultural heritage, Chinook names are sprinkled throughout the landscape. Below are some Chinook words you will encounter on the Olympic Peninsula.

chuck	water, river, stream
cultus	bad or worthless
elip	first, in front of
hyas	big, powerful, mighty
illahee	the land, country, earth, soil
kimtah	following after, behind
klahanie	outdoors
klahowya	greeting, "how are you?" or welcome
klootchman	woman
kloshe nanitch	take care, stand guard
la push	the mouth (of a river)
ollalie	berries
potlatch	give, gift
sitkum	half of something, part of something
skookum	big, strong, mighty
tenas	small, weak, children
tillicum	friend, people
tupso	pasture, grass

Hurricane Ridge

For many, the Hurricane Ridge region represents the créme de la créme when it comes to day hiking on the Olympic Peninsula. Nowhere else in these rugged mountains can you access alpine meadows and lakes with such ease. Nowhere else on the peninsula are you granted almost nonstop, stunning horizon-spanning views. Many of the area's hikes start at high elevations and remain high, weaving along lofty ridges as panorama-providing pathways.

But with such notoriety come masses of view-seekers. Many of the trails in this area can get downright crowded, especially on nice weekends (both summer and winter). The Hurricane Ridge Road (Heart o' the Hills Parkway), which enables such easy access to this high country, is a double-edged sword. On one side, it allows perhaps far too many people for the fragile alpine environment to absorb. But on the other side, it provides access to almost anyone. Indeed, more than a few got their first taste of the Olympics because of this popular parkway, gaining a love and respect for this special place. That's what happened to me a quarter of a century ago.

79 Lake Angeles

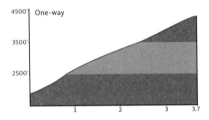

RATING/ DIFFICULTY	ROUND-TRIP	ELEV GAIN/ HIGH POINT	SEASON
★★/3	7.4 miles	2350 feet/ 4196 feet	June–Nov

Maps: Green Trails Port Angeles No. 103, Custom Correct Hurricane Ridge; **Contact:** Olympic National Park, Wilderness Information Center, (360) 565-3100, www.nps.gov/olym; **Notes:** Dogs prohibited; **GPS:** N 48 02.345, W 123 25.916

Known for its craggy peaks, wilderness coast, and deep lush forests, Olympic National Park contains quite an array of spectacular natural features. But when it comes to alpine lakes, the park seems lacking. Sure, scores of aquatic gems sparkle in the backcountry, but compared to the Cascades, the Olympics come up short. Lake-loving day hikers need not shy away, however, for there are a handful of attainable alpine gems. Lake Angeles is one

of them. It's also one of the largest lakes in the Olympics, and the most popular.

GETTING THERE
From Port Angeles leave US 101 near milepost 249, following Race Street south 1.2 miles to Hurricane Ridge Road (Heart o' the Hills Parkway) and passing the Olympic National Park Visitors Center and Wilderness Information Center. Proceed on Hurricane Ridge Road for 5 miles. Just before the park entrance booth, turn right (west) to reach a large trailhead parking area.

ON THE TRAIL
From high above on Klahhane Ridge, 20-acre Lake Angeles looks like a teardrop. Occupying a glacial cirque, the lake is ringed on three sides by steep rocky walls. Through most of the summer, tumbling creeks of snowmelt feed the isolated body of water. A small island formed by rockfall and adorned with subalpine firs sits in the middle of the emerald lake.

Beautifully set, Lake Angeles is well-loved by hikers from near and far. The boot-beaten path to its shores attests to this. But this is not an easy hike—the trail gains over 2300 feet in 3.5 miles. Well-shaded, however, you shouldn't have any trouble overheating while grunting to your objective.

The well-worn path immediately sets out climbing, paralleling Ennis Creek, before making a sharp turn east and heading over to another creek drainage. The trail then makes a sharp turn back west, crosses the creek, and begins to climb straight up a rib, the divide between Ennis and Lake Creeks. Never easing up, the trail works its way into the deep cirque housing the lake.

At 3.7 miles a sign indicates the lake is near. Turn left down a short spur and behold, Lake Angeles. Cool air rushes down the bare slopes above, rippling the lake surface. Sunlight twinkles off of the small waves. It's a soothing scene,

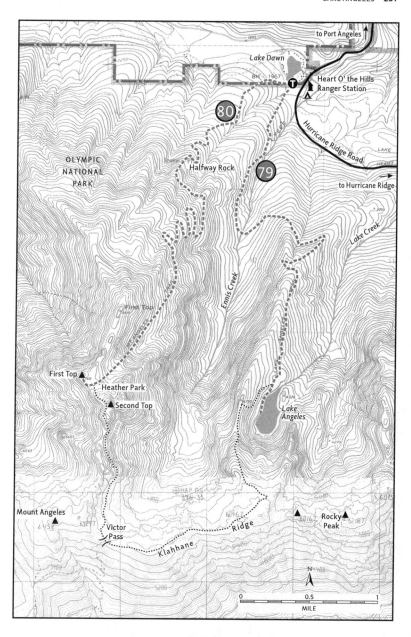

but you won't be alone here. You've earned the right to find a nice spot, however, to enjoy this Olympic aquatic gem.

EXTENDING YOUR TRIP

If the rugged surroundings intrigue you and you're full of energy, continue climbing 2000 more feet in 2 more miles to the open slopes of Klahhane Ridge (Hike 81). You can peer right down on the twinkling lake and out beyond to the "big lake," the ocean waters of the Strait of Juan de Fuca. A grueling 12.5-mile loop can also be made by following the ridge to the Heather Park Trail (Hike 80) and then back to your vehicle. Snowfields can linger along the ridge into midsummer, so check conditions before striking out.

80 Heather Park

RATING/ DIFFICULTY	ROUND-TRIP	ELEV GAIN/ HIGH POINT	SEASON
★★★★/4	10 miles	3800 feet/ 5740 feet	Mid- June–Nov

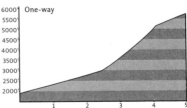

Maps: Green Trails Elwha North–Hurricane Ridge No. 134S, Custom Correct Hurricane Ridge; **Contact:** Olympic National Park, Wilderness Information Center, (360) 565-3100, www.nps.gov/olym; **Notes:** Dogs prohibited; **GPS:** N 48 02.345, W 123 25.916

Climb a steep ridge high on the shoulder of Mount Angeles to a prominent pinnacle with panoramic views of the Olympic Peninsula. From this point, known as First Top, enjoy first-rate views that encompass snowy Mount Olympus all the way to salty Pillar Point on the Strait of Juan de Fuca. And gracing this heavenly haven on the mountain of angels are delightful rock gardens and fields of blooming heather. Divine, yes, but it's a devil of a climb!

GETTING THERE

From Port Angeles leave US 101 near milepost 249, following Race Street south 1.2 miles to Hurricane Ridge Road (Heart o' the

Lake Angeles as seen from high above on Klahhane Ridge

Hills Parkway) and passing the Olympic National Park Visitors Center and Wilderness Information Center. Proceed on Hurricane Ridge Road for 5 miles. Just before the park entrance booth, turn right (west) and proceed to the large trailhead parking area.

ON THE TRAIL

The trail starts from the west end of the parking lot. If any cars are parked here, chances are the occupants are on the adjacent Lake Angeles Trail. It's a tough hike to Heather Park, but the trail is in good shape. You will be too after tackling this hike.

Start through a uniform forest of second-growth Doug-fir. The original forest burned in the early twentieth century thanks to homesteaders who didn't heed Smokey's sound advice. Through a thick understory, the trail steadily climbs, at times steeply. At 2 miles pass Halfway Rock, a glacial erratic marking the not-quite-midway point to Heather Park. The trail eases somewhat before launching into more switchbacks.

Now skirting along the northeast slope of First Top, a thinning forest reveals glimpses of the amazing views that await you at the summit. Craggy Second Top hovers ahead. The trail soon breaks out into the open, snaking steeply around basalt ledges bursting with blossoming wildflowers.

At 4.2 miles the way levels out, entering a small basin (elev. 5300 ft) tucked between First and Second Tops. This is the beginning of Heather Park, a subalpine bowl of flowers, boulders, heather, and stunted evergreens. Come upon a small creek before making a final climb to wind-blasted and sun-baked Heather Pass. Piper's bluebell, cinquefoil, and Olympic onion add colorful touches to the drab shale and scree littering the pass.

The view is amazing. But it's better from First Top, 100 feet higher and reached by following a small way path just to the right. From

Olympic-endemic Piper's bellflower grows on the ledges around Heather Park.

this basaltic shoulder of Mount Angeles, gaze out in every direction for supreme viewing. Port Angeles and the Strait of Juan de Fuca lie to the north 1 vertical mile below. To the east, follow the strait to islands flanked by snow-capped peaks. To the west, follow the strait as it parts the peninsula from Vancouver Island and leads to the Pacific. And to the south, take in Mount Angeles, Hurricane Hill, the Bailey Range, Mount Appleton, and Snider Ridge—all under Mount Olympus's watchful eye.

EXTENDING YOUR TRIP

Strong hikers can continue 1.5 miles beyond Heather Pass, dropping below Second Top's cliffs before climbing a high shoulder separating it from Mount Angeles. From there the trail drops into a high open basin and then climbs to Klahhane Ridge (Hike 81). A loop of 12.5 miles can be made by following the Lake Angeles Trail (Hike 79) back to the trailhead. It's a tough hike over loose scree and past some steep, semi-exposed areas. Snowfields often linger along the ridges beyond Heather Pass well into summer. But if conditions are good and you're up for the challenge, it's one of the most scenic hikes in the park.

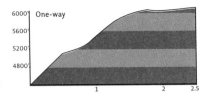

Maps: Green Trails Elwha North–Hurricane Ridge No. 134S, Custom Correct Hurricane Ridge; **Contact:** Olympic National Park, Wilderness Information Center, (360) 565-3100, www .nps.gov/olym; **Notes:** Dogs prohibited. National park entry fee required; **GPS:** N 47 59.225, W 123 27.652

81 Klahhane Ridge

RATING/ DIFFICULTY	ROUND-TRIP	ELEV GAIN/ HIGH POINT	SEASON
★★★★/4	5 miles	1700 feet/ 6046 feet	Mid-June– Oct

Of the four ways to reach the rugged, rocky, and wide-open Klahhane Ridge, the Switchback Trail is the shortest. Ascending 1500 feet in 1.5 miles, this direct approach wastes

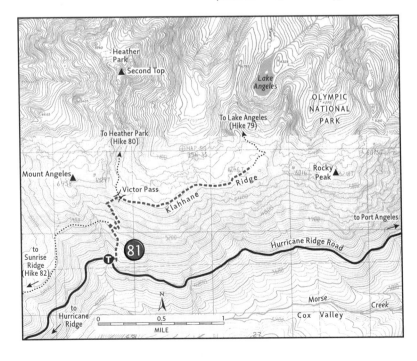

no time ruthlessly reaching the high ridge crest. You, however, may need to take your time. The south-facing ascent guarantees an early-season entry into the high country, but also exposes you to plenty of direct sunlight. Pack extra water, sunscreen, and your camera for this memorable hike.

GETTING THERE
From Port Angeles leave US 101 near milepost 249, following Race Street south 1.2 miles to Hurricane Ridge Road (Heart o' the Hills Parkway) and passing the Olympic National Park Visitors Center and Wilderness Information Center. Proceed on the Hurricane Ridge Road for 14.8 miles to a small parking lot for the Switchback trailhead on the north side of the road.

ON THE TRAIL
Get an early start, not only to avert overheating, but also to witness a myriad of critters scurrying about. They, too, prefer to avoid the midday heat. Once you reach the barren basalt ledges of Klahhane Ridge, however, chances are good that you'll be greeted with a refreshing breeze. Far-reaching views from Vancouver Island's endless summits to the jumbled wall of peaks in the Olympic interior also await you.

Immediately begin climbing. After 700 feet of vertical ascent in just 0.6 mile, come to the junction with the Mount Angeles Trail. To the left this trail leads 3.1 miles to Hurricane Ridge via Sunrise Ridge (Hike 82), a delightful high-country romp through rolling alpine meadows.

Your eyes are set on Klahhane Ridge, so proceed right for some more grueling climbing. At 1.4 miles and 1400 feet of elevation gain, come to Victor Pass and a second junction. The trail left, often snow-covered until midsummer, leads to Heather Park. Take the trail right, the Lake Angeles Trail, to begin a cloud-probing stroll over the exposed ledges and precipitous cliffs of Klahhane Ridge. In a few spots, the trail has been blasted right into the rock, assuring safe passage, though hikers prone to vertigo may want to opt for Sunrise Ridge (Hike 82).

Venture east along Klahhane, dipping a little and climbing a little for 1.25 miles to a 6046-foot knoll, a logical turnaround point for day hikers. Beyond, the trail drops mercilessly 2000 feet to tear-shaped Lake Angeles (Hike 79). If you continue a little ways from the knoll,

Rick and Marti take a break at Victor Pass along Klahhane Ridge.

you'll be able to see it, one of the largest lakes in the Olympics, way, way down below.

Common sense tells you to save Lake Angeles for another day and enjoy the views instead. To the south, Elk Mountain and the Grand Ridge dominate the skyline. Craggy, glacier-covered Mount Cameron peeks out behind. The deep green Cox Valley lies directly below in the foreground. To the north are the Strait of Juan de Fuca, Vancouver Island, and British Columbia's Coast Ranges. Mount Baker rises abruptly in the east. Directly below are Port Angeles and Ediz Hook jutting into the strait.

Klahhane is a Chinook word meaning "outdoors." Upon completing this hike, you'll probably add "great" when describing this prominent ridge.

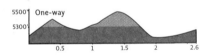

82 Sunrise Ridge

RATING/ DIFFICULTY	ROUND-TRIP	ELEV GAIN/ HIGH POINT	SEASON
★★★★/2	5.2 miles	1000 feet/ 5500 feet	Mid-June– Oct

5500' One-way
5300'

0.5   1   1.5   2   2.6

Maps: Green Trails Elwha North–Hurricane Ridge, No 134S, Custom Correct Hurricane Ridge; **Contact:** Olympic National Park, Wilderness Information Center, (360) 565-3100, *www.nps.gov/olym*; **Notes:** Dogs prohibited. National park entry fee required; **GPS:** N 47 58.203, W 123 29.702

Sunrise Ridge delivers the same jaw-slacking views as Hurricane Hill, but without the asphalt and crowds. Chances are also good that on Sunrise Ridge you'll encounter some resident wildlife, especially in the morning. Deer, bear, coyote, and the ubiquitous chipmunk all make themselves at home along this delightful trail. And wildflowers—they grow in profusion, from magenta paintbrush, to spreading phlox, penstemon, lupine, bistort, and larkspur. When your nose isn't glued to the ground admiring a myriad of blossoms, your eyes will be strained from scanning the horizons.

GETTING THERE

From Port Angeles leave US 101 near milepost 249, following Race Street south 1.2 miles to Hurricane Ridge Road (Heart o' the Hills Parkway) and passing the Olympic National Park Visitors Center and Wilderness Information Center. Proceed on the Hurricane Ridge Road for 17.5 miles to the Hurricane Ridge Visitors Center. The trail begins on the north side of the large parking area.

ON THE TRAIL

From the parking lot, head north on the Mount Angeles Trail, the first 0.3 mile following the paved High Ridge Nature Trail. Real tread begins after cresting a small knoll. Just beyond, in a small saddle, come to a junction. The trail left leads 0.1 mile to Sunrise Point, a 5500-foot viewpoint on the ridge. It's a nice spot, but it gets better down the trail. Carry on, dropping 250 feet from the saddle, leaving the hubbub of Hurricane Ridge behind.

Undulating between groves of subalpine fir and resplendent alpine meadows, the trail works its way over and around a handful of knolls. Gaze north, out across the Strait of Juan de Fuca to massive Vancouver Island and its scads of mountains. Scan the strait eastward to snowy Mount Baker rising above a myriad of islands and inlets. Turn your attention south to the Olympic interior, to an emerald sea punctuated by craggy summits adorned in ice and snow. Mount Olympus, the centerpiece of this magnificent wilderness setting, dominates the southwestern horizon.

Of course, it's impossible to ignore the

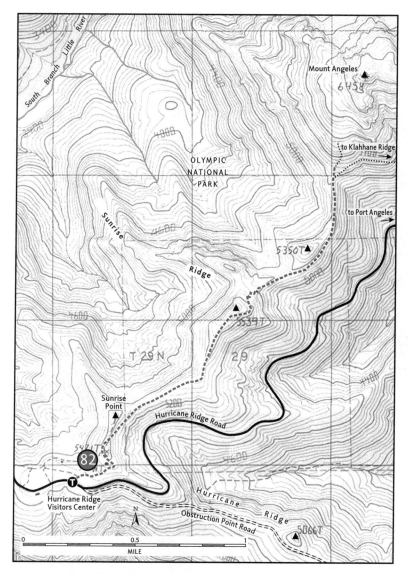

to Klahhane Ridge

to Port Angeles

OLYMPIC
NATIONAL
PARK

Sunrise

Ridge

5350 T

5535 T

T 29 N

29

Sunrise
Point

5200

Hurricane Ridge Road

5471 T

82

T

Hurricane

Ridge

Hurricane Ridge
Visitors Center

N

5066 T

Obstruction Point Road

0   0.5   1
MILE

imposing peak in front of you—the one
growing taller with each step—6454-foot
Mount Angeles. At 2.6 miles the trail delivers you right to the base of this locally prominent peak. A climbers path takes off to the
left, while the Mount Angeles Trail continues

always continue on the Mount Angeles Trail, climbing 800 feet to the rugged aerie of Klahhane Ridge.

83 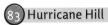 Hurricane Hill

Summer

RATING/ DIFFICULTY	ROUND-TRIP	ELEV GAIN/ HIGH POINT	SEASON
★★★/2	3 miles	650 feet/ 5757 feet	June–Oct

Winter

RATING/ DIFFICULTY	ROUND-TRIP	ELEV GAIN/ HIGH POINT	SEASON
★★★★★/4	6 miles	950 feet/ 5757 feet	Dec–Mar

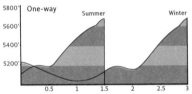

Maps: Green Trails Elwha North–Hurricane Ridge No.134S, Custom Correct Hurricane Ridge; **Contact:** Olympic National Park, Wilderness Information Center, (360) 565-3100, *www.nps.gov/olym*. Winter Hurricane Ridge Road conditions, (360) 565-3131; **Notes:** Dogs prohibited. National park entry fee required. Dec–Mar the road is open Fri–Sun weather permitting; **GPS:** N 47 58.594, W 123 31.069

A paved path to an emerald knoll with horizon-spanning views from snowy Olympus and Mount Baker to the azure waters of the Strait of Juan de Fuca. Choked in the sunny summer months with sauntering tourists, Hurricane Hill has helped introduce young and old, local and foreign, to the wonders and delights of the Olympic high country. This hike is perfect for kids in the summer, and even hard-core hikers need not

The Sunrise Ridge Trail marches off towards Mount Angeles.

right, skirting the southern slopes of the rocky mountain. Feel free to venture a ways up the steep climbers path through more meadows and subalpine forest. Stop when the trail reaches scree, unless you're trained and prepared to make a class 3 scramble. In any case, the views along Sunrise Ridge are as good as any from Mount Angeles.

EXTENDING YOUR TRIP

A half mile beyond the climbers path junction, the trail intersects the Switchback Trail (Hike 81). If you can arrange for it, make your hike one-way by hiking down it. Of course, you can *shun it. And when winter spreads its white coat upon the open slopes, it's a whole different adventure.*

GETTING THERE

From Port Angeles leave US 101 near milepost 249, following Race Street south 1.2 miles to Hurricane Ridge Road (Heart o' the Hills Parkway) and passing the Olympic National Park Visitors Center and Wilderness Information Center. In the summer, drive 17.5 miles to the Hurricane Ridge Visitors Center and continue 1.5 miles farther on the narrow Hurricane Hill Road to trailhead parking. In the winter, stop at the visitors center. Water and restrooms available at the visitors center.

ON THE TRAIL

Summer: For summertime visits, the way is quite simple and straightforward. Follow the procession of people in front of you on the paved path 1.5 miles to the 5757-foot pinnacle, where views abound. Take in the mountains, from Mount Baker in the Cascades, to Mount Garibaldi in British Columbia's Coast Ranges to the interior Olympic peaks. Enjoy views of the green cirque below that forms the ridge between Hurricane Hill and Sunrise Point. Wildlife, including bears, are often seen feeding below. People-friendly deer will probably be loitering on the summit. Don't feed them—they need to fend for themselves if they are to survive the winter.

Winter: For winter visitors, Hurricane Hill offers one of the most-accessible snowshoe routes in the Olympics. Although not overly difficult, windy and icy conditions can make the route treacherous. Hurricane Hill is subject to blinding snowstorms and howling, frostbite-inducing winds. Snow along the ridge forms cornices and

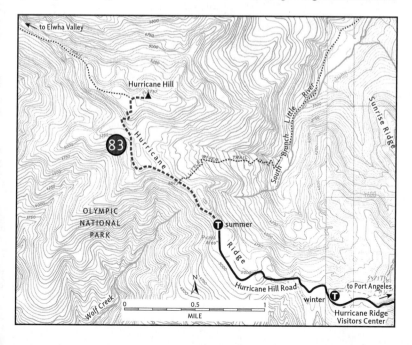

No crowds in winter on Hurricane Hill—looking west towards Mount Appleton

the steep slopes are subject to avalanches. But when conditions are optimal—stable snow and stable weather—the trek to Hurricane Hill is in-credibly rewarding. Always check with the park about conditions before setting out. The park also offers guided snowshoe hikes along the ridge on winter weekends, perfect for introducing novices to snowshoeing.

Along the way enjoy a winter wonderland landscape, with Mount Olympus and the Bailey Range forming a great white wall to the southwest. Venture out on the broad western shoulder of Hurricane Hill for breathtaking views down into the Elwha Valley. In winter, Hurricane Hill is a whole different world.

EXTENDING YOUR TRIP

Summertime hikers can head down off of Hurricane Hill on three different one-way adventures to the valleys below. For the best of the three, veer off the trail just below the summit on the trail leading down to the Elwha Valley. Long before the Hurricane Ridge Road was built, this was one of the ways to access Hurricane Hill. Roam for 1.25 miles on this path through glorious alpine meadows teeming with deer, grouse, and views to a 5000-foot knoll. Beyond, the trail plummets 4500 feet in 4.25 miles to the valley—a good one-way trip with a car shuttle, or a round trip for masochists. The 6-mile Wolf Creek Trail is the easiest additional hiking option, while the 8-mile Little River Trail is the most difficult and loneliest.

84 PJ Lake

RATING/ DIFFICULTY	ROUND-TRIP	ELEV GAIN/ HIGH POINT	SEASON
**/4	1.8 miles	1000 feet/ 5050 feet	July–Oct

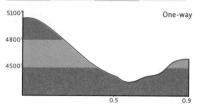

Maps: Green Trails Elwha North–Hurricane Ridge No. 134S, Custom Correct Hurricane

Ridge; **Contact:** Olympic National Park, Wilderness Information Center, (360) 565-3100, *www.nps.gov/olym*; **Notes:** Dogs prohibited. National park entry fee required. Heavy winter snowfall can delay opening of Obstruction Point Road; **GPS:** N 47 56.750, W 123 25.528

A tiny lake tucked in a hidden bowl on Hurricane Ridge, PJ Lake entertains few hikers due to its rough-and-tumble approach. On a trail pockmarked with deer tracks, drop steeply for 600 feet before climbing 350

Secluded PJ Lake

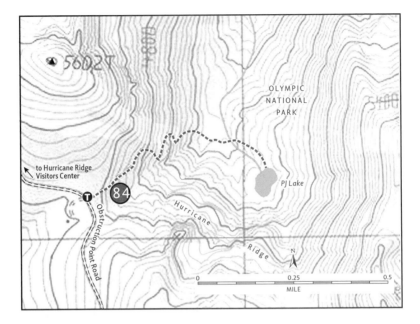

feet to reach this emerald pool—all in less than a mile! Is it worth it? If you cherish solitude and the opportunity to spot wildlife up close, yes. Wildflowers and a pretty cascade offer a little incentive too.

GETTING THERE

From Port Angeles leave US 101 near milepost 249, following Race Street south 1.2 miles to Hurricane Ridge Road (Heart o' the Hills Parkway) and passing the Olympic National Park Visitors Center and Wilderness Information Center. Proceed on the Hurricane Ridge Road for almost 17.5 miles. Just before the large parking lot at Hurricane Ridge, make a sharp left turn on Obstruction Point Road. Follow this very narrow (and harrowing to some) gravel road for 3.8 miles to the Waterhole, a former picnic area. The trail begins on the left side of the road.

ON THE TRAIL

Start in a stand of subalpine fir before rapidly dropping through open forest, huckleberry patches, and meadow clumps. Watch your footing—critter burrows blemish the tread. When not looking down, gaze out to a window view of the Dungeness Spit. The steep hillside often teems with browsing deer. Remind them to stop cutting the switchbacks.

After dropping 600 feet in 0.6 mile, angle east in a cool glen, crossing two streams. The second one cascades 30 feet over a mossy ledge. Now climb 350 feet, reaching pretty little PJ Lake at 0.9 mile from the trailhead, and find yourself in a semi-open bowl flanked with Alaska yellow cedars, big silver firs, and brushy avalanche chutes. The lakeshore is graced with purple asters and columbine, and jumping trout and frogs break the silence of the basin. A grassy bench near the lake's outlet invites picnicking.

If you've hiked in during late summer, allow time for harvesting huckleberries on your way out. It'll make the return more manageable, not to mention delicious.

85 Grand Ridge

RATING/ DIFFICULTY	ROUND-TRIP	ELEV GAIN/ HIGH POINT	SEASON
★★★★★/3	5 miles	700 feet/ 6600 feet	Mid-July– Oct

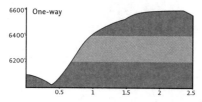

Maps: Green Trails Mt Angeles No. 135, Custom Correct Hurricane Ridge; **Contact:** Olympic National Park, Wilderness Information Center, (360) 565-3100, www.nps.gov/olym; **Notes:** Dogs prohibited. National park entry fee required; **GPS:** N 47 55.105, W 123 22.927

Grand Ridge is appropriately named. The views are grand, the wildflowers are grand, and trekking across its wide open slopes is a grand experience. But it gets grander. Reaching an altitude of 6600 feet, this trail is among the highest in the Olympics and one of the most scenic, with nonstop views of jagged glacier-covered peaks, deep valleys of unbroken old growth, and miles upon miles of wildflower-saturated meadows and tundra.

GETTING THERE

From Port Angeles leave US 101 near milepost 249, following Race Street south 1.2 miles to Hurricane Ridge Road (Heart o' the Hills Parkway) and passing the Olympic National Park Visitors Center and Wilderness Information Center. Proceed on the Hurricane Ridge Road for almost 17.5 miles. Just before the large parking lot at Hurricane Ridge, make a sharp left turn on the gravel Obstruction Point Road. Follow this narrow (and harrowing to some) gravel road 7.7 miles to its end at the trailhead. Privy available.

ON THE TRAIL

The complete trek across Grand Ridge from Obstruction Point to Deer Park is 7.5 miles, with a whole lot of up and down. It ranks as one of the all-time great ridge traverses in the Olympics. But unless you can arrange for a pick-up at the other end, it's a tough 15-mile round trip that only a few hardy souls are willing to make. The 5-mile out and back traversing the slopes

A hiker heads across Grand Ridge.

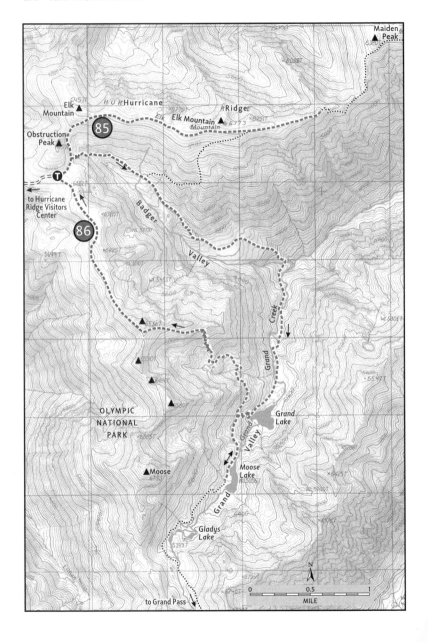

of Elk Mountain, the highest point on the ridge, should do the trick for most. You'll be able to take in Grand Ridge's finest views, with plenty of time to stop and smell the copious flowers along the way.

In wide-open country, start off by descending slightly toward the Badger Valley. In 0.2 mile the Badger Valley Trail takes off right (see Hike 86), dropping steeply below into emerald oblivion. Your trail angles left, rounding Obstruction Peak before traversing the barren, wind-battered, and sun-dried south face of Elk Mountain. Some years, snows linger in the shadows of Obstruction Peak, making travel dangerous. If the steep gullies haven't melted out, consider hiking to Grand Valley instead (Hike 86).

Once the snow is gone, however, it's high and dry on the ridge. Pack plenty of water. After 1 mile of huffing and puffing the grade eases, allowing you to concentrate on the fascinating alpine tundra cloaking Elk Mountain. Put your nose to the ground to admire floral arrangements of lupine, columbine, tiger lily, paintbrush, cow parsley, rosehip, penstemon, larkspur, gentian, cinquefoil, and a handful of other showy blossoms. Watch the meadows for movement too. You may spot one of the horned larks that calls Grand Ridge home.

At 2 miles and an elevation of 6600 feet—the highest maintained tread in the park—come to a junction with the Badger Valley cutoff, an option for an interesting, albeit difficult return. Continue on relatively flat terrain for another 0.5 mile, basking in mountain breezes and soaking up views. From the sparkling waters of the Strait of Juan de Fuca to the snowy summits of Mounts Olympus, Cameron, Carrie, and Deception, grand views emanate.

At 2.5 miles the trail makes a steep plunge down a rocky slope on its way to Maiden Peak. This is a good place to start retracing your steps, savoring this alpine beauty a little bit longer.

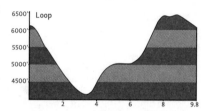

86 Grand Valley

RATING/ DIFFICULTY	LOOP	ELEV GAIN/ HIGH POINT	SEASON
★★★★★/4	9.8 miles	2400 feet/ 6450 feet	Mid-July– mid-Oct

Maps: Green Trails Elwha North–Hurricane Ridge No. 134S, Custom Correct Hurricane Ridge; **Contact:** Olympic National Park, Wilderness Information Center, (360) 565-3100, www .nps.gov/olym; **Notes:** Dogs prohibited. National park entry fee required; **GPS:** N 47 56.750, W 123 25.528

In a park where more than a few valleys can vie for the name "grand", this one is the grand contender. A necklace of sparkling alpine lakes adorning bold mountain faces spans this mile-high valley. Wildflowers, old growth, alpine tundra, deer, marmots, bear—they're all here in this outdoor cathedral. Your ticket into this wild kingdom comes at minimal cost—the trail is mostly downhill on a good grade, though you do pay the piper on the way out on a grueling ascent. But it's all worth it.

GETTING THERE

From Port Angeles leave US 101 near milepost 249, following Race Street south 1.2 miles to Hurricane Ridge Road (Heart o' the Hills Parkway) and passing the Olympic National Park Visitors Center and Wilderness Information Center. Proceed on the Hurricane Ridge Road for almost 17.5 miles. Just before the large parking lot at Hurricane Ridge, make a sharp turn on Obstruction Point Road. Follow this narrow (and harrowing to some) gravel road 7.7 miles to its end at the trailhead. Privy available.

ON THE TRAIL

The quickest way into Grand Valley is via the Grand Pass Trail, climbing along Obstruction Ridge and then brutally descending to Grand Lake. Consider this loop as an alternative.

Moose Lake in the Grand Valley

ONLY IN THE OLYMPICS

Because the Olympic Peninsula is in essence a biological island—isolated by eons of glacial ice followed by the "moats" of the Strait of Juan de Fuca and Puget Sound—many of its life forms are found nowhere else on the planet. The peninsula is home to eight plant endemics and fifteen animal endemics.

Among the region's unique fauna are the Olympic marmot, Olympic yellow-pine chipmunk, Olympic snow mole, Olympic Mazama pocket gopher, Olympic ermine, Olympic torrent salamander, Olympic mudminnow, Olympic grasshopper, arionid jumping slug, and the Quileute gazelle beetle.

Among the peninsula's unique flora are the Olympic mountain milk vetch (a plant endangered because of introduced mountain goats), Piper's bellflower, Olympic mountain groundsel, and Flett's violet.

Among original (but not endemic) inhabitants that are missing today from this biologically diverse landscape is the gray wolf. Extirpated by early settlers and the Park Service itself (talk about a misguided predator policy), the majestic howl of *Canis lupis* hasn't been heard in the Olympic backcountry since the 1920s. Conservationists hope that this noble creature and important component of the Olympic ecosystem can someday be reintroduced.

Sure, it's longer and, sure, there's more overall climbing involved, but the gentle descent will save your knees and you'll get to traverse the quiet Badger Valley en route. Bursting with flowered meadows and fluttering with animal activity, this valley is neglected by those in a hurry to get to Grand Valley. Don't expect any badgers, though—it was named after a ranger's horse. There are lots of Olympic marmots, however—close enough.

Start by heading toward Grand Ridge (Hike 85), making a right turn after 0.2 mile onto the Badger Valley Trail. Descend in the wide U-shaped valley, hopping over rivulets and brushing against clumps of flagrant greenery. Try not to fall into a marmot burrow.

After passing the Elk Mountain cutoff at 1.1 miles, enter subalpine forest. Undulating between meadow and forest, cross Badger Creek at 2.8 miles (elev. approx. 4000 ft). Then, with Grand Creek at your side, begin the gradual climb to Grand Lake. The forest thins as you ascend and cross brushy avalanche chutes and march over glacial moraine. After gaining 800 feet in just under 2 miles, come to a marshy area that announces that Grand Lake is nearby.

It's a pretty big lake in a pretty big bowl. Cascading waters from above echo over the placid lake waters. Grand Lake is appealing, but the next lake is much grander. Proceed on stones steps and tight switchbacks through a flower-studded meadow of swaying golden grasses to a junction. Your return is via the trail right. Head left. After an easy 0.5 mile, emerge on an open ledge above the sparkling waters of Moose Lake (elev. 5075 ft)—like Badger Valley, a misnomer. There are no moose here; the lake was named for Frank Moose, whoever he was.

With easily one of the most spectacular backdrops of any Olympic alpine lake, Moose is surrounded by black-shale pinnacles garlanded with verdant forest. Roam the lakeshore—the open ledge yields to grassy shoreline. Share the crystal waters with fly-snapping trout.

When you must relinquish this grand kingdom to the deer and marmots, prepare yourself for the excruciating exodus. The trail back climbs 1400 steep feet in 2.4 miles. Look back over your shoulder while catching your breath. Grand Valley's aquatic jewels twinkle in the late afternoon sunlight.

Once you crest Obstruction Ridge, enjoy nearly 2 miles of alpine tundra with sweeping views over the Lillian River valley all the way to Olympus. Grunt up one last speed bump, and then enjoy a downhill glide to close the loop.

EXTENDING YOUR TRIP
One mile beyond Moose Lake is little Gladys Lake, set in a high grassy and moraine-filled bowl. Continue another mile to 6400-foot Grand Pass for an awesome view of glacier-covered Mount Cameron and the wild and lonely Cameron Creek valley.

Elwha River Valley

Comprising nearly 20 percent of Olympic National Park's landmass, the Elwha River is the largest watershed in the park. Cutting a deep green valley in a sea of rugged peaks capped with ice and snow and adorned in alpine meadows, the Elwha consists of some of the finest hiking country anywhere.

While backpackers retrace the historic Press Expedition's 1889–90 traverse across the Olympics, or access routes to remote Hayden Pass or the astonishing Bailey Range traverse, there is plenty of spectacular country attainable to day hikers in the Elwha too. All along the river's northern reaches, wildlife-rich meadows, forests that have stood for centuries, and miles of stunning landscapes can be explored in a day or less.

Strong day hikers can push themselves farther—into the surrounding high country to remote alpine lakes and meadows. They can gaze out from above to a landscape nearly void of human interferences, witnessing just how grand and wild the Elwha country remains.

87 Griff Creek

RATING/ DIFFICULTY	ROUND-TRIP	ELEV GAIN/ HIGH POINT	SEASON
★★★/4	3.6 miles	1500 feet/ 1875 feet	Year-round

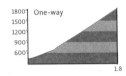

Maps: Green Trails Joyce No. 102, Custom Correct Elwha Valley; **Contact:** Olympic National Park, Wilderness Information Center, (360) 565-3100, www.nps.gov/olym; **Notes:** Dogs prohibited. National park entry fee required; **GPS:** N 48 00.994, W 123 35.407

Ascend a steep and arduous hillside to a sun-kissed ledge that grants panoramic perspectives of the wide and wild Elwha River valley, from snow- and ice-covered Mount Carrie down to the twinkling turquoise waters of Lake Mills. One of the Olympic National Park's least hiked trails, Griff Creek guarantees plenty of solitude—even when the Elwha Valley is hopping with activity.

GETTING THERE
From Port Angeles follow US 101 west for 9 miles. At milepost 240, before the Elwha River Bridge, turn left onto Olympic Hot Springs Road (signed "Elwha Valley"). Follow this good paved road, and in 2 miles enter Olympic National Park. In 2 more miles reach the Elwha Ranger Station. Park here. The trail begins behind the building. Water and restrooms available.

ON THE TRAIL
Don't let the distance fool you. This is not an easy hike. The trail climbs 1500 feet in a little over 1.5 miles. But here's the payoff: though

you're likely to run into deer, hare, and other critters, chances of encountering a fellow human are slim to none. Despite being named after Griff Creek, the trail travels along a dry ridge nowhere near the waterway. Pack lots of water.

Begin in a daisy-dotted meadow just to the rear of the Elwha Ranger Station. Traverse a park compound, entering a cool and mature forest of fir and cedar. Griff Creek can be heard roaring in the distance, but that sound soon becomes a memory. Despite being lightly traveled, the tread is good and the trail is regularly maintained.

At 0.5 mile cross a seasonal creek bed. The way now wastes no time rising from the moist valley floor to a dry south-facing slope. As you ascend via a series of tight, steep switchbacks the forest canopy thins, revealing teaser views of what lies ahead. At 1.6 miles emerge on a dry ledge. Manzanita and madrona frame a view east to the prominent Elwha River range pinnacle, Unicorn Peak.

Next, hike one sweeping switchback that delivers you to the top of that ledge. A sign

The author enjoys the view of Lake Mills from the Griff Creek Trail.

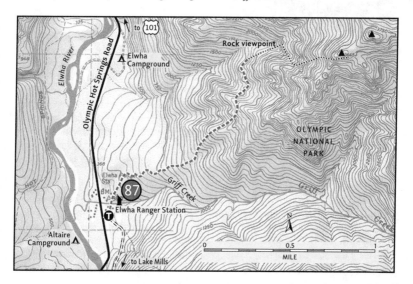

indicates "Rock viewpoint el. 1875 feet." Drop your pack, grab your water bottle, and stake a claim to this picture-perfect promontory. Lake Mills and the Elwha River lie directly below. Mount Carrie towers above. Directly across the wide valley admire the imposing and inhospitable wall of Baldy and the Happy Lake Ridge guarding the Hughes Creek drainage.

EXTENDING YOUR TRIP

Most day hikers will be content, calling it quits at this first viewpoint. But another fine lookout is reached at 2.3 miles (elev. 2400 ft). Beyond that, the trail climbs an insane 800 feet in 0.5 mile on rough and rocky tread to a ledgy terminus with an impressive view of Hurricane Hill, Griff Peak, and the Unicorn. There are also other obscure trails of the Elwha Valley to consider. Cascade Rock is reached in 2 miles after climbing 1500 feet. The West Elwha Trail takes off from the Altaire Campground on a 3-mile up-and-down course along the river. There's good car camping at both Altaire and Elwha Campgrounds.

88 Geyser Valley

RATING/ DIFFICULTY	ROUND-TRIP	ELEV GAIN/ HIGH POINT	SEASON
★★★★/2	7.8 miles	600 feet/ 1300 feet	Year-round

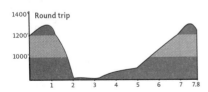

Maps: Green Trails Elwha North–Hurricane Ridge No. 134S, Custom Correct Elwha Valley; **Contact:** Olympic National Park, Wilderness Information Center, (360) 565-3100, www.nps.gov/olym; **Notes:** Dogs prohibited. National park entry fee required; **GPS:** N 47 58.055, W 123 34.941

Geyser Valley is a misnomer: there aren't any geysers in this valley. The Press Expedition of 1889–90—that group of intrepid souls intent on exploring the Olympic interior—either mistook thumping grouse or swirling low clouds when they bestowed their geothermic moniker on this valley. But geyser or no, you won't be steaming after hiking this beautiful region of the Elwha Valley. Stroll alongside the Elwha River's churning waters and lounge on its grassy and rocky banks. Snoop around pioneer homesteads, and scope for elk and bear feeding in surrounding pastures. Wildlife and history spout from the Geyser Valley.

GETTING THERE

From Port Angeles follow US 101 west for 9 miles. At milepost 240, before the Elwha River Bridge, turn left onto Olympic Hot Springs Road (signed "Elwha Valley"). Follow this good paved road, and in 2 miles enter Olympic National Park. In a hair over 2 more miles, just past the Elwha Ranger Station, turn left onto Whiskey Bend Road. Follow this narrow gravel road 4.5 miles to its end at the trailhead. Privy available.

ON THE TRAIL

Start by heading down the Elwha River, a super-highway trail. This well-trodden path has been delivering visitors into the Olympic wilds ever since James Christie and company blazed a route across these parts well over a century ago. Begin by gently climbing thorough mature forest and then younger timber (thanks to a series of early twentieth-century fires).

At 0.8 mile a small spur leads right to the Elk Overlook. Here scan the mighty river flowing 500 feet below. The large grassy bend was once part of the Anderson Ranch homestead and is now a favorite grazing ground for resident elk. Continue through open forest, coming to a junction at 1.2 miles with the Rica Canyon Trail. Head right on it, dropping 500

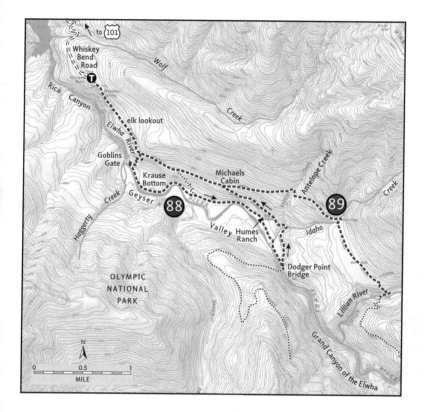

feet in 0.5 mile through a 1970s fire-damaged forest to the river bottom. Take the short spur to Goblins Gate, a rocky narrow chasm funneling the Elwha's swiftly moving waters.

Now work your way upstream on the Geyser Valley Trail. Traverse meadows and fir groves. Rub shoulders with the churning river at wide bends and rocky ledges. At 2.7 miles come to the Krause Bottom Trail. The trail left climbs 0.5 mile back to the Elwha River Trail. Head right for more delightful riverside walking. At 3.4 miles you'll arrive at Humes Ranch on a grassy bluff. Inhabited until 1934, a small cabin still remains and has been restored by the Park Service.

A trail leads left back to the Elwha, but you have more valley to see. Continue right, dropping off of the bluff. Pass a campsite by a sprawling meadow, and then climb onto a high river bank that grants sweeping views of the river. Work your way across Antelope Creek, which may be tricky during rainy periods, and come to a junction with the Long Ridge Trail at 4 miles.

Before turning left and heading back to your vehicle, consider a 0.6-mile side trip on the Long Ridge Trail. Cross a huge recent mudslide swath, dropping to the Dodger Point Bridge at the mouth of the Grand Canyon of the Elwha. This deep, dark gorge is an impressive sight to behold.

To close the loop climb gently 1.3 miles along the Long Ridge Trail back to the Elwha River Trail at Michaels Cabin, a 1906 homestead. Continue left on the Elwha River Trail, ignoring all side trails to return to your vehicle in 2.3 miles.

EXTENDING YOUR TRIP

Just past the Dodger Point Bridge, an old but discernible trail drops to the river's shoreline. Hikers with good routefinding skills might be able to follow this trail for 2 miles to the old Anderson Ranch site.

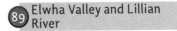

89 Elwha Valley and Lillian River

RATING/ DIFFICULTY	ROUND-TRIP	ELEV GAIN/ HIGH POINT	SEASON
★★/3	9.6 miles	700 feet/ 1600 feet	Year-round

Maps: Green Trails Elwha North–Hurricane Ridge No. 134S, Custom Correct Elwha Valley; **Contact:** Olympic National Park, Wilderness Information Center, (360) 565-3100, www.nps.gov/olym; **Notes:** Dogs prohibited. National park entry fee required; **GPS:** N 47 58.055, W 123 34.941

A hike along the mighty Elwha River is a trip into the very heart of the Olympic Peninsula. From its remote point of origin on the rugged southern slopes of Mount Barnes, practically at the exact center of the national park, the Elwha flows 45 miles to the Strait of Juan de Fuca, draining over 300 square miles of surrounding wilderness and passing through one of the largest tracts of old growth left in America. But you don't need to travel far to experience this historic and wildlife-rich river valley. The hike to Lillian River, one of the Elwha's major tributaries, will suffice.

GETTING THERE

From Port Angeles follow US 101 west for 9 miles. At milepost 240, before the Elwha River Bridge, turn left onto Olympic Hot Springs Road (signed "Elwha Valley"). Follow this

This trail hugs the mighty Elwha in the Geyser Valley.

Michaels Cabin on the Elwha River Trail

good paved road, and in 2 miles enter Olympic National Park. In a hair over 2 more miles, just past the Elwha Ranger Station, turn left onto Whiskey Bend Road. Follow this narrow gravel road 4.5 miles to its end at the trailhead. Privy available.

ON THE TRAIL

If you're itching for a small taste of the Olympic interior, or looking for a good long winter hike, the Elwha River Trail should satisfy your restlessness. Following the route of the famed 1889–90 Press Expedition, this well-maintained trail will deliver you with ease to the same points that the Press Party struggled to get to.

From the trailhead, the trail bypasses the narrow gorge known as the Grand Canyon of the Elwha, traversing slopes high above it. At 1.2 miles you'll come to a junction with the Rica Canyon Trail, which drops steeply to Geyser Valley (Hike 88). After another 0.5 mile reach the Krause Bottom Trail, which

also drops to Geyser Valley. Continue on the main trail, and after another 0.6 mile arrive at Michaels Cabin, a 1906 homestead once occupied by predator hunter "Cougar Mike." The resident wildcats have rebounded nicely since Michael's departure.

The Long Ridge Trail veers right at the cabin, but continue left on the Elwha River Trail. Climb a little, leaving the sound of the Elwha well in the distance. Between Antelope and Idaho Creeks, look for a handful of old trees bearing original ax blazes from the Press Expedition. Through stands of second-growth forest teeming with an understory of salal (fires swept the region in the early 1900s), the trail reaches an elevation of 1600 feet.

At 4.3 miles reach a junction with the Lillian River Trail. Stay on the Elwha River Trail and come to Lillian River in another 0.5 mile and after the trail steeply drops 300 feet. Here, amid good campsites, find yourself a nice picnic site by the pristine tributary. Contemplate how long it took the Press Expedition to get to this spot (two months), and then, avoiding smugness, pat yourself on the back for your rapid passage.

EXTENDING YOUR TRIP
Head up the lonely Lillian River Trail for 2.8 miles. Chance of encountering fellow hikers: low. Bears, elk, and deer: high.

90 Lake Mills

RATING/ DIFFICULTY	ROUND-TRIP	ELEV GAIN/ HIGH POINT	SEASON
★★/2	4 miles	300 feet/ 800 feet	Year-round

800'
One-way
700'

0.5   1   1.5   2

Maps: Green Trails Elwha North–Hurricane Ridge No. 134S, Custom Correct Elwha Valley; **Contact:** Olympic National Park, Wilderness Information Center, (360) 565-3100, *www .nps.gov/olym*; **Notes:** Dogs prohibited. National park entry fee required; **GPS:** N 48 00.115, W 123 36.266

A quiet trail to a small backcountry campground on Lake Mills, this hike makes for a good leg stretcher on a rainy afternoon. It's also the perfect place to watch the transformation of the Elwha River back to a wild and free-flowing waterway. The removal of the Glines Canyon Dam is scheduled to begin in 2008, after which Lake Mills will become a distant memory. Hike this trail to celebrate the restoration of a great river.

Dam to be removed on Lake Mills

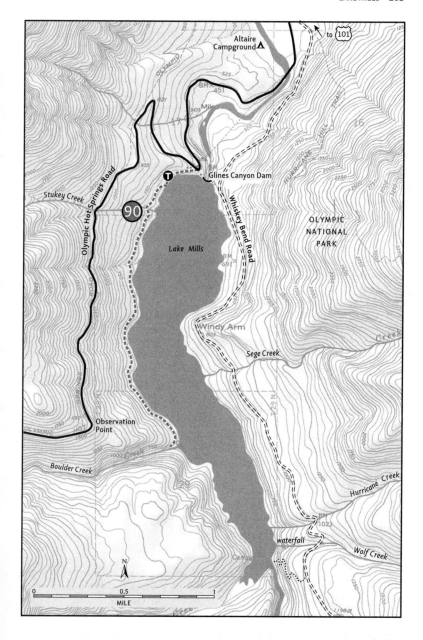

Altaire Campground ▲

to (101)

BM 451

Glines Canyon Dam

Stukey Creek

Olympic Hot Springs Road

90

T

Lake Mills

Whiskey Bend Road

OLYMPIC NATIONAL PARK

Windy Arm

Sege Creek

Creek

Observation Point

Boulder Creek

Creek

Hurricane Creek

waterfall

Wolf Creek

Camp

N

0   0.5   1
MILE

NO DAM. GOOD!

For millennia the Elwha River ran wild and free. From its origins deep within the Olympic Mountains, the mighty waterway tumbled and flowed 45 miles to its outlet on the Strait of Juan de Fuca. Its legendary salmon runs fed the Klallam people. Hundreds of thousands of the anadromous fish, some weighing 100 pounds, made their way up the Elwha each year. But all that changed in 1911 when a dam was constructed just 5 miles up the river.

The Elwha Dam, the lower of two dams, was built without a fish ladder. Then in 1926 an upper dam was built at Glines Canyon. It, too, was constructed without a fish ladder. After thousands of years, the salmon runs of the Elwha ceased—a blow to a culture, an ecosystem, and a nation. The power generated from the dams is small, and in modern times used only by a local paper mill. To many citizens, conservationists, and anglers, the destruction of one of the greatest salmon runs in the state was not at all justified.

By the 1980s the country's love affair with hydropower projects had begun to change. Many Americans realized that there were real costs involved with this so-called clean energy source. Those costs were degradations to our environment. A movement mounted to remove the two dams, and a wide consortium of the public protested the dams' reauthorizations. Congress got involved in this contentious issue, resulting in the Elwha River Ecosystem and Fisheries Restoration Act of 1992, which authorizes the dams' removal.

The act was a major victory for the river, salmon, the greater Olympic ecosystem, the Klallam people, and the country. It marked a major shift in policy. Now, after a decade of planning, public commenting, and review, the dams are about to come down. Removal is scheduled to begin in 2008 and to continue for a few years. One hundred years after the mighty river was harnessed, it will once again run free.

GETTING THERE

From Port Angeles follow US 101 west for 9 miles. At milepost 240, before the Elwha River Bridge, turn left onto Olympic Hot Springs Road (signed "Elwha Valley"). Follow this good paved road for 5.5 miles (entering Olympic National Park at 2 miles). At a sharp turn above the Glines Canyon Dam, turn left (use caution on this blind corner) onto a dirt road (signed "boat launch"). Proceed 0.2 mile to the trailhead. Privy available.

ON THE TRAIL

The Lake Mills Trail begins by the boat launch on this man-made body of water. As far as lakes go, Mills isn't anything special. Still, many people have come to love it since its inception in 1927. They've paddled, fished, and admired snow-capped mountains reflecting in its dark waters. While many hikers eagerly anticipate the dam's removal, a few will be lamenting the lake's demise.

The real charm of this trail, however, is the forest it traverses. Mossy alder groves, a handful of madronas, and plenty of big old firs will greet you along the way. There are lots of creeks to cross too. After periods of heavy rainfall you may find that one or two test the waterproofing of your boots.

After a pleasant start along the lakeshore, the trail climbs almost a couple hundred feet above it. Enjoy some good lake views and then plunge back to the shoreline. Hop across a few more creeks, and at 1.9 miles come to a backcountry campsite. Proceed for another 0.1 mile to the trail's end at a small bluff above crashing Boulder Creek. Retrace your steps, visualizing the trail running along a free-flowing river like Boulder Creek.

EXTENDING YOUR TRIP

Across Lake Mills on the Whiskey Bend Road is the trailhead for the Upper Lake Mills Trail. Hike a short, steep 0.4 mile, losing 350 feet of elevation, to the lake's inlet. Here, marvel at the delta that has formed due to the impounded river. A hidden waterfall on Wolf Creek near the trail's terminus is worth snooping around for.

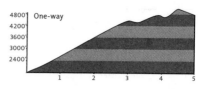

Maps: Green Trails Seven Lakes Basin–Mt Olympus No. 133S, Custom Correct Lake Crescent–Happy Lake Ridge; **Contact:** Olympic National Park, Wilderness Information Center, (360) 565-3100, *www.nps.gov/olym*; **Notes:** Dogs prohibited. National park entry fee required; **GPS:** N 47 59.005, W 123 37.540

91 Happy Lake

RATING/ DIFFICULTY	ROUND-TRIP	ELEV GAIN/ HIGH POINT	SEASON
★★★/4	10 miles	3900 feet/ 5280 feet	June–Oct

You may have a hard time staying jovial on your way to Happy Lake. Reaching this subalpine lake requires a stiff climb up a high dry ridge. But once you crest Happy Lake Ridge,

View along Happy Lake Ridge

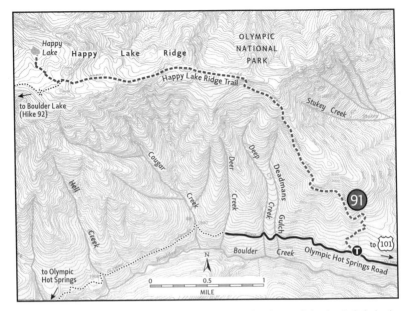

a smile is sure to come to your sweaty face. Open forest, quiet meadows, and heather parklands grace the way. Enjoy breathtaking views, too, of the sweeping Elwha Valley and the impressive snow and rock wall known as the Bailey Range.

GETTING THERE

From Port Angeles follow US 101 west for 9 miles. At milepost 240, before the Elwha River Bridge, turn left onto Olympic Hot Springs Road (signed "Elwha Valley"). Follow this good paved road for 8.7 miles (entering Olympic National Park at 2 miles) to the trailhead, located on the right.

ON THE TRAIL

Happy Lake was named by three pioneering bachelors extolling their emotional state in their femaleless society. The fishing must have been pretty darn good! The happy three are long gone, and many women have since

graced the shores of this lovely little backcountry lake. But don't expect much company of any kind on your trek. While the nearby Boulder Creek valley teems with hikers, Happy Lake remains quiet. You'll probably have the whole place to yourself—happy?

Waste no time gaining elevation. Come near a small creek in 0.25 mile, the last reliable water until the lake. Cutting through thick carpets of salal, the trail next winds its way up Happy Lake Ridge. At 1.5 miles a small spring may be flowing; big trees and a brushy slope indicate its past irrigations. The climb then stiffens, huckleberry bushes and bear grass now lining the way. A small clearing is passed, providing a good view of Mount Carrie to the south.

After almost 3 miles of unrelenting climbing, the trail reaches the ridge crest (elev. 4500 ft). Now heading west along the ridge, enjoy much easier going, the trail ascending a small knoll before leveling out. At 3.5 miles come upon a stunning view spanning from

Appleton Pass all the way to Obstruction Point. Hurricane Hill and Mount Angeles can clearly be seen in the east across the deep cut of the Elwha Valley.

Continue along a narrowing crest, taking in views both north and south. The ridge broadens again as its highest point is neared. Traversing subalpine forest and heather parkland, the way makes one final climb, topping out at 5280 feet after 4.5 miles. Consider walking up one of the adjacent knolls for excellent views; otherwise, head down the Happy Lake Trail, which takes off right.

Descending 400 feet through lovely subalpine country, the jovial tarn is reached in 0.5 mile. Situated in a small cirque, the grassy-shored lake is a happy sight. And hungry mosquitoes may be happy to see you. Consider visiting in fall, when the bloodsuckers are gone and the hillside is carpeted in crimson. As far as the fishing goes, it's still pretty good.

EXTENDING YOUR TRIP

The Happy Lake Ridge Trail continues from its junction with the Happy Lake Trail for 5.2 miles to Boulder Lake (Hike 92). Amble just a little ways beyond the junction for some excellent views north into the Barnes Creek basin.

92 Boulder Lake

RATING/ DIFFICULTY	ROUND-TRIP	ELEV GAIN/ HIGH POINT	SEASON
★★★/4	12 miles	2600 feet/ 4350 feet	June–Oct

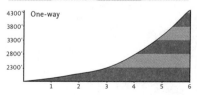

Maps: Green Trails Elwha North–Hurricane Ridge No. 133S, Custom Correct Lake Cres-cent–Happy Lake Ridge; **Contact:** Olympic National Park, Wilderness Information Center, (360) 565-3100, *www.nps.gov/olym*; **Notes:** Dogs prohibited. National park entry fee required; **GPS:** N 47 59.210, W 123 39.115

Hike to an emerald lake in a subalpine setting. The trip is long, but the terrain is welcoming and the surroundings peaceful. Miles of magnificent old growth shade the way. Come in midsummer and enjoy a swim. Visit in late summer and reap a bounty of succulent huckleberries. Make the trip on a

Aquamarine Boulder Lake—Boulder Peak in the background.

chilly autumn day and look forward to a hot-springs soak on the way out.

GETTING THERE

From Port Angeles follow US 101 west for 9 miles. At milepost 240, before the Elwha River Bridge, turn left onto Olympic Hot Springs Road (signed "Elwha Valley"). Follow this good paved road for 10 miles (entering Olympic National Park at 2 miles) to its end and the trailhead. Privy available.

ON THE TRAIL

The first 2.3 miles of this hike are a drag, utilizing a paved road long-closed by the Park Service. It was a prudent move to cut down on crowding and problems at the popular Olympic Hot Springs, but it makes for a boring approach. Bicycles aren't allowed (even if they were, three washouts would prove difficult to negotiate), so you'll just have to suck it up. I usually hike this section in running shoes and change into boots when the real trail starts, ditching my shoes for the return.

After plodding the pavement, arrive at a junction at a former car campground, now a popular backcountry camping area, Boulder Creek Camp. The trail left goes a short distance to a series of hot-spring pools tucked on ledges above crashing Boulder Creek. Avoid them in the summer—they're crowded and probably won't get the health inspector's thumbs-up. Besides, it's hot in the summer—what's the point? In the off-season, however, these pools, the only natural soaking area in the Olympics, are really inviting.

For Boulder Lake, continue right, climbing to well-used campsites and the start of real trail. Walk a gentle short mile through cool and inspiring ancient forest to another junction, and take the trail to the right (the left-hand trail heads to Appleton Pass, Hike 93). Angling along a slope crowded by coniferous giants, the trail climbs at a moderate grade, allowing you

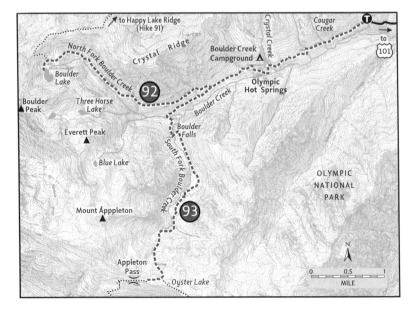

to absorb the beauty and tranquility of your surroundings. Boulder Creek's crashing and thrashing fades into the distance. Silence.

At about 4.5 miles the trail approaches North Fork Boulder Creek and steepens, making a final push to the lake. At 5.9 miles a junction is reached. Boulder Creek is a pebble's throw away to the left (the right-hand trail heads to Happy Lake Ridge; see Hike 91).

Cross marshy meadows and reach the lake, which is perched in a semi-open bowl at the base of 5600-foot Boulder Peak. Inviting shoreline ledges that harness the sun's warmth, perfect for a nap or lunch break, can be found just a short distance to the south. Enjoy the green hue of the lake's waters, and enjoy the silence of the surrounding environment. Well, not quite silent. Chattering chickarees, busy nuthatches, flittering dragonflies, and surface-breaking fish add some commotion. But it's peaceful just the same.

An arduous hike to one of the most spectacular mountain passes in the Olympics— Appleton Pass sits a mile high on the Elwha–Sol Duc divide. Offering glimpses of peaks, forested valleys, and thousands of acres of wilderness in both watersheds, Appleton Pass is a remote outpost in the heart of the Olympics. On the demanding journey there, encounter resplendent meadows, primeval forest, and captivating cascades. But even if you're not up for this laborious trip, just a few miles along this trail still has its rewards.

GETTING THERE

From Port Angeles follow US 101 west for 9 miles. At milepost 240, before the Elwha River Bridge, turn left onto Olympic Hot Springs Road (signed "Elwha Valley"). Follow this good paved road for 10 miles (entering Olympic National Park at 2 miles) to its end and the trailhead. Privy available.

ON THE TRAIL

Start off on a long-abandoned section of the Olympic Hot Springs Road. The paved but rapidly crumbling road travels 2.3 miles to a junction at Boulder Creek Camp. The Olympic Hot Springs are just a short distance to the left, and you may want to consider soaking in them after your return. But skip the idea in the summer—you won't find space, and your aching body doesn't need to fight off a viral attack while it's recovering.

Continue right, through campsites to the start of bona fide trail. At 0.8 mile come to a junction for Boulder Lake (Hike 92). Continue left through imposing ancient firs, cedars, and hemlocks. The forest has a dry feel, as Mount Appleton and the Bailey Range create a bit of a rainshadow effect here on their eastern sides.

About 0.75 mile beyond the junction, the trail crosses North Fork Boulder Creek, which is prone to jumping its channel. You may have to negotiate a few washed-out

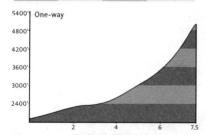

93 Appleton Pass

RATING/ DIFFICULTY	ROUND-TRIP	ELEV GAIN/ HIGH POINT	SEASON
★★★★★/5	15 miles	3400 feet/ 5050 feet	July– mid-Oct

Maps: Green Trails Elwha North–Hurricane Ridge No. 133S, Custom Correct Seven Lakes Basin–Hoh; **Contact:** Olympic National Park, Wilderness Information Center, (360) 565-3100, www.nps.gov/olym; **Notes:** Dogs prohibited. National park entry fee required; **GPS:** N 47 59.210, W 123 39.115

A PRESSING TRIP

In February 1890, having made camp at several spots along the lower Elwha River since December, James H. Christie led a group of five rough and ready men, a couple of dogs, and a pack of mules on an arduous three-month journey across the Olympic Mountains. Christie's ambition to explore the last of the uncharted mountain ranges in the continental United States was met with much interest and enthusiasm in the new state of Washington.

Funded by the *Seattle Press* newspaper, Christie's voyage was named the Press Expedition, and upon the party's emergence at Lake Quinault in May 1890, it became the first successful European American north-south crossing of the Olympics.

Many of the place names that dot the Olympics today were bestowed by Christie and company: Mount Ferry (for Washington's first governor), Mount Seattle (after the city), Mount Barnes (for an expedition member), the Bailey Range (for the publisher of the *Seattle Press*), and Mount Christie (for Christie himself, no less).

An objective of many modern-day Washington backpackers is to hike a route that roughly follows the Press Expedition's original course: a 45-mile journey from Whiskey Bend up the Elwha over the Low Divide and out the North Fork Quinault River. What took the intrepid Press Party over three months to complete is now—thanks to manicured trails—easily covered in three to five days.

areas before actually crossing the creek.

In another 0.5 mile two short side trails lead left to pretty little Boulder Falls, a series of cascades set in a mossy ravine. This is a good destination for hikers not intent on going all the way to Appleton Pass. A handful of swimming holes beneath the lower falls may be tempting, but remember, they ain't no hot springs!

Beyond the falls, the trail crosses the creek and climbs more steeply. Traversing a deep rugged valley, forest cover thins, allowing previews of what lies ahead. Bubbling springs and copious huckleberry bushes may entice you to abandon your strenuous march.

After about 5.5 miles the trail enters an open basin, getting rougher while the views get better. Look back at Lizard Head Peak; Mount Appleton looms above. Dazzling wildflowers paint the basin in reds, purples, and yellows, and numerous creeks tumble down the rugged encircling slopes.

The trail makes a few steep and sweeping switchbacks through clumps of mountain hemlock and sprawling meadows, finally arriving at the 5050-foot pass after 7.5 grueling miles.

EXTENDING YOUR TRIP

Oyster Lake lies a short distance to the left and 100 feet higher, reached by a well-defined way path. If time and energy permit, wander beyond the lake to some of the most amazing views in the Olympics.

Lake Crescent

With over 5000 surface acres, Lake Crescent is the largest lake within the Olympic Mountains and is among the largest natural bodies of freshwater in western Washington. Arched like a crescent, the 9-mile-long lake is known for its crystal clear waters and stunning mountain reflections. A couple of pockets of private

Opposite: Picturesque Oyster Lake at Appleton Pass—Mount Appleton in the background

cabins (grandfathered in after the park's creation) line the lake, but the majority of shoreline acreage is undeveloped and managed by Olympic National Park.

Hiking options in the Lake Crescent area range from easy lakeshore wanderings to steep grunts up surrounding ridges and peaks. Unfortunately, while the lake may evoke a feeling of tranquility, the constant hum of vehicles on US 101 disrupts the peace. Still, it's possible to escape this noisy intrusion by hiking along a babbling creek—or along the lakeshore or an adjacent ridge top when strong winds whistle a more harmonious hymn.

Lake Crescent is a great place to set up a base camp for exploring adjacent trails and those located in the nearby Sol Duc Valley. A fine national park campground complete with beach and boat launch can be found at Fairholm on the lake's western end, while the Lake Crescent Lodge and Log Cabin Resort offer cushier alternatives. And watch out: the lake's alluring waters may just have you packing your kayak along with your trekking poles.

Hop aboard the Spruce Railroad Trail for a scenic and historic hike along the sparkling shores of massive Lake Crescent. For 4 nearly flat miles you'll saunter along one of Olympic National Park's most alluring natural features. Nine miles long, over 600 feet deep, and surrounded by steep ridges and peaks, Lake Crescent seems more like a fjord. With a microclimate of warmer and drier conditions than areas just a few miles away, this trail is a good hiking choice on an overcast afternoon.

GETTING THERE

From Port Angeles follow US 101 west for 17 miles to the Olympic National Park boundary.

94 Spruce Railroad Trail

RATING/ DIFFICULTY	ROUND-TRIP	ELEV GAIN/ HIGH POINT	SEASON
★★★/2	8 miles	250 feet/ 700 feet	Year-round

Maps: Green Trails Lake Crescent No. 101, Custom Correct Lake Crescent–Happy Lake Ridge; **Contact:** Olympic National Park, Wilderness Information Center, (360) 565-3100, www.nps.gov/olym; **Notes:** Dogs prohibited; **GPS:** east trailhead N 48 05.597, W 123 48.151, west trailhead N 48 04.062, W 123 49.534

Bridge over the Punchbowl on the Spruce Railroad Trail

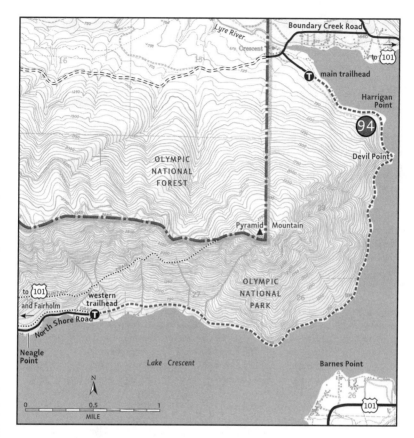

Turn right onto East Beach Road (signed "Log Cabin Resort, East Beach"). Follow this narrow paved road for 3.2 miles. Just beyond the Log Cabin Resort, turn left onto Boundary Creek Road (signed "Spruce Railroad Trail"). Follow it for 0.8 mile to the eastern trailhead. Privy available.

ON THE TRAIL

One of few trails in Olympic National Park permitting mountain bikes, this low-country path is also one of the park's best choices for a winter hike. Gaining very little elevation, the Spruce

Railroad Trail hugs the pristine shoreline of Lake Crescent, the largest lake within the Olympic Mountains, renowned for its crystal-clear waters. You can peer down over 40 feet into its depths. And when strong breezes aren't whistling down the lake valley, those same pristine waters capture stunning reflections of the surrounding ridges.

Start by hiking through an old orchard graced with big moss-draped maples. On an old roadbed you'll skirt around some cabins then drop down toward the lakeshore to the old railroad bed. You're now hiking what was

DISCOVERING THE OLYMPIC PENINSULA TRAIL

Hikers traveling along US 101 through the Jamestown S'Klallam Indian Reservation in Blyn are sure to notice some fancy new bridges spanning Jimmycomelately Creek servicing what looks like a trail. And it is! It's a recently opened section of what will become the longest trail on the Olympic Peninsula, the Olympic Discovery Trail. And if you are unfamiliar with this pan-peninsula path, it's time you discovered it.

The idea for the Olympic Discovery Trail was born in 1988 along with the Peninsula Trails Coalition, formed upon the dismantling of a local rail line. The coalition quickly realized the potential and unique opportunity now afforded for the development of a hiker-bicyclist trail from La Push on the Pacific all the way to Port Townsend on Puget Sound. Through public forums, grant money, and a corps of dedicated volunteers, trail work began in 1991 at Sequim's Railroad Bridge Park.

The Olympic Discovery Trail will ultimately extend over 100 miles, in essence spanning the northern half of the Olympic Peninsula. As of 2006 over 30 miles of the trail, mostly in the Sequim and Port Angeles areas, are open. Another 30 miles of trail, mainly in the Lake Crescent area, should be opened by 2010. Besides offering local people a safe nonmotorized transportation route, the Olympic Discovery Trail also provides miles of year-round hiking for both residents and visitors alike.

once a 36-mile rail line built during World War I to haul Sitka spruce—once coveted for airplane manufacturing—to mills in nearby Port Angeles. Ironically, the Great War ended days before the line was completed. The Spruce Railroad did, however, serve commercial logging interests for thirty-five years. In 1981 the National Park Service converted 4 miles of the railbed into trail.

Although it runs close to the shoreline, the trail often remains high above it and lake views are occasionally obscured by large trees. But when the trail breaks out of the canopy of giant firs, hemlocks, and scaly-barked contorted madronas, the views across glimmering waters are breathtaking. You'll reach the trail's most scenic section, Devil Point and Punchbowl after only 1 mile of hiking. Cross the Punchbowl on a bridge, from which you can admire the lake's impressive depth and the lofty emerald peaks and ridges surrounding it.

Beyond the Punchbowl the trail resumes its course above the lake. At 2.5 miles you'll come to some good viewpoints along the lake's narrowest section at the arch of its crescent. Directly across from you, Barnes Point—formed by river outwash—juts into the lake. Craggy Mount Storm King hovers above it.

At 3 miles you'll round a bluff. The railroad passed through a tunnel here and it is still discernable (but advisable to stay out of). Another tunnel was bypassed back at Devil Point (look for it on your return). At 4 miles you'll reach the western trailhead. Fuel up for the chug back to your vehicle.

EXTENDING YOUR TRIP

An extension of the Spruce Railroad Trail can be followed for several more miles west. It's being incorporated into the North Olympic Discovery Trail (see "Discovering the Olympic Peninsula Trail" in this Lake Crescent section), which will eventually allow you to extend your hike all the way to La Push or Port Townsend if you so desire.

95 Mount Storm King

RATING/ DIFFICULTY	ROUND-TRIP	ELEV GAIN/ HIGH POINT	SEASON
★★/4	3.8 miles	1700 feet/ 2400 feet	Apr–Nov

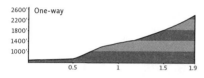

Maps: Green Trails Lake Crescent No. 101, Custom Correct Lake Crescent–Happy Lake Ridge; **Contact:** Olympic National Park, Wilderness Information Center, (360) 565-3100, *www.nps.gov/olym*; **Notes:** Dogs prohibited; **GPS:** Storm King Ranger Station N 48 03.469, W 123 47.306

Huff and puff up a short steep trail to an eagle's-eye view of Lake Crescent. From a vertigo-inducing aerie peer straight down to the deep-blue waters of one of the Olympic Peninsula's most famous landmarks. Despite its difficulty, this trail entertains its fair share of hiking neophytes and Sunday-afternoon strollers due to its proximity to the Marymere Falls Nature Trail. Aside from knocking the wind out of unconditioned hikers, this trail can be dangerous because of its exposed ledges. Keep an eye on children and avoid this trip during bad weather.

GETTING THERE

From Port Angeles follow US 101 west for 20 miles to Barnes Point at milepost 228 and turn right (signed "Lake Crescent Lodge and Marymere Falls"). In 0.2 mile, at a stop sign, turn right and proceed to a large parking area. The trail begins on the Marymere Falls Nature Trail near the rustic Storm King Ranger Station. Picnic site and restrooms available.

ON THE TRAIL

Join swarms of people on the first 0.5 mile of this hike, as it uses the well-groomed and well-trodden Marymere Falls Nature Trail (see Hike 96). At a giant boulder that came crashing down Storm King many moons ago, a small sign indicates the way to go for Storm King's lookouts (left and up!).

Under a climate-controlled old-growth canopy, ascend steeply and quickly. As the trail works its way up the south-facing hogback, the dampness dissipates. Madronas and salal now decorate the way. From here on up, the terrain is dry and the hike can be quite hot during the summer months. Get an early start, or consider Storm King as an evening enticement.

Lake Crescent as seen from the Storm King Trail

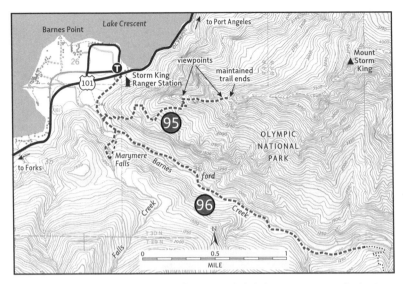

As you rise above the Barnes Creek valley and busy US 101, the crash of rushing water and the hum of zooming traffic fills the air. Enjoy a short reprieve from the steepness as the trail traverses a fir-filled bench. Then head into low gear again as the grade intensifies. Occasional window views of Aurora Ridge interrupt the monotony of the grunt.

After 1.4 miles, which feels more like 3, arrive at a series of belvederes (elev. 2000 ft) on a ledge that drops off precipitously to the north. Enjoy a stunning view of Lake Crescent directly below, with Pyramid Mountain hovering over the jewel. Savor the scenery and bask in the sunshine, or carry on if you desire. A second viewpoint is reached in another 0.5 mile and after 400 more feet of elevation gain. The lake is hidden from there, but the deep, wide, verdant Barnes Creek valley is fully revealed.

EXTENDING YOUR TRIP

The trail officially ends at the second viewpoint, but a scramble path continues. Experienced and equipped hikers may want to carry on a little father to more views of Lake Crescent. But the tread deteriorates and the way becomes increasingly exposed.

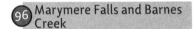

96 Marymere Falls and Barnes Creek

Marymere Falls

RATING/ DIFFICULTY	ROUND-TRIP	ELEV GAIN/ HIGH POINT	SEASON
★★/1	2 miles	200 feet/ 800 feet	Year-round

Barnes Creek

RATING/ DIFFICULTY	ROUND-TRIP	ELEV GAIN/ HIGH POINT	SEASON
★★/3	6 miles	800 feet/ 1300 feet	Year-round

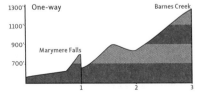

Maps: Green Trails Lake Crescent No. 101, Custom Correct Lake Crescent–Happy Lake Ridge; **Contact:** Olympic National Park, Wilderness Information Center, (360) 565-3100, *www.nps.gov/olym;* **Notes:** Dogs prohibited; **GPS:** N 48 03.469, W 123 47.306

A pretty little waterfall popular with the summer masses or a lonely valley coveted by those seeking solitude and old-growth splendor—it's your choice. From a secluded valley tucked between Mount Storm King and the Aurora Ridge, Barnes Creek winds its way down to Lake Crescent. Falls Creek tumbles down the steep slopes of Aurora Peak, ultimately as Marymere Falls in a damp glen just above Barnes Creek. Two diverse waterways, two diverse hikes, two diverse experiences. Of course, you can always hike them both.

GETTING THERE

From Port Angeles follow US 101 west for 20 miles to Barnes Point at milepost 228 and turn right (signed "Lake Crescent Lodge and Marymere Falls"). In 0.2 mile, at a stop sign, turn right and proceed to a large parking area. The trail begins on the Marymere Falls Nature Trail near the rustic Storm King Ranger Station. Picnic site and restrooms available.

ON THE TRAIL

Head up the well-groomed and well-traveled nature trail, pass under US 101, and in 0.5 mile come to a junction. The trail right follows Barnes Creek to the Lake Crescent Lodge on Barnes Point, a nice alternative return. Turn left instead, following the softly gurgling creek upstream under a cool canopy of old-growth giants. Pass the Mount Storm King Trail (Hike 95) and soon afterward come to another junction.

Marymere Falls: Head right for the falls, crossing Barnes Creek on a sturdy bridge and then climbing 200 feet to a cool narrow ra-

vine. Marymere Falls plummets 90 feet into this dark, dank slot. A short loop provides several vantages for viewing the cataract. Consider visiting in winter when plenty of runoff promises the most spectacular showing.

Barnes Creek: For relief from the hordes of shutter-finger tourists, continue straight at the Marymere Falls Trail junction. Immediately notice the change in tread, from superhighway to quiet byway. Amble alongside the creek in lush bottomlands punctuated with giant conifers. Climb a little on a steep hillside; then drop steeply to the river bottom 1 mile from falls trail junction. A bridge once spanned Barnes Creek at this point. It is now necessary to ford; easy in summer, potentially dangerous in winter.

Frosty morning at Barnes Creek

Once across the wilderness waterway the trail continues on an up-and-down course, hugging the creek shore then pulling away, all while traversing delightful maple groves and impressive stands of old-growth timber. At 1.5 miles from the falls trail junction cross a tributary creek on a log bridge; then descend back to Barnes Creek to some inviting gravel bars made for feet-soaking.

At 2 miles from the falls trail junction cross another tributary, returning yet again to Barnes Creek, this time among a set of soothing cascades. Find yourself a nice lunch spot or head up the trail another 0.25 mile through towering firs and hemlocks. Beyond, the trail merges with the Aurora Divide Trail and begins a brutal ascent of 3400 feet in 4.5 miles to Aurora Ridge. Opt for the foot soak instead.

EXTENDING YOUR TRIP

Upon your return to the trailhead, consider wandering on the 0.5-mile Moments in Time Nature Trail. It offers stunning views of Aurora Ridge and, across Lake Crescent, of Pyramid Mountain. Nice beaches are accessed along this trail, too, making it a wise option on a warm summer's day.

97 Pyramid Mountain

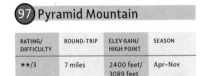

RATING/ DIFFICULTY	ROUND-TRIP	ELEV GAIN/ HIGH POINT	SEASON
★★/3	7 miles	2400 feet/ 3089 feet	Apr–Nov

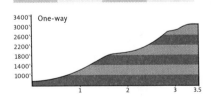

Maps: Green Trails Lake Crescent No. 101, Custom Correct Lake Crescent–Happy Lake Ridge; **Contact:** Olympic National Park, Wilderness Information Center, (360) 565-3100, www.nps.gov/olym; **Notes:** Dogs prohibited. Warning: A section midway along the trail is prone to landslides. While the tread is periodically restored, the area is exposed, potentially dangerous, and may be intimidating for some to cross; **GPS:** N 48 03.954, W 123 51.548

🏔 *Hike a prominent peak that hovers over the crystal-clear waters of Lake Crescent. A World War II enemy airplane spotter cabin still teeters on the precipitous summit. Trees have overtaken the wide views once afforded to lookout personnel, but nearby ledges still offer breathtaking glimpses straight down to the lake and out across to Mount Storm King. Graced with a microclimate of mild temperatures and moderate precipitation, the trail to Pyramid Mountain melts out early, providing peak-probing hiking in la primavera.*

GETTING THERE

From Port Angeles follow US 101 west for 27 miles to Fairholm on the western end of Lake Crescent (milepost 221). Turn right on Camp David Jr. Road (aka North Shore Road) and proceed for 3.2 miles to a small pullout adjacent to the North Shore Picnic Area. The trail begins on the opposite side of the road.

ON THE TRAIL

The hike to Pyramid Mountain is pretty straightforward. Locate the trail and head up the mountain! Immediately intersect the Olympic Discovery Trail, a long-distance rail trail that traverses the peninsula (see "Discover the Olympic Peninsula Trail," in this Lake Crescent section, and Hike 94). On an easy grade and through a dry forest of Doug-fir, salal, and madrona the trail contours along the western ridge of the mountain.

After a mile the forest grows more impressive, with big specimens now hovering

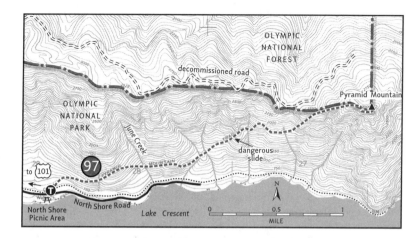

overhead. At 1.4 miles come to June Creek, your last water source if it's flowing at all. The grade now steepens, and the trail skirts a series of small slides. At 1.75 miles you'll approach a big landslide area (elev. 1900 ft). Scraped bare of vegetation, the slide is several hundred feet across and highly exposed. Trail tread is only a few inches wide in spots. Do not cross it if you are prone to vertigo or are the least bit uncomfortable. Instead, enjoy the limited views of Lake Crescent from this sunny spot. Those who do make the slide crossing will find no other obstacles along the way. Now in cool forest, the trail switchbacks and steadily climbs.

At 2.75 miles reach the ridge crest and the edge of an old clear-cut, compliments of the Forest Service. They couldn't even leave a buffer along the park boundary. In 3 miles the trail comes on a logging road. The Forest Service, perhaps making amends for its ridgetop logging disgrace, is currently converting the road into trail. A final 0.5-mile push up a steep hillside of old-growth conifers is all that's keeping you from the 3000-foot summit.

From the forested peak, scout out a ledge to peer 0.5 mile straight down to Lake Crescent. In the distance, Lake Sutherland and the

Lake Crescent as seen from Pyramid Mountain

Strait of Juan de Fuca can be seen. The old cabin was built in 1942 to spot enemy aircraft intent on reaching Puget Sound. It's one of only two that remain of the original thirteen that once sat on Olympic peaks during World War II. This hiker-historian would like to see it restored as a reminder and a memorial to our servicemen and women.

Sol Duc River Valley

No matter how you spell it, Sol Duc or Sole-duck, it still means "sparkling water," and has early Native inhabitants to thank for its name. One of the longest rivers in the Olympic Mountains, the Sol Duc drains some of its prettiest and most dramatic landscapes: dozens of alpine lakes, deep valleys of old growth, sprawling alpine meadows, rugged ridges and craggy peaks. Waterfalls, emerald pools, and even hot springs grace this majestic river.

Hiking opportunities in the Sol Duc Valley range from gentle to challenging and include some of the best ridge running in the Olympics. Overall the Sol Duc is an enchanting valley, its sparkling waters and stunning scenery soothing to both mind and soul.

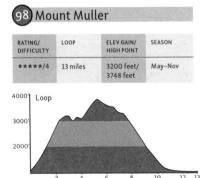

98 Mount Muller

RATING/ DIFFICULTY	LOOP	ELEV GAIN/ HIGH POINT	SEASON
★★★★★/4	13 miles	3200 feet/ 3748 feet	May–Nov

Maps: Green Trails Lake Crescent No. 101, Custom Correct Lake Crescent–Happy Lake Ridge; **Contact:** Olympic National Forest, Pa-

cific Ranger District, Forks, (360) 374-6522, *www.fs.fed.us/r6/olympic*; **Notes:** Northwest Forest Pass required; **GPS:** N 48 04.563, W 124 00.786

Roam for miles on a high ridge carpeted in a mosaic of brilliant wildflowers. Catch your breath not from climbing (although it's tough), but from watching a continuous reel of premiere showings starring glistening white Mount Olympus and deep-blue Lake Crescent. If that's not enough to slack your jaw, Mount Baker hovering over the Strait of Juan de Fuca will most certainly captivate you. Constructed in 1994, the Mount Muller Loop is one of the newest additions to our trail system and among the all-time supreme scenic high-country romps.

GETTING THERE

From Port Angeles follow US 101 west for 32 miles to an electricity substation at milepost 216, 4.5 miles beyond Fairholm. Turn right on Forest Road 3071 (signed "Mount Muller–Littleton Loop"), proceeding 0.3 mile to the trailhead. Privy available.

ON THE TRAIL

Back in 1975, Forest Service employee Molly Erickson was convinced that Mount Muller and Snider Ridge were the most beautiful places in the Forks Ranger District—and that someone should put a trail on them. Twenty years later, Erickson and a slew of her Forest Service compatriots did just that, designing and building over 20 miles of trail on the long northern ridge above the Sol Duc Valley.

These dedicated Forest Service workers not only built an amazing trail that delivers one stunning view after another; they named features along the way and dedicated meadows to each other, making hiking the loop a whole lot of fun. The trail is shared by equestrians and mountain bikers, but no need to worry

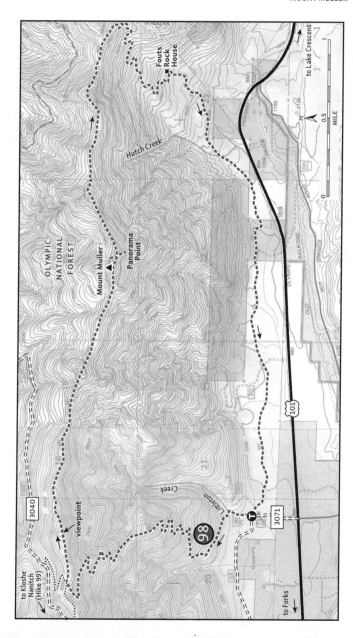

Amazing views of Lake Crescent and wildflowers along the Mount Muller Loop

about crowds. Your main concern should be carrying enough water—most of the way is bone dry.

Do the loop clockwise, tackling the steep climb early in the morning before the day heats up. Start in a dark damp glen housing Littleton Creek, your last sure water until Hutch Creek, 9 miles farther. The way starts off easy before reaching a series of switchbacks that climb 2000 feet in 2.5 miles. In early summer, twinflower lines the trail like rows of tiny street lights. As you climb you'll traverse acres of young forest interrupted by big charred stumps.

After 3 long uphill miles, crest the ridge (elev. 3200 ft). Here at Jim's Junction, a trail leads left 3.5 miles to Kloshe Nanitch (Hike 99), one goes straight 0.5 mile to FR 3040, and another goes right 2.5 miles to Mount Muller. Head right on an up-and-down ridgeline march across miles of meadows, drinking in panoramic perspectives of the U-shaped Sol Duc Valley.

After a short stroll through a stand of silver fir, come to a glorious viewpoint of the emerald wall, Aurora Ridge, and the massive snow and ice heap, Mount Olympus. Hikers not wishing to make the long loop may consider this point far enough. For those eating the whole enchilada, carry on. After climbing to 3400 feet in Millsap Meadow, the trail rapidly loses 400 feet, bottoming out in Thomas Gap before steeply regaining lost ground.

On an up-and-down course, pass through Millsap, Jasmine, Allison, and Markham Meadows. Marvel at their multitude of blossoming flowers: paintbrush, tiger lily, thistle, bleeding heart, vetch, star flower, hawkweed, daisy, bear grass, columbine, lupine, lace, strawberry, bunchberry, and queen's cup among them.

At 5.5 miles a side trail leads left for 0.1 mile to the semiforested 3748-foot summit of Mount Muller. Bag it. Now proceed on the main trail to another side path, this one leading right 0.1 mile to Panorama Point, a series of outcrops in a sea of meadows. If you think the view can't possibly get better, wait until you see Lake Crescent sparkling below. Like sentinels, Pyramid Mountain and Mount Storm King guard the pristine waters of the fjordlike lake.

After soaking up views and sunshine, continue up and down along the ridge crest, dashing behind ledges and undulating between forest and meadow. From Cahill's Overlook (at 7 miles), drop rapidly to Mosely Gap, a 2800-foot low point on the ridge. One last uphill struggle, and then begin a long descent back to the valley.

Take a break to check out Fouts Rock House, two giant boulders rubbing shoulders at 8.5 miles. A mile beyond, cross Hutch Creek, a good spot for refilling depleted water bottles. The final 3 miles are mostly uneventful, traversing forest on a mostly level route. Not very exciting after what you've experienced, but a necessary price to pay for this satisfying journey. At 12.8 miles (13 if you went up Muller) Littleton Creek's soft babble welcomes you back to the trailhead.

99 Kloshe Nanitch

RATING/ DIFFICULTY	ROUND-TRIP	ELEV GAIN/ HIGH POINT	SEASON
★★★/4	6.4 miles	2200 feet/ 3160 feet	Apr–Nov

Maps: USGS Snider Peak; **Contact:** Olympic National Forest, Pacific Ranger District, Forks, (360) 374-6522, www.fs.fed.us/r6/olympic; **GPS:** N 48 03.138, W 124 06.180

Teetering on an outcrop on Snider Ridge high above the glacially carved Sol Duc Valley is the Kloshe Nanitch lookout. A replica of the 1920s wooden cupola-like house that once graced this high ledge, it is every bit as graceful as the original. Chinook Jargon for "stand guard" or "stand watch," Kloshe Nanitch once served as a fire lookout in the early days of the

The author takes a closer look at the Kloshe Nanitch Lookout.

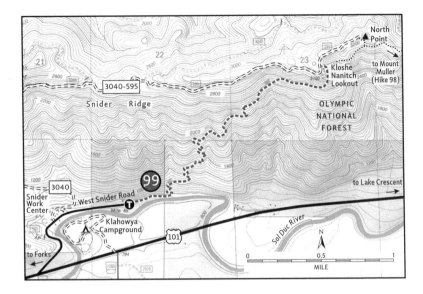

Olympic National Forest. But while fires are now patrolled by aircraft, thousands of acres of the rugged surroundings can still be spotted from this restored post.

GETTING THERE

From Port Angeles follow US 101 west for 37 miles to the Klohowya Campground. Proceed west for another 0.5 mile, turning right on West Snider Road (just past the Sol Duc River Bridge, signed "Snider Work Center"). In 0.4 mile come to the Forest Service work center and continue straight on the paved road. In 0.6 mile the road ends at the trailhead (unsigned as of 2006).

ON THE TRAIL

Your journey to this historic fire lookout begins appropriately enough on an abandoned section of US 101. Walk the old road, asphalt losing ground to moss and shrubbery, along a bend in the Sol Duc River. After 0.2 mile pass a deep swimming hole (remember it on your return) and come to a sign indicating the start of true trail.

Through second-growth fir forest carpeted with salal and pipsissewa, the trail steadily climbs, switchbacking up the south side of Snider Ridge. Cross several streams rushing down steep ravines, although by late summer most will be running dry. At about 2 miles the grade eases through a stand of hemlocks and then launches into some tight switchbacks (more like Z-backs) before approaching a small ledge offering a preview of the views lying ahead.

At 3 miles, after skirting beneath some cliffs, come to a junction (elev. 2980 ft). The trail right travels 3 miles along Snider Ridge to connect with the Mount Muller Loop (Hike 98). Head left, breaking out into a wildflower-studded meadow beneath the historic lookout. Make one last short and steep climb to arrive at the snow-white structure sitting on a ledge at the edge of the long ridge (elev. 3160 ft).

You may find that you have company. The lookout can also be reached via a series of rough Forest Service roads. More than likely, though, you'll have Kloshe Nanitch and its adjacent picnic grounds to yourself. Head over to the wrap-around balcony and *stand watch*. Scan the Sol Duc Valley from beginning to end, from craggy Mount Appleton and the snow-patched High Divide all the way to the Pacific. A blanket of clouds on the western horizon marks the coastline. On a clear day you can see James Island near La Push. That big jumble of snow- and glacier-covered mountain to the south is Olympus, of course.

EXTENDING YOUR TRIP

For a 1.5-mile loop, at the summit follow Forest Road 3040-595 for 0.4 mile north toward North Point. An unmarked but maintained trail then takes off right down the side of the ridge, connecting with the Snider Ridge Trail. Turn right, returning to the main trail after skirting above a series of cliffs. Consider staying at the nearby Klahowya Campground, one of the loveliest car camps on the Peninsula. Be sure to hike the 0.5-mile Pioneer Path while you're there.

100 North Fork Sol Duc River

RATING/ DIFFICULTY	ROUND-TRIP	ELEV GAIN/ HIGH POINT	SEASON
★★★/3	12.4 miles	1200 feet/ 2400 feet	Mar–Dec

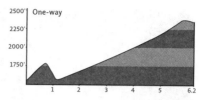

Maps: Green Trails Seven Lakes Basin–Mt Olympus Climbing No. 133S, Custom Correct Lake Crescent–Happy Lake Ridge; **Contact:** Olympic National Park, Wilderness Information Center, (360) 565-3100, *www.nps.gov /olym*; **Notes:** Dogs prohibited. National park entry fee required. As of summer 2006, the washed-out bridge over the North Fork Sol Duc has not been replaced, requiring a ford (easy in late summer, dangerous in spring); **GPS:** N 48 00.645, W 123 54.660

The Sol Duc River may be a happening place with its hot springs resort, riverside campgrounds, and miles of popular trails, but not so for the North Fork. Here you're likely to run into only elk and deer. Is the trail rough? Hardly. It's one of the most enjoyable riverside trails on the peninsula. It's just that it really doesn't go anywhere—no peak, no lake. And in today's goal-oriented society, these types of

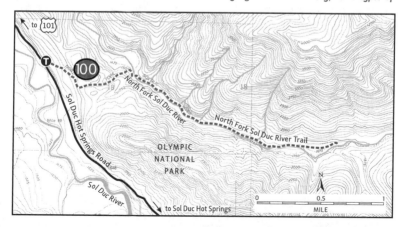

North Fork of the Sol Duc River

trails are overlooked. But if it's miles of solitude you're seeking, and peace of mind that only wilderness can instill, this is your trail.

GETTING THERE

From Port Angeles follow US 101 west for 29 miles, passing Lake Crescent. About 2 miles beyond the Fairholm store, turn left onto the Sol Duc Hot Springs Road. (From Forks head east 28 miles on US 101, and turn right just past milepost 219.) Follow this road for 8.2 miles (passing the park entrance booth). Parking is on the right side of the road, and the trail begins on the opposite side of the road.

ON THE TRAIL

The trail starts from an overlook above the Sol Duc. The North Fork is nowhere to be found.

It's hidden behind a small ridge, the only real climb you'll be doing on this hike. Start by heading up that obstacle through a forest of hemlock interspersed with a few big Doug-firs. Leave the roar of the Sol Duc behind, soon supplanted by the songs of thrushes and wrens. After a climb of about 350 feet start descending, losing all elevation gained. At 1 mile behold the North Fork Sol Duc in all of its wild glory.

If the bridge is still out and you decide to ford the river, choose a spot about 1000 feet downstream where the river fans out and the current is moderate. Once on the other side, look forward to miles of riverside roaming. At 1.25 miles cross a careening tributary. Through mossy maple glades, under towering conifers, and along basalt ledges lapped by the river, this trail is a true delight.

At about 2 miles pass some large Sitka spruce trees that might make you feel like you're in one of the coastal rain forests. A few grassy openings are traversed along the way, and chances are always good for spotting big game in these clearings. At 3 miles you'll come to a riverside campsite, perfect for snacking or calling it quits if you prefer a shorter hike.

If wanderlust persists, carry on. After passing a few big mossy boulders, the trail moves away from the riverbank, climbing above it on a steep slope. The river can now be heard crashing through a canyon, while you traverse a stately forest of Doug-firs. As you hike deeper into the lonely valley, numerous side creeks need to be crossed, and a few may leave your boots a tad bit wet.

At 6.2 miles the trail drops back down to the river in a dark and cool ravine. You can ford it and continue, but most day hikers will be content turning around here. Recall some of your favorite spots on the hike in, they'll be your rest stops on the way out.

101 Sol Duc Falls

RATING/ DIFFICULTY	LOOP	ELEV GAIN/ HIGH POINT	SEASON
★★/1	5.3 miles	400 feet/ 2000 feet	Mar–Nov

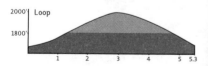

Maps: Green Trails Seven Lakes Basin–Mt Olympus Climbing No. 133S, Custom Correct Seven Lakes Basin–Hoh; **Contact:** Olympic National Park, Wilderness Information Center, (360) 565-3100, www.nps.gov/olym; **Notes:** Dogs prohibited. National park entry fee required; **GPS:** N 47 58.200, W 123 51.763

An easy loop from the Sol Duc Hot Springs Resort, perfect for early or late-season hiking. Ramble beneath towering old trees to a misty, mossy ravine that the Sol Duc River careens into. Watch determined dippers hunt for insects in the splash zone. Return along the pristine river until the fetid smell of sulfur signals you've arrived back at the springs.

GETTING THERE

From Port Angeles follow US 101 west for 29 miles, passing Lake Crescent. About 2 miles beyond the Fairholm store, turn left onto the Sol Duc Hot Springs Road. (From Forks head

Sol Duc Falls

east 28 miles on US 101, and turn right just past milepost 219.) Follow this road for 12 miles (passing the park entrance booth). Just past the Eagle Ranger Station turn right into the Sol Duc Hot Springs Resort. Parking is located to the far right (west) of the main lodge.

ON THE TRAIL

This is a social hike from the hot springs resort through campgrounds and finally to the falls. Start by walking over the Sol Duc River Bridge, locating the trail on the northeast corner. Closely following the river, the trail first travels through the resort's RV park before emerging in the lower loop of the Sol Duc Campground after 0.4 mile.

Follow the campground loop road a short distance, picking up the trail and following it to the upper loop of the campground. Once again, walk a short distance on pavement to pick up the trail. Then through big timber, saunter 1.3 pleasant and peaceful miles to a junction. The trail left leads 0.25 mile to a large parking lot—the reason for the hordes of people you'll now be encountering.

On a well-trodden path continue for a nearly level 0.5 mile to a Civilian Conservation Corps–built shelter where the thundering sound of swiftly moving water barreling over a ledge announces that you've reached the falls. The best views are from the mist-sprayed bridge—quite inviting on a warm summer's day. The Sol Duc fans into two, crashing 50 feet into a narrow chasm where the sun rarely shines.

After enjoying the spectacle, cross the bridge and climb a small bluff to a junction.

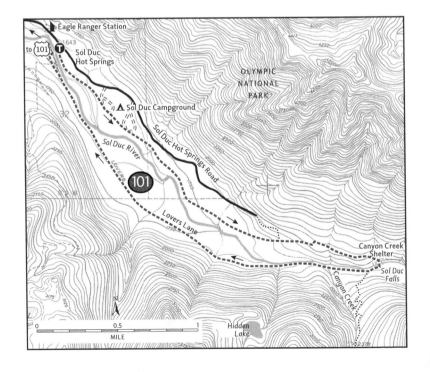

Hang a right onto the Lovers Lane Trail, although it's open to all, lovelorn, loveless, and loved alike. In a short distance cross Canyon Creek, which drains Deer Lake high above. Follow the peaceful path through lush bottomlands, crossing a couple more crashing tributaries before arriving back at the resort at 2.8 miles from the falls. Your nose will tell you when you're close.

EXTENDING YOUR TRIP

The campground and resort you've hiked through make great bases for exploring this and other area trails. Beyond the falls, the Sol Duc Trail travels through deep primeval forest for almost 5 miles, gaining only 1000 feet in elevation. From there it's off to the high country.

102 Mink Lake and Little Divide

Mink Lake

RATING/ DIFFICULTY	ROUND-TRIP	ELEV GAIN/ HIGH POINT	SEASON
★★/2	5 miles	1500 feet/ 3120 feet	May–Oct

Little Divide

RATING/ DIFFICULTY	ROUND-TRIP	ELEV GAIN/ HIGH POINT	SEASON
★★★/4	8.6 miles	2500 feet/ 4100 feet	Late June– mid-Oct

Early morning reflections on Mink Lake

Maps: Green Trails Seven Lakes Basin–Mt Olympus Climbing No. 133S, Custom Correct Seven Lakes Basin–Hoh; **Contact:** Olympic National Park, Wilderness Information Center, (360) 565-3100, *www.nps.gov/olym*; **Notes:** Dogs prohibited. National park entry fee required; **GPS:** N 47 58.159, W 123 51.849

Leisurely hike to a quiet backcountry lake ringed with grassy meadows and big trees, or break a sweat to the Little Divide, the loneliest outpost in the Sol Duc country. Lacking the panoramic vistas that the High Divide is notorious for, Little Divide trades views for solitude. You're far more likely to encounter deer, elk, and bear than fellow hikers in this neck of the Sol Duc.

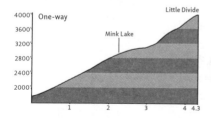

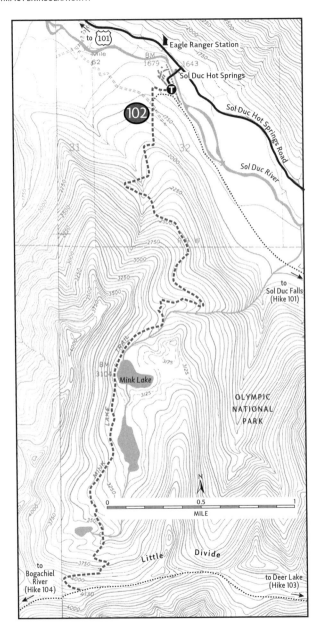

GETTING THERE

From Port Angeles follow US 101 west for 29 miles, passing Lake Crescent. About 2 miles beyond the Fairholm store, turn left onto the Sol Duc Hot Springs Road. (From Forks head east 28 miles on US 101, and turn right just past milepost 219.) Follow this road for 12 miles (passing the park entrance booth). Just past the Eagle Ranger Station turn right into the Sol Duc Hot Springs Resort. The trailhead and parking are located to the far right (west) of the main resort building.

ON THE TRAIL

Mink Lake: Start in cool, dank second-growth timber, bearing right at a junction. The trail left leads 2.8 easy miles to Sol Duc Falls. The way to Mink Lake heads off first on old road, then on good tread, entering mature woods in 0.5 mile. Winding above the Sol Duc Valley, the trail rounds a knoll and then tags along Mink Creek as it weasels its way to its source in 2.5 miles. A side trail leads left to campsites and lunch spots on the lake's grassy and sunny southern shore. Darting dragonflies provide captivating air shows.

Little Divide: If not content sitting by this placid body of water, cinch up your pack and hit the trail once again. On much lighter tread make your way toward Little Divide. In a short distance, pass another quiet grassy-shored lake, this one partially hidden in thick woods. One mile beyond Mink Lake the forest thins, revealing a tiny pool off to the right surrounded by heather.

Leaving the Mink Creek drainage, the climb steepens. Look back for a nice view of Mink Lake; Aurora Ridge is off in the distance. Now through heather and huckleberry, the trail attains Little Divide (elev. 4100 feet) at a junction with the Bogachiel River Trail. Amble a short distance left on a hogback ridge shrouded in ancient forest for glimpses and peeks down to the emerald Bogachiel Valley and out to snowy Mount Olympus. The views aren't grand, but the solitude and serenity are.

EXTENDING YOUR TRIP

Continue following the Bogachiel Trail east on an up-and-down, at times steep journey across the Little Divide to Deer Lake. Pass lonely meadows and tarns along the way. Follow the Deer Lake Trail to the Lovers Lane Trail back to your start for a 13.6-mile round trip.

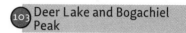

103 Deer Lake and Bogachiel Peak

Deer Lake

RATING/ DIFFICULTY	ROUND-TRIP	ELEV GAIN/ HIGH POINT	SEASON
★★/3	7.5 miles	1600 feet/ 3550 feet	June– mid-Oct

Bogachiel Peak

RATING/ DIFFICULTY	ROUND-TRIP	ELEV GAIN/ HIGH POINT	SEASON
★★★★★/5	16 miles	3450 feet/ 5474 feet	mid-July– Oct

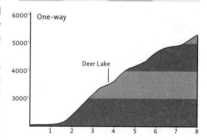

Maps: Green Trails Seven Lakes Basin–Mt Olympus Climbing No. 133S, Custom Correct Seven Lakes Basin–Hoh; **Contact:** Olympic National Park, Wilderness Information Center, (360) 565-3100, www.nps.gov/olym; **Notes:** Dogs prohibited. National park entry fee required; **GPS:** N 47 57.310, W 123 50.103

A moderately difficult hike to a large subalpine lake frequented by many of its namesake critters or an all-day challenging grunt to perhaps the most beautiful viewpoint in the Olympics. This is the famed High Divide

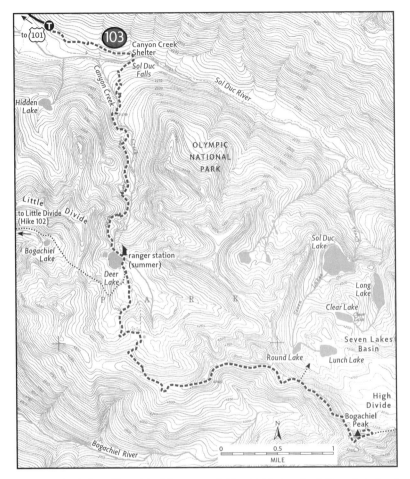

country, a land of sparkling alpine lakes, re-splendent alpine meadows, and awe-inspiring alpine views. Usually reserved for backpackers with time to explore, strong and tenacious day hikers can get a small taste.

GETTING THERE

From Port Angeles follow US 101 west for 29 miles, passing Lake Crescent. About 2 miles beyond the Fairholm store, turn left onto the Sol Duc Hot Springs Road. (From Forks head east 28 miles on US 101, and turn right just past milepost 219.) Follow this road for 14 miles (passing the park entrance booth) to its end at a large trailhead parking lot. Privy available.

ON THE TRAIL

Deer Lake: The hike to both Deer Lake and Bogachiel Peak starts off easy enough on a 0.8-mile nearly level sojourn through spectacular

A hiker descends Bogachiel Peak—Mt Olympus in background.

old growth to pretty Sol Duc Falls. Then the party's over and it's time to work. Cross the Sol Duc, pass the Lovers Lane Trail, and commence to climb. On a steep, sometimes rocky path work your way up the dark ravine housing Canyon Creek. At 1.5 miles, cross high above the tumbling waterway on a wide and sturdy bridge. After another 0.5 mile the grade eases somewhat.

After another push, cross Canyon Creek once more, this time at the outlet to Deer Lake (elev. 3550 feet). Nestled in a forested and grassy bowl, the lake's waters reflect a soft green. Surrounded by yellow cedar, mountain hemlock, silver fir, and a thick understory of huckleberries, it's a pretty and serene spot. Deer often browse along the lakeshore and it's not uncommon to see them in the shallow lake as well.

A backcountry ranger station and multiple campsites can also be found at the lake. A rough path circles the lake and reveals a smaller hidden "fawn" lake. Call it a day here or carry on to higher ground.

Bogachiel Peak: For Bogachiel Peak, continue past the lake, bear left at a junction, and climb to more-open country. Winding through heather fields, subalpine forest, and by a dozen pothole tarns (a.k.a. mosquito incubators), the trail works it way up to the high ridge dividing the Sol Duc and Bogachiel watersheds. Alternating between groves of mountain hemlock and open meadows, the trail continues to climb. Far-reaching views across rainforest valleys all the way to the Pacific can now be had.

Look for what guidebook writer Robert Wood called the snake pit. It's a cluster of contorted mountain hemlocks resembling a serpentine lair. The trail soon rounds the ridge crest, working its way around a high isolated basin, headwaters of the Bogachiel River. Mount Olympus peeks its icy head over the next ridge, and Bogachiel Peak—still a ways away—beckons. In September, bugling elk from down below can often be heard. And it's not rare to run into berry-munching bears, so be aware.

Drop into a big rocky depression where a trail descends to Seven Lakes Basin, one of the prettiest spots this side of Shangri-la. Next, on steep open slopes, angle around Bogachiel Basin. Snow often persists well into summer here, making it potentially dangerous to proceed. After a series of tight switchbacks, reach the ridge crest (elev. 5100 feet). Bogachiel Peak is reached via a short side trail a short distance left on the High Divide Trail.

While you clamber to bag the 5474-foot former lookout site, no doubt the incredible views by this time will have bowled you over. They are beyond breathtaking. The alpine jewels of the Seven Lakes Basin shimmer below. The snow-capped Bailey Range marches off into the eastern horizon. The emerald swath of the Hoh rain forest spreads out nearly 1 vertical mile below. And rising above it all, staring you right in the face, is Mount Olympus. Its glaciers and snowfields are blinding on a sunny summer day.

It doesn't get any more spectacular than this. It was on Bogachiel Peak in September 1989 when I first fell in love with the Olympics. How could I not?

Opposite: Crashing cascade on the Big Creek Trail

The Rain Forests

One of the Olympic Peninsula's most famous attractions, the temperate rain forest offers one of the most unique hiking experiences in the country. Such forests are found only in Chile, New Zealand, and the Pacific Northwest, and those of the Olympic National Park are perhaps the most accessible. Good trails lead to and through all of the major rain forest valleys.

Here you'll hike among some of the largest living organisms in the world. While tropical rain forests rank supreme in biodiversity (number of species), the temperate rain forests of the Olympic Peninsula contain the highest amount of biomass (living matter) on the planet. Giant conifers cloaked in epiphytes and growing upwards of 300 feet dominate a saturated forest floor shrouded in mosses, ferns, horsetails, and ground pines. The damp, heavy air of the rain forest teems with spores. Hike into this special environment and you can feel the forest breathe. Sense its pulse. Grasp its fortitude.

And while parts of this region can receive over 200 inches of rainfall a year, it's not unusual to be kissed by the sun while hiking deep into the Olympic rain forest. Days are often dry in August and September—the dry season—and it's not uncommon to get a reprieve from the rain in the middle of the winter. Pack sunglasses with your poncho and waterproof those boots; there are miles of trails to be explored in this fascinating bioregion.

104 **Bogachiel River**

RATING/ DIFFICULTY	ROUND-TRIP	ELEV GAIN/ HIGH POINT	SEASON
★★★/3	12 miles	400 feet/ 500 feet	Year-round

500' One-way
400'
300'
    1   2   3   4   5   6

Maps: Green Trails Spruce Mountain No. 132, Custom Correct Bogachiel Valley; **Contact:** Olympic National Park, Wilderness Information Center, (360) 565-3100, *www.nps.gov /olym*; **Notes:** Dogs prohibited at national park boundary (at 1.5 miles); **GPS:** N 47 52.933, W 124 16.503

The Bogachiel River snakes through Washington's forgotten rain forest. No main roads run along this major Olympic river, nor penetrate its wild valley. There are no visitors centers here either. No interpretive trails or developed campgrounds amid the towering spruce and fir. There's nothing fancy here at all—just a quiet backcountry trail through pure rainforest wilderness.

GETTING THERE

From Forks travel south for 5 miles on US 101. Turn left (east) onto Undie Road, located directly across from the entrance to Bogachiel State Park. Follow this road for 5.6 miles to a gate and the trailhead (the last 2 miles are unpaved and during heavy periods of rain are prone to flooding and developing giant mud holes).

ON THE TRAIL

Your first impression of the Bogachiel River Trail may have you wondering, "I thought this was a wilderness trail through old-growth rain forest." It is—just give it a couple of miles. The trail begins in a dark forest of second growth. It was logged during the 1940s in the name of national defense.

Descend on a muddy track to Morganroth Creek. During the rainy season (most of the year) expect to get your feet wet crossing it. A small interpretive path leads left to a marshy area. The Forest Service has plans to extend this trail into a small loop. The main trail continues right, intersecting then utilizing an old road bed for some level and easy strolling.

At 1.5 miles come to the national park

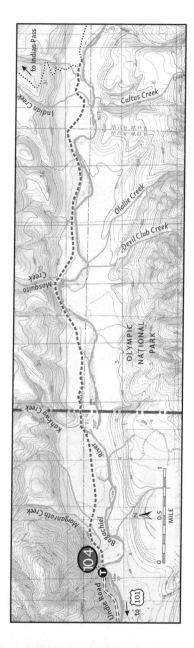

Giant Sitka spruce along the Bogachiel River

boundary. Pooches are not permitted beyond this point. Along rich bottomlands the trail brushes up against the river. At 2.5 miles negotiate a steep bluff (with the help of a rope) to skirt an area claimed by the river. Drop back down to river level and get your feet wet again hopping across Mosquito Creek. Big trees finally appear (I told you it gets better). Despite light use, the trail is in remarkable shape, thanks in large part to the tireless work of the Washington Trails Association. But while only a handful of hikers trek up this valley each year, the elk that pass through are legion. Keep your eyes out for these elegant beasties.

Ancient giants dwarf you as you continue up the trail. Except for the river's soothing churn and sweet serenades from resident wrens, the primeval forest is quiet. Lichens drape overhead. Fern boughs burst open from the forest floor. Dew-dripping moss clings to everything. Only the glaucous sheen of alder bark breaks the deep green of the rain forest.

After 6 miles of peaceful passage, you'll come to a junction with the Rugged Ridge Trail and a most inviting riverside camping area. This is a good spot to turn around, or if inclined, spend the night. During low water flows, venture out onto the gravel banks of the river. During downpours admire the torrents from the elevated embankment.

EXTENDING YOUR TRIP

The Bogachiel River Trail continues deep into the Olympic backcountry for 18 more miles. Wander up the Rugged Ridge Trail to Indian Pass for some real solitude. Car-camp at Bogachiel State Park for a cushy night in the rain forest. Don't forget the tarps!

prohibited. National park entry fee required; **GPS:** N 47 51.580, W 123 56.023

The most famous of all the Olympic rain forests, the Hoh is one of the busiest places in Olympic National Park. A visitors center and a couple of well-groomed nature trails attract bus loads of admirers from Seattle to Seoul, Boston to Berlin. And its not just camera-toting tourists that invade this valley; pan-toting backpackers and caribiner-clanking climbers flock here too. The Hoh River Trail also provides access to Mount Olympus and the High Divide. But who can blame all of these people for coming here? The Hoh rain forest truly is one of the world's most spectacular places.

GETTING THERE

From Forks travel south on US 101 for 12 miles to the Upper Hoh Road. (From Kalaloch head north on US 101 for 20 miles.) Head left (east) on the Upper Hoh Road for 18 miles to its end at a large parking lot, visitors center, and trailhead. Water and restrooms available.

ON THE TRAIL

While the Hoh rain forest is a busy place, most hikers visit during the summer months and on autumn weekends. Come in the spring or even winter and experience a valley more sedate. Besides, with fewer people in the off-season, chances are good of witnessing members of the resident elk herd. But even if you end up hitting the trail on a busy day, the crowds thin out dramatically after only a couple of miles.

The hike to Five Mile Island is far enough to experience the old-growth grandeur and pure wildness of this valley, yet close enough that it can be done by most hikers, young and old. The trail is impeccably groomed, and the way virtually level, with minimal elevation change. Five Mile Island, with its wide grassy banks along the mighty rainforest river, was

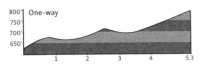

105 Hoh River–Five Mile Island

RATING/DIFFICULTY	ROUND-TRIP	ELEV GAIN/HIGH POINT	SEASON
★★★★/2	10.6 miles	300 feet/800 feet	Year-round

Maps: Green Trails Seven Lakes Basin–Mt Olympus Climbing No. 133S, Custom Correct Seven Lakes Basin–Hoh; **Contact:** Olympic National Park, Wilderness Information Center, (360) 565-3100, *www.nps.gov/olym*; **Notes:** Dogs

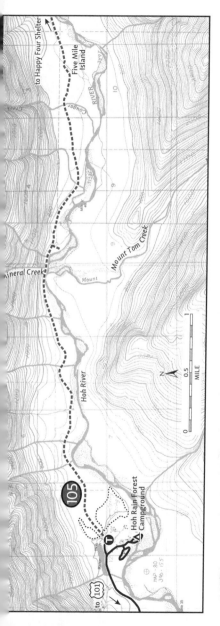

designed for whiling the afternoon away.

Start by following the paved Hall of Mosses Trail for 0.2 mile to a junction. Now on bona fide tread begin your journey through this valley of primeval forest. A cacophony of birdsong from wrens, nuthatches, woodpeckers, chickadees, and thrushes can be heard over the distant hum of the river. Pass by colonnades of spruce and under awnings of moss-cloaked maples. Licorice ferns and club mosses cling to overhanging trees like holiday decorations on New York's Fifth Avenue. And while the surroundings are lush, the understory is fairly open. Browsing elk keep the shrubs and bushes well trimmed.

Hoh rain forest

In 1 mile get your first unobstructed view of the river. Gaze out to the High Divide and snow-capped Mount Tom, a peak on the Olympus massif. Pass the Mount Tom Creek Campsite at 2.3 miles; then climb above the river, catching glimpses of deep emerald pools below. Cross Mineral Creek by a lovely cascade. Five minutes later another cascade delights. At 2.9 miles come to a junction with the Mount Tom Trail. If you'd like, follow this path right 0.25 mile to open gravel bars and spectacular valley views.

Veering away from the river, the main path continues. Traverse impressive stands of Sitka spruce and at 4 miles come to the Cougar Creek cedar grove. Stand in awe beneath these trees, older than the great cathedrals of Europe—and just as inspiring. At 5.3 miles arrive at Five Mile Island. Formed by river channels, the island is an inviting grassy bottomland graced with maple glades. Sit by the churning river and enjoy views up the valley all the way to Bogachiel Peak. If it's raining, the nearby Happy Four Shelter (0.5 mile farther) will provide cover for your lunchtime break.

EXTENDING YOUR TRIP

The Hoh Campground at the trailhead is a delightful place to spend the night. By all means check out the two adjacent nature trails and the visitors center to gain a better appreciation of this fascinating corner of the planet.

A hiker heads out onto the gravel bars of the Big Flat on the South Fork of the Hoh.

Maps: Green Trails Mt Tom No. 133, Custom Correct Mount Olympus Climber's Map; **Contact:** Olympic National Park, Wilderness Information Center, (360) 565-3100, *www.nps .gov/olym*; **Notes:** Dogs prohibited; **GPS:** N 47 47.957, W 123 57.267

Hikers from around the globe find their way to the Hoh rain forest. After all, it is world famous. But if your idea of experiencing the Olympic rain forest is sans bucketloads of people, cast your attention to the Hoh's little known South Fork. Local fly fishermen are familiar with this wild and lonely valley, but most hikers aren't. Getting to the trailhead can be confusing, but the

106 South Fork Hoh River– Big Flat

RATING/ DIFFICULTY	ROUND-TRIP	ELEV GAIN/ HIGH POINT	SEASON
★★★/1	6 miles	200 feet/ 800 feet	Year-round

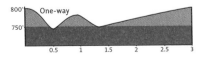

hike is easy and not very long. The payoff is solitude.

GETTING THERE

From Forks travel south on US 101 for 14.5 miles. Drive 2 miles beyond the Hoh River Bridge and turn left onto the Clearwater Road at milepost 176 (signed "Clearwater–Hoh State Forest"). Proceed on this paved road for 6.9 miles to a junction. Turn left onto Owl Creek Road (signed for the South Fork Hoh Trail and campground). In 2.3 miles bear right onto Maple Creek Road, following signs for the campground. After 5.4 miles cross the South Fork Hoh River and pass the campground entrance. Continue for another 2.3 miles, bearing right at an unmarked junction. In 0.5 mile the road ends at the trailhead (unsigned as of spring 2006).

ON THE TRAIL

The trail starts in Washington State Department of Natural Resources (DNR) land that has been intensively logged over the decades. Through scrappy trees choked in mosses, drop down to a flat outwash area. Cross nu-

merous streams in various stages of flow and after 0.5 mile reach the national park boundary. Now we're talking trees—real old trees, real big trees.

Pass a monstrous Sitka spruce recently laid to rest by a winter storm. Climb onto a bench, pause and look around in bewilderment. Do you feel small? Gargantuan Doug-firs, western hemlock, and Sitka spruce tower above you like skyscrapers in an ecotopian Manhattan. At 1 mile you'll come to a crashing creek that may prove tricky to cross after a heavy rain.

Continuing under a canopy of ancient giants, the trail drops to a lush bottomland known as Big Flat. At 1.3 miles you'll come to a backcountry campground. A side path diverts right, leading to open gravel banks on the South Fork Hoh. The main trail continues left through grassy swales and alongside colonnades of maples. At 2.25 miles, past more impressive spruce trees, the trail finally greets the river.

Soon a large washout is encountered, but the trail has been rerouted around it. Cross a lazy side creek on a sturdy log. Ten minutes beyond, about 3 miles from your start, the

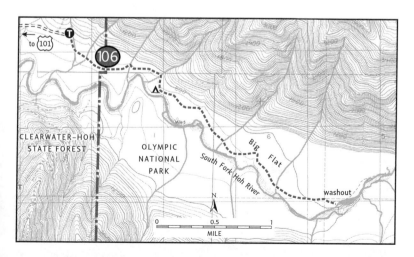

trail abruptly ends. The South Fork in one of its winter huffs lopped off a huge part of its bank, taking a good piece of trail with it. More tread can be picked up farther upstream, but some difficult bushwhacking is required to get to it. Instead, plop down on the nice grassy bank before you and let the solitude serenade you.

EXTENDING YOUR TRIP

The DNR South Fork Hoh River Campground located downstream from the trailhead has a handful of inviting sites right on the river.

Maps: Green Trails Kloochman Rock No. 165, Custom Correct Queets Valley; **Contact:** Olympic National Park, Wilderness Information Center, (360) 565-3100, *www.nps.gov /olym*; **Notes:** Dogs prohibited. Queets River ford required, only safe during low flows. As of 2006 the Queets River Road is closed at milepost 8 due to a washout; **GPS:** N 47 37.469, W 124 00.856

Big trees, a wilderness valley flourishing with wildlife, and no crowds. The peninsula's wildest rainforest valleys are up the Queets River, and many a hiker has never ventured into this enchanting corner of Olympic

107 Queets River

RATING/ DIFFICULTY	ROUND-TRIP	ELEV GAIN/ HIGH POINT	SEASON
★★★★/4	10 miles	200 feet/ 425 feet	Late July– Sept

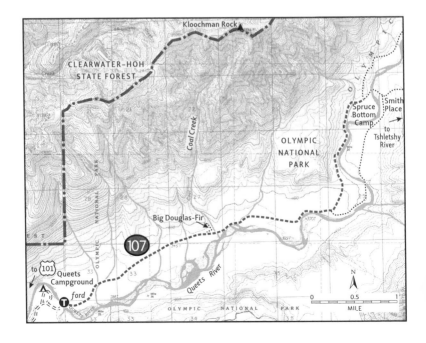

National Park. The main deterrent is accessibility, both to and on the trail. The gravel 14-mile Queets River Road can often be agonizing to drive. And once you reach the trailhead, you'll find there's no bridge over the river! This keeps more than a handful of adventurers from ambling up the trail. But if you persist you're guaranteed a lonesome journey.

GETTING THERE

From Hoquiam travel north on US 101 for 57 miles. (From Forks travel south on US 101 for 45 miles.) Just after milepost 144 turn right (east) onto the gravel Queets River Road. Proceed on this road for 13.8 miles to its end and the trailhead. Privy available.

ON THE TRAIL

From the trailhead kiosk look down the steep riverbank to see what lies ahead: the Sams River rushing into the Queets. Both need to be forded if you're intent on exploring this wild valley. The crossing can be intimidating, but in the drier months of August and September the rivers are usually only knee-deep. A set of old running shoes and sturdy trekking poles should help get you across safely. Do not attempt to cross early in the season or after heavy periods of rain. Remember, too, that on hot days the water will be higher on your return due to the melting snow feeding the river. If it looks unfavorable, head over to the Sams River Trail instead (Hike 108).

Once you've crossed the wide river, you'll get to experience a wilderness Olympic valley the way it should be experienced—crowds in absentia. Giant firs, towering spruce, and humongous hemlocks 200-plus feet tall and several hundred years old humble your stature and status. Moss-draped maples and lichen-blotched alders line the trail. Boughs of ferns 4 feet tall crowd the understory.

Although the Queets is in essence a wilderness, it has experienced man's presence for

The hike begins with a ford of the Queets River.

centuries. Native Americans long hunted this remote valley. A few hardy pioneers homesteaded it. At 1.6 miles a dilapidated barn is evidence of the latter's tenure.

From this small clearing, Kloochman Rock can also be seen peeking above the remote valley. At 2.3 miles a short side trail leads left 0.25 mile to one of the biggest and oldest Douglas-firs in the world. With a trunk 14 feet around, this tree began its life sometime around the first millennium.

Through lush bottomlands the Queets River Trail heads deeper into the heart of the Olympic Mountains. At 4 miles a side trail leads right (requiring a ford) 2 miles to Smith Place, the remains of an old hunting cabin.

The main trail continues left, arriving at Spruce Bottom Camp at 5 miles. The bottomlands and gravel bars here make a nice destination for day hikers. Sit and enjoy the solitude and quiet, interrupted only by the soft rippling of the river and the frantic chirping of passing dippers.

EXTENDING YOUR TRIP

A short distance beyond Spruce Bottom, a side trail leads right, fording the Queets to reach Smith Place. Continue on the old trail for 1 mile to the truly remote rainforest river, the Tshletshy. Backtrack to Smith Place and return to the main trail via the primitive trail following the Queets's east bank (this route requires a ford). The main Queets River Trail can also be followed upriver for another 10 miles, where it peters out near Pelton Creek.

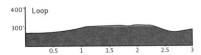

108 Sams River

RATING/ DIFFICULTY	LOOP	ELEV GAIN/ HIGH POINT	SEASON
★★★/1	3 miles	50 feet/ 300 feet	Year-round

400' Loop
300'
0.5 1 1.5 2 2.5 3

Maps: Custom Correct Queets Valley; **Contact:** Olympic National Park, Wilderness Information Center, (360) 565-3100, *www.nps.gov /olym*; **Notes:** Dogs prohibited. As of 2006 the Queets River Road is closed at milepost 8 due to a washout; **GPS:** N 47 36.985, W 124 01.924

Enjoy an easy loop in the Queets River valley without having to ford the river. Saunter along an open bank

above the wild Queets, hike under some of the largest spruce trees in the park, and look for resident elk while traversing old homestead farms. The Sams River Loop is ideal for introducing children to the rain forest. Unlike nature trails at the Quinault and Hoh, you'll have this entire living classroom for yourselves.

GETTING THERE

From Hoquiam travel north on US 101 for 57 miles. (From Forks travel south on US 101 for 45 miles.) Just after milepost 144 turn right (east) onto the gravel Queets River Road. Proceed on this road for 12.5 miles to the Queets Ranger Station. Park here. The trail begins across the road.

ON THE TRAIL

On soft tread frilled with mosses and oxalis, the trail begins its journey across a lush bottomland. This section of trail is often wet and muddy. Pass by wetland pools teeming with crooning frogs. At 0.3 mile come to a collapsed bridge at a channeled creek. Crossing is possible on a nearby fallen tree, but use caution.

Just beyond the creek is the first of several homestead clearings. Blackberry bushes and apple trees are all that remain. Between the melodic chirps of feasting birds, listen to the voices in the wind speak of the hardships and joys of living in the rain forest. Pick up tread again across the meadow in a grove of mossy maples.

A large outwash area is encountered in 1 mile. You may have to do some creek-channel hopping. Soon, the trail comes upon the churning Sams River. Take time to walk out on its wide gravel bars. Enjoy views of Kloochman Rock and surrounding ridges cloaked in deep greenery. Look for elk track etched into the sand.

Now climb a small bluff flanked with giant

Opposite: The Sams River flows into the Queets.

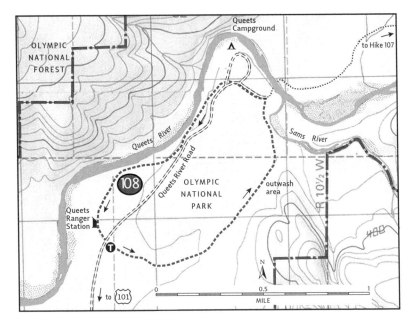

spruces that reach straight for the clouds. At 1.5 mile you'll come to the Queets River Road and the trailhead for the Queets River Trail. Turn left on the road, pass the campground entrance, and pick up the Sams River Loop once again.

This half of the loop spends most of its time high on a bluff along the Queets. Scan the lofty conifers that embrace the river for perched eagles and kingfishers. Inspect trailside snags for industrious woodpeckers. Listen for owl hoots coming from the dark forest.

Continue along the river to another large homestead clearing. Elk evidence is everywhere, from droppings and tracks to flattened clumps of grass. Accessible gravel bars along the river, perfect for lounging and feet-soaking, can be found at the clearing's edge. The trail continues through a stately maple glade, delivering you back to the ranger station at 3 miles.

EXTENDING YOUR TRIP

The primitive and quiet car campground at the end of the Queets River Road makes for a cushy night out in this wild rainforest valley. Bring your own water, or filter from the river.

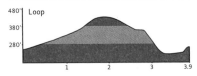

109 Quinault National Recreation Trails

RATING/ DIFFICULTY	LOOP	ELEV GAIN/ HIGH POINT	SEASON
★★★/2	3.9 miles	300 feet/ 450 feet	Year-round

Maps: Green Trails Lake Quinault No. 197, Custom Correct Quinault–Colonel Bob; **Contact:** Olympic National Forest, Pacific Ranger

District, Quinault, (360) 288-2525, *www.fs.fed
.us/r6/olympic*; **Notes:** Northwest Forest Pass
required. Dogs should be leashed; **GPS:** N 47
27.594, W 123 51.728

*The Quinault National Recreation
Trail system offers a mélange of hiking options to choose from. With nearly 10
miles of well-maintained interconnecting
trails, your choices are as varied as spring
wildflowers on these popular paths. Trails
lead from campgrounds and a historic lodge
to waterfalls, cedar bogs, monster trees,
and along crystal-clear creeks and a scenic
lakeshore. Spend a half day or half a week
exploring this delightful area. The Rainforest Lake Loop is one suggestion. Feel free to
expand, contract, or combine it with other
trails.*

GETTING THERE

From Hoquiam travel north on US 101 for 35
miles. Turn right (east) onto the South Shore
Road, located 1 mile south of Amanda Park.
Proceed on this road for 1.3 miles to a large
parking area signed "Rainforest Nature Trail
Loop." Water and restrooms available.

ON THE TRAIL

Step into the Quinault rain forest and immediately be propelled into a world of primeval
beauty. Start your journey under a canopy of
towering, emerald giants: ancient Sitka spruce,
western red cedar, and western hemlocks that
were mere saplings when Christopher Colum-
bus set sail for the Americas.

The Quinault Valley left a deep impression
on president Franklin D. Roosevelt when he
visited here in 1937. It inspired him to protect a

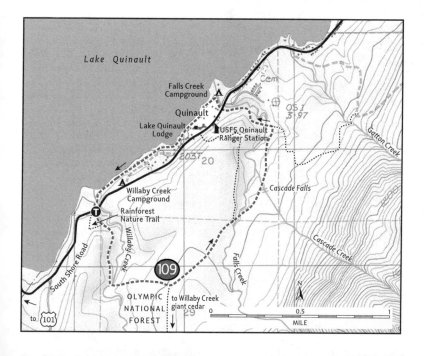

good chunk of the adjacent lands within a new national park. The Quinault rain forest, however, has remained within the national forest. But it's managed for recreation and wildlife, not timber production.

From the trailhead the well-groomed path passes a colossal Doug-fir to emerge on a high bank above Willaby Creek. Search the sparkling creek waters for salmon. Gaze up at the towering forest canopy for eagle nests. Then turn right and begin your journey into the past. At 0.25 mile is a junction; a short nature trail heads right, returning to the parking lot.

Cascades on Cascade Creek—Quinault National Recreation Trail

Continue on the main path, crossing Willaby Creek at about 0.5 mile. A half mile farther you'll reach another junction. The trail to your right travels 1.7 miles and climbs over 1000 feet to the Willaby Creek giant cedar. A ford over Willaby Creek is necessary and can be difficult in high water.

The loop continues forward to a cedar bog bursting with pungent patches of skunk cabbage. Traverse this saturated landscape via a boardwalk and come to another junction at 1.8 miles. The trail to your left heads 0.6 mile to the Quinault Lodge; proceed right instead. Cross Falls Creek, and after 0.5 mile of gentle climbing, cross Cascade Creek at lovely Cascade Falls. Admire the tumbling waters and then carry on. At 2.4 miles turn left at a junction (the right trail goes to Gatton Creek). Span Falls Creek again, climb a little, and then drop back down to reach the South Shore Road at 2.8 miles.

Cross the road, stop to admire Falls Creek Falls, skirt a campground, and then come to Lake Quinault, one of the largest bodies of water on the Olympic Peninsula. Close the loop by following the lakeshore for 1 mile, passing quiet coves, humble cabins, and the majestic 1926 Lake Quinault Lodge. In times of heavy rainfall, this section of trail is prone to inundation. If that's the case, return via the South Shore Road, or head up the Lodge Trail and retrace some of your route. The forest may be ancient, but this hike never gets old.

EXTENDING YOUR TRIP

From the Forest Service's Quinault Ranger Station it's a 3-mile one-way hike to the world's largest Sitka spruce via the quiet Gatton Creek Trail. On the north shore of Lake Quinault the 0.5-mile Maple Glade and 1.3-mile Kestner Homestead Loop trails make great rainforest strolls and are kid-friendly. A number of car campgrounds on Lake Quinault make ideal base camps for exploring the region.

110 Fletcher Canyon

RATING/ DIFFICULTY	ROUND-TRIP	ELEV GAIN/ HIGH POINT	SEASON
★★/3	4 miles	1100 feet/ 1450 feet	Year-round

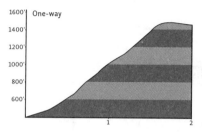

Maps: Green Trails Mt Christie No. 166, Custom Correct Quinault–Colonel Bob; **Contact:** Olympic National Forest, Pacific Ranger District, Quinault, (360) 288-2525, www.fs.fed.us /r6/olympic; **GPS:** N 47 31.700, W 123 42.395

Venture up a deep and dark canyon into a lonely corner of the 11,961-acre Colonel Bob Wilderness. The hike is short, but steep in places, and the terrain can be rough. But what will you receive for your sweat and toil? An excellent chance of observing a few of the wild denizens of this rugged rift in the Quinault Ridge. Stay alert for elk, cougar, bear, and perhaps even an endangered marbled murrelet while exploring this remote part of the Quinault rain forest.

GETTING THERE

From Hoquiam travel north on US 101 for 35 miles. Turn right (east) onto the South Shore Road, located 1 mile south of Amanda Park. Proceed on this road for 12 miles (passing the Forest Service's Quinault Ranger Station at 2 miles). The trail begins at the end of a small spur on the south side of the road. If the spur is flooded (often in winter), park instead on the north side of the South Shore Road.

Big trees dwarf a hiker in Fletcher Canyon.

ON THE TRAIL

The trail starts by an apartment-size boulder housing an array of ferns and lichens. Ignore the kiosk sign that says "Col Bob Trail 4 miles." The trail beyond the 2-mile mark has long been abandoned. Overgrown to jungle proportions, even Sasquatch now avoids it. Immediately start climbing on a sometimes steep, sometimes rocky route. Numerous creeks cross the trail, making it a challenge if you're intent on keeping your boots dry.

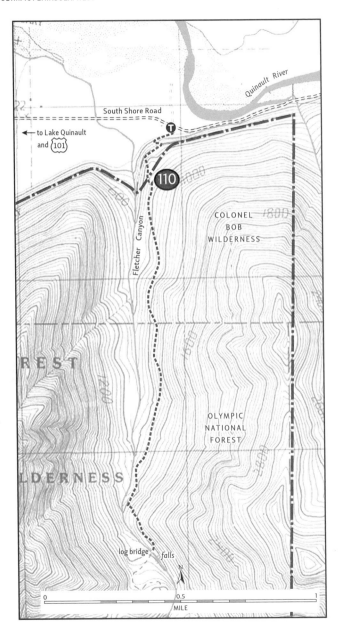

After gaining a couple of hundred feet, the trail rounds a bed and enters the deep and dark canyon. Soon enter the Colonel Bob Wilderness. Under an emerald canopy of stately hemlocks and firs with frothing Fletcher Creek crashing in the distance, continue climbing. Waves of sword ferns appear to roll down the vertical canyon walls.

After about 1 mile the way gets rougher, growing rockier and rootier. Finally, the trail approaches the creek. Enter a magical spot where big mossy boulders corral the feisty waters. Stare across to the sheer vertical wall at the far side of the canyon, where you can also see the scars of avalanches and rockslides.

With good tread now a memory, the trail darts over slick rocks and skirts along damp ledges on a somewhat steep course. At 2 miles, after a slight descent, break out into a small clearing alongside Fletcher Creek. A huge cedar log acts as a bridge over the gurgling waters, and another pretty waterfall can be seen just upstream. This is a good spot to call it quits. Beyond, the trail peters out into a tangle of brush. Sit by the creek and enjoy a corner of the rain forest were few bootprints have been left behind.

Winter hiking in the Graves Creek valley

111 Graves Creek

RATING/ DIFFICULTY	ROUND-TRIP	ELEV GAIN/ HIGH POINT	SEASON
**/3	7 miles	1200 feet/ 1880 feet	May–Nov

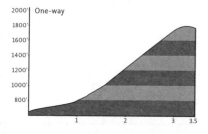

Maps: Green Trails Mt Christie No. 166, Custom Correct Enchanted Valley–Skokomish; **Contact:** Olympic National Park, Wilderness Information Center, (360) 565-3100, *www.nps.gov/olym*; **Notes:** Dogs prohibited. Road from Quinault River Bridge is subject to temporary closures during winter; **GPS:** N 47 34.370, W 123 34.191

Perhaps the loneliest of the Quinault rainforest valleys, Graves Creek promises solitude among a multitude of ancient trees. And while chances are slim of running into other wayward souls, a chance encounter with an elk is possible. Through a deep canyon, Graves Creek booms and crashes on its way to the Quinault River, at times disappearing into a tight chasm. But the valley is never free from its thundering outbursts and explosive rants.

GETTING THERE

From Hoquiam travel north on US 101 for 35 miles. Turn right (east) onto the South Shore Road, located 1 mile south of Amanda Park. Proceed on this road for 13.5 miles (passing the Forest Service's Quinault Ranger Station at 2 miles), coming to a junction at the Quinault River Bridge. Continue right, proceeding 6.2 miles to the road's end and the trailhead. Privy available.

ON THE TRAIL

Start this hike on the popular Quinault River Trail to Pony Bridge (Hike 112) and Enchanted Valley. Immediately cross Graves Creek on a sturdy bridge high above the churning waterway. In 0.25 mile come to a junction. Turn right onto the Graves Creek Trail, trading a well-worn pathway for narrow tread adorned with encroaching mosses.

Through a jungle of big trees draped in mosses and flanked with ferns, begin climbing out of the Quinault Valley. Numerous creeks flow across and, during heavy rain periods, down the trail. At 0.75 mile and after 400 feet of climbing, reach a bench high above Graves Creek. With caution, locate the waterway below as it tumbles through one of several box canyons lying along its route.

As you climb gradually, the valley walls grow steeper and Graves Creek's thundering roar intensifies. In late spring numerous cascades fall from the surrounding slopes, adding to the commotion. As you continue deeper into the valley, the trail dips close to the wild waterway at a few spots. Then it's more cascades, more rumbling, more climbing above the forbidding passages.

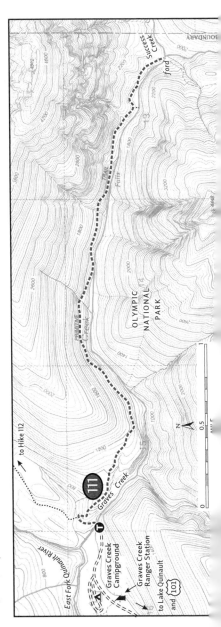

At 2.5 miles cross the first of two large avalanche chutes. Despite the low elevation (1700 feet) snow often lingers late into the spring. At 3 miles find a steep side trail heading down to a secluded pool on the creek. The main trail continues through big timber, traverses an open flat, and then at 3.5 miles descends to Success Creek. Here at the confluence of Success and Graves Creeks, two fords must be made if you wish to continue. Day hikers will want to call it quits here. Find a nice rock, pull out your lunch, and watch the dippers look for theirs.

EXTENDING YOUR TRIP

Strong hikers may want to continue all the way to Lake Sundown, 4.4 miles and 2000 vertical feet farther. Consider car-camping at the Graves Creek Campground, a mere 0.3 mile from the trailhead. From the campground, enjoy a nice 1-mile loop trail through lush river bottomland.

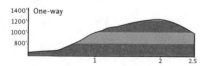

112 Quinault River–Pony Bridge

RATING/ DIFFICULTY	ROUND-TRIP	ELEV GAIN/ HIGH POINT	SEASON
★★/2	5 miles	900 feet/ 1200 feet	Year-round

Maps: Green Trails Mt Christie No. 166, Custom Correct Enchanted Valley–Skokomish; **Contact:** Olympic National Park, Wilderness Information Center, (360) 565-3100, www .nps.gov/olym; **Notes:** Dogs prohibited. Road from Quinault River Bridge is subject to temporary closures during winter; **GPS:** N 47 34.370, W 123 34.191

Big trees, a narrow canyon, and a little taste of the Enchanted Valley Trail, a

19-mile path deep into the Olympic interior. Explore the same primeval rainforest valley that explorers of the 1890 O'Neil Expedition set out across. Witness a wilderness not unlike the one those intrepid souls experienced. Come here in the heart of winter and find yourself among one of the largest elk herds in America.

GETTING THERE

From Hoquiam travel north on US 101 for 35 miles. Turn right (east) onto the South Shore Road, located 1 mile south of Amanda Park. Proceed on this road for 13.5 miles (passing the Forest Service's Quinault Ranger Station at 2 miles), coming to a junction at the Quinault River Bridge. Continue right, proceeding 6.2 miles to the road's end and the trailhead. Privy available.

ON THE TRAIL

The Quinault is one of the grandest of the rainforest rivers. Draining much of the Olympics' southwest corner, the Quinault is comprised of two main branches: the North and East Forks. This hike takes you along a portion of the East Fork, through a deep glacially carved valley.

Start by crossing Graves Creek on a large log bridge. In 0.2 mile come to a well-signed junction. Continue left on a wide and well-graded trail, an old road that once extended almost to Pony Bridge. Along a bench, away from the river, traverse moisture-dripping groves of towering hemlock, spruce, and fir. In winter scads of hoofprints mar the surrounding saturated ground. Stay alert for elk. The trail meanders a little over a small rise. Scores of creeks and rivulets run under, over, and sometimes down the trail.

At 2 miles the old road ends. Pass an old picnic table rapidly losing a fight with the elements; then begin to drop a couple of hundred feet to the river. Finally, at 2.3 miles, the

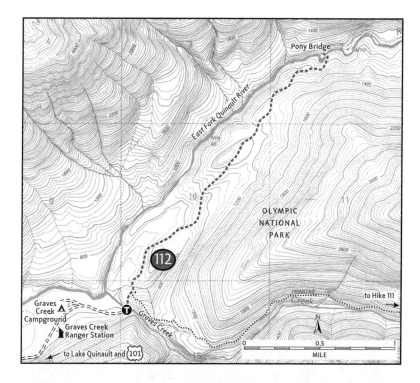

East Fork Quinault comes into view. Through a fern-ringed narrow canyon of slate and sandstone, the crystal-clear waters bubble and churn. Walk a little ways to Pony Bridge, which spans this scenic gorge. Enjoy an unobstructed view of emerald pools swirling below and horsetail falls streaking the canyon walls. If you've trekked this way on a rare sunny day, retreat a few hundred feet on the trail to find a rough path leading down to some lunch rocks along the river.

EXTENDING YOUR TRIP

Want to see more of the East Fork valley? Continue up the Enchanted Valley Trail on an up-

and-down course along the river. Fire Creek, 1 mile farther, makes a good destination.

113 North Fork Quinault River–Halfway House

RATING/ DIFFICULTY	ROUND-TRIP	ELEV GAIN/ HIGH POINT	SEASON
★★★/3	10.2 miles	400 feet/ 900 feet	Year-round

Opposite: Pony Bridge in the Quinault Valley

Maps: Green Trails Mt Christie No. 166, Custom Correct Quinault–Colonel Bob; **Contact:** Olympic National Park, Wilderness Information Center, (360) 565-3100, *www.nps.gov/olym*; **Notes:** Dogs prohibited. North Shore Road is subject to temporary closures during winter; **GPS:** N 47 34.542, W 123 38.889

🏠 *Hike along a wild river sporting big bends and wide gravel bars that'll have you thinking you're in Alaska. Massive Sitka spruce, gargantuan western hemlocks, and corridors of mossy maples and speckled alders grace the way. Retrace part of the Press Expedition's 1889–90 route across the Olympics, and visit the former site of a lodge that provided warmth and hospitality to trekkers during the 1920s and '30s. Along the North Fork Quinault River, you can embrace the pure wildness and raw beauty of the Olympic rain forest.*

GETTING THERE

From Hoquiam travel north on US 101 for 35 miles. Turn right (east) onto the South Shore Road, located 1 mile south of Amanda Park. Proceed on this road for 13.5 miles (passing the Forest Service's Quinault Ranger Station at 2 miles), coming to a junction at the Quinault River Bridge. Turn left and cross the bridge. Then immediately turn right onto the North Shore Road, proceeding 3.5 miles to the road's end at the ranger station and trailhead. Privy available.

ON THE TRAIL

Like many trails following rivers deep into the Olympic interior, the first couple miles of the North Fork Quinault River Trail were once a road. Building roads up these narrow, wet valleys was difficult enough, but maintaining them proved to be even more challenging. Winter storms and spring floods have a way

Lush rain forest in the North Fork of the Quinault Valley

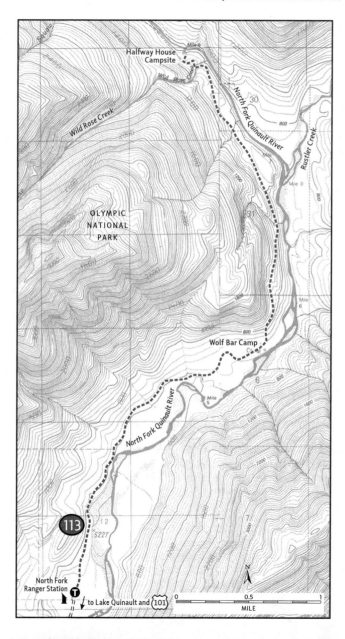

Halfway House
Campsite

Wild Rose Creek

Wild Rose Creek

North Fork Quinault River

Rustler Creek

Mile 8

30

800

1000

Mile 9

OLYMPIC
NATIONAL
PARK

800

Mile 6

800

Wolf Bar Camp

800

1200

Mile 5

1600

North Fork Quinault River

2200

113

12

522T

3000

N

North Fork
Ranger Station

T

to Lake Quinault and 101

0   0.5   1
MILE

of wreaking havoc on them. Over the decades and faced with limited budgets, the Park Service allowed some of these disaster-prone roadbeds to be converted to trail—a plus for wilderness and solitude seekers, but a minus for hikers seeking easier access into the backcountry. The decision to convert, not always met with approval, occasionally induces rifts within the hiking community (see "All Washed Up" in the Dosewallips River Valley section).

The North Fork Quinault's first 2.6 miles were converted long ago, making for an easy and enjoyable hike to a wide riverbank camping and picnicking spot known as Wolf Bar. Much of the way is right along the roaring river. And as in the past, the river continues to jump its bank, forcing reroutes and new tread to be built.

About 1 mile from the trailhead the first of several side creeks is crossed. While easy during summer, winter rains can make this and the other crossings difficult. At 1.5 miles traverse a huge gravel outwash area arranged with boughs of sword ferns and columns of maples swathed in moss. Next, cross a channel bed that may or may not be flowing. Traverse an alluvial island; then negotiate the channel once more. Now travel over more outwash, through groves of towering old growth and along newly exposed riverbanks.

At 2.6 miles arrive at Wolf Bar, a suitable destination for a shorter hike. Head out on the broad gravel bar for views of the surrounding steep-sided ridges adorned in swirling clouds. When the rain is in remission, worship the sun from this extensive outwash.

Beyond Wolf Bar the trail climbs a terrace, pulling away from the river. On an up-and-down course through thick forest, but always within earshot of the North Fork, the trail winds up the deep valley. At 5 miles, come to Wild Rose Creek, requiring a ford that may be dangerous during high water. The Halfway House site lies just beyond. Now a backcoun-

try campsite, nothing remains of the old lodge. But the area's charm is still in full swing. Find a piece of ledge to sit on to watch the swirling, gurgling river negotiate a narrow chasm.

114 Irely Lake and Big Creek

Irely Lake

RATING/ DIFFICULTY	ROUND-TRIP	ELEV GAIN/ HIGH POINT	SEASON
★/1	2.2 miles	200 feet/ 700 feet	Year-round

Big Creek

RATING/ DIFFICULTY	ROUND-TRIP	ELEV GAIN/ HIGH POINT	SEASON
★★★/3	8 miles	850 feet/ 1350 feet	Mar–Nov

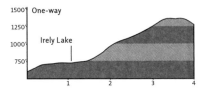

Maps: Green Trails Mt Christie No. 166, Custom Correct Quinault–Colonel Bob; **Contact:** Olympic National Park, Wilderness Information Center, (360) 565-3100, *www.nps.gov /olym*; **Notes:** Dogs prohibited. North Shore Road is subject to temporary closures during winter; **GPS:** N 47 34.049, W 123 39.317

A leisurely, kid-friendly jaunt to a quiet body of water teeming with wildlife, or a more moderate push through ancient forest along a crashing waterway—it's your choice. The forests of Big Creek, like those throughout the Quinault Valley, are impressive. Over 140 inches of rain fall here each year, saturating the forest floor and supporting massive cedars, lofty firs, hovering hemlocks, and clumps of shoulder-high ferns. Elk are abundant in this verdant valley, while hikers remain scarce.

GETTING THERE

From Hoquiam travel north on US 101 for 35 miles. Turn right (east) onto the South Shore Road, located 1 mile south of Amanda Park. Proceed on this road for 13.5 miles (passing the Forest Service's Quinault Ranger Station at 2 miles), coming to a junction at the Quinault River Bridge. Turn left and cross the bridge. Then immediately turn right onto the North Shore Road, proceeding 2.9 miles to a parking area located on your right. The trail begins on left side of the road.

ON THE TRAIL

Irely Lake: Begin under a lofty canopy, compliments of a support team of colossal cedars and spruce. After a small climb of 100 feet come to a flat that's bisected by Irely Creek. Turn south, following the skunk-cabbage-laced creek. Be careful on the rotten puncheon (planking that has deteriorated due to constant saturation). Beavers are active along this stretch, their handiwork causing occasional inundation of the trail.

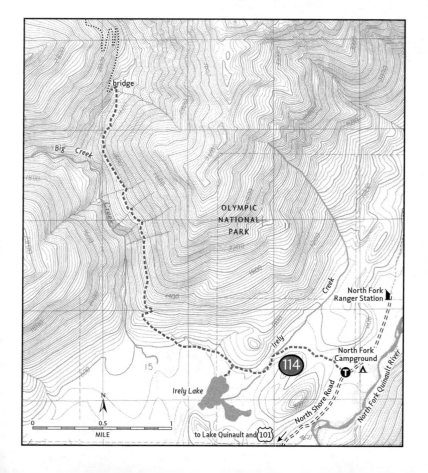

Starting a winter hike to Irely Lake

creeks that often flood during periods of high rain (which is often). The tread gets rougher and rockier, heading deeper into the saturated, verdant forest. If you could overdose on chlorophyll exposure, it would happen here.

Cross a maple flat frequented by elk before beginning a steep climb high above Big Creek. The cedars are enormous along these steep slopes. Several behemoths lay toppled across the trail, victims of strong winter storms. Wind is the number-one agent of succession in the rain forests of the Olympic Peninsula. Strong gusts ensure openings in the canopy, allowing new growth to compete with the entrenched elders.

At about 2.5 miles traverse a massive mudslide from the winter of 2006. Slain giants lie jumbled in a mélange of rocks and earth. Continue skirting steep slopes, and then at 4 miles abruptly drop toward the crashing creek. With a small cascade on your right, work your way down a short rocky ledge to the sturdy bridge that spans the thundering North Fork Big Creek. It's an impressive sight of hydrological force. Break out the granola bars and enjoy the show.

EXTENDING YOUR TRIP

You can continue on the Big Creek Trail, but the way gets steeper and rougher. One mile farther and 1000 feet higher beyond the bridge is the world's largest yellow cedar. Another mile and another 1000 feet of elevation gain delivers you to the Three Little Lakes and the beginning of the Skyline Trail, one of the premier backpacking routes in the park.

Cross the small creek on a log bridge; then head for higher and drier ground. At 1 mile reach a side trail that leads 0.1 mile down to a grassy spot on Irely Lake. The lake, more a big marsh, is a good place to sit still (if mosquitoes aren't present) and scope out birds. Ducks, woodpeckers, blackbirds, and songbirds are present in large numbers.

Big Creek: Beyond Irely Lake the trail traverses muddy lowlands, crossing several

115 Petes Creek–Colonel Bob Peak

RATING/ DIFFICULTY	ROUND-TRIP	ELEV GAIN/ HIGH POINT	SEASON
★★★★/5	8.2 miles	3500 feet/ 4492 feet	Late June– mid-Oct

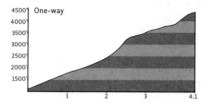

Maps: Green Trails Grisdale No. 198, Custom Correct Quinault–Colonel Bob; **Contact:** Olympic National Forest, Pacific Ranger Station, Quinault, (360) 288-2525, *www.fs.fed .us/r6/olympic*; **Notes:** Northwest Forest Pass required; **GPS:** N 47 27.433, W 123 43.905

Climb a prominent peak on the western edge of the Olympic Mountains. From this 4000-plus-foot aerie above the saturated Quinault Valley, stare down upon sprawling rain forest. Enjoy an unobstructed view of shimmering Lake Quinault too, and from Mount Olympus to the Pacific take in an ocean of peaks and peek at the ocean. It's a tough climb to this rugged outpost on the periphery of the Olympics, but the panorama it provides is a worthy pursuit.

GETTING THERE

From Hoquiam travel 25 miles north on US 101. Just past milepost 112 turn right onto Donkey Creek Road (Forest Road 22, signed for Wynoochee Lake). Follow this paved road for 8 miles to a junction. Turn left onto FR 2204 and continue 11 miles (the pavement ends in 3 miles) to the trailhead at Petes Creek. Privy available.

ON THE TRAIL

The hike to this peak is just like the man it was named for: straightforward and to the point. Colonel Robert G. Ingersoll was a Civil War veteran, politician, orator, and free thinker who never stepped foot on this peak, but some admiring climbers who did thought the peak

should be named for him. The good colonel eventually got a wilderness area named after him too, the only wilderness on the west side of the Olympic National Forest.

It's just over 4 miles to the summit, but it'll feel a lot longer. Most of the way is steep, with several rocky sections. Is it worth it? Absolutely! Colonel Bob offers views into country rarely seen from high above. It's one of the very few hiker-accessible summits in the western reaches of the Olympics.

Start your journey on the Petes Creek Trail,

Heather enjoying lunch on the summit of Colonel Bob Peak—Lake Quinault in the background

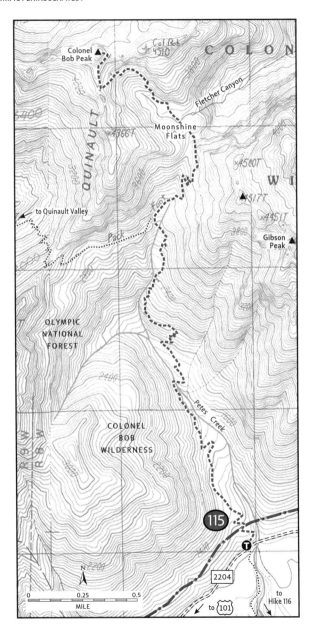

Colonel
Bob Peak

Col Bob
4510

C O L O N

Fletcher Canyon

QUINAULT

4866T

Moonshine
Flats

4500T

W I

4517T

4451T

Gibson
Peak

to Quinault Valley

Pack

OLYMPIC
NATIONAL
FOREST

2400T

Petes Creek

COLONEL
BOB
WILDERNESS

R 9 W
R 8 W

115

T

N

2204

to Hike 116

to 101

0   0.25   0.5
MILE

immediately entering ancient forest and the Colonel Bob Wilderness. In just under a mile cross the creek. You may get your feet wet, you may not; some years the creek runs underground. The climb stiffens as the trail works its way up the west slope of neighboring Gibson Peak.

At 1.5 miles traverse a brushy avalanche slope. Another larger slope is encountered soon afterward and views open up of the Humptulips Valley. Steeply zigzag through rugged terrain and at 2.4 miles come to a junction with the Colonel Bob Trail (elev. 3000 ft). Head right, climbing yet more steep brush-choked slopes and finally receiving a reprieve at a gap (elev. 3700 ft) above Fletcher Canyon (Hike 110).

The trail now heads northwest, dropping a bit to a tarn—boulder- and creek-graced Moonshine Flats. One mile and 1000 feet of elevation gain still need to be covered. Through subalpine forest and skirting basalt cliffs, the rough trail steeply switchbacks to the summit cone, the final 100 feet on steps blasted into the rock.

One look from this former fire lookout site quickly validates all your pain and suffering. Lake Quinault twinkles below. Mount Olympus glistens to the north, while Mount Rainier hovers in the east over rows of scrappy hills and ridges. And fanning out below from your aerie hub is an emerald network of luxuriant rainforest valleys—a burgeoning kingdom of biomass.

EXTENDING YOUR TRIP

Colonel Bob can also be hiked from the Quinault Valley, but it's a long trek (7.2 miles one-way) gaining over 4200 feet of elevation. However, the first 4 miles along Ziegler Creek to the Mulkey Shelter are through beautiful old-growth forest. The trail is good, rises just 1900 feet, and makes for excellent year-round kid- and dog-friendly hiking.

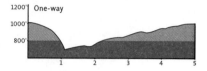

116 West Fork Humptulips River

RATING/ DIFFICULTY	ROUND-TRIP	ELEV GAIN/ HIGH POINT	SEASON
★★★/2	10 miles	700 feet/ 1000 feet	Late July– Oct

Maps: Green Trails Grisdale No. 198, Custom Correct Quinault–Colonel Bob; **Contact:** Olympic National Forest, Pacific Ranger Station, Quinault, (360) 288-2525, www.fs.fed.us/r6/olympic; **Notes:** Northwest Forest Pass required. River fords required, only safe during low flows; **GPS:** N 47 27.433, W 123 43.905

With spectacular groves of old-growth forest, meadows teeming with wildlife, and views of rugged surrounding peaks, the West Fork Humptulips River bottom is one of the most varied of the rainforest valleys. Devoid of visitors and traversing the edge of one of the largest roadless areas in the Olympic National Forest, this hike offers a true wilderness experience. The river must be forded eight times, but if amphibious adventuring is not for you, 1.5 miles of dry trail (and kid-friendly hiking) can be enjoyed year-round from the northern terminus of this hike at the Campbell Tree Grove.

GETTING THERE

From Hoquiam travel 25 miles north on US 101. Just past milepost 112 turn right onto Donkey Creek Road (Forest Road 22, signed for Wynoochee Lake). Follow this paved road for 8 miles to a junction. Turn left onto FR 2204 and continue 11 miles (the pavement ends in 3 miles) to the trailhead at Petes Creek. Privy available.

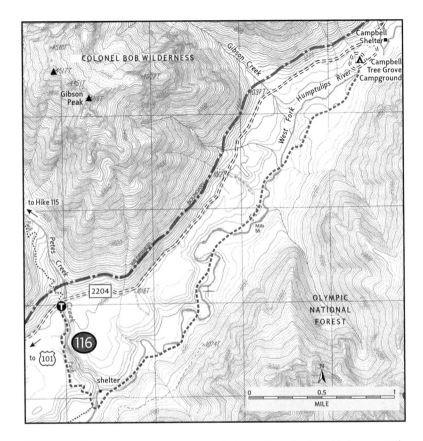

ON THE TRAIL

Because this hike involves eight river fords within a 2.5-mile stretch, consider wearing a pair of old running shoes so you can keep plodding without having to continuously stop to lace up your boots. The terrain and tread between the crossings is generally level, a little brushy in spots, but not rocky or rough. It's a great hike on a late summer's day. The river warms up nicely, assuring no red feet along the way.

Start by heading 1 mile down the Lower Petes Creek Trail on a wide and gentle path, first through a grove of old cedars and hem-

locks and then along an old clear-cut. With the sound of the West Fork Humptulips amplifying, the trail leaves the level terrace, dropping steeply 300 feet to meet the West Fork Humptulips River Trail on the lush river bottom. Head left a short distance, encountering the river and your first ford. Scan the wide gravel bank looking for a shallow and gently flowing crossing.

Once across, a grassy meadow graced with big maples lures you to continue. An old cedar-shingled shelter sits snuggly in the quiet grove. The trail wastes no time fording the river again. With the soothing song of the river constantly in range, head up the remote valley surrounded by rugged peaks of the Colonel Bob Wilderness to the west and Stovepipe and Moonlight Dome to the east. The trail traverses the western edge of the 6000-acre Moonlight Dome Roadless Area, one of the last large tracts of unlogged, unprotected national forest land in the rainforest valleys. Wilderness designation would suit this primeval piece of public property just perfectly.

Through groves of massive spruce and firs, across grassy openings, and through gently flowing ripples, wander up this de facto

The West Fork of the Humptulips from the first ford

wilderness valley. At 3.5 miles complete your last ford. Now enjoy 1.5 miles of dry-foot trekking on excellent tread. At 5 miles, you may be shocked to encounter a bridge. Cross the river on it to the Campbell Tree Grove, one of the loveliest stands of old growth in the Olympics. Rest up and enjoy the return wade!

EXTENDING YOUR TRIP

The trail continues beyond the Campbell Tree Grove for nearly 5 miles. But the 7-mile stretch south of Petes Creek makes for easier and more interesting walking. The Campbell Tree Grove is a quiet and inviting place to set up a base camp for exploring area trails.

MEET THE ROOSEVELTS

The fact that nearly 1 million acres of wild land is protected on the Olympic Peninsula as a national park is primarily the work of two presidents: one a Republican, one a Democrat, both Roosevelts.

Lieutenant O'Neil was one of the first people calling for protection of the area as a national park back in 1890 after his second scientific and exploratory journey. In 1897 President Grover Cleveland created the Olympic Forest Preserve, but it lacked strong protection. An avid sportsman, President Theodore Roosevelt used the Antiquities Act of 1906 (which he signed into law) to proclaim 600,000 acres as Mount Olympus National Monument, primarily to protect the dwindling elk herds from unregulated hunting. Today the elk bear his name and number over 5000.

National monuments, however, don't enjoy the same protections as national parks; timber, mining, and development interests began putting pressure on the government to open up the area to exploitation. In 1937 President Franklin D. Roosevelt visited the area, staying at the Lake Crescent and Lake Quinault Lodges and prompting him to declare, "This must be a national park!"

In 1938, four weeks before O'Neil's death, FDR signed a bill designating 898,000 acres as Olympic National Park. Most of the coastal strip was added to the park in 1953 with a stroke from President Truman's pen (a Democrat). In 1988 Republican president Ronald Reagan signed a bill declaring nearly 95 percent of the park as wilderness, the strongest protection afforded by law.

But work on the park isn't complete. Conservationists and park officials have expressed an interest in further expanding the park's boundaries. Hopefully, Congress and the president, both Democrats and Republicans, will agree and follow their predecessors' enlightened examples.

Opposite: Sea stacks and tide pools south of Cape Alava

olympic peninsula: coast

Olympic Coast

Majestic sea stacks, secluded coves, deserted strands of smooth sandy beaches, contorted salt-sprayed maritime forests, and tidal pools bursting with urchins, starfish, limpets, barnacles, and all kinds of squishy and crunchy sea critters—this is what you can expect to find while hiking along the Olympic Peninsula's coast.

The Olympic Coast mostly remains roadless and isolated, with the wildest beaches remaining in the continental United States. And while good portions of this wild, windswept, and rain-drenched world require tenacity and determination to visit, a surprisingly good amount of this country is relatively accessible. Even along the coast's southern limits—the only area where a road runs parallel to this beautiful land teetering on the far northwest edge of the Pacific Northwest—the feeling is still of remoteness from the civilized world.

Nowhere along these pristine beaches that sport sea and river otters, oystercatchers and bald eagles, grey whales and sea lions, guillemots, puffins, murrelets and murres will you ever have to share the way with cars, trucks, and SUVs—mechanized menaces still permitted to mar the beaches farther south. But it almost didn't turn out so well for the Olympic Coast. A coastal highway, oil drilling, and surfside development nearly wreaked havoc on this sacred land of the Makahs, Quileutes, Hohs, and Quinaults. Most of the coastal strip wasn't added to Olympic National Park until 1953, and Shi Shi Beach only joined the protected ranks in 1977 after officials had to evict back-to-the-earth squatters who left plenty of traces.

From Kalaloch's miracle strand of broad sandy beaches to Cape Flattery's towering cliffs over tumultuous currents, there's plenty of good hiking to be had in Washington's wild northwestern corner.

117 Kalaloch–Browns Point

RATING/ DIFFICULTY	ROUND-TRIP	ELEV GAIN/ HIGH POINT	SEASON
★★★/1	4 miles	25 feet/ 25 feet	Year-round

25'   One-way

0.5   1   1.5   2

Maps: Green Trails La Push No. 163S, Custom Correct South Olympic Coast; **Contact:** Olympic National Park, Wilderness Information Center, (360) 565-3100, *www.nps.gov/olym*; **Notes:** Dogs must be leashed. Browns Point can only be rounded during low tides, consult tide chart; **GPS:** N 47 36.771, W 124 22.570

The wide sandy beaches of Kalaloch are the perfect introduction to the wild Olympic Coast. Although the highway is never far, towering bluffs and hidden coves give this area a remote feeling. Perfect for children and Rover too (dogs are allowed on these beaches, but they must be leashed), spend days exploring this area's extensive tide pools and headlands. The hike to Browns Point, a jumbled collection of rock islands and surf-splashed cliffs, makes a fine half-day objective.

GETTING THERE

From Hoquiam follow US 101 north for 70 miles to Kalaloch. (From Forks travel 34 miles south on US 101.) Turn left (west) into Kalaloch Campground (just beyond the lodge and ranger station), and park in the picnic day-use area. Water and restrooms available.

ON THE TRAIL

From the picnic area bluff descend 25 feet, hopping over a tangled pile of drift logs to reach the beach, and then head north on the wide and smooth expanse of sandy shoreline.

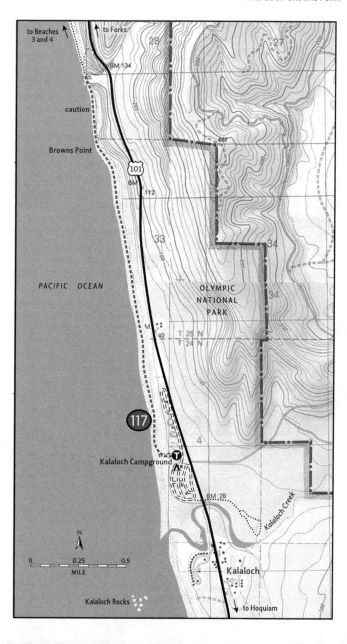

Beached logs at Browns Point–Kalaloch Beach

Throughout most of the summer a shroud of fog impairs the view. But on clear fall and spring days you can see all the way to Hoh Head on the northern horizon. Destruction Island, a 60-acre barren outpost over 3 miles from shore, can also be seen when the skies are clear. Uninhabited, it's one the Pacific Coast's most important seabird colonies.

In 1 mile high grassy bluffs rising to your right increase the feeling of remoteness. At 1.6 miles a series of ledges and cliffs encroaches

upon the surf. If the tide is high, this is as far as you can safely go. Turn around and enjoy the beaches south of the Kalaloch Campground.

But if the tide is low, work your way over, around, and even through (there's a small sandstone arch, look for it) the rocks and ledges making up Browns Point. Explore tidal pools and cliffside caves. Admire orange and purple starfishes tightly cemented to barnacle-clad rocks. Peer down at spongy urchins and other sea critters in nature's little saltwater baths. But remember, the intertidal zone is a fragile ecosystem. Please don't remove or disturb its inhabitants. That's the job for raucous oyster-catchers in search of tasty morsels.

Come to the other side of Browns Point at 2 miles. Beyond, Beaches 3 and 4 offer more wide sandy stretches. Don't forget to check your tide chart for the return if you decide to go farther.

EXTENDING YOUR TRIP

Pitch your tent at Kalaloch, one of just a few oceanside campgrounds in the state. Hike the delightful 1-mile Kalaloch Creek Loop Trail or explore more beaches. North of Browns Point, you can hike 4 miles to Ruby Beach (Hike 118). South of Kalaloch, over 3 miles of sandy shoreline await your footprints.

118 Ruby Beach

RATING/ DIFFICULTY	ROUND-TRIP	ELEV GAIN/ HIGH POINT	SEASON
★★★/2	6 miles	80 feet/ 80 feet	Year-round

Maps: Green Trails La Push No. 163S, Custom Correct South Olympic Coast; **Contact:** Olympic National Park, Wilderness Information

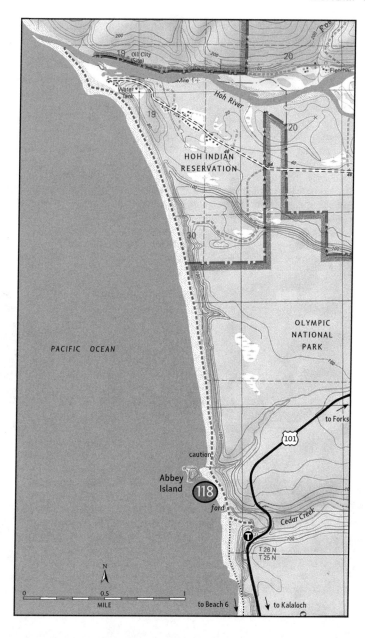

19 Oil City (Site)

Water Tank

Mile 1

Hoh River

19

HOH INDIAN
RESERVATION

20

Pas

20

Fletcher

30

PACIFIC   OCEAN

OLYMPIC
NATIONAL
PARK

to Forks

101

caution

Abbey
Island

118

ford

Cedar Creek

T

T 26 N
T 25 N

N

0   0.5   1
MILE

to Beach 6 ↓   ↓ to Kalaloch

Center, (360) 565-3100, *www.nps.gov/olym*; **Notes:** Dogs must be leashed. Consult tide chart before hiking beach; **GPS:** N 47 42.591, W 124 24.816

Consider Ruby Beach to be Olympic wilderness coast lite. You'll get the same great wilderness taste as Cape Alava, Shi Shi Beach, and Third Beach, but for a lot less calories. The hike to Ruby Beach is a mere 0.25 mile, but it's a glorious 0.25 mile. Through a wind-blasted maritime forest, follow a well-groomed trail lined with salt-sprayed shrubs to the mighty Pacific. Emerge behind a barrier of surf-tossed logs and consider your options: south to Beach 6 or 3 lonely miles north to the mouth of the Hoh River.

GETTING THERE

From Hoquiam follow US 101 north for 77 miles, 7 miles beyond Kalaloch. (From Forks travel 27 miles south on US 101.) Turn left (west; signed "Ruby Beach") and proceed 0.1 mile to a large parking area and the trailhead. Privy available.

ON THE TRAIL

Make the 0.25-mile jaunt to the sea. Most hikers might be content right where the short trail meets the sea. They'll wander a bit and photograph the contorted sea stacks that greet them. Perhaps they'll comb the beach looking for treasure or try to capture the beauty of offshore Abbey Island on a memory card, whiling away the afternoon at this spectacular spot. But if the tide's low

Ruby Beach—Abbey Island in background

and your ambitions are high, consider hiking north for nearly 3 miles to the mouth of the Hoh River.

Check your tide chart. You'll need a low one to rock-hop across Cedar Creek and to safely round the small headland just north of it. After that it's an easy, straightforward hike to the mouth of one of the peninsula's most famous rivers. On a wide sandy beach beneath bluffs rising 150 feet, hike all the way to where the rain- and glacier-fed Hoh River empties into the world's largest ocean.

En route you're sure to see bald eagles perched in high snags hanging precariously above the eroding bluffs. You may even encounter a deer or two out on the deserted beach. At the river you're likely to meet anglers in pursuit of a prize salmon.

Spend some time exploring the mouth of the river (which lies within the small Hoh Indian Reservation), and then plan for your return. Don't forget about the tides. Let Abbey Island act like a beacon to guide you back to Ruby Beach. Early settlers to the area thought that the imposing block of an island resembled a cathedral, hence the name. Whether the island looks like a house of worship to you, like an abbey this island and coastline are indeed sacred. And despite easy access, Ruby Beach is as beautiful and wild as any of the Olympic Peninsula's famed wilderness beaches.

EXTENDING YOUR TRIP

During a low tide you can hike south to Beach 6. Look for small caves carved into the steep bluffs lining the beach.

119 Second Beach

RATING/ DIFFICULTY	ROUND-TRIP	ELEV GAIN/ HIGH POINT	SEASON
★★★/2	4 miles	350 feet/ 250 feet	Year-round

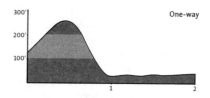

One-way

Maps: Green Trails La Push No. 163S, Custom Correct South Olympic Coast; **Contact:** Olympic National Park, Wilderness Information Center, (360) 565-3100, www.nps.gov /olym; **Notes:** Dogs prohibited. As of summer 2006, the trail is closed due to a dispute between the Park Service and the Quileute Indian Nation, call the park for current status; **GPS:** N 47 53.890, W 124 37.429

Just south of the village of La Push are three Olympic Coast charms: First, Second, and Third Beaches. Each one is sandy and broad and hemmed in by dramatic bluffs and headlands. And while they're in close proximity to each other, you can't hike from one to the next because those headlands block the way. With roadside access, First Beach is the easiest to get to and so can be crowded. Third Beach requires a 1.2-mile slog down a forested trail. But Second Beach is just right: a hike just long enough to discourage crowds, yet short enough to encourage all who want to see this beautiful beach.

GETTING THERE

From Port Angeles follow US 101 west for 55 miles to the junction with State Route 110 (signed "Mora–La Push"). (From Forks the junction is 2 miles north.) Continue west on SR 110. In 7.7 miles at Quillayute Prairie, SR 110 splits. Take the left fork (La Push Road), and drive 5.2 miles to the trailhead, located on the south side of the road (you'll pass the Third Beach/Hike 120 trailhead and the Quileute tribal office).

ON THE TRAIL

Well-constructed and well-maintained, the trail starts on the Quileute Indian Reservation. Immediately cross a small creek lined with imposing Sitka spruce before beginning a short climb. At the height of the land enter Olympic National Park, and then begin a short, steep descent to the beach, the distant surf growing louder with each step you take. Soon, start catching glimpses of offshore sea stacks through the surrounding towering spruce. Before you know it, emerge on the log-lined shore. Take a deep breath. The beauty of this place just may leave you short of breath.

You can hike a short distance along the beach northward. Do it, for it'll lead you to a natural arch. But to really stretch your legs and get the most out of Second Beach, head south. Over 1 mile of sandy beach awaits your footprints.

Immediately offshore is a consortium of battered islets and sea stacks known as the Quillayute Needles. Crying Lady Rock is the largest of the batch. These forbidding landmarks are

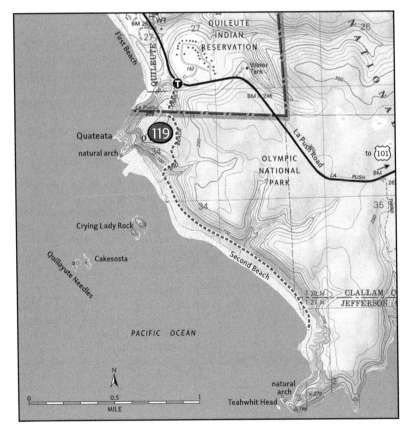

Starfish on tidal rocks at Second Beach

Maps: Green Trails La Push No. 163S, Custom Correct South Olympic Coast; **Contact:** Olympic National Park, Wilderness Information Center, (360) 565-3100, *www.nps.gov/olym*; **Notes:** Dogs prohibited; **GPS:** N 47 53.435, W 124 35.941

An easy hike to one of the Olympic Coast's famed wilderness beaches. Walk the wide sandy beach to the foot of a waterfall tumbling from a towering bluff right into the crashing surf. Feeling more energetic? Leave the crowds behind by grunting over Taylor Point to a secluded beach flanked by steep sea stacks and flower pot islands.

part of the Quillayute Needles National Wildlife Refuge. Inhospitable to humans, they're productive breeding grounds to thousands of seabirds, oystercatchers, murres, gulls, petrels, cormorants, and auklets among them.

Continue wandering. Taste the salty spray coming off the crashing breakers. Eventually you'll come to an impasse, the headland named Teahwhit Head. But before you turn around and retrace your steps, scan the rugged bluff. Teahwhit Head is also graced with a natural arch. In retrospect you may conclude that with two arches, an awesome seascape, scores of pelagic birds, and an inviting sandy shoreline, Second Beach is second to none.

GETTING THERE

From Port Angeles follow US 101 west for 55 miles to the junction with State Route 110 (signed "Mora–La Push"). (From Forks the junction is 2 miles north.) Continue west on SR 110. In 7.7 miles at Quillayute Prairie, SR 110 splits. Take the left fork (La Push Road) and proceed 3.8 miles to the trailhead, located on the south side of the road. Privy available.

ON THE TRAIL

Start off on an old road through a scrappy forest of Sitka spruce, hemlock, and alder. The trail has been greatly improved over the last decade. No longer are you at risk of being swallowed by a mud hole on the way to Third Beach. After 0.5 mile the trail veers left, leaving the old road and entering a more attractive forest.

Continue walking and soon you'll hear the surf and taste the salty air. Begin a slow descent, and after 1.3 miles of hiking, voilà—the beach! Hemmed in by two imposing headlands, Teahwhit Head and Taylor Point, Third Beach extends for about a mile along Strawberry Bay. Hard to imagine that this wild sweep of coastline was once explored for oil. Luckily for the integrity of the environment and for us

120 Third Beach

RATING/ DIFFICULTY	ROUND-TRIP	ELEV GAIN/ HIGH POINT	SEASON
★★★/2	3.6 miles	280 feet/ 280 feet	Year-round

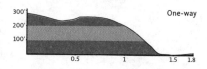

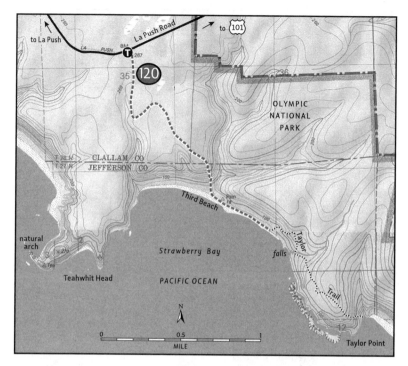

hikers, the drillings never proved abundant or profitable.

If you care to escape Third Beach's frequent crowds, hike left (south) 0.5 mile toward the overland trail to admire a waterfall plunging from its heights straight into the pounding waves below.

EXTENDING YOUR TRIP

To see some really spectacular maritime scenery, head over Taylor Point via the overland trail. Sand ladders and ankle-twisting terrain climb 250 feet up and over the imposing headland. Travel through a grove of old-growth Sitka spruce before making a steep descent back to sea level. After 1.75 difficult miles of overland travel, a quiet and secluded beach is your reward. To go farther requires planning for tides. Find a smooth drift log and savor the surrounding sea.

121 Hole-in-the-Wall

RATING/ DIFFICULTY	ROUND-TRIP	ELEV GAIN/ HIGH POINT	SEASON
★★★★/1	4 miles	None/ sea level	Year-round in all but highest tides

Opposite: Footprints in the sand at Third Beach—waterfall on Taylor Point in the background

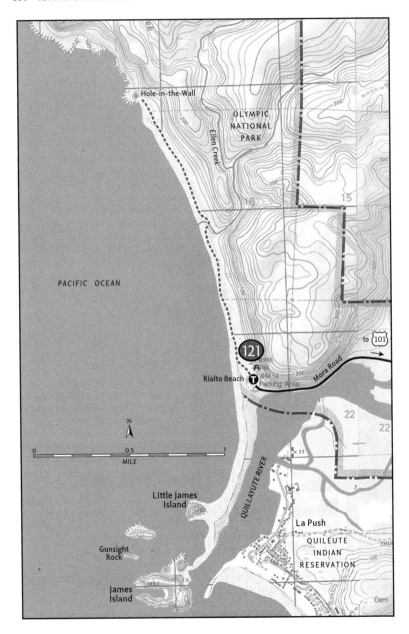

Hole-in-the-Wall

OLYMPIC
NATIONAL
PARK

Ellen Creek

16   15

PACIFIC OCEAN

to 101

121

Rialto Beach

BM 14
Parking Area

Mora Road

N

0   0.5
MILE

QUILLAYUTE RIVER

22   22

Little James
Island

La Push

Gunsight
Rock

QUILEUTE
INDIAN
RESERVATION

James
Island

Cem

Maps: Green Trails Ozette No. 130S, Custom Correct North Olympic Coast; **Contact:** Olympic National Park, Wilderness Information Center, (360) 565-3100, *www.nps.gov/olym*; **Notes:** Dogs must be leashed, prohibited beyond Ellen Creek. Exploration of Hole-in-the-Wall is only possible at low tide, consult tide chart; **GPS:** N 47 55.269, W 124 38.291

Hike to a real hole in the wall of a place: a genuine natural sea arch carved by surf and wind in an out-of-the-way section of the wild Olympic Coast. And while the Hole-in-the-Wall is an outstandingly beautiful place, the hike there via Rialto Beach doesn't exactly suffer from a dearth of spectacular scenery. Flanked by sea stacks, lined with giant logs, windswept and strewn with cobblestones, Rialto has all the makings of an Olympic wilderness beach. But unlike its wild counterparts, you don't have to hike very far to get here. The beautiful beach begins right from the parking lot.

GETTING THERE
From Port Angeles follow US 101 west for 55 miles to the junction with State Route 110 (signed "Mora–La Push"). (From Forks the junction is 2 miles north.) Continue west on SR 110. In 7.7 miles at Quillayute Prairie, SR 110 splits. Take the right fork (Mora Road), proceeding 5 miles to the road's end and the trailhead. Water and restrooms available.

ON THE TRAIL
Rialto Beach stretches northward from the Quillayute River for over 3 miles. From the parking lot it's a 2-mile hike to the beach's northern boundary at Hole-in-the-Wall. This dramatic sea arch can only be hiked through during low tides. However, the beach can be hiked during almost any tide. But before you bound across the surf-blasted beach, gaze seaward out to high-bluffed, forest-capped James Island. Guarding the mouth of the Quillayute like a sentinel, for centuries this island acted as a natural fortress, protecting the Quileute people from northern invaders.

Begin your hike northward across Rialto Beach. Like a giant split-rail fence, surf-battered logs line the beach. Admire their symmetry, but never climb on them during high tides; a wave can easily jostle them loose, trapping and endangering you.

A salt-blasted maritime forest rises behind the rows of downed timber. Look for eagles perched in the higher trees. Along the gently sloping beach, listen for the ringing *crik-crik-crik* of the black oystercatcher. Watch the

Rialto Beach from Hole-in-the-Wall

swelling surf for guillemots, scoters, grebes, and harlequin ducks. Don't forget to admire the scenery too. Sculpted sea stacks, shelved ledges, and battered offshore islands will keep you oohing and aahing.

At 1 mile you'll come to Ellen Creek, the end of the line for four-legged beach hikers. Crossing Ellen Creek may be tricky. Look for a log, or take your boots off and plod through the tannic and chilled waters. Hole-in-the-Wall, now coming nicely into view, lies 1 mile farther.

Once you hit the Hole-in-the-Wall, if the tide is out stroll through it for a whole new meaning to barrier-free hiking. Comb the adjacent tidal pools. Hike up the short overland trail that guarantees passage around this landform if the tide is in. The view of Rialto from the crest of the bluff is a classic, endlessly replicated in murals, photos, and memories.

EXTENDING YOUR TRIP

The Chilean Memorial, which lies about 2.25 miles farther, makes for a good all-day beach hike. Be sure to carry and consult a tide chart, though, for two spots are impassable in high tides and you don't want to be trapped.

122 Quillayute River Slough

RATING/ DIFFICULTY	ROUND-TRIP	ELEV GAIN/ HIGH POINT	SEASON
★/1	1.8 miles	30 feet/ 30 feet	Year-round

Maps: Green Trails La Push No. 163S, Custom Correct South Olympic Coast; **Contact:**

Evening along the Quillayute River

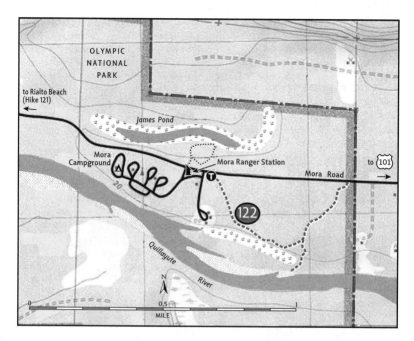

Olympic National Park, Wilderness Information Center, (360) 565-3100, *www.nps.gov/olym*; **Notes:** Dogs prohibited; **GPS:** N 47 55.089, W 124 36.160

A quiet trail from a popular campground along a rainforest river lined with giant spruce. Hike this trail early in the morning or late in the evening for wildlife- and bird-watching. The Quillayute River is famous for its steelhead and salmon fishing, so you may want to consider bringing your fishing pole along as well.

GETTING THERE

From Port Angeles follow US 101 west for 55 miles to the junction with State Route 110 (signed "Mora–La Push"). (From Forks the junction is 2 miles north.) Continue west on SR 110. In 7.7 miles at Quillayute Prairie, SR 110 splits. Take the right fork (Mora Road), proceeding 3.3 miles to the Mora Ranger Station. Park here. The trailhead is located on the east side of the parking lot.

ON THE TRAIL

Mora Campground is a great place to car-camp for exploring nearby Rialto Beach. But it's not necessary to venture too far from your site, as the Quillayute River Slough Trail originates from the campground itself. Many hikers ignore it or miss it—all the better for quiet ramblings.

The trail starts out flat and gentle through a forest of scaly-barked spruce carpeted with mosses. Look for large burls on some of the big trees. After about 0.25 mile the trail crests a small ridge above one of the many sloughs along the Quillayute. Formed by three main rainforest rivers—the Bogachiel, Sol Duc, and Calawah—the Quillayute snakes and oxbows to the Pacific at La Push. The river takes on an almost southern appearance of a lazy waterway cutting through lush bottomlands.

At 0.5 mile you'll come to a junction. The trail right leads a short distance to the slough, along the way passing a massive old Sitka spruce. The trail left leads 0.3 mile to Mora Road at the national park boundary. Hike them both before returning to the campground. Take your time, however, enjoying the natural riches of this productive environment.

EXTENDING YOUR TRIP

Also originating from the Mora Campground is the James Pond Trail. This short 0.5-mile loop leads to an oxbow pond surrounded by lush vegetation. Ducks, herons, and eagles are frequently observed at this peaceful body of water.

123 Ozette Triangle

RATING/ DIFFICULTY	LOOP	ELEV GAIN/ HIGH POINT	SEASON
★★★★★/3	9.4 miles	350 feet/ 175 feet	Year-round

200'
100'
Loop
2 4 6 8 9.4

Maps: Green Trails Ozette No. 130S, Custom Correct Ozette Beach Loop; **Contact:** Olympic National Park, Wilderness Information Center, (360) 565-3100, *www.nps.gov/olym*; **Notes:** National park entry fee required. Dogs prohibited. Coastal section can be difficult during high tides, consult tide chart; **GPS:** N 48 09.642, W 124. 43.890

✪ *With sea stacks, sea otters, sea lions, and ocean scenery for as far as you can see, the 9.4-mile Ozette Triangle is one of the finest hikes on the Olympic Coast.*

Easily accessible and a loop hike, the Triangle (named for the loop's shape) is a perfect introduction to America's wildest coastline south of Alaska. You won't be alone on this section of wilderness beach, however, for Ozette's admirers are legion. But there's plenty of room, and if you venture this way on a winter weekday you might just find yourself alone with the harlequin ducks.

GETTING THERE

From Port Angeles follow US 101 west for 5 miles to the junction with State Route 112. Turn right (west) on SR 112, continuing for 46 miles to the community of Sekiu. (Alternatively, take US 101 to Sappho and drive SR 113 north to SR 112 and then on to Sekiu. This way is longer, but not as curvy.) Drive 2.5 miles beyond Sekiu and turn left onto the Hoko-Ozette Road. Follow this paved road for 21 miles to the Ozette Ranger Station and trailhead. Water and restrooms available.

ON THE TRAIL

From Lake Ozette, one of the largest natural bodies of freshwater in the state, the loop begins its 3.3-mile journey to the sea. Cross the lazy and brackish Ozette River on an arched bridge, coming to a junction in 0.25 mile. Take the trail right (the left trail is your return route), proceeding through a thick forest of western cedar and Sitka spruce. Most of the way is via a cedar-planked boardwalk, convenient for traversing the saturated terrain but slippery during periods of rain. The Park Service has begun replacing many of the rotting cedar planks with nonslippery plastic ones.

Continue through lush maritime forests drenched in sea mist. Towering ferns line the elevated path, and in early spring the boardwalk is lined with thousands of nature's lanterns: blossoming skunk cabbage. At 2.25 miles pass through Ahlstroms Prairie, an early homestead site long-since reclaimed by the dense greenery that thrives in this water-logged climate.

Raucous gulls and the sound of crashing surf announce that the ocean is nearing, and at 3.3 miles a slight descent delivers you to the wild beaches of Cape Alava. Now for real fun! Turn south and follow the shoreline for 3.1 adventurous miles. Look out to offshore islands. Search the ocean waters for seals, whales, and scores of pelagic birds. Look in tidal pools for semisubmerged starfish tenaciously clinging to barnacle-encrusted walls. Look for oyster-catchers cruising down the aisles of this open fish market. Look up in the towering trees hugging the shoreline for perched eagles.

Search for Makah petroglyphs etched into the Wedding Rocks, a cluster of shore-hugging boulders about halfway along the coast. Respect these historic and sacred artifacts, which predate European settlement in the Northwest. If the tide is low, continue along the surf. If it is high, use the steep but short trails (signed) that bound over rough headlands. Continue on wide beach and approach another spot that may require a detour if the surf is high.

At 3 miles from Cape Alava and after 6.3 miles of hiking, you'll arrive at Sand Point. Over 2 glorious miles of some of the finest sandy beaches in all of Washington extend south from this point.

When you must relinquish this heavenly environment back to its rightful owners—the seals, oystercatchers, otters, and sanderlings—return to Lake Ozette via another 3-mile-long boardwalk trail through expansive cedar bogs

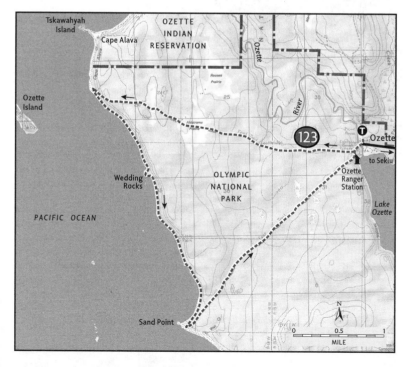

A hiker inspects the petroglyphs at the Wedding Rocks on the Ozette Triangle Hike.

and under a dense canopy of majestic Sitka spruce. The sound of the surf slowly fades in the distance, but the Ozette Triangle will chime in your memories for quite some time.

EXTENDING YOUR TRIP

The Park Service maintains a small and attractive car campground at Lake Ozette, convenient for exploring area trails. North of Cape Alava, 2 miles of wide, sandy, and scenic beach can be explored to the Ozette River. Fording the river can be extremely dangerous. Please stay off of Tskawahyah Island, a sacred spot for the Makah people. The area across from the island was once the site of a flourishing Makah village. Artifacts from it are on display in the Tribal Museum in Neah Bay.

124 Shi Shi Beach and Point of the Arches

RATING/ DIFFICULTY	ROUND-TRIP	ELEV GAIN/ HIGH POINT	SEASON
★★★★/3	8 miles	200 feet/ 200 feet	Year-round

Maps: Green Trails Cape Flattery No. 98S, Custom Correct North Olympic Coast; **Contact:** Olympic National Park, Wilderness Information Center, (360) 565-3100, *www.nps.gov /olym*; **Notes:** Dogs prohibited. Makah Recreation Pass required, available at Washburn's General Store in Neah Bay. Point of Arches is inaccessible at high tide, consult tide chart; **GPS:** N 48 17.623, W 124 39.905

Revered through the ages, Shi Shi Beach has its share of disciples, from First Peoples to first-time visitors, naturalists, bird-watchers, hard-core hikers, beach bums, conservationists, politicians, and just plain ordinary folk. And Northwest hikers have consistently rated Shi Shi as one of the region's most beautiful beaches. Though this natural gem's history has had a few blemishes, including access issues, thankfully many of those problems have been washed out to sea.

GETTING THERE

From Port Angeles follow US 101 west for 5 miles to the junction with State Route 112. Turn right (west) on SR 112, continuing for 64 miles to the community of Neah Bay. (Alternatively, take US 101 to Sappho and drive SR 113 north to SR 112 and then on to Neah Bay. This way is longer, but not as curvy.) Just past the Makah Tribal Museum is Washburn's, where you can purchase the required recreation

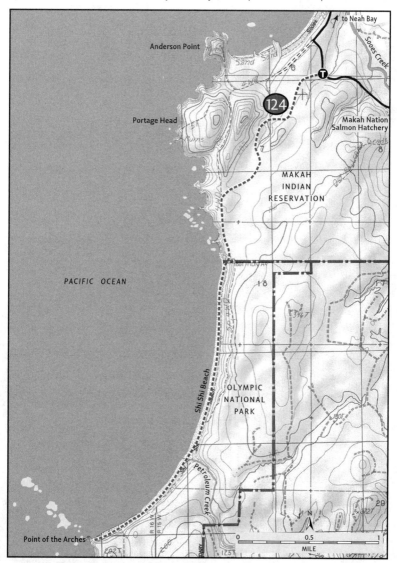

pass. Continue west on Bayview Avenue for 1 mile, following signs for "Cape Flattery and Beaches." Turn left on Fort Street, and in 0.1 mile turn right on 3rd Street. In another 0.1 mile turn left on Cape Flattery Road. Follow this road 2.5 miles to a junction just before the tribal center. Turn left onto Hobuck Road and—staying on the main paved road, following signs for the fish hatchery—drive 4.3 miles to the trailhead, located on your right. Privy available.

ON THE TRAIL

One of the last additions to Olympic National Park, Shi Shi Beach's inclusion in 1976 was met with a fair amount of resistance. Abutting landowners had to be convinced to allow public access. Land developers had to be discouraged from turning the area into an enclave of second homes. And once the Park Service acquired title, they had to remove counterculture squatters and tidy up the mess left behind. Even then the fight to secure Shi Shi for the public wasn't over; in the late 1990s the trail was closed in a land-access dispute. But after much wrangling and negotiating, the Park Service and landowners broke the impasse. The Makahs developed a new trailhead and built a new trail to the beach, and it's top-notch in both design and standards.

The first mile winds through pockets of mature Sitka spruce, traversing rain-saturated bogs via cedar-planked boardwalks and bridges. The new trail then intersects part of the old trail, where 0.5 mile of somewhat muddy terrain must still be negotiated. Eventually this part of the trail will be rehabilitated. At 1.75 miles you'll reach the national park boundary. Now, the only thing separating you from the spectacular beach is a steep trail down a 150-foot bluff.

Brace your knees and emerge at the northern end of the 2-mile sandy beach. Taste the salty air. Feel the pounding surf at your feet. Embrace the raw beauty of this wilderness beach and immediately forget about the civilized world. Dunes and bluffs hem the sandy shoreline. Giant logs dance in the thundering breakers. Eagles belt out high-pitched welcomes from overhanging snags.

In 1.3 miles from the bluff descent you'll come to Petroleum Creek. Cross it and continue. Point of the Arches, a mile-long cavalcade of sea stacks and natural arches, comes into better view. It's 1 mile farther to reach them. During a low tide, there's no better place on the Olympic Coast for admiring these wind- and water-sculpted landforms. The only thing grander than Shi Shi's natural beauty is its resilience in the face of forces that would have prohibited us from enjoying and admiring this national treasure.

EXTENDING YOUR TRIP

Nearby Hobuck Beach contains 1 mile of wide sandy shoreline. Its accessibility makes it ideal for children and hikers looking for an easy beach hike.

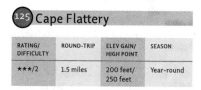

125 Cape Flattery

RATING/ DIFFICULTY	ROUND-TRIP	ELEV GAIN/ HIGH POINT	SEASON
★★★/2	1.5 miles	200 feet/ 250 feet	Year-round

Maps: Green Trails Cape Flattery No. 98S, Custom Correct North Olympic Coast; **Contact:** Makah Indian Nation, (360) 645-2201; **Notes:** Dogs prohibited. Makah Recreation

Opposite: Deserted and beautiful Shi Shi Beach

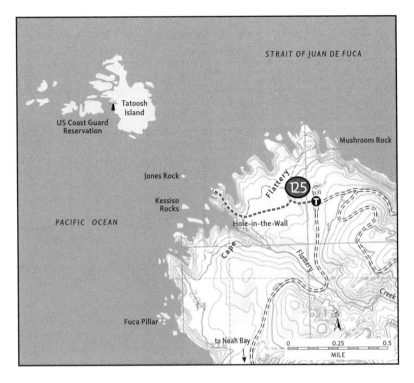

Pass required, available at Washburn's General Store in Neah Bay; **GPS:** N 48 23.065, W 124 42.940

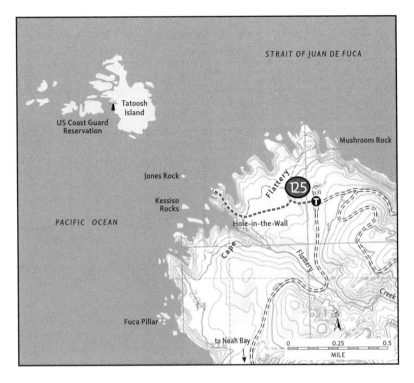 *Hike to the northwesternmost point in the continental United States. Here, where the Strait of Juan de Fuca meets the Pacific, Cape Flattery protrudes into a sea of tumultuous waters. A land of dramatic headlands, sea stacks, and deep narrow coves, Cape Flattery exhibits sheer rugged beauty. Scores of seabirds ride the surf and scavenge the sea stacks. Watch for whales and sea lions too. And the sunsets . . . they're simply divine.*

GETTING THERE

From Port Angeles follow US 101 west for 5 miles to the junction with State Route 112. Turn right (west) on SR 112, continuing for 64 miles to the community of Neah Bay. (Alternatively, take US 101 to Sappho and drive SR 113 north to SR 112 and then on to Neah Bay. This way is longer, but not as curvy.) Just past the Makah Tribal Museum is Washburn's, where you can purchase the required recreation pass. Continue west on Bayview Avenue for 1 mile, following signs for "Cape Flattery and Beaches." Turn left on Fort Street, and in 0.1 mile turn right on 3rd Street. In another 0.1 mile turn left on Cape

Opposite: Forbidding headlands at Cape Flattery

Flattery Road. In 2.5 miles pass the Tribal Center, and 0.5 mile farther the pavement ends. Proceed for another 4.6 miles to the trailhead. Privy available.

ON THE TRAIL

Thanks to the Makah Indian Nation, the stewards of this land, a well-constructed trail leads to this remote corner of the Northwest. Start through a mist-drenched forest of Sitka spruce. Utilizing boardwalks and steps, drop to a series of promontories that provide stunning vistas of rugged Cape Flattery. At 0.75 mile reach the final viewing platform teetering on the edge of terra firma.

Admire the cape's abrupt contours of sea stacks, caves, and forbidding sheer cliffs. A hostile environment of strong currents, swift breezes, and frequent storms—all forces responsible for creating this stunning landscape.

But nature has a way of adapting to such brutal conditions. Look carefully at this intimidating world where sea meets land and you'll see life. Lots of life! Puffins and guillemots surf the turbulent waters. Murres nest in the fortresslike cliffs. Oystercatchers probe the tidal pools left behind on offshore reefs. Sea otters, once on the brink of extinction, bob in the protected coves. Whales can often be spotted farther out.

People, too, have adapted to this landscape, which is often draped in fog and receives over 100 inches of annual rainfall. Directly offshore is Tatoosh Island. Named for a Makah chief, this 20-acre treeless island once served as a summer fishing camp for the Makahs. The U.S. Coast Guard first constructed a lighthouse on the island in 1857. The current structure is automated. Now only sea lions, seals, and scads of seabirds live on Tatoosh.

The Makahs have declared Cape Flattery a nature sanctuary—an enlightened move for this wild world sitting on the brink of the continent.

Appendix I: Recommended Reading

Eifert, Larry and Nancy. *Olympic National Park Nature Guide*. Port Townsend, WA: Estuary Press, 2001.

Manning, Harvey, Bob Spring, and Ira Spring. *Mountain Flowers of the Cascades and Olympics*. 2nd ed. Seattle: Mountaineers Books, 2002.

Olympic Mountain Rescue. *Olympic Mountains: A Climbing Guide*. 6th ed. Seattle: Mountaineers Books, 2006.

Whitney, Stephen R., and Rob Sanderlin. *Field Guide to the Cascades and Olympics*. 2nd ed. Seattle: Mountaineers Books, 2003.

Wood, Robert L. *Across the Olympic Mountains: The Press Expedition, 1889–90*. Seattle: Mountaineers Books, 1967.

———. *Men, Mules, and Mountains: Lieutenant O'Neil's Olympic Expeditions*. Seattle: Mountaineers Books, 1976.

———. *Olympic Mountains Trail Guide*. 3rd ed. Seattle: Mountaineers Books, 2000.

Appendix II: Conservation and Trail Organizations

Bainbridge Island Land Trust
PO Box 10144
Bainbridge Island, WA 98110
(206) 842-1216
www.bi-landtrust.org

Conservation Northwest
1208 Bay Street #201
Bellingham, WA 98225
(360) 671-9950
www.conservationnw.org

Friends of Willapa National Wildlife Refuge
PO Box 1130
Ocean Park, WA 98640
(360) 665-0115
www.willapabay.org

Great Peninsula Conservancy
3721 Kitsap Way, Suite 5
Bremerton, WA 98312
(360) 373-3500
www.greatpeninsula.org

Jefferson Land Trust
1033 Lawrence Street
Port Townsend, WA 98368
(360) 379-9501
www.saveland.org

The Mountaineers Club
300 3rd Avenue W
Seattle, WA 98119
(206) 284-6310
www.mountaineers.org

North Olympic Land Trust
104 North Laurel Street, Suite 114
Port Angeles, WA 98362
(360) 417-1815
www.northolympiclandtrust.org

Olympic Forest Coalition
606 Lilly Road NE, Suite 115
Olympia, WA 98506
www.olympicforest.org

Peninsula Trails Association
PO Box 1836
Port Angeles, WA 98362
www.olympicdiscoverytrail.com

Washington's National Park Fund
PO Box 4646
Seattle, WA 98194
www.wnpf.org

Washington Trails Association
1305 4th Avenue, Suite 512
Seattle, WA 98101
(206) 625-1367
www.wta.org

Index

About the Author

Craig Romano was raised in New Hampshire where he fell in love with the natural world. He has traveled extensively, from Alaska to Argentina and Sicily to South Korea, seeking wild and beautiful places. He ranks Washington State, his home since 1989, among the most beautiful places in the world and he has thoroughly hiked it from Cape Flattery to Puffer Butte, Cape Disappointment to the Salmo-Priest. But he still misses the East Coast, especially when it comes to getting a decent Italian meal.

Craig holds a BA in history, a master's degree in education, and an AA in Forestry. He teaches part time in the Edmonds and Shoreline, Washington, school districts and works part time in Europe's Pyrenees mountains as a guide for Walking Softly Adventures.

An avid hiker, runner, kayaker, and cyclist, Craig has written about his passions for many publications, including *Backpacker*, *Canoe and Kayak*, *Northwest Travel*, *Northwest Runner*, *AMC Outdoors*, *The North Columbia Monthly*, and *Northwest Outdoors*. He also writes recreational content for Hike of the Week (*www.hikeoftheweek.com*) and Canada's The Weather Network (*www.theweathernetwork.com*). He is the author of *Best Hikes with Dogs: Inland Northwest* and *Columbia Highlands: Exploring Washington's Last Frontier*, and he contributed to *Best Wildflower Hikes in Washington*, all published by The Mountaineers Books.

Craig's solo backpacking trip on the High Divide back in 1989 still ranks as one of his most memorable and cherished life experiences.

Author on First Top researching book

1% For Trails and Washington Trails Association

Your favorite Washington hikes, such as those in this book, are made possible by the efforts of thousands of volunteers keeping our trails in great shape, and by hikers like you advocating for the protection of trails and wild lands. As budget cuts reduce funding for trail maintenance, Washington Trails Association's volunteer trail maintenance program fills this void and is ever more important for the future of Washington's hiking. Our mountains and forests can provide us with a lifetime of adventure and exploration—but we need trails to get us there. One percent of the sales of this guidebook goes to support WTA's efforts.

Spend a day on the trail with Washington Trails Association, and give back to the trails you love. WTA hosts oer 750 work parties throughout Washington's Cascades and Olympics each year. Volunteers remove downed logs after spring snowmelt, cut away brush, retread worn stretches of trail, and build bridges and turnpikes. Find the volunteer schedule, check current conditions of the trails in this guidebook, and become a member of WTA at *www.wta.org* or (206) 625-1367.

THE MOUNTAINEERS, founded in 1906, is a nonprofit outdoor activity and conservation club, whose mission is "to explore, study, preserve, and enjoy the natural beauty of the outdoors. . . ." Based in Seattle, Washington, the club is now the third-largest such organization in the United States, with seven branches throughout Washington State.

The Mountaineers sponsors both classes and year-round outdoor activities in the Pacific Northwest, which include hiking, mountain climbing, ski-touring, snowshoeing, bicycling, camping, kayaking, nature study, sailing, and adventure travel. The club's conservation division supports environmental causes through educational activities, sponsoring legislation, and presenting informational programs.

All club activities are led by skilled, experienced instructors, who are dedicated to promoting safe and responsible enjoyment and preservation of the outdoors.

If you would like to participate in these organized outdoor activities or the club's programs, consider a membership in The Mountaineers. For information and an application, write or call The Mountaineers, Club Headquarters, 300 Third Avenue West, Seattle, WA 98119; 206-284-6310. You can also visit the club's website at www.mountaineers.org or contact The Mountaineers via email at clubmail@mountaineers.org.

The Mountaineers Books, an active, nonprofit publishing program of the club, produces guidebooks, instructional texts, historical works, natural history guides, and works on environmental conservation. All books produced by The Mountaineers Books fulfill the club's mission.

Send or call for our catalog of more than 500 outdoor titles:

The Mountaineers Books
1001 SW Klickitat Way, Suite 201
Seattle, WA 98134
800-553-4453
mbooks@mountaineersbooks.org
www.mountaineersbooks.org

The Mountaineers Books is proud to be a corporate sponsor of The Leave No Trace Center for Outdoor Ethics, whose mission is to promote and inspire responsible outdoor recreation through education, research, and partnerships. The Leave No Trace program is focused specifically on human-powered (nonmotorized) recreation.

Leave No Trace strives to educate visitors about the nature of their recreational impacts, as well as offer techniques to prevent and minimize such impacts. Leave No Trace is best understood as an educational and ethical program, not as a set of rules and regulations.

For more information, visit *www.LNT.org*, or call 800-332-4100.

OTHER TITLES YOU MIGHT ENJOY FROM THE MOUNTAINEERS BOOKS

Day Hiking: South Cascades
Dan Nelson, Photographs by Alan Bauer

Day Hiking: Snoqualmie Region
Dan Nelson, Photographs by Alan Bauer

Day Hiking: Oregon Coast
Bonnie Henderson

Best Hikes with Kids: Western Washington & the Cascades
Joan Burton & Ira Spring
Big fun for little feet—discover the best hikes for kids

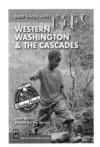

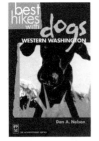

Best Hikes with Dogs: Western Washington
Dan Nelson
Where to hike with Fido—all trails recommended as dog safe and dog fun!

Tent and Car Camper's Handbook Advice for Families & First-Timers
Buck Tilton, Kristin Hostetter
The lowdown on car and tent camping—no experience necessary

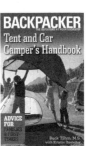